WIEHLERCHRONIK 2000 - co-author
400 years of history of Mother's family

LEMKECHRONIK 2002
A history of father's family

Nicht mehr als ihr ertragen könnt 2004
Autobiography - German edition

Crossing Frontiers - 2009
Autobiography I - English edition

A Life Fully Lived (Loving Hildegard) 2010
Autobiography II (A story of an immigrant family)

Mennonite Artists' Home - 2010, co-author

A Life Fully Lived

Loving Hildegard

The story of an immigrant family

Helmut Lemke

AuthorHouse™
1663 Liberty Drive
Bloomington, IN 47403
www.authorhouse.com
Phone: 1-800-839-8640

© 2010 Helmut Lemke. All rights reserved.

No part of this book may be reproduced, stored in a retrieval system, or transmitted by any means without the written permission of the author.

First published by AuthorHouse 10/14/2010

ISBN: 978-1-4520-3719-6 (sc)
ISBN: 978-1-4520-3720-2 (e)

Printed in the United States of America

This book is printed on acid-free paper.

Because of the dynamic nature of the Internet, any Web addresses or links contained in this book may have changed since publication and may no longer be valid. The views expressed in this work are solely those of the author and do not necessarily reflect the views of the publisher, and the publisher hereby disclaims any responsibility for them.

Cover Photo:
Hildegard looking over the Greek island of Santorini
Front page photo:
Hildegard meditating

To my children

*Michael, Krista, Hanno,
their spouses
my grandchildren
and those who knew Hildegard well*

Acknowledgements:

I want to thank my children for their critical support, for questioning and adjusting some of the facts in my stories.
I want to express my appreciation to our friend, Margret Shaw, for giving advice and editing my manuscript and to our long-time friend Jean Roux, who patiently gave advice and did the proofreading.
Dr. Evan Kreider kindly gave permission to include one photo to the illustrations.

Contents

1. In Memoriam	1
2. Meeting Hildegard	3
3. Leaving Germany	9
4. New Beginning in Canada	13
5. Starting our life together	18
6. Our first employment in Canada	25
7. Changing Careers	29
8. Second Thoughts about Canada	33
9. Becoming Canadian Mennonites	38
10. Preserving our heritage	40
11. Building a new Church	46
12 For the Love of Music.	48
13. Our first home	52
14. Searching for new ways.	64
15. Our 'Hauskreis'	66
16. Revisiting Germany	75
17. Family Activities	82
18. Getting involved	91
19. Spiritual Renewal – Jesus People	97
20. Retracing our roots	102
21. Leaving Sherbrooke	126
22. St. Margaret's	130
23. A place of refuge	138
24. Challenges in growing up	151
25. Our new house.	165
26. Metamorphosis	173
27. New Challenges	182
28. Exchange teaching	187
29. Visiting Italy	195
30. Bielefeld our new home.	199
31. Holiday in Greece and elsewhere	207
32. More adventures in Europe	219
33. Retirement	237
34. Closing the circle	240
35. Early retirement activities	246

36. The empty nest.	260
37. Oh Canada, our home and native land!	269
38. Family events and surprises	293
39. Meeting relatives and in-laws	299
40. Becoming grandparents	317
41. New Discoveries	330
42. The new Millennium	346
43. Returning to her 'Father's House'	365
44. Our last journey	374
45. The final story	385
Aus Hildegard's (Liebes) Briefen	400
Exerpts from letters written by Hildegard (and Helmut)	400
Excerpts from letters of appreciation and sympathy from friends of Hildegard during her illness and at her memorial service..	407
Leaving My Father's House, - One Woman's Journey	409

Preface

When my wife, Hildegard, unexpectedly died of lung cancer, I felt I had to write our life story to deal with the grief and agony of her loss. Writing our story slowly changed my sorrow into quiet thankfulness for the privilege I had, to share my life with her for fifty-one years.

Hildegard was an exceptional woman, beautiful, intelligent and transparent. She had a very positive attitude towards life, was loving and compassionate. She could listen intently to other people, make them feel important to her and respond thoughtfully. Many expressed this in letters of appreciation and sympathy at her memorial service.

I relived our life again, remembering the short meeting with her when we were students and then learning to know her more intimately through letters across continents, which motivated me to immigrate. We started our life together, adjusting and contributing to a new culture and new customs, finding work and changing careers. We started a family raising three children in the turbulent sixties and seventies.

Our lives were enriched through our involvement with other people, artists and musicians, draft dodgers, hippies, Jesus people, young offenders and marginalized people.

I remember the challenges to our relationship when Hildegard left the church and went through a metamorphosis, changing from a more traditional woman to finding her identity as a woman with new visions and responsibilities and a new faith.

We shared wonderful retirement activities together, exploring the beauty and diversity of our world - it all ended too soon.

This story developed into a biography of our family, a sequel to my autobiography, 'Crossing Frontiers,' in which I shared my childhood and war experiences.

A Life Fully lived (Loving Hildegard) is based on my memory, on reflections about Hildegard, our family and friends.

I wrote it as honestly as I could remember and verify through letters, diary and journal entries. To refresh my memory, I communicated with our friends and my children who suggested that I smooth over some of the 'rough edges' referring to their life stories.

I hope my children and grandchildren will treasure it later as a memorial of their mother and grandmother.

Helmut Lemke   April 2010

1. In Memoriam

When Gillian starts to play the harp, tears fill my eyes. Hildegard had seen Gillian grow up to become a beautiful young woman and an accomplished harpist. Now she plays her harp in memory of 'Tante Hildegard' at her memorial service.

Many people gather in Peace Mennonite Church to pay tribute to Hildegard. She always liked this place of worship because of its simplicity and pleasant design by an architect friend of ours. Hildegard needed beautiful surroundings to blossom and enjoy life.

Dr. Evan Kreider, who officiates at the memorial, characterizes her life and spiritual journey very thoughtfully. He admires her honesty and transparency in the way she interacted with people and in matters of her faith which has deeply influenced him. He will remember this celebration of Hildegard's life as 'A life fully lived'.

Hildegard loved music. Evan has arranged a quartet of musicians from the church we attend and they sing songs by Schubert and Mendelssohn; they are very suitably chosen for the occasion.

It is a tense and quiet mood when close friends bring words of gratitude and appreciation and talk about the inspiration Hildegard had been to them. Tears come to the eyes of many when our children passionately express what their mother had meant to them and what they learned from her.

It is moving when Madison's letter to her Oma is read.

I am participating in the 'celebration of Hildegard's life' but feel like an onlooker from a different planet. I still cannot accept that this is to be final. I will never be able to see her smile and hear her cheerful laughter, never share impressions, creative ideas, dreams and future plans with her. Never again? –

We pour her ashes into the earth, as she had wanted it, in the wooded area of a small cemetery. There her remains lie now under a rough granite boulder, into which both of our names have been engraved, she lies in the shadow of the trees.

We had selected this spot several years ago already; a solitary niche flanked by two large cedar trees. The trunk of one had grown in a curve first and then changed its direction and straightened up. This unusual tree had attracted her attention, as trees in general did; she liked round forms.

Anna, her daughter-in-law, puts a beautiful bouquet of white roses which she had arranged with dark boxwood green from our garden, in front of the stone.

I take Ruth and Eva, Hildegard's older sisters, from the memorial service back to my house. They stay for a short time with me; we reflect on the service and Hildegard's last days with us and then they leave for home. I am now alone in the big house. Still not really conscious of what has happened. I go into Hildegard's bedroom, look at her pillow and think: "I cannot talk to you anymore, cannot stroke your cheeks and give you a good-night-kiss…."

The library door is open and I notice on the writing desk lies an early photo of her, a picture of a charming teenager. As I pick it up, tears come to my eyes. My thoughts wander back – I fell in love with this girl fifty-six years ago.

2. MEETING HILDEGARD

Bluffton College, Ohio; I have been studying here for a year on a scholarship from the Mennonite Central Committee, (MCC). The year is over now and I have a few months to spend before I go back to Germany. I had discussed with Gerhard, a fellow student from Germany, studying at Eastern Mennonite College, the idea of exploring the United States together after our final semester. He is from Karlsruhe and we came over on the same ship from Germany.

We meet in Kansas and hitch-hike from there together to the Pacific coast, which is still possible and safe to do in 1952.

Dr Shelly, my counselor at Bluffton, has arranged stays for me in *Mennonite Voluntary Service Camps* along our way. I am quite familiar with MVS camps. I had taken part in several of these international camps in Europe and am interested to see how they operate here in the States. Many young Mennonite men in America opt for alternative military service. They would rather serve socially and mentally disadvantaged people in mental hospitals, help in refugee camps and peace teams, than go to war and kill or maim people.

Visits to these MVS camps have an added benefit for us, as it gives us a place to stay over-night and enjoy a warm meal.

"One family we have to visit", Gerhard tells me, "are the Schefflers". He knows them as a Mennonite Pastor's couple from youth retreats in Germany where he had befriended 'Onkel Hugo, Tante Susa and the girls'. They had emigrated from Germany to the state of Washington, to a remote little town called Ritzville, a year ago and have told him they would gladly accommodate us for a few days.

They used to live in West Prussia, close to where I was born and knew my parents quite well. Tante Susa sang in my Father's church choir. I know

Ruth, the second of the girls, with whom I worked in a MVS Camp in Espelkamp, Germany, and I liked her and thought it would be nice to see her again.

Our journey takes us to Arizona. The MVS members serve in a Mennonite Mission in an Indian Reservation in the desert east of the Grand Canyon. This is our first opportunity to meet American Native people. We help the volunteers with the building of a school for Native children and visit them in their children's summer Bible Camp. We sing a German lullaby for the kids and we encourage them to join us in the refrain

"Aber Heidschi Bumbeitschi bum bum.". and they love it.

In California we run into trouble. A Sheriff stops his car in front of us; he has seen our sign 'Foreign Students' which so far has served us well and provided interesting rides. He asks for our passports. Gerhard does not have his with him. He makes it quite clear to us that hitch-hiking in California is illegal and he is going to arrest us.

We have to get into his car and he takes us to the San Bernardino police station. The officer at the desk to whom we report dispels our fear and, instead of putting us in a cell, he issues Gerhard a temporary ID card and wishes us a good trip.

Two days later we arrive at the bus station in Ritzville. We ask a woman how to get to the Schefflers. "Oh you mean the new immigrants from Germany," she answers "They live on the other side of town. I'll take you there in my car". She drops us off on Broadway Street on the outskirts of the town close to the little airport. "It is the house with the tall red and white hollyhocks in the front yard".

I feel a little uneasy when we knock at the door. Though Gerhard had informed them that we were coming, I am still a stranger. Nobody is at home. We decide to play a little trick on them. We leave our luggage beside the front door, hide on the other side of the boulevard and wait to observe how they will respond to those strange suitcases when they come home. After awhile a young man stops at the house, unlocks the door and puts the suitcases inside. As he is about to leave again, we go over and introduce ourselves. He says he is Herbert Janzen, Tante Susa's nephew. He invites us to come inside and tells us the family will arrive soon. We sit on the sofa and look around the living room. Everything is clean and orderly, simple but tastefully furnished. After a short time we hear a car pulling into the driveway. Two women are getting out of a shiny black Buick and walk towards the entrance. They are astonished and happy to see us. Gerhard introduces me to Tante Susa and then to Hildegard. She is a tall, lively, good looking teenager. We shake hands, as is the custom among Germans. A little later, after he has parked the car in the garage, Onkel Hugo comes in. He is a stately middle-aged man with black hair and a short mustache. He welcomes us and makes us feel at ease. He tells me that he still has good memories of my parents back in West Prussia which makes me feel more at home. At the supper table questions go back and forth; they want to know what has happened in Germany since they left. Gerhard tells them that Onkel Hugo's former congregation in Southern Germany misses them very much. I join the conversation and tell them about our Mennonite Young People in Northern Germany, mostly refugees from West Prussia, with whom I am very much involved.

Hildegard shares with me later that since she came to Ritzville she cannot get over her culture shock. She is still homesick for the lovely wooded rolling hills of the Palatinate which are so different from this somewhat barren land. The people here are superficially very friendly but more focused on material things and having fun. The girls are mainly thinking of boys and dating compared to her many interests which they do not share.

We talk until late into the night and the next morning they are late getting ready for work. They usually walk to their workplace. Since I got my driver's license at Bluffton, I can drive them to work in their new Buick. I take Onkel Hugo to the Safeway store. He has a job there in the vegetable department. Hildegard tells me, when they came to Ritzville she worked first in the harvest on different farms and then in the local restaurant as a waitress. One day she served the manager of the Safeway store his coffee and he asked her if she wanted to work for him as a cashier. She accepted.

Not long after this 'promotion', the bank manager came into the store. He had noticed how well and efficiently she served the customers and asked her if she would like to do this kind of work in his bank as a teller, a somewhat more respectable position with better pay and better working conditions. So she switched her work place again. I drop her off at the local bank where she still works.

Hildegard is the only one of the four daughters who is living at home with her parents; the other three are 'farmed out' to wheat farmers in the area to help with the harvest and with other chores. Onkel Hugo had made arrangements to visit them and so we all get into the Buick and drive first to Mammy and Daddy Gering, as Eva calls her employers. She takes care of Mrs. Gering, who has been diagnosed with cancer, and helps in the household. Leon Gering, a well-to-do wheat farmer, had assisted the Schefflers with finding and financing their house and car. After a good lunch with the Gerings we visit Ruth. She is pleased to see me again and we refresh old memories from 'Camp Espelkamp' where we helped to convert former German ammunition barracks into homes for refugees. She is busy and we go on to visit Gertraud, the youngest. She has been 'adopted' by a wealthy wheat farmer to help in the household while finishing her final years in the local high school.

On the way back, Hildegard confides to me her interest in art and literature which she cannot share with her new friends in town, not even intimately with her own sisters.

When we come home and the others have gone to bed she asks me into her room and shows me her art collection. Inspired by her art teacher in her school in Germany, she had started to collect a variety of art reproductions. She had cut out from Life magazines pictures of Giotto's frescos depicting the life of Christ in the Padua Chapel, several pages of Grünewald's Isenheim Altar, works by several Impressionist and Expressionist artists, reproductions on post cards and calendars from ancient Egyptian and Greek sculptures to Barlach and Matare. She spreads them out on the carpet around us. We discuss the changing art periods and the different styles, share our knowledge about the work and life of the artists and the impact they had on society and how they affect us. Her appreciation of art is genuine and sincere and she talks about it unaffectedly and naturally, asks questions and considers my answers thoughtfully. I am astonished at her intuition and knowledge of the subject. She tells me that her involvement with art has led her to discover and appreciate beauty. When I look in her bright open eyes I can see right into her and feel that her outer beauty is paralleled by her inner beauty. I just love that girl. It is past midnight when we part and I thank her for sharing her intimate thoughts and feelings with me.

Hildegard 1952   Helmut Hitchhiking

Visiting Scheffler

On the last day of our stay in Ritzville she does not have to work. It is very hot and we go swimming in the town's swimming pool to cool off. She drives us around town and to the Mennonite Church in the country. On the way back we stop at the Safeway store to see where her dad is working. She parks the car very close to a fire hydrant and when we leave again she turns too close to the fire hydrant and it scratches the fender of the car. She stops the car, goes back to the store and tells her father about the incident. I admire her honesty in reporting this mishap right away. Shaken by what had happened she asks me to drive home.

I still remember that last day after supper when we were doing the dishes together we sang this sentimental German folksong:

> Zum Abschied reich' ich dir die Hände
> und sag' ganz leis' Aufwiedersehn,
> Ein schönes Märchen geht zu Ende, es war doch so schön
> (For parting I stretch out my hands to you and say softly good-bye
> A beautiful fairytale is coming to an end, it was so enjoyable)

The next morning Hildegard drives us to the highway and when I say good bye to her I ask her if she would mind if I write to her occasionally. In her natural, open way she says: "Not at all, I would love that." Later she told me that at that point no sparks had yet been crossing over, she just thought it might be interesting to correspond with a student of architecture at a German university, sharing similar interests; that was all.

We are on the road again, on our way back east. We get a few short rides and then strike it lucky. An ex-soldier who had been discharged from the army is going home. He drives alone, sees our sign 'Foreign Students', stops and invites us in. He is glad to have company for the next one thousand and five hundred miles. His destination is Ohio, not far from Bluffton. He drives until late into the night, stops only for a few hours of sleep in the car and continues early in the morning. We do not mind, it saves us looking and paying for night quarters.

He lets me out at the road to the College and I spend a few days packing my belongings and writing my first letter to Hildegard, telling her about our trip as well as thanking her and her family for hosting us. I tell her how much it has meant to me to learn to know her and how much I enjoyed her sharing her interests with me.

The time comes to say good-bye to Bluffton and the USA and sail back to Germany on the SS America.

3. Leaving Germany

My mother and the other residents in the parsonage where we live are happy to see me back again and celebrate my return.

I enroll at the Technical University of Braunschweig for my fifth semester in architecture. To bring some balance to my serious studies I join the Lutheran Student congregation. They have rented a house not far from the University for students to congregate during lecture breaks. They can share their problems with the student pastor or with friends, join discussion groups or sing in the choir. I love music, join the choir and play the trumpet in the brass octet. I enjoy the company of my fellow students, the activities and the Sunday services in the large gothic cathedral.

I hear through my connections with MCC that Mennonites, mainly West Prussian refugees, meet as a congregation once a month in one of Braunschweigs Protestant churches. I contact them and attend their service. After the meeting I introduce myself to the elder of the congregation and in our conversation he tells me he is concerned about the young people and asks me if I would be willing to care for them.

I talk to the young people and we agree to come together as a group twice a month. Katja knows a Lutheran pastor in her neighborhood and he allows us to meet in the basement of his church. We get acquainted with each other, share our life stories, talk about our faith, sing, and go on hikes and ski tours together.

I write to Hildegard about my activities and she shares what she is doing. She is now studying at Bethel College on a Mennonite scholarship. We write to each other more frequently now and in each letter we share more intimately and honestly our thoughts and experiences. This is not easy for me because by nature I am more of an introvert. Intentionally

I do not aggrandize my activities or make empty compliments to please or win her.

Two years have passed since I departed from her in Ritzville and our relationship has become quite intimate. She has moved from Bethel College to the University of Washington. For her twentieth birthday I send her a tiny red book with love letters from famous writers, artists, poets and musicians with the title: "Wie lieb ich Dich" (How I Love You!) and write into it: 'This is what I want to say to you but cannot say it as eloquently.' She answers with a poem by Shakespeare:

> Let me not to the marriage of true minds admit impediments
> Love is not love which alters when it alteration finds,
> Or bends with the remover to remove.
> O no, it is an ever fixéd mark that looks on tempests
> And is never shaken
> It is the star to every wand'ring bark
> Whose worth's unknown, although his height be taken
> Love's not time's fool, though rosy lips and cheeks
> Within his bending sickle's compass come,
> Love alters not with his brief hours and weeks,
> But bears it out even to the edge of doom.

She signed the letter for the first time with: Deine Hildegard (<u>Your</u> Hildegard).

The ending of this letter makes my heart beat faster. I cannot wait to see her again and plan to immigrate to Canada after my graduation. Before that happens I would like to see more of Germany especially the southern part.

At the end of the summer semester, our art history professor takes us students on an art excursion. He wants to show us the real cathedrals, castles and medieval towns about which he had talked in his lectures. He guides us through art galleries and points out what is typical and unusual in paintings and sculptures in different time periods. Art becomes alive when Professor Flesche explains that to us. I appreciate this trip immensely, learn to understand and value our art treasures much better and see parts of Germany which I did not yet know.

A little later, Dr. Kristen, our professor for chemistry and material application, wants to show us the production of materials which we may consider using in our designs. He takes us on a tour of factories which manufacture different construction materials.

This tour has an unforeseen and tragic ending.

We are travelling on the Autobahn and see a truck pulling a trailer loaded with tar paper rolls approaching. It does not slow down when it changes lanes at a detour on the Autobahn; the trailer sways and tilts, hits our bus and rips the whole left side of the bus open. The driver is killed and several of us are injured. Ambulances take us to a nearby hospital. I suffer a concussion and cuts and bruises, and have to stay in hospital for almost three weeks.

This accident has an unexpected benefit for me. The insurance company pays me a two thousand one hundred DM compensation for my injuries. This solves one problem, it will cover the price for my voyage to Canada and leave a little over to expand my wardrobe and buy some gifts and things that I need to take along.

For the conclusion of my studies to receive my degree, I have to write the 'Diplomarbeit' (thesis) I have chosen to design a central bus station for the city of Braunschweig. It takes longer than I had expected to do the required research and I have to add another semester to finish it.

My final oral and written examinations are now completed and the thesis which I handed in has been accepted; I am ready to cross the ocean.

The next thing I have to do is get my immigration papers. I stand in line to fill out application forms for a passport and an entry visa to Canada.

While waiting for my immigration and travel documents to be approved, I take on a short term job with an architect in Braunschweig. Working for him gives me some practical experience for my future work in Canada and will provide me with some extra cash.

I pay visits to relatives and friends. Members of my youth group surprise me to say good-bye. They give me a signed copy of a book on 'Beautiful Germany' to remind me not to forget them.

An antique overseas trunk in a second hand store has caught my eye; it seems to be just the right size for all my belongings, my clothing, books, architectural drawings and my musical instruments. I had been given a trumpet, acquired a set of recorders and a violin which I picked up in a second hand music store. They all have to be wrapped up carefully and put into the trunk.

Russian soldiers had smashed my father's good violin, when they ransacked our home at the end of the war; it made me sad and angry and I felt that I would not touch another one anymore. I had taken violin lessons and had just come to the point where I appreciated playing it. When I saw the violin in the music store on display, old memories came back, and I could imagine playing the violin again someday.

Many stores had been destroyed during the war and here and there one is opening up again, displaying some merchandise. Mother and I are strolling through the city to see if we can find a sewing machine to take along for my sister. We walk by a jewelry store and see a nice ladies wrist watch in the window, a rarity. I point it out to Mother, "That might look good on Hildegard's arm; it would be a lovely engagement gift". We buy it and ask the cashier to wrap it in a fine gift box. I am glad to have a gift for her when we meet again.

The hardest part of leaving Germany is parting from my mother. We had shared so many daring episodes together in the war and post war periods. Could I now leave her behind? She does not want to come with me until I have established myself in the new country and be a burden to us children at this time. She knows that I will be with my sister who immigrated five years ago and I know she is in good care in the Handorf parsonage and can be with her siblings and other relatives. This makes it a little easier for both of us to say good-bye.

4. New Beginning in Canada

It is my third crossing of the ocean. This time it is a rather rough voyage. Hurricane-like storms toss our small boat around. The doors to the outer decks are tied together with ropes for fear that passengers might go outside and be swept overboard. The dining room is almost empty. The waiter has set the table for us few passengers and at the next sway of the ship the dishes slide on the floor and break, even setting them on a wet tablecloth does not help;. He serves us only half portions. I am glad when we arrive at the North American continent, on the safer shores of the St.Lawrence River.

Going through the Canadian immigration in Quebec causes no problem. I am quickly sending a letter to my sister in Vancouver to tell her of my approximate arrival date and hope it will arrive before I am there.

For four days the train is traveling through very diverse landscapes. I look out of the window and see the landscape passing by. It gives me an impression of the beauty and vastness of a place which I will now call my home country. Sleeping at night on hard wooden benches is not so comfortable and I am relieved when we arrive in Vancouver. My sister and brother–in-law have received my letter in time and are at the station, welcoming me with open arms and take me to their home. They are renting the main floor of an older one family residence in the vicinity of Vancouver's 'German-town'. A small, cozy room on the attic floor furnished with a bed, a closet, a writing desk and an easy chair will be my abode for the next months, that is all I need and I am quite happy to have my own floor.

Little two-and-a-half year old Ralf, Magdalena and Gustav's first son, looks inquisitively through the open door when I put my belongings away. I invite him in, take him on my knee, play 'Hoppe Hoppe Reiter' with him and slowly he accepts Uncle Helmut as a part of the family and we become friends.

I cannot wait to contact Hildegard; she is now in her last year studying foreign languages at the University of Washington. With some anticipation I dial her number in Seattle and am delighted to hear her voice. She wants to know about my trip and we are both looking forward to see each other. Her Dad has an appointment next Sunday to preach in a Mennonite Church in nearby Abbotsford, he will pick her up and bring her over.

It is now over three years since we first met; at that time she was open and friendly with me. Through our correspondence, we have become much more intimate with each other; I wonder how she will respond now when we see each other. I will find out shortly.

The black Buick that I still remember from Ritzville stops in front of 947, 30th Ave. in Vancouver. Onkel Hugo, Tante Susa and Hildegard step out. I rush down the stairs to meet them. They greet me heartily and I am very happy to see them again. Magdalena has already set the table and we drink coffee together and taste the delicious cake she has baked for this occasion. Soon Hildegard's parents will have to leave for Abbotsford where Rev. Scheffler has been offered the position of pastor of a German-speaking Mennonite congregation.

Magdalena knows Ruth, Hildegard's older sister, from voluntary service camps in Germany and they have become friends. The two sisters had visited Vancouver a few years ago and had stayed with Magdalena, so she knows Hildegard too. She remembers her as an amiable person, full of life and ideas.

After a while of catching up on news, I take Hildegard up to my room. We are alone and when I look at this graceful, handsome young woman, she seems to me to be even more beautiful than when I first met her. In her natural, open way she is very attractive.

We had shared our feelings for each other in our letters and now we can verbalize them. I hold her hands, look into her deep clear eyes for a while, and can see right into her.

This time sparks fly back and forth. I get the courage to ask her if she will share her life with me and become my wife and life partner. I don't remember if I sank down on one knee when I proposed to her to emphasize my serious intention. Moved by my question, she nods, "Yes, I will", with her winning smile. Our lips meet for the first time and we hold each other close for a while.

There is one more hurdle to take. I will have to ask her parents for the 'hand of their daughter'.

On their way home Onkel Hugo and Tante Susa drop in again to say good-bye. When they are alone in the living room, I start out, "I know you must have noticed that Hildegard and I are in love with each other". I make a pause and continue, "I just asked her if she would consider becoming my wife and life partner and she said that she gladly would." Then I ask them if they would accept me into their family and give their blessing to our union. Onkel Hugo first acts as if this is news to him and asks questions about my work, not having a steady job yet, how I see our future, if I think I could provide for a family -- Tante Susa gets more and more agitated, "Why don't you tell him that we like him and that we would love to have him become part of our family," she blurts out. Hugo smiles "We have to make sure that things are in order and will work out, Mother". Then he shakes my hand, "Yes, we will give our blessing, Helmut". After they have left, I tell Hildegard what happened. She wants to know all the details.

We sit together with Magdalena and Gustav and talk about our engagement preparations. They assure us that they will help to arrange it. We set the date for Saturday Oct 1, 1955. That is in two weeks. I notice Hildegard does not wear a wrist watch, so I am sure my engagement gift is suitable and she will appreciate it. The next day I take Hildegard to the railway station and she takes the train to Seattle, back to her studies.

Hildegard grew up in a Christian home, in Kaiserslautern, Germany. I think she inherited the best qualities of her parents, the positive, inquisitive and joyful attitude of her father and the sense of justice, honesty and work ethic of her mother and her ability to create a pleasant home atmosphere on a tight budget, which she did from her husband's lean salary as a Mennonite pastor.

I had responded to an ad in the paper, an architect's office is looking for an architect to help with the construction of a model for a design of a large bank in Vancouver. I present the portfolio of my student work and my Diplomarbeit, which has several pictures of models of my work, to the head architect. He is impressed and hires me. I am now employed, my first employment in Canada. I board the bus to downtown every day, walk to the Marine Building, the second highest building in town at that time, and take the elevator to the top floor, where McCarter and Nairn have their offices. During my lunch break I step out onto the balcony and enjoy the panoramic view of the city of Vancouver, the mountains and the ocean, my new home town; it is wonderful.

We finish the model in three weeks and that means my job is over. It takes a while until I find another job, this time with a Belgian architect. Work for architects is scarce at this time. When he interviews me he says he can pay me only two hundred dollars a month to start with and will raise my salary when he gets more contracts. I am astounded to be offered the salary of a household help for an architect with five years of university training and I fear it will be hard to raise a family on that salary. But I trust that things will change and get better. I do not pay much for room and board at my sister's place and live frugally, so I can even open a savings account.

We celebrate our engagement with a small circle of friends and relatives. The day before, we had gone to a jeweler and selected a pair of simple golden rings. On our engagement day we put them on each other's ring finger on the left hand, which is the custom in Germany. We will change it to the right hand when we get married. I do not remember many details of the celebration. We know now that we belong to each other and we are both very happy.

Hildegard is delighted and thankful when I strap the elegant ladies watch on her arm. Mother, who helped me select it, cannot celebrate with us but I know she is with us in her thoughts and prayers. My sister cannot join us either; she is in hospital, giving birth to her second son. Benno did not want to wait his turn, he was a week early.

Since I cannot get a visa to the USA as a recent immigrant, Hildegard comes to visit me in Vancouver. Gustav is generous and lends me his Volkswagen to pick her up from the railway station and I am very grateful for that.

I am always looking forward to her coming and enjoy being with her. During the day we take long walks to the beautiful sights of Vancouver, to Little Mountain Park, along the Sea Wall and the famous Stanley Park, we visit art exhibits and go to concerts. In the evening, after supper, we sit in my room and share our thoughts and experiences from the last two weeks.

I notice that she is sometimes quiet and thoughtful. When I ask if something troubles her, she confides to me that she would like to know more about what I think and feel inside. In my letters I had described so skillfully my experiences and was able to express my inner feelings and intimate thoughts so well that she loved to read them several times. But now, when we are together, I seem to have difficulty expressing them verbally. She tells me later that this was a great concern to her at the time of our engagement and she wondered if it would affect our communication in our married life and be a hindrance to real intimacy. I did not really know what she meant by that. I loved her dearly and would have done anything to make her feel at ease and happy but I did not know how to dispel her concern. I had no role models; my father had died too early.

Most of the time we enjoy doing things together. We have a lot in common. We grew up in the same country with very similar customs, speak the same mother tongue, sing the same songs, share many interests especially in music, art and literature and even share a relative. My uncle married her aunt.

5. Starting our life together

Hildegard is now in her last semester. She enjoys her studies and does well in all her subjects. We plan to get married after her graduation and discuss with her parents a suitable date. Aug, 18, 1956 seems to work out for all of us and we put that date on our calendar.

Gertraud, Hildegard's younger sister, has fallen in love with a young man in her father's former congregation on Vancouver Island. They decide unexpectedly and without discussing it with us, to get married before the date we had set for our wedding. We are upset when we hear that. We think it is inconsiderate and will be too much of a burden to the parents to cope with two weddings within five weeks; it will be draining their energy and their financial resources. But they insist on it and we accept their decision gracefully.

I hope there will be a change in my employment situation. My boss is awarded a new contract to design a conference and exhibition building in Vancouver. I remind him of his promise to raise my salary if this happens but he is still reluctant. So I keep my eyes open and find out that a Dutch architect is hiring new staff. I go to his office. Mr. Van Norman, a warm hearted, middle-aged portly man, looks through my folder, likes my work and tells me I can start on the first of next month. The salary he offers me is almost double what my present employer pays me. I am happy and tell Mr. Noppe that I have found another job. He is fair and gives me a two week holiday pay.

I have applied at the American Consulate for a visa. It is approved and I can now enter the US. Gertraud invites me for her wedding and Hildegard encourages me to come. She wants to introduce me her fiancé to her friends in Ritzville. It does not take much persuasion as I love to pose with her.

Everybody in the Scheffler household is running around preparing for Gertraud's and Werner's wedding. The ceremony is in the Ritzville Mennonite Church. The young couple looks lovely. I do not remember many details about the celebration, except that Hildegard was the most beautiful bridesmaid. For us it is a kind of rehearsal for our wedding.

After the reception is over we help to clean up and collect the gifts. When most of the guests are gone, we leave too. We want to be alone and have some privacy. We take the long way home, driving down the lonely country road. We stop on a small side lane off the road, watch the sun setting over the wide golden wheat fields and see the tumbleweeds rolling across the road. We reflect on the festivities we took part in and try to imagine us being in front of the altar and then living a life together afterwards -- wonderful thoughts. It is getting dark and we sit quietly close to each other. Hildegard puts her head in my lap. I stroke her hair and she touches my hand and whispers," I am looking forward to the time when we are married and can be close together." It is late when we arrive home. The next day I have to go back to Canada and back to my work.

Hildegard finishes her studies at the University. She graduates with a BA. "Magna cum laude" in foreign languages. She has also become an honorary member of a German and an American university sorority, the Delta Phi Alpha and the Phi Beta Kappa, for outstanding scholarship. We celebrate this honor appropriately.

Now we have time to prepare the details for our wedding.

We almost have to postpone our wedding date. Gustav gets sick and asks me to drive to the nearby drugstore to get some antibiotics. On an unmarked street crossing a drunken barber staggers towards my Volkswagen and throws his half empty beer bottle into my open window. I duck to avoid a hit and by doing so turn the steering wheel towards the curb and drive right into the back of a parked car. There are several bystanders on the sidewalk who know the man and they tell the police, when they arrive, what has happened. We have a court hearing and the fellow is sentenced to pay for the repair of Gustav's car and for the treatment of my injuries. This is ten days before our wedding. Fortunately the doctor can pull the stitches from the cuts on my head before that date. The swelling on my lips and nose have gone down and I am fit again and we can go ahead with our arrangements.

I arrive in Ritzville the day before the celebration and help with some of the preparations. Women from the church and friends are busy preparing the food and arranging the decorations. I offer some suggestions but basically they want me out of the picture. Hildegard does not have much time for me either, she has to try on her wedding dress and veil which I am not allowed to see. After supper, most of the activities stop and the women go home. Finally we have a little time together to talk and prepare our minds and hearts for the great day ahead of us.

The next morning Hildegard's father, who is going to perform the marriage ceremony, calls both of us into the sanctuary and talks to us about the meaning of a vow and the importance of this promise to each other before God and prays with us. He discusses briefly the procedure with us since we did not have the usual rehearsal. For me our marriage is an original experience for the two of us, not a flawless performance for an audience. I want to leave room for impromptu changes if necessary.

I had asked my friend Herbert to be my best man at the wedding. We get a shock when he phones from the border that his Morris Minor has broken down and he cannot get parts for his British car in America, so he will not be able to arrive in time to attend the wedding. We have to improvise now. One of my two relatives who had come from Vancouver is willing to step in.

We deviate from another custom. In America the father gives his daughter away to her future husband. We skip that part. In a way I like that custom, giving the daughter into the care of her future husband after she has been living with her parents, but this 'giving away' had already happened four years ago when Hildegard left home and went to University in Seattle. We do it the German way. We enter the church together arm in arm singing "Jesu geh voran" (Jesus still lead on) with the organ accompanying softly.

We say our vows and exchange our rings. Our Father is blessing our union.

At the reception a friend of the family gives a talk, using the metaphor of a tree whose roots go deep into the ground, it loses its leaves and bears fruit. Every stage has its proper application but my thoughts are with my beautiful bride so I don't remember much anymore.

The Gering's offer us their guest suite on the top floor of their home for our first night together. It is very hot all day long and I suffer this unusual heat in my black suit and tie. Hildegard can endure this temperature a little better in her simple, open white wedding-dress. Even at night it is still 35 degrees when we go to bed and a sweltering 32 degrees when we get up in the morning -- not the most romantic environment for a honeymoon night!

Helmut and Hildegard (wedding picture)

Hildegard has made arrangements to spend our honeymoon at Coeur d'Alene Lake for the next two weeks. Dad Scheffler lends us his Buick and we drive to our little cottage which we have all to ourselves directly on the lake. It is wonderful walking along the beach, swimming in the warm water, sitting in the shade sketching the dock and the boats. We both enjoy being close together.

A number of small boats are moored at the dock. We rent one for a spin on the lake and it is fun. The next morning we pack a lunch, pay the rent for half a day's usage, board one of their nicest boats and head off towards the far end of the lake. We cruise at a gentle speed over the calm water and once in a while we spot a school of fish swimming beside our boat in the clear water. The sun is shining and warming our backs. We enjoy the ride and the water and are not paying much attention to the weather, so we are not aware of a heavy black cloud that is approaching fast on the sky behind us. All of a sudden a strong wind arises and our boat starts to sway.

Now I discover a character trait in Hildegard that I did not know, she is fearful when she faces danger. When she sees the black cloud and feels the wind getting stronger she begs me to go home as quickly as possible by the shortest route. This is easier said than done. The waves rise higher and the water sprays into the boat. I try to steer the boat against the waves so that we will not roll over and that is not always the shortest way. She is terrified, clings to me and asks if the boat could capsize and we would drown. That is a possibility but I do not reveal that to her. I remain calm and assure her I will do my best to get us back safely and tell her that I have been in rough waters before having been a member of the rowing team in our school. It is a challenge to avoid those breakers. When we finally tie the boat to the dock, I take her in my arms and she is trembling.

She recovers quickly and we enjoy the sunshine during the last days

Our honeymoon comes to an end and we have to leave this memorable place. We both enjoy being in nature in beautiful simplicity.

When we arrive back in Ritzville we still have a few days before we have to leave for Vancouver. Dad gives us his old 1946 Chevy as a wedding gift. It was given to him when he was pastor of a congregation on Vancouver Island. We pack all of Hildegard's belongings and our wedding gifts into the car and say good-bye to her parents and sisters. A new era of life begins for us as a couple.

At the border we face a problem. The immigration officer inspects our papers. We tell him that we just got married and are moving to Vancouver and that Hildegard wants to immigrate to Canada. We have to fill out lengthy forms. All our luggage counts as personal effects and is duty free. He asks us "And who owns the car with the American license?" We tell him it is also a wedding gift. "And when was it transferred to you?" he asks Hildegard. We tell him and he explains to us the US – Canada border regulations. "If you own the car for less than six months you have to pay duty when you import it to Canada". We cannot argue about that but when he tells us how they calculate the amount of duty, we object. The value of the car was assessed at $50 by a used-car dealership and he wants to charge us $157.38. We have the choice to leave the car at the border or agree to pay the duty. He grants us three months to pay. We are annoyed but we pay.

Before I went to Ritzville I had rented a small apartment on the first floor of an old patrician home in Vancouver, close to the university. It is now an engineer's fraternity house. We have two rooms in it, the front room, which may have been the living room of the former owner with large high windows through which we have an amazing view of the city, Burrard Inlet and the coastal mountains. For us it will serve as living, dining and bedroom. The second room, adjacent to the living room, is long and narrow; it also has high windows with a view. It will be our kitchen with a breakfast nook and utility. The bathroom we will have to share with other students on the first floor. I had chosen this place because of its good view, its affordability and closeness to the university. Hildegard will have to take one year of education and teacher training at UBC in order to be able to teach in BC; this is her plan for the next years.

It is late when we arrive in Vancouver. We park our car in front of the fraternity house, rear seat and trunk packed to the rim with our belongings. We walk through the front yard, a few steps up to the entrance; I don't remember if I carried Hildegard over the threshold, I think I did. A grandiose staircase leads up to the second floor to our apartment. Hildegard has never seen the apartment before and knows of it only from my description. When I turn the lights on, I wonder how she will respond to my choice.

She is too tired to say much but she likes the spaciousness of the room and the view of the lighted city with the dark silhouette of the coastal mountains behind it.

I carry the suitcases up while she prepares a snack for us. She urges me to wait with emptying the car until tomorrow, she is too tired to help me but I feel it is safer to unload it now. She learns to know a character trait of mine which she will have to get used to in one way or another for most of the following fifty years. I call it determination, she thinks it is stubbornness.

When we awake the next morning, the sun is shining into our room and Hildegard enjoys the view at daylight even more than last night. Walking through the rooms she already has ideas of how to furnish them and where to hang which pictures. She values the workmanship of our multipurpose beds, which my cousin Erwin has built and given to us as his wedding gift. I had bought few pieces of furniture in the Bauhaus style. She likes it because of its pleasing, practical form.

The kitchen is narrow but will do for our purposes. Neither of us is pleased with having to share a bathroom with other male students. We will have to introduce some regulations for the maintenance and proper use of it.

After a few days our place is transformed; it looks cozy, a little Spartan but livable, everything seems to be well placed and color-coordinated. In time, when our finances allow it, we will add some more furniture and accessories.

I enjoy my work at the new architect's office. We are 19 architects and engineers from almost as many countries, from Australia, Sweden, Estonia, Germany, Ireland, England and Jan, who uses the excuse when he does something wrong, "That is the way we do it in Holland". We Europeans look down somewhat on the two Canadian architects.

6. Our first employment in Canada

Next month Hildegard will start her post graduate studies at UBC. It is the first year that the Teacher Training Department has been elevated from 'Normal School' to the Faculty of Education of the university. In the first years some courses are taught by former high school teachers and their teaching methods reflect that somewhat narrow background. It is different from our former more liberal university experiences

Hildegard finishes her education courses with honors and several school boards want to recruit her to teach in their school district. There is a shortage of teachers. She decides to accept a position in Burnaby as a French teacher in the Kensington Junior High School.

We rent one side of a duplex at the end of Ellesmere Ave. on Capitol Hill, not too far from the school. It is a small one bedroom place with a magnificent view of the coastal mountains and Indian Arm, a fjord of the Burrard Inlet. The owner has it newly painted, lime green and coral, colors which go very much against our sense of color harmony. So before we move in, we ask if it can be repainted. She agrees to pay for the paint, and we do the painting, sepia brown and pale yellow.

Hildegard's father now has a position as pastor of a German Mennonite congregation in Abbotsford and they can visit us more often. On their first visit Mother brings us as a housewarming gift a set of dishes, green with a strong brown and ocher abstract design. I look at Hildegard and see that she does not like it either. I tell Mother politely that I don't think it would fit well into our décor and would affect our enjoyment of eating from it. She is dumbfounded and after she finds her speech again says "Then I will give it to Gertraud, she will appreciate it". Hildegard and I are somewhat embarrassed but I want to be honest.

The news about our polite rejection of the gift spreads quickly. Some of our relatives are shocked about our audacity in rejecting Mother's gift given so lovingly, others are surprised at our courage to be so honest. This honesty has its rewards; from this time on people are more thoughtful in choosing gifts for the young Lemkes and we receive few ill-designed objects or trinkets as gifts.

To live in our new apartment in winter is a challenge. The central heating system is in the basement and is only accessible from the outside. On some winter mornings I get up at six o'clock, put my winter coat over my pajamas, climb down the small outside stairs from the kitchen into the boiler-room and that sometimes in minus twenty- two degree weather and start the fire. The logs for it I have to split myself. Then I crawl back into bed which Hildegard has kept warm for me. When she gets up it is already cozy warm. One benefit this hardship has for us - the rent for our apartment is reasonable. We outlive three consecutive renters who lived on the other side of the duplex. We are quite content and happy in our small home and give expression to that by singing our old German folksongs in harmony while doing our work. Our neighbors on the other side of the duplex hear us singing lustily and ask if we are practicing for a choir,

Just before school starts the principal hires Marguerita, whose main subject is also French. Now Hildegard has to share the French classes with her and has, in addition to French to teach English and Health and Personal Development (HPD). This course is a little problematic for her to teach since she grew up with a different cultural background, customs and values. She does not like to teach from the prescribed textbook, so she tries to draw out some information from her students and then compare it with her own 'personal development'. She takes the best out of both and teaches that. Her students find it interesting, especially the girls, who adore her. She finds that out later.

At a friend's place in Christina Lake, where we have our summer cottage, Hildegard meets Diana, a hefty middle-aged woman. They both help a friend painting her cabin. When Diana hears Hildegard's name she recognizes her and cries out, "My Mrs. Lemke!, my favorite teacher. I remember you well; you were one of my best teachers, always very elegantly dressed but you did not shave your legs". They laugh and hug each other.

About forty years after she had quit teaching, Hildegard and her sister take a walk on a cold winter day and pass the pub a few blocks away from our house. They see a man at the Mountain Shadow Inn shoveling snow from the entrance of the pub. He takes a rest, turns around and sees these two muffled up women passing by. He looks at them, "Aren't you Mrs. Lemke", he asks, "my former French teacher from Kensington?" When Hildegard assures him that this is her name, he sheepishly tells her "But I cannot call you Mrs. Lemke anymore" She allows him to call her Hildegard. "I am the owner of the pub" and he points at the building, "It is cold outside; come in and I will treat you to a bowl of hot soup". As they are enjoying the soup, he tells her that he did not like French but it came alive and was fun the way she taught it.

I take our daughter, Krista, for a driver's test. While we are waiting in the license office for the examiner, I hear a voice in the background, "Be nice to her, she is the daughter of my favorite teacher."

The principal is not very considerate towards Hildegard, his inexperienced new teacher. In her first year of teaching he gives her one of the worst English classes in the school, students with low IQs and some young offenders with criminal records. She has to be very strict with these boys at the beginning to keep order in the class. This has some repercussions.

One night a group of these boys come into our street, when it is already dark, and throw a dozen eggs at the house next door, assuming it is the house where Hildegard lives. The neighbor is not happy at all about the mess. A few weeks later we hear objects hitting our roof, door and window. We go outside and see the yellow egg yolk running down the roof and door. This time they have targeted the right house. It is the same gang.

The principal, a good detective, finds out who the boys are and punishes them for their mischief. A month later they take revenge again and burn their English test papers on the running board of our car. We do not say much about it this time but it is scary for Hildegard this first year teaching and I have to cheer her up occasionally. These 'attacks' stop after the two incidents.

7. Changing Careers

Hildegard has been teaching for a year, when I lose my job. BC is entering an economic recession and there is now very little work for architects. Mr. van Norman, my employer, tries his best to keep his staff on the pay roll but when the bank refuses him any further credit he has to downsize and one by one we are laid off. The last one, the senior architect, takes an original oil painting from the office wall as a pledge. He is going to return it, when the boss pays him the last three months wages he owes him. The recession hits many architects. My former employer has to close his office as well. He retreats to his own ranch in the interior of BC and becomes a cowboy.

I hit the road again with my folder of sample drawings, designs and references under my arm. I have a list of fourteen architects who practice in Vancouver and I visit each one of them. I follow up those visits once a week with the ones who asked for my résumé, to find out if they received new contracts.

After a few months of trying to find a job, I give up and venture on a different career, teaching. My degree in architecture and one year Bluffton College give me enough credits to be accepted at UBC for a post graduate year in education. I take many of the basic courses Hildegard had taken a year ago. They are exactly the same this year and she allows me to use her lecture notes. In my selected specialties, Art and German, I get high marks. In Philosophy and Psychology of Education, my European viewpoint sometimes deviates from that of my 'progressive' professors, but I still finish both courses with good marks.

I graduate in 1958 with a BC teaching certificate. My last teaching practicum was in the Burnaby South Senior Secondary School. It happens that this school needs a teacher for German and Art. The principal offers me that position and I gladly accept it. Hildegard and I are now teachers in the same School District. We break a Burnaby by-law prohibiting husband and wife from teaching in the same district; however, the shortage of teachers is enough reason for the School Board to change its rules.

Teaching was the first profession I wanted to pursue after high school graduation. Right after the war, German Universities suffered from a shortage of professors and facilities. To enroll in a university that had been damaged in the war, a student has to help rebuild the university to provide needed additional lecture rooms and laboratories before he is admitted. Only a limited number of students are admitted to many faculties. Because of this "numerus clausus", I was not accepted into the faculty of education but could enroll in my second choice, the faculty of architecture.

We are now both foreign language teachers. Hildegard teaches French to junior students and I teach German to senior students. She is a born teacher. She presents her subject efficiently and enthusiastically, as is her temperament. She involves students in conversations and role plays and tells stories and her students like the young good-looking, creative teacher.

My first year of teaching German, the language I have spoken for the first thirty years of my life, proves to be more difficult than I had expected. I cannot easily anticipate the problems students face learning a foreign language. As I gain more experience, I can identify their problems more readily and can answer many questions before they are even asked.

I enjoy teaching my mother tongue, especially German literature, to the advanced classes. I also introduce them to German history, culture and customs and the correct etiquette when visiting a German family. A few times I invite my graduating class to our home to practice this last skill; Hildegard is a good hostess and involves students to speak German, they love it.

In art I try a number of creative approaches. Besides drawing and painting, we do sculptures in different media, pottery, architectural and textile design, batik and silk screening.

A great favorite is jewelry making, especially copper enameling, which is fashionable during the Hippie period and draws more students into my art classes. In graphic design we create ads for the local newspaper using black and white photography and students are excited seeing their pictures evolve in the developer-bath in the darkroom.

The drama teacher asks my help with the stage design for the school's drama productions, mainly Broadway Musicals. My students learn to paint large backdrops and movable settings. Inspired by this work they venture into other large scale painting.

Our school adds a new Technical Education wing to accommodate the increasing student population. The building contractor shields the excavation site off with an eight foot high plywood panel fence which looks rather drab. I suggest to him that we could transform the fence into an outdoors art gallery. It would be an interesting feature for our school. With his permission and help our students paint pictures on the side of the 4x8 foot panels that face the school. The panels are up for tender and all students may apply to paint them. This is a hot project and a lot of fun, so much so that students would rather paint outside than attend their regular classes.

Reporters from local newspapers come to get a good story for their paper. They photograph our students painting some of the 103 panels, print them on the front page and our art department gets some free publicity...

Since we both now have secure jobs in Burnaby, we want to establish ourselves here. Hildegard and I begin looking for property in this area, close to our workplace. We find a building lot on Ridge Drive on the sunny southwest slope of Burnaby Mountain. It is accessible on a gravel road. If we climb up a little, we have a beautiful panoramic view of the coastal mountains, the water of Burrard Inlet and the city. We negotiate with the owner and he tells us, "This is a gold-mine; wait until the area is more developed and the price of a lot with this view will increase greatly", and he is right. So we pay $3500, (the equivalent to a teacher's annual salary) for a double lot which borders on Burnaby Mountain

Park. We are now proud owners of a piece of property in Burnaby, BC. We achieve this in four years after my immigration to Canada, in our third year of marriage.

The first thing we do on our property is build a bench on the highest point of our lot Whenever we have time we drive out, sit on the bench, take in the beautiful view and dream of our future home.

8. Second Thoughts about Canada

In 1959 we have paid off our mortgage and to celebrate this event we plan a trip back to Germany. Hildegard had said to me shortly after we were married, "You never asked me if I would consider coming back to Germany before you emigrated." That is right, I never did and I don't know why. When then I ask, "Would you have come?" she thinks for a moment and replies "I don't know".

On this trip we want to find out if we have made the right decision to settle in Canada.

We have planned a demanding agenda for the two months we want to spend in Europe. We begin our trip in Frankfurt and travel first to Kaiserslautern. Hildegard is very anxious to see the old town where she spent the first seventeen years of her life and she wants to introduce me to the city, to her relatives and friends. The house on Lilienstrasse five, where she was born, a typical three story town house, built with the local red-brown sandstone, is now painted a light blue. It looks so different, it alienates her and she does not dare to go inside.

She cannot wait to visit her old high school, the *Höhere Weibliche Bildungsanstalt*. She walks through her old classrooms and meets her former science teacher, Miss Lauterbach. She tells Hildegard what has changed in education since she left and asks what she is doing. Years later, when we have children, she sends us the best-seller in German children's books every year at Christmas and the children love the stories.

We walk down the Eisenbahnstrasse to the railway station. Hildegard remembers the shrill whistle of the old steam locomotives, which are now diesel-driven.

She had taken the train to school in Kaiserslautern from the nearby village of Stockborn, to which the family had been evacuated because of bomb threats during World War II. Hildegard knows the village well; it belonged to her father's congregation.

We trek from one farm to the next and hear the stories of their families. They tell us about the good old days and the changes that have taken place since Hildegard left. Her most memorable couple, Onkel Hannes and Tante Emma, who had no children and had sort of 'adopted' the Scheffler girls, offer us their guest room to stay overnight and we sleep wonderfully in the old wooden double-bed with thick fluffy eiderdown pillows and duvets.

We cannot leave the village before Hildegard finds out what has become of her first little boyfriend, Werner. They had played with marbles in the yard and he had been creative in inventing new games. Now he is a well-established farmer and has a family. He is rather reserved and interaction with him is somewhat difficult.

Having grown up on a farm, I enjoy being in the country again and getting involved with the people who live and work there, especially with those who had a vital influence on Hildegard's formative years. It helps me to understand her better and when she later talks about these old friends, I can put a face to the name.

Neudorferhof, a small settlement in the winegrowing part of the Palatinate, is also one of Hildegard's father's spiritual charges. Eva, Hildegard's oldest sister, had been an apprentice in farm management at Onkel Adolf and Tante Mariechen's farm and vineyard. They invite us for dinner and let us taste some of their wines of the last vintage.

Further north we stop at *Eischeiderhof* in the Eifel Mountains. The Scheffler girls spent many holidays on this well-managed estate of the Fuchs family. We are privileged to spend two nights there. All have pleasant memories of their former beloved Pastor's family and are happy to see Hildegard again.

Fritz, one of Tante Fuchs' sons, had a crush on Ruth, Hildegard's older sister, but he did not have the courage to propose to her. Later when he had a family he called his first daughter Ruth. Heini, the oldest son, thought Eva, with her training in farming, would make a good farmer's wife on his estate but he too was afraid of being rejected. He never got married. Both Ruth and Eva later said they might have considered these respective proposals.

Hildegard wants to see the *Maare*, her former 'swimming pools,' again. We drive through a forest and in a clearing before us we see three craters of former volcanoes. They are now small, almost circular, deep lakes. This volcano area, the Eifel, is known for its mineral springs and on the way back we pass one whose water runs like an artesian fountain into a basin; it is accessible to the public and I drink a glass of this rather tart-tasting mineral water.

Now it is my turn to introduce Hildegard to my relatives who live in North Germany. Cousin Günther is the first one we visit. He lives in a well built red brick house right on the edge of the Lüneburger Heide (heath). I remember him as a young boy, in his grandfather's smithy, now he is a reputable police chief in the town of Schneverdingen. I had written to him when I asked for information for my Lemke Chronicle, now he and Hanna are very happy to see us after such a long time and we share what had happened in all those years.

They offer us their spacious guest suite for the few days we spend with them and they treat us regally. The sun is shining and he takes us on a bike ride on narrow trails and board walks through the blooming heather. Up on a hill we watch a bearded shepherd with his long coat and shepherd's crook herding his small black faced Heidschnucken sheep, surrounded by watchful sheepdogs, a pastoral sight.

Günther, like his father and grandfather, is a beekeeper and has several beehives in his backyard. He gives us a glass of yellow heather honey as a farewell gift.

Right after the war the Lüneburg heath had been the training ground for British and French tanks. One can still see deep tracks in the sand and piles of dirt from their sharp turns.

I introduce Hildegard to other relatives and friends whom I have not seen for decades. They love Hildegard's friendly, animated way and the ease with which they can communicate with her.

We visit my favorite classroom teacher, Dr. Sundermeyer. He is delighted to see me again and meet Hildegard." Your coming back is a good reason to have a class reunion!" so he phones some former classmates and a few days later a dozen of us meet in a restaurant in Peine, not far from our old school. Hildegard happens to sit beside Dr. Sundermeyer. He is charmed by her winning smile, her openness and the intensity with which she can listen and respond. He, too, is a very good communicator.

From Germany we drive west to Paris. We are looking forward to visiting the Louvre and see the paintings of old and new masters. Hildegard has several reproductions of these masters in her art folio. It is exciting to see the originals now hanging on the walls or standing on pedestals in this famous art gallery.

To stand before old city halls and water-spouting fountains in Paris and go through the Versailles palace is more impressive than analyzing them from art history books. Hildegard remembers some of these sites from her French studies.

We also enjoy the famous French cuisine and sip the renowned French wines which are served with each dinner.

We continue our trip into Switzerland. In Zurich we look into the ninth century *Fraumünster Abbey*, which emperor Louie the German had dedicated to his daughter Hildegard. We walk through the *Großmünster*, known for the disputes between Protestant reformer Zwingli and the Anabaptist leaders, Konrad Grebel and Felix Manz. The outcome of these dialogues had terrible consequences later for the Anabaptists and Mennonites.

We drive around beautiful Lake Luzern, surrounded by high alpine Mountains. In Bern we are fascinated by Rodin's large sculpture group of the *Burghers of Calais*. We take time to walk around the individual larger than man-size sculptures displayed in the open market plaza and admire Rodin's masterful portrayal of tension and agony in the faces and bodies of the desperate, humiliated burghers when they surrender the key of their city to the enemy.

A visit to Bienenberg, the Bible School where Hildegard's father had taught for three years, concludes our time in Switzerland.

In Munich we happen to get involved in the *Evangelischer Kirchentag*, a special day in the year for all German Protestant churches to gather and celebrate their faith. About one hundred thousand people from all over Germany and neighboring countries listen to talks by important theologians, participate in discussion groups and prayer meetings or listen to musical performances. Since I had lived in the Protestant parsonage and had attended their services, I thought we would qualify to participate. For three nights, we stay with two Catholic teachers who have offered their house to participants of the Kirchentag, free of charge.

For another four days we visit several churches and art galleries. Among the latter are the Alte Pinakothek with a variety of Old Dutch masters and German, French and English painters and sculptors and the Neue Pinakothek with many paintings from French Impressionists and German Expressionists. My favorite masters, Franz Marc and Wassily Kandinsky, are well represented.

We return our car, which has served us so well for these seven weeks, to cousin Erich and take the train to the airport.

It is hard to depart from these familiar and interesting places and the people we love. When we board the plane to Vancouver, we talk about our beloved home country, weighing the pros and cons of having immigrated to Canada. At the end we come to the conclusion: we have chosen wisely to buy property in British Columbia, settle down there and build our future in Canada, in spite of all the historic beauty of Europe and the friends and loving relatives we have left behind. It will be easier for us and our children to establish ourselves here. Germany will always be an attraction for us and our children to visit.

9. Becoming Canadian Mennonites

Before I immigrated to Canada I had known a number of Canadian Mennonites through MCC and heard that there are several different Mennonite churches in Vancouver and vicinity. When I arrived in Vancouver I searched out a few of them. Naturally I want to go to the same church as my sister. But to become a member of the Mennonite Brethren church, which she and Gustav attend, I would have to be re-baptized by immersion. Magdalena and I had been baptized in West Prussia by sprinkling. I hesitate to join their church., as I did not want to devaluate my baptism. I also find the MB church too legalistic. My cousin Erwin, who is co-pastor in the First United Mennonite Church, invites me to attend their services. When Hildegard comes to Vancouver we join First United Mennonite Church. Most of the church members are immigrants from the German settlements in the Ukraine and South America. At church they speak High German but in daily life they speak Low German. We German Mennonites, or 'Prussians', as we are referred to by them, do not speak Low German anymore; our Grandparents were the last generation who did. We also do not share all the same customs, so it is not easy for us to integrate and we remain 'outsiders'. We also have university degrees and are suspected of being too liberal. Hildegard has difficulty with the simple, not very challenging Sunday sermons and the often pat answers given to complex questions about faith.

We sing in the choir and become friends with its conductor, Paul and his wife, and befriend three young couples, the children of the pastor, who, like us, are also teachers.

One Sunday in the morning service, Ältester Wiens introduces new visitors, John Wiebe and his wife Monika from Germany. I turn around, see them standing and wonder; this Monika looks familiar to me. After the service we introduce ourselves to them and Monika tells me that we have met at young peoples' retreats in Northern Germany. She was then still a young vivacious teenager. We have a lot of memories to share. We invite them for lunch to our place and they tell us their story.

John, who lives in Abbotsford, had studied at the Music Academy in Detmold, Germany. Some of his musician friends had studied there and lauded its quality of instruction. Inspired by them, he went to Detmold and enrolled in a three year course in voice, instrumental instruction and conducting.

At that time John's younger brother, Herbert, was doing alternative military service as a 'Pax Boy' near Detmold. They were helping a Mennonite refugee congregation in Bielefeld to build their first church. Monika's father, Lothar, was involved in the design and construction of that church. He is senior art instructor in a High School in Bielefeld. His family befriended the lonely Canadian Pax Boys and invited them to their home. They introduce them to German culture and customs and provide a good meal.

At one of these visits, Herbert tells Lothar that his brother, John, is studying music in Detmold and Lothar tells Herbert to bring him along. Hans, as they call him, becomes a frequent visitor at the Hein's home. He finds their oldest daughter, Monika, attractive. They fall in love, get married and she decides to immigrate to Canada.

John plans to study education at UBC, to become a music teacher. He takes the same program that Hildegard and I had taken a few years ago. We can give him some valuable hints and help them to get acquainted with Vancouver. Monika comes originally from the same area in West Prussia where I was born and we have many things in common.

The Wiebes and we are about the same age, attend the same church, share an interest in music, art and literature and soon we become good friends.

10. Preserving our heritage

Several Mennonites as well as Baptists, Lutherans and other denominations have their main church service in German. To help the children understand and participate in the service, these churches founded 'Samstagsschulen'. Parents encourage their children to learn or improve their German in these 'German Saturday schools'. Many children hate having to spend their free Saturday in German School, but they come. Hildegard volunteers to teach a senior class for a couple of years and I am school superintendent during that time.

The new German Consul in Vancouver, Dr.Liebrecht, is impressed by the effort of these churches to retain German Language and Culture and is willing to support them. After all, among the three point six million British Columbians there are about ninety-five thousand of German origin. So he sets out to visit the German schools and happens to drop in on Hildegard's class as she discusses Rilke's poems with her students. To hear Rilke interpreted in this environment seems to surprise him. He talks to Hildegard afterwards for a while and is impressed and charmed by her personality and style of teaching and a friendship develops. We correspond with him long after he retires from Consular duties and returns to Germany.

Dr.Liebrecht tells us of the existence of a German-Canadian Cultural Society. We attend one of their meetings and learn to know Mrs. Kastens, its president. She had been a high school teacher in Berlin. Her roots are also in East Prussia. After the war the Russians had taken her to Siberia and she had to spend several years there under forbidding conditions. We have had similar experiences and it does not take long before we befriend her and her husband.

Mrs. Kastens asks Hildegard to accept the position of 'Kulturbeirat', (Culture Council), in the society and to assist her in organizing interesting programs. The Cultural Society's goal is to make German-Canadians aware of their cultural heritage and cherish it and to familiarize Canadians in general with the contributions of German scholars, humanists, scientists and artists to our society.

The German Consulate and Frau Kastens have access to German Government and private German organizations. Upon our request, they will provide guest speakers for us, who will inform us about events in science, politics and art in Germany. After their talks we sit together with a cup of coffee and refreshments and socialize in a more informal manner.

One of these guests at our meeting is the well-known German minstrel, Karl Wolfram. We appreciate his performance of medieval art and folksongs which he accompanies on original instruments of different periods, lute, theorbe, zither and hurdy-gurdy. We talk with him after the performance and can persuade him to come to our house for an encore. We also invite some of our music-loving friends. I quickly make a fire in our fireplace. Hildegard places candles around the room and puts some refreshments on the table. She has a gift of transforming a room, creating a warm and cozy atmosphere appropriate to the occasion, in this case a romantic medieval one.

Wolfram spots our harpsichord and is surprised to find such an instrument in a private home. He remarks that the real period cembalo has gut strings on a wooden frame; ours has a metal frame inside because of the humid coastal climate. He is a purist and tells us that he sings only songs where text and music are from the same period. He offers to sing a few more songs for us and we all enjoy his encore in a more intimate environment.

On another occasion we invite the German author, Dr.Willy Kramp, and he shares from his work and his time. He, too, accepts an invitation to come to our house to see how German-Canadians have established themselves. He admires the design and fine décor and the grand view from the windows of our house. Hildegard wins his heart. He writes in our guest-book

> Ich habe mich wie bei nahen Verwandten
> gefühlt – in Ihrem schönen Hause!
> 24. 10. 65   Willy Kramp

(I felt like being with close relatives in your beautiful home Oct. 24, '65)

Hildegard keeps up a correspondence with him for several years. He writes after this visit

> "Ihr Haus war das einzige Haus während meiner ganzen Reise, das nach meinem eigenen Geschmack war. Ich spürte, dass Sie – sozusagen – Ihre heimatlichen Hausgötter mitgenommen hatten und das Ihre innere Welt Ihnen auch dort in der Fremde Heimat geschaffen hatte. Es ist gut zu wissen, dass es so etwas in unserer unheimlatlichen Welt gibt".

(Your house was the only one during my entire trip that was to my own aesthetic taste. I felt -so to speak- that you had taken your ancestral gods (values) with you and that your inner world had created a home for you in a foreign country. It is good to know that something like this is still possible in our alienated world.)

The audience at our German-Canadian Cultural Society meetings is usually German immigrants and students who take German courses at UBC and some of their professors.

At one of our programs an elderly couple comes in and looks a little lost. I welcome them and introduce them to other members of our society. Hildegard and I get into a more intimate conversation with them after the meeting. They are a German-Jewish couple on a stopover in Vancouver. We invite them to our home later and they tell us that they had lived in Israel, in America and plan to go back to Berlin, where they once lived. "We are still Germans and we love our German culture", they tell us. When Hildegard apologizes to them about what Germans had done to their Jewish fellow citizens, he looks at her and says, "I was in Berlin when the Berlin Wall was built. When the police officer told me to step back, so that they can lay the concrete blocks to divide Germany, I said, 'Yes, officer', and stepped back. I did not complain and say what you are doing is wrong. I know that many Germans did not approve of what the Nazis did but they too stepped back." These two were an unusual, kind couple. Later on, they sent us a card from Berlin

Jean and Hildegard

Adelheid and Monika

Ulli   John

Frau Kastens likes to give evolving local German-Canadian artists an opportunity to perform in public. Reinhard, a relative of ours, works in Siegfried's German bookstore, the 'Book Nook'. He tells us enthusiastically about Ulli, the brother-in-law of Siegfried, who writes beautiful poetry and illustrates some in a color-felt-pen technique. We mention that to Frau Kastens. She invites him to one of our German Canadian Cultural Society meeting to read from his work. We had not yet met him.

She introduces Ulrich Schaffer, a student of Germanistics and American literature. He reads from his poems, handwritten, still unpublished. After his reading, in the discussion afterwards, we talk about his poetry and German and American literature in general. We appreciate his spirit and attitude and before we depart we exchange addresses.

Hildegard draws like-minded people easily into a more intimate relationship. We invite Ulli and his fiancée, Waltraud, together with John and Monika to our home. In our conversation around the coffee table we discover that they, too, are German refugees like Monika and I and that they immigrated to Canada around the same time that we did. Ulli had been studying in Hamburg and is now doing postgraduate work at UBC; Waltraud is a teacher in an elementary school. They are both leading the young peoples' group in their Baptist church as we do in the Mennonite church. We continue our get-togethers and soon a bond develops between us three couples. As Mennonites and Anabaptists we share a deep Christian faith which becomes an important component in our friendship.

11. Building a new Church

More Mennonite immigrants arrive from South America and Europe and we need more room to house the newcomers in our church building. Some suggest extending the existing facilities but several of us would like to take wings, fly out of the old nest and settle somewhere else. This means we would have to find property on which to erect a new building. The church council asks me, as an architect, to come up with some good ideas. I take on the challenge, do some research, find out in which area most of our people live, look for available property in that vicinity and ask the planning department for rezoning. Hildegard and I visit a few new churches, talk to the pastors to find out what they like in their new church building and what they do not. Using their input and my experience, I do a number of sketches and present them to the council and later to the congregation. We agree on a design and from it we build the new church on Sherbrooke Street.

Shortly before I designed the Sherbrooke church, a church planting group of Mennonites in Richmond had asked me to design a meeting hall for their new congregation, later they wanted to add a larger sanctuary to it. Another congregation, the Mountain View Mennonite Church commissioned me to design a Sunday school complex for their church and upgrade the sanctuary. I enjoyed doing both jobs.

Cousin Erwin is ordained to be the pastor of the new Sherbrooke Mennonite congregation. Those who like change in leadership and style and live in the area flock to the new church.

Hildegard and I are excited and willing to help establish a new congregation. The pastor asks us to be sponsors of the young peoples group. We accept and hope to inspire our younger generation. They accept us, without the prejudices which some of their parents have against "Prussians". They trust us and we have a good relationship with them. John and Monika join the new congregation and John becomes its music director. He forms a church choir which sings in Sunday services and for special occasions.

At this time, a self-appointed prophet speaks in the Baptist church about end-time events. Waltraud is impressed and thinks we should listen to him too. Hildegard had heard her parents and sisters speak about end-times and is interested, so we invite him to our home. He walks up to the big window in our living room, looks over Burrard Inlet and the coastal mountains and comments, "You will be safe here." We are puzzled and ask, "Safe from what?" He says, "God gave me a vision: 'Vancouver was hit by a big earthquake, all the high rise buildings collapsed and a huge tsunami swept over the city and the Fraser valley, leaving a terrible destruction behind," and he adds, "But the tsunami would not come up to the level of your house; you will be safe." Hildegard, who had survived bombing raids in Germany during the war and seen the destruction of sections of her city, has flashes of that time and asks him, "What can we do about that?" He replies, "This is a sign of the end-times which will come soon. Pray for the salvation of your family and the people around you and look for a place of refuge".

We know seismologists have predicted a shift of continental plates along fault lines which go through our area. This will result in an upheaval of the earth of a tremendous magnitude and could happen within the next two hundred years. This seems to support his statement. He gives a date when this will happen and then I get suspicious and question if his vision is from God, as he claims. I assure Hildegard she need not worry; we survived the horrors of WWII and will be able to endure this if it should happen during our lifetime. But we store some water bottles and boxes with non-perishable food in the basement. A few months later this incident fades and we once again go joyfully about our daily business in home and church.

12 For the Love of Music.

John has been musical director in our church for a while and realizes the limitations of a church choir. He would like to extend his musical activities beyond what he can expect from ordinary church members. He visualizes an ensemble which could perform more 'demanding' music, a dream he had when he left the music academy in Detmold. We invite a few music friends to our house, discuss the matter and come to the decision to form a choir which would enjoy singing cantatas, motets and masses. We even come up with a name for the new choir, the "Motet Singers". John's background and contact with good musicians from various other churches, helps him to sign up qualified singers. Soon our small group grows to a thirty voice choir and we sing and perform motets and cantatas from Schütz, Bach, and Brahms to Hindemith, a Capella and with a small orchestra. We sing in churches, community halls for special occasions and cut two records with Hugh McLean at the organ.

It was common in the old country for Mennonite families to have a keyboard instrument in their home and the children, at least the girls, would take piano lessons. So we want to continue that tradition and get a piano. When Hildegard resigns from teaching she asks the school board to refund her contributions to the teacher's pension plan. The amount she receives is just enough to cover the price for a good piano. We ask John for advice. He thinks we should be a little more adventurous and invest in a harpsichord. He knows a harpsichord builder in town who has just emigrated from Munich and is now building harpsichords here in Vancouver. After all, the music we love and perform is mainly from the period where this instrument, the cembalo or harpsichord, was played.

We visit the harpsichord builder, Sabathil, in his factory. He shows us the different models he builds and suggests one that would be suitable for "Hausmusik" and is in a price range we can afford. We agree to order one.

The new Harpsichord fits perfectly into our living room and matches our teak furniture. Hildegard tries it out for a while. She can play piano but feels a little unsure with the different keys and touch of the instrument. To improve her performance, she asks Mrs. Sabathil if she is willing to give her lessons and she does.

We are excited about our new instrument. We like the soft sound of the plucked strings on different sound levels. We love to gather around it as a family and make music, Hildegard on the harpsichord and the rest of us singing in harmony or joining in with recorder, clarinet, oboe or trumpet. We both want to introduce our children to good music and, by example, inspire them to appreciate and perform music on instruments of their choice.

Hanno, Hildegard, Krista, Helmut, Michael

Serenade at our Golden Wedding
Krista, Hanno, Madison, Michael

My mother is glad that I continue my father's tradition and encourages us to sing or play as a family – a little von Trapp family- at small church or family events. When the children get older performances of this kind fade out.

Knowing that we have a harpsichord draws other music lovers to our house. John gets a small ensemble of musicians together and for several years our living room becomes a centre for *Hausmusik*. Gerhard, a German church organist, plays the harpsichord, John viola, Jake cello and Harald plays the flute. We all love to hear the quartet play.

The Hippie and Jesus People era is especially conducive to making music. Members of our house group and church compose songs, often adapted from scripture texts, and play them accompanied by guitars at our worship services.

We often listen to the songs of the Medical Mission Sisters. I sometimes play songs, based on scripture texts, from their records to my class in school instead of reading the prescribed text from the King James Bible. At that time we still were required to start each school day with a Bible reading and the Lord's Prayer.

We get acquainted and become friends with Merv and Merla Watson, a musical family. They often travel to Israel and have composed contemporary Christian music often based on the Psalms and specially adapted to Messianic-Jewish audiences. They have cut a number of records and tapes of which we have several.

13. Our first home

Since I have established myself as senior art teacher at Burnaby South Senior Secondary School, a fairly steady position, we can think of starting a family. We decided, after we returned from our exploration trip to Germany, to make Canada our home and Burnaby the place where we want to settle.

It will be a challenge to design a house on a steep sloping lot, taking into account such a gorgeous view.

I draw a few possible designs, we plan the details and build a scale model. Hildegard is very creative and helpful. We plan the house to be built in two stages. When we have paid off most of the mortgage for the first stage we will add the second stage.

I am architect, general contractor and construction worker in one. Cousin Herbert, whose house I had designed before, and Gus, my brother-in-law, whom I helped to build his first house, are my faithful companions. By helping Gustav to build his house I learned a lot about the Canadian wood frame construction, which is uncommon in Germany. Doing most of the work myself, keeps the building cost down.

Hildegard is very actively involved, ordering materials, supervising the construction when I am not there, helping to nail sub floors and siding and bringing meals and drinks to the building site when we can't go home to eat. 1960 is a hot summer; it does not rain while we are building the shell of the house until the roof is on.

We have to go back to school again after the holidays and are glad that doors and windows are installed and the house can be locked up at night. We are working now two jobs, during daytime teaching and in the evening and sometimes early in the morning finishing the house.

We give notice to our landlady that we are leaving and are excited and happy to move into our new house. It is not completely finished when we move in and the building inspector does not approve of our moving into an unfinished house. He threatens to cut off water and electricity; I have to be diplomatic in persuading him to issue an occupancy permit which is required for connection to the city's water and electricity grid.

We live in the first stage of our house for a year but to live in a house where we have to enter through the back door and have the dining room serve also as living room is very inconvenient. We abandon our five year plan to pay off the mortgage before we start building the final stage and change it to a two year plan. We had already poured the foundation for the whole house during the first stage so it does not take that long to complete the second stage.

Hildegard once more takes active part in the construction and we have some photos showing her standing on the ladder holding up roof rafters while I nail them in.

We are both looking forward to having a family and want our children to be born into our own finished house.

On one morning in late spring, I am woken up very early by sounds coming from the woods through our open window. We are sleeping in the bedroom of our new house already which is facing the forest. I listen for a while and think these sounds must be bird songs. I look at my watch; it is four o'clock. I sneak out of the bedroom quietly. Hildegard is still sleeping. I hang my new Uher four speed tape recorder over my shoulder, go up the stairs from the patio across the backyard into the forest. Very quietly I move deeper into the woods, always listening. I set my tape recorder at fast speed and start recording these varied songs. Occasionally I can see a colorful dot between the leaves; it looks like the bulging red breast of a Robin making those short caroling sounds up and down. There is the outstretched neck and open beak of the mocking bird singing long continuous phrases and repeating them several times. It is interrupted by the deeper piping whistle of the Oriole or the staccato clack, clack of the blue jay. The birds seem to inspire each other to sing, sometimes I hear a solo and then an orchestra, all singing at full volume. It sounds eerie at this time in the morning. When the sun comes up all of a sudden the songs stop and it is quiet in the woods.

I go back to bed again and the bird songs accompany me in my dream. In the evening I play the recording for Hildegard at slow speed. We notice that the long continuous sounds are actually drawn out tremolos which the birds can hear but we cannot.

We appreciate our home and the park right behind it. We blaze a small private trail through the woods up to the mountain ridge. From its top we have a panoramic view of the city to the south. Burrard Inlet with the Indian Arm, a steep fjord of it, and the coastal mountains are on the north side. There is no public access to the park from our street and the deer are not afraid to graze occasionally on our back lawn. It is not always that idyllic. We have a peaceful supper after a busy day in our dining room when we hear voices in the woods at the end of our property. It sounds as if a tree is falling. I go up to see what is going on. The two older sons of our neighbor are hacking at our trees. I am annoyed and ask them why they are doing that on my property when theirs is twice as wide. They feel they do not owe me an answer. So I confiscate their axe and tell them their father can claim it back from me. I have not met their father yet. He is known to be very outspoken and controlling. Not long after I have put the axe away, the phone rings. An angry man's voice asks me who I think I am and tells me in no uncertain terms, "You have no right to affront my sons in this way and confiscate their property. You may do this in the country you come from, in Nazi Germany, but here in Canada the woods belong to all Canadians and we operate on different terms. You'd better return the axe." He is a lawyer. I ask him, "If the forest belongs to all Canadians don't they have a communal obligation to care for the park or can everyone go and cut trees where he wants? Why did your boys not cut trees on your property which is larger than mine? They can claim their axe at any time, since you now know about their activities in the woods." I try to be as polite and factual as possible. Later I meet his wife on the street and she apologizes for her husband's anger; "The boys will come and pick up the axe." Over time, our relationship improves.

In 1962, when Hildegard knows that she is expecting a baby, she hands in her resignation to the Burnaby School board. I think it is not easy for her to give up a job which she likes and in which she is very competent and creative, but the anticipation and joy of having a family makes that decision easier. Hildegard wants to stay at home and be a full-time mother, guiding the children in their most vulnerable years and be available for them when they need her. We both agree on that.

Our firstborn arrives on Hildegard's twenty-ninth birthday after eighteen hours of excruciating labor pain. Hildegard is thankful when it is all over and happy when the little boy is put into her arms. He weighs seven pounds and thirteen ounces, (3544g) is healthy, has a ferocious appetite and knows how to get his nourishment.

We call him Michael ('who is like God'), a name common in both German and English. Hildegard has given herself a beautiful birthday gift, he is a Sunday child.

She is well prepared for bringing him home. For the first weeks she puts his cradle in our bedroom for the night, so that she can easily breastfeed him. It is a lovely sight to see these two together. Hildegard is a beautiful, devoted mother.

We put Michael into his own room after seven weeks when he sleeps through the night. In one of the antique stores we find an old wooden rocking chair with wide arm rests. It is comfortable and practical for Hildegard to nurse him in it and rock him to sleep. He sometimes falls asleep already during his feeding time.

The first festivity in our new house is the blessing ceremony of Michael. We Mennonites do not baptize babies. If they grow up in a Christian home, observe and receive instruction in Christian principles they will develop a faith of their own and can express their wish to be baptized. To give them a good start in life we bless them in a special ceremony. A few months after Michael's birth, we invite Grandfather Scheffler and Cousin Erwin, our pastor, to join the gathered extended family in the new living room (on the plywood floor, the carpet has been ordered but shipment has been delayed). They take little Michael in their arms and pray for God's protection, physical and spiritual health, growth and guidance for his life.

Michael enjoys the full attention of his parents for one and a half years, then he has to share it with a little sister, Krista. We name her after my sister Christa who did not return from the war. He seems to be quite happy to have a little playmate and is very gentle with her. I build a bunk bed for the two, but put the beds at a right angle to each other so that they fit into the corner of the room. It creates a little covered niche underneath the top bed in which they love to play and hide from each other and from Mother.

Hanno, our third one, is in a hurry to find out what this world has to offer. We hardly have time to get Hildegard to the hospital before he arrives. He is the heaviest and weighs 8 lb. 2oz. (3690g) at birth, a healthy baby. Hildegard remembers his peculiar cry, like a rooster. She always knows that it is he when the nurse brings him to her.

Most of our children's furniture and some toys we design ourselves and make to measure. We have fun decorating our children's room, making it beautiful and functional. Hildegard has the idea of making special curtains for the high bedroom windows, with designs based on fairy tale themes. I design the fairy princesses, witches and dwarfs and Hildegard appliqués the colorful shapes on a forest-green cloth. Later when she reads those fairy tales to them with great fervor, she can point to the curtains and the children see the two dimensional characters take on shape, walk out and join them in the story.

Hildegard is a very caring mother. She spends a lot of quality time with the children, is very creative in feeding their imaginations and inspires them to invent new games to play alone or with each other. She does not miss teaching; the small class of three needs all her attention.

All three like books and follow the stories which Mom usually reads to them with great intensity. Michael turns the pages of picture books and magazines very carefully and can spend a long time with them. He is quite disturbed if by accident he tears a page.

Once I have Hanno on my lap and read him a story. One illustration in the book shows a burning house in a city. He points at the picture and responds quite excitedly, "But Daddy stop, we have to extinguish the fire."

We read an article about the mental capability of small children and make an experiment with Michael to test the validity of it. We print flash cards with common words in German, read them to him, pointing to each letter (it is easier in German because it is a very phonetic language) He seems to have fun with it and after a short time he can read all the words on the twenty flash cards. I think he is about two years old. We do not continue the same experiment with the other two.

We watch the children develop their distinct personalities. Michael is the reasonable one, he follows rules and instructions if they are explained to him and make sense or we can persuade him. Not so Krista. She knows what she wants, she is normally quite sweet but can also have a temper tantrum if things do not work out the way she thinks they should. She will throw herself on the floor and cry. The only way Hildegard can get her out of it, is to pick her up and give her a long loving hug. Usually she wants to please us and is quite conscientious. She is the first one to learn to walk and to use the potty, I think before she is two. Hanno is a little trickster, full of ideas and most of the time a happy amiable fellow.

Hildegard tries to introduce our children to routines and to take on little chores. We think this will help them to learn to manage their activities better and prepare them for life later when they have to take on responsibilities. Hildegard is very organized herself and they can observe how she manages her time and activities.

At mealtime we eat together as a family, thanking God for providing and Mother for preparing the food. Sitting around the table with us, gives the children a feeling of being a family and an opportunity to share success stories or miseries of the day, we listen attentively and suggest solutions or give advice if appropriate.

In the evening they have a set time to go to bed. We suggest quiet activities beforehand, announce cleanup time and help them to get ready, if they still need that. One of us will read them a bedtime story or sing a lullaby to or with them, cuddle and tuck them in. If something went wrong during the day and still troubles them we talk about it, pray with them, bless them and wish them a good night. They stay in bed until they fall asleep. Then Hildegard and I have the rest of the evening to wind down, share with each other or read.

Things do not always go that smoothly. Sometimes we feel we have to use more severe means to guide the children. If they have gotten into trouble we will discuss with them what went wrong, point out the consequences of their action and show them how to improve. If they have been repeatedly disobedient, behaved badly or disrespectfully they will get a spanking, depending on the severity of the offence and their age. Occasionally Hildegard tells me somewhat desperately that one of the kids deserves a spanking and delegates action to me. I do not like to administer corporal punishment and do it only in extreme cases if other means do not work. I never spank them on their first offence or in anger. I explain to them afterwards why I think this was necessary, assure them that I still love them and offer a forgiving hug. Hanno sometimes throws his arms around my neck and weeps. I hold him close until he calms down, then he is relieved, smiles, runs to Mom and apologizes. For Krista it is not always that easy…

We try to teach our children to become independent thinkers and not to do things because that is the way people do them. We try to tell and show them that it is sometimes necessary to do things differently, to make decisions not coerced by peer pressure or fashion but based on common sense and their own judgment. That is sometimes hard.

There is the story with the 'Lederhosen' (leather pants). When my sister's boys, Ralf, Benno and Gerald were starting school, they received Lederhosen with the appropriate suspenders and matching jackets from relatives in Germany. They looked spiffy in their little 'Bavarian' outfits and everyone admired them and they wore them more or less proudly but I think also with mixed feelings, at least to school. They outgrew their outfits and passed them on to our boys who are about ten years younger than their cousins. Leather pants can last for several generations.

Michael and Hanno are not very enthusiastic about inheriting leather pants and wearing them to school when nobody else does. At the beginning their fellow students tease them: "Oh, you are still wearing plastic pants." The Gauer's boys were told, you got these pants and you wear them.

We try to persuade them, to stand up for themselves, to dare to be different. Michael finds them practical, they don't tear and wear through and the dirt can be wiped off, so he accepts them more easily. Not so Krista. She gets a pair of cute red girl's leather pants with dainty suspenders from Tante Martha, my favorite aunt in Germany. Krista is the most hesitant to wear them to school and does it only on special occasions, but she likes to wear them at home or if we visit German relatives and friends who admire them.

John and Monika's children are about the same age as ours, two boys, and a girl in the middle. We share our experiences with raising our children. Sometimes they are hair-raising stories. Occasionally we exchange children's outfits. The kids grow out of them so quickly and starting a new household with only one salary means we both have to economize. Monika's mother sends quality children's outfits from Germany and material for Monika to sew her own.

John has a workshop in his basement, as I do. We build furniture, toys and practical things for the household. We are both 'skilled' handymen and do this as a hobby and as a balance to our academic work as teachers.

Now and then, we do things together as families, go on excursions, take canoe trips, play games or make music, occasionally we spend holidays together. These shared activities enrich our friendship.

All our children like music. At age five we enroll Michael in an Orff music class where he learns about rhythm and playing different instruments in a little ensemble. He likes to sing. We do that often as a family, so he joins the school choir. That is sissy stuff in the eyes of his peers. Boys of his age don't sing - that is for girls. He goes even a step further and with three other boys forms a barbershop quartet and they enjoy singing the difficult close harmony. I am proud of him and back him up. Both Michael and Krista join a children's choir outside of school for a number of years. They are all dressed alike and perform for community events and festivities. All three take piano lessons and play in the school bands,

Michael oboe, Krista clarinet and Hanno trumpet. Later, in High School they take guitar lessons so as to be able to accompany our singing. Of course they also love to play street hockey with the neighbor children.

When our children were born my mother lived with us for a few years to help out. She had immigrated two years after I had arrived in Canada. We had urged her to come because of the political unrest in Eastern Europe. The Russian tanks had rolled into Czechoslovakia and we did not know where they would go from there.

It was not easy for Mother to leave the country where she was born and had lived in for over sixty years of her life. She had siblings there and had been a substitute mother for several nieces and nephews. She had been active in the Lutheran parsonage assisting pastor Brandes in church work, visiting sick and troubled people and they valued her counsel. Here in Canada she had her children and some relatives that made up for the loss of family and friends left in Germany.

To adjust to the new country, Mother first stays with my sister's family. They had just purchased their first house in Vancouver. Magdalena enjoys her help with the children. Mother is eager to adapt to her new environment. To be able to communicate with neighbors and make friends, she enrolls in night school courses in English for newcomers. Soon she is in demand as an occasional babysitter for relatives and friends. She is always available and helpful.

Mother knew Hildegard only from photos and from what I enthusiastically had told her. She knew her parents quite well from West Prussia. Now as she lives with us and learns to know Hildegard more intimately she assures me that I made a very good choice. The two get along very well and Hildegard tries out a number of her recipes to cook my favorite West Prussian meals. She also uses Mother's recipe for baking whole grain bread.

The children love their Oma. She plays board games with them inside and floor hockey on the patio. She is sorry that she could not be at our wedding but she brings us a wonderful wedding gift, a full set of

Rosenthal dishes for twelve people, white with platinum rim, a beautiful design.

Hildegard is a very efficient housewife and mother and there is not much work left for Oma to do, so she accepts an offer from our neighbor next door to watch her children for a few hours a day while she is at work. Her three children are quite messy at home, something my mother cannot stand. With the little English she has learned she teaches them to keep order, put toys and clothing in closets and boxes. She does this in a kind and loving way. When their mother comes home she is very surprised at how clean her house is and how Mother can deal with the children in spite of her language difficulties.

We notice that Mother's life is lacking fulfillment, she feels isolated because of her language problem. Back in Germany she had managed our farm after Dad died; she had her own household and was independent. Here she is dependent on our family for communication and support. When she works for other people she is almost subservient, anxious to do everything right. I have not experienced Mother that way. We talk with her about the situation and decide to rent an apartment for her in the German district of Vancouver, close to where some of our relatives live and where she can walk to our church and listen to German services. She soon wins new friends. A young German immigrant family lives across the street from her. When Mother passes by their house she hears them speak German to their children. The next time she meets them she introduces herself. They have four children. Mother enjoys being with children and she learns to know the family more intimately. She tells us about her new acquaintances. Ortrun, the mother of the four children is an accomplished pianist and organist and sings in a renowned Vancouver choir. We invite her family to our house. Their children are about the same age as ours. We have many common interests and become good friends with them.

In the area where Mother lives are many German establishments, She can walk to a German delicatessen store to buy groceries for cooking her own meals A bank employee speaks German, there is a German speaking Mennonite dentist and a doctor and she can walk to visit church members of her own age. Mother seems to be much happier now that she can once more care for herself. Her German and Canadian old age pensions provide enough income that she can live independently. She loves to visit us for a few days once and awhile and then return home to her own place.

A Mennonite society builds an apartment block for seniors, the Menno-Court, in that area and Mother is the first one who can choose her apartment there. She chooses one with a view of the playground so that she can observe children playing. A number of her friends from church become her neighbors now. She and Hanna, whom she knows from our Mennonite church in West Prussia, visit each other often and undertake activities together. Hanna has a car and takes Mother along to visit relatives and friends in the country and they go on holidays together.

When Mother gets older and finds it difficult to lift her cooking pots to make her own meals, she moves to Pinegrove, an assisted living home. She still likes to come over to stay with us for a couple of days or visit Magdalena. We also visit her often and spend a few hours with her in her home. We celebrate her birthdays in grand style with friends and relatives in the fire side room of the church or the assembly room in her home. She enjoys the grandchildren contributing to the celebration in the old tradition. They recite a poem or play a few pieces on the piano or other musical instruments for Oma.

Oma is very generous and always interested in the well-being of her children and grandchildren. She encourages them to get a good, versatile education that will prepare them for life. When they visit her she always has some cookies or chocolate in her drawer. Occasionally she asks me;"How much money do I still have in my bank account?" (She has asked me to take care of her financial arrangements,). If it is more than she thinks she needs for herself she tells me, "Put some cash in an envelope for Ingrid's birthday next week", or, "How is Michael doing at medical school?" We tell her he loves it and is progressing well. "Oh, I am happy to hear that, his studies must be costly, I would like to contribute something to his education."

Oma usually celebrates Christmas with us. We still have candles on the Christmas tree and sing our German Christmas songs as we did in Germany. It is Krista who now accompanies us on the harpsichord and she likes it. When the candles are burned down and it is time for distributing gifts, Oma pulls envelopes out of her handbag and hands them to the children, "I cannot buy you gifts anymore; take this money and fulfill your wishes with it", she says. They in return will give Oma a big heartfelt hug and a thank you. She loves her grandchildren and often inquires as to how they are, so that she can accompany them in her thoughts and prayers.

At age ninety two Oma falls and breaks her hip and we take her to hospital. Her two granddaughters visit her as often as they can and push her in her wheelchair through the hospital park. She loves to be outside, seeing the trees and flowers. Michael had just graduated from Medical School and is doing his practicum in Orthopedics in Vancouver. He comes to the hospital for a visit. He asks the attending physician if he can see the x-rays and explains the accident to Oma. She proudly tells her roommates that the Doctor is her grandson.

She is proud of her grandchildren. Her hip heals again and she can return to her home in Pinegrove.

14. Searching for new ways.

The 'sixties' are politically turbulent years. Tension between the two superpowers, Russia and the USA, grows. The border between East and West Germany is fortified with a barbed wire fence and land mines to stop people leaving the Russian Zone and escaping to the American or British Zone. In 1961, the Russians and East Germans build the infamous Berlin Wall, hoping to close the loophole, which hundreds of thousands of people used to escape communist East Germany. It had still been possible to travel from East Germany to East Berlin in the subway and go 'shopping' in West Berlin. From West Berlin's Tempelhof airport they could then fly to West Germany.

The arms race and the space race fuel the Cold War. We are afraid that the conflict between Russia and America, escalated by the Russians storing missiles in Cuba, could start the third World War.

America gets involved in the Vietnam Conflict.

Young people get agitated, they want some stability and security and rebel against the policies of their governments. Tension grows. Good political jokes give voice to their frustration.

They do not accept the values of the establishment anymore and seek alternative lifestyles where peace, justice, personal freedom and love are valued. Some try to find it in eastern philosophy and meditation. Others become dropouts or use drugs to be lifted into a higher consciousness.

On the positive side, the younger generation becomes more creative. They write new stage plays expressing their values and outlook on life and develop new art styles in painting, sculpture and installations. Music has more volume and rhythm. Folksongs include lyrics that express the disappointment and the hope of the present generation. Rock an' Roll blossoms and finds expression in exotic and suggestive dancing. Young people express their otherness from the 'conservative generation' by wearing unusual casual clothing in colorful patterns, often oversized. They walk in sandals or go barefoot. They become known as the 'Hippies' or 'Flower Children.'

15. Our 'Hauskreis'

Some of us younger Mennonites are influenced by these societal changes. We are searching for spiritual impulses to live more consciously and to make our life more meaningful.

I attended a Mennonite College at Bluffton and Hildegard at Bethel. Exchanging ideas with fellow students and professors gave us some direction and opened our eyes to look at ourselves and our world around us more critically. We want to learn to be honest with ourselves and others and live our faith convincingly.

Hildegard's father had introduced her to Stauffer's critical, historical review of the New Testament. He felt that might be more challenging for her way of thinking than for his, and he was right. Hildegard becomes more critical of the often narrow, literal exegesis of scripture as it is presented in some of our churches.

We share these concerns with the Wiebes and Schaffers. We are all teachers, are active in our churches, live by the same Christian values and like to dialogue.

To become aware of our faith and its application in our personal life stimulates our conversations. Some of our friends are attracted to our honest and open way of communicating with each other and we invite them to join us, among them are several of Ulli's and Waltraud's Baptist young people, including their new young pastor and his wife. We meet in homes and we three core couples take responsibility for our new group, our 'Hauskreis'. The opportunity for personal sharing is still part of our activities; we want to learn from each other. We have no organized program, Ulli or sometimes Hildegard come up with a topic that is relevant. We share openly and uninhibitedly our thoughts and feelings around each topic and about events that captured our attention during the week.

The teachings of Jesus, the wisdom of current theologians, spiritual and political leaders are guidelines for our search to understand God's ways for us. We worship God, sing and pray together. Rüdiger writes and composes some of the songs we sing and accompanies them on his guitar.

Hauskreis from l. Ulli, Hildegard - Hildegard
Holger, Bobby, John

Ruediger and Jesus people in our backyard

Our small fellowship grows numerically. In one of our annual weekend retreats at our house, we are thirty participants from nine congregations. We grow in inner strength. We are willing to share our experiences with other Christian groups if and when we are invited. Once Hildegard accompanies Ulli and Rüdiger to Edmonton where they participate in a Baptist young people's retreat as guest speakers.

Our home churches become somewhat suspicious of our group since we are inter-denominational and do not operate under their or any church leadership. We feel we need new impulses besides those which our churches are able give us in order to grow.

One of these unanticipated 'impulses' comes from a prophet of 'the end times.' I do not remember how he came into our orbit, perhaps through our connection with St. Margaret's Church. Gordon is a small man with a long, thin, reddish beard and piercing eyes. His wife, Emily, taller than he, is a kind, likable, submissive woman. He bases his prophecies on Revelation and the Old Testament prophets especially Daniel and Jeremiah. And like they, he prophesies, 'Our society is corrupt, selfish, greedy, gluttonous and immoral and God's judgment will come over us if we do not repent; God's judgment is near'; and he knows the timing of it! That makes me suspicious. He also has a consolation: We can be saved if we live a pure Christian life and get rid of all our 'idols'. Hildegard is startled by his message and does not know how to respond.

Since Gordon and Emily have no place to stay, she invites them to stay in our home.

Gordon comes into the living room and sees Hanno's stuffed toy frog on the fireplace and Krista's beautifully crafted macramé owls on the wall. He turns around and tells us these animals are an abomination to God and we should get rid of them. He looks at our bookshelf and points out that some of those books should not be in a Christian home. He also talks about finding a place of refuge to escape the last judgment.

One cannot reason with him. He quotes scripture, sometimes out of context and he is 'right', God has revealed that to him in his word, in dreams and visions. I question that, but do not say much anymore. Perhaps there is still a trace of, 'What if he is right?' in me. When they are gone, Hildegard, the fearful soul, wants to go into action. I try to convince her that, according to the Bible, God made <u>all</u> the fish in the sea and <u>all</u> the fowl in the air and judged them to be good. Why would he now single out frogs and owls to be bad? I do not want to confuse her and let her do what she thinks should be done. She collects a box of books and throws them into the fire, among them Hitler's 'Mein Kampf' which she had gotten from one of her colleagues in school to 'translate' and which I had not yet read.

She tries to explain to Hanno why he should put his frog into the fire, he does not quite understand why but obeys his mother. I make a deal with Hildegard about Krista's beautifully crafted owls. I will remove them from the house and take them to my school. The librarian is happy to decorate the library with them.

We mull over the 'place of refuge', which we had considered already when we heard about the impending great earthquake and the possibility of a nuclear war, predicted by Prophet 'Schulz' before.

New members come to our group and bring new ideas and new questions. At one of our evening gatherings Ulli, who takes post graduate courses at UBC, tells us about a stimulating deeper life meeting at the Lutheran chapel on campus. The Christian Student Fellowship had invited an inter-denominational team of young Christians, a Methodist preacher, a Catholic priest and a Lutheran theologian to share with students their experience about the impact the Holy Spirit has had in revitalizing their faith and life, which has given them new joy in Christ.

They are acquainted with an ecumenical revival known as the 'Charismatic Movement.'

Ulli and Rüdiger have listened to them, found their exposition very helpful and feel that our group could benefit from their teaching.

I want to find out more about it, leave the group and drive to the Lutheran Centre at UBC.

When I quietly enter the chapel I hear a soft, melodious chanting, a kind of music I had never heard before I find a seat in the back row and listen and am moved by these 'ethereal' sounds. The group of about twenty students are sitting in a half circle, half have their eyes closed, some their hands slightly raised, sing without songbooks, no director, no instruments. It moves me and I am drawn to harmonize with them but I cannot understand the words and cannot identify the language. When they stop singing one of their leaders stands up and speaks to the group about the perception of God as a threefold presence in our lives. "We hear much about God the creator and the Father, we know Jesus, his teaching and mission, but the role of the Holy Spirit is often somewhat nebulous for us." He continues to expound on the mission and gifts of the Holy Spirit for us today. His message gives me a lot to think about.

At the end of the meeting, I ask one of the leaders about the singing at the beginning. "We were singing in the spirit", he says. I am puzzled and he asks me if I have time. He takes me into a side room and explains to me the gift of glossolalia as mentioned in the New Testament. It is a mystery, a language given to the individual who asks for it which he might not understand himself, but which can be interpreted by the recipient or someone else. He offers to pray for me if I want to receive that gift. I want a closer relationship with Jesus and, if this is a way to achieve this, I am ready.

On my way back in the car I cautiously use my new gift of tongues and praise God in a new way. When I come home, I share my experience at the Lutheran Centre with the group, some of whom are still at our place, waiting for me to come home. Hildegard, who is always open for new ideas, wants to hear all about it and the next evening she goes with some other women from the group to find out for herself and they have a similar experience.

The baptism of the Holy Spirit now adds another dimension to worship in our group, a greater joy, acceptance and love that we did not feel to that extent before.

Hildegard and I now pray or sing occasionally in the spirit especially if we do not know how to pray for people or occasions. For me this seems to give me a more intimate relationship to God.

A week later Hildegard feels we should share our experience with our pastor. We tell him faithfully what we have experienced and he listens carefully and asks questions. Then we kneel down together and praise God for his grace. He thanks us for sharing what has happened in our lives.

At this time we receive a phone call from Pastor Erhard. He has been invited by a German-speaking Lutheran congregation in Vancouver to be their new pastor. Previously he had been in Paraguay instructing Mennonite teachers how to improve teaching religion to their students. He had befriended Ernst, the president of the Mennonite Seminary in Montevideo, a distant relative of the Schefflers. Ernst had told him and his wife that if they feel lonely in Vancouver at the beginning and cannot find a supporting Christian fellowship, to contact the Lemkes. The former Pastor of the Markus Gemeinde, whom we know, had focused more on the social aspect of the gospel and Erhard is christo-centric. The congregation has to get used to this shift and is somewhat reserved. He does not feel fully accepted and supported at the beginning. So he contacts us and we invite him and his wife to visit us. Erhard comes originally from Saxony in Germany and his wife Louis, was born in Indonesia. We talk about their new position and expectations. Our interest in their ministry and Hildegard's positive attitude soon wins their hearts and trust. We pray for a good start and progress in their work and they ask if we could meet once a week with them, share and pray together for God's guidance and empowerment in their work. We do this for about a year until he is able to gather a like-minded supporting group from his own congregation. We continue to visit each other occasionally as friends.

Through Erhard we make contact with another German minister, Pastor Sigmar. He is a protestant pastor from Heidelberg on a search for spiritual impulses to revitalize his congregation. He had heard about reform movements in North America and has contacted the German-Lutheran Church in Vancouver. Pastor Erhard shares with him what is happening in his congregation and suggests that he contact us, if he wants to hear more about new ways to activate church life. So Pastor Sigmar phones and asks if he could meet with us. We tell him he is welcome to stay with us. Our Hauskreis meets the next day and we invite him to join us, he can see then how we are worshiping and living our faith.

He observes with an open mind and heart and occasionally participates. When the group has left, we reflect on the meeting and tell him that it is not easy to transplant something that has grown on a prepared soil, out of a special relationship, into another environment.

We have been meeting for several years and have grown into a loving and participating fellowship. We trust the Holy Spirit to empower us to live an active Christian life. He listens thoughtfully and appreciates what he is hearing.

On the weekend John, our boys and I, take him on a canoe trip to Pitt Lake and share more in a neutral environment with him. We row the Widgeon Creek upstream into the wilderness. Loons, eagles, otters, herons and other wildlife cross our way. We hope that being with us in God's versatile creation will give him a fresh outlook on life, a thankful and joyous attitude which his church will find contagious.

About a year later Jandirk from Oldenburg, Germany, contacts the Lutheran church and speaks to pastor Erhard. He is interested in immigrating to Canada and wants to find out how Christians in established churches live and participate in church activities here. He has also heard about the charismatic movement in North America and wonders if and to what extent it has influenced or penetrated main line churches. Erhard tells him the best people he knows to speak to both topics, are the Lemkes. Jandirk phones us and we invite him to be our house guest. He mentions that he belongs to the 'Marburger Kreis', an interdenominational group of committed Christians similar to our Hauskreis. We ask if he wants to participate in our next meeting. He appreciates being included and is surprised at how open, accepting and spontaneous our members are. In his group, they are more reserved.

In regard to the charismatic movement, we tell him we find that it has influenced many churches. For the conservative churches, which believe that they already possess what the charismatics claim is a new insight and revelation, the influence is often negative. It can lead to arguments and church splitting.

Churches which have integrated charismatic theology into their church life, experience a renewal. We, in our group, think and hope that the gift of the Holy Spirit will transform Christians to live a more fruitful and fulfilled life and that in love they will accept and encourage each other as brothers and sisters in Christ.

Jandirk asks me if it is good to invest in real estate in Canada. At this point house prices go up but the market is unstable. He decides to buy a house and a realtor does the paperwork for him. After he has owned it for a few years, house prices drop and the realtor suggests selling. He sells it at a considerable loss. I suggest that he buy my first house, which I have just vacated and which is now for sale. It has a better location with a marvelous view and will keep its value.

He buys it and asks me if I would manage it. Inken, Jandirk's wife, however, decides not to emigrate and they sell again. Shortly afterwards house prices climb and years later they have doubled.

Jandirk's daughter, Antje, is inspired by her dad's stories about Canada. She has to wait a year after high school graduation before she can start her studies at university and wants to fill the time. She thinks Canada might be a good place, where she can improve her English and have some adventure. We find an 'au pair' job for her with a nice young couple from our church who have three little girls and she is eager to come to Canada.

At the airport, a suspicious, uncompromising immigration officer suspects Antje wants to work illegally in Canada and causes her trouble. She will not allow Antje to immigrate and is about to send her back to Germany on the next plane. I am waiting for her at the arrival deck to pick her up and am quite surprised when I hear my name over the public address system, "Mr. Lemke, could you come to the immigration office please". I have to explain the apparent problem to her supervisor and he grants Antje a permit to stay.

She enjoys her time in Canada and develops a good relationship with her 'adopted' family. They give Antje time off to explore our beautiful country and make new friends with whom she goes on a sailing trip. We have become good friends with her and her parents and continue our visits with them in Germany and here in Canada.

16. Revisiting Germany

We have paid off a good part of our mortgage on our house and have been able to save money for extended holidays with the family. Our children have joined the Forest Warden Club. With experienced guides they explore the forests in our coastal mountains and learn to identify native trees, wildflowers and animals. They learn how to recognize edible plants, make a safe fire and survive in the wilderness. Occasionally we accompany them on some of their outdoor camps as assistant guides. The children think it would be fun to travel in a recreational vehicle through our beautiful country, to areas to which they have not been yet and apply what they have learned in their club activities.

Hildegard and I plan to inquire about a camper on our summer vacation in Germany. We think our children are still too small to enjoy coming with us on such a long trip. We are, however, somewhat hesitant to leave them behind for two month. Our extended family encourages us to go; they will take good care of them while we are gone, they assure us. Gertraud invites Michael to spend the holiday with his cousins in Black Creek on Vancouver Island and Opa and Oma Scheffler are willing to come to our house and look after Krista and Hanno who are now four and six years old.

To help the grandparents keep the two young ones occupied and to prepare them for our future vehicle, I build a camper model from plywood with a cab in front, a steering wheel, gas pedal and brake. I make the back big enough for a space to sleep and cook and they even can expand the roof. The children love it and I hope playing in it with their friends will occupy their time and will enable the grandparents to get some rest.

Grandparents Scheffler, Hanno, Michael, Krista

Krista, Hildegard, Hanno, Helmut, Michael

One of our first destinations, after we land in Germany, is the city of Wiedenbrück where Volkswagen's Westfalia Campers are assembled. We had made arrangements with the factory and notified them of our coming. They pick us up from the railway station and serve us coffee and cookies when we arrive. We get permission to observe the assembly line and view our new vehicle which still has to be polished. We like it, sign the contract, pay $3009 and board our brand new Westfalia camper. Hildegard is afraid of handling it and leaves the driving to me. She prefers to be the navigator and she is perfect at that. Her good sense of direction and ability to read maps helps a great deal to get us safely and quickly to all the places on our itinerary. I have fun cruising along and looking down from my elevated driver's seat at the Mercedes and BMWs beside me.

It seems we have too many relatives on our list whom we want to visit. Hildegard's live in the south and mine in the north of Germany. They are happy to see us again and when they see our new camper, they generously share their surplus bedding, dishes and cutlery with us to furnish it properly. We just have to buy a little gas camping stove to be fully outfitted for camping.

We appreciate the freedom from school and family obligations and the dependence on hotels or relatives. We are self-sufficient now. We are happy and much in love with each other. Since we take our home with us, we have more flexibility to go or stay where we want. On this trip, we manage to have more time for ourselves, to stroll through parks and towns and visit museums and art galleries. We love to sit in serene old gothic or decorative baroque cathedrals and meditate. Or, if we are lucky listen to an organist playing the old pipe organ.

We visit Bavaria and the Alps and stop at our friend Anke's place in Garmisch Partenkirchen, a typical, picturesque Bavarian village.

Unexpectedly we have the opportunity to get tickets for the famous Passion play in Oberammergau which is performed only once every ten years. We had heard in Vancouver that tickets were already sold out for this performance three years ago. Anke tells us, a number of Jews have returned their tickets lately because the play is 'too anti-Jewish'. Early the next morning we drive to Oberammergau about half an hour's drive. We line up at a hotel where their guests have returned tickets and get two seats close to the front. For four hours we watch local artists recreate the story of Jesus' suffering and crucifixion. We go back to our camper quietly and thoughtfully.

Another reason to go to Germany was to participate in a retreat for educators in Schloss Craheim, in northern Bavaria, a Baroque castle built for Freiherr Crafft von Truchsess von und zu Wetzhausen. In 1968 he leased the castle to 'The Ecumenical Centre for the Unity of Christians'. This retreat in Craheim is led by Wilhard Becker, a Baptist pastor, Pater Mederlet, a Catholic priest, and Dr. Arnold Bittlinger, a Protestant theologian. They give lectures, seminars, training and counseling sessions for young people, professionals and church leaders. Ulli had told us about Craheim and had invited us to this retreat. It is intended for teachers and is about 'Christian relationships and responsibilities'. The guest speaker is Dr. Christenson, a charismatic Protestant minister from California. His German is passable but his deliberations lack some of the distinctive details which he has described so well in his books in English. The lively discussions after the lectures are very interesting and sometimes heated. The Germans are forthcoming with their critical comments, often unaware of the different way of thinking and dealing with the subject by Americans and their more cautious way of responding.

Ulli introduces us to Heide, a lively young high school teacher from Heilbronn who is also attending the retreat. He had known her from the Baptist 'Rufer movement'. She likes Hildegard and they become friends. The Schaffers and Heide come to our room; we reflect on the lectures, discuss critical points and pray for God's guidance and a meaningful outcome of the retreat.

From our nicely furnished room in the castle on the hill, we have a wide view of the fields and the countryside below.

Countess Amalia, a relative of the owner of the castle, visits the retreat. As foreigners, we get more attention and Hildegard gets into a conversation with her. The two connect well. She invites us to her home after the conclusion of the seminar and introduces us to her family. We keep up a correspondence with her for awhile.

After the retreat is over, the Schaffers travel with us in our camper to Berlin. My Uncle Gustav lives in Berlin-Schöneberg and I have been looking forward to visiting him and cousin Röschen and her children. Röschen's husband died after the war. We introduce the Schaffers to them. Since they have very limited room, the Schaffers stay in our camper and explore Berlin on their own, while we visit with my relatives. Uncle Gustav is my father's oldest brother. He is my favorite uncle, a wise and generous man. He tells us very sad stories from the Russian occupation of Berlin in April 1945.

When the Russian troops entered the city, they ransacked the houses in the wealthier suburbs, raped the women and took all their valuables and food supplies. They were starving in the first year. All the stores were empty. Since no trains were running, they rode their bicycles early in the morning into the country and begged farmers or garden owners to sell them some food. In the evening, they would return with a few potatoes, turnips or cabbage in their rucksack and sometimes their rucksack remained empty because many other Berliners did the same and the supplies were limited.

Uncle Gustav worked as a representative of a well-known company in the eastern part of Berlin, which is now Russian Zone. There was not enough work for him to support his family, so he decided to defect to West Berlin. He left his house and all his belongings in East Germany and came with only a briefcase to the West.

His grandchildren told me later, they had, with great fear and trepidation of being discovered, smuggled some valuables hidden in their school backpacks to the West. They lived in East Germany but their nearest school was in West Berlin and they were allowed to take the underground train to school. Often they were questioned and searched at the border.

Uncle Gustav had to start fresh again in West Berlin. Experience and hard work earned him back his position in the company where he had worked before. Now he is retired. He takes us on a day trip to Grunewald, one of the most prestigious residential areas in West Berlin. A number of mansions are nestled in a wooded area around artificial lakes. From the Grunewald tower we have a panoramic view of Berlin. Our eyes can follow the line of the Berlin Wall.

It is extremely hot in Berlin and Uncle Gustav introduces us to the 'Berliner Weisse' a mixture of raspberry concentrate and beer, very thirst quenching, we love it. We visit other relatives and take a tour through the city before we depart from Berlin.

Uncle Gustav and cousin Röschen provide us with some food for the journey and we say good-bye to our lovely, generous relatives, join the Schaffers in our camper and together we travel south.

At home, in our Hauskreis, we had wondered if it would benefit us to live in community, like some Hippie groups do. Ulli knew, from his former study years in Germany, of groups which live communally. Some for religious or economical reasons, others have common interests and form an artists' colony We want to find out what are the benefits and difficulties of living together. We visit different groups who live communally but are not convinced that this is the way we want to live in Canada. We also want to observe life in communities which have been touched by the charismatic movement and see how it has influenced or transformed Christian life in Germany.

The Schaffers are our neighbors in Burnaby now. The property next to us was for sale and we bought the double lot together since they do not have the finances to pay for the whole lot. They choose the front lot, which has access from the street and we buy the back part which borders on Burnaby Mountain Park with no street access. I design their house and help with the supervision of the construction. It is the first house of their own. They are excited about it and furnish it according to their taste, which is somewhat different from that which is common. We have about a thirty foot strip of lawn between our houses which we use 'communally'. The sandbox for our children is half on their and half on our side and our children play together in it.

We had told Heide in Craheim about beautiful British Columbia and she is interested in seeing it and Schaffers invite her to spend her holidays here. She stays awhile with Schaffers and visits us. Hildegard's joyful outlook on life makes her feel comfortable with us and she asks if she can spend the rest of her stay with us.

She becomes a good friend of the family and calls Hildegard a true friend and mentor with whom she can be completely open and honest. From now on, she comes more often to Canada to visit us during her summer vacations and sometimes spends Christmas with us. Being single, she enjoys living with our family.

17. Family Activities

Our children grow up in a healthy home atmosphere which Hildegard so capably can provide. She plays creative games with them and encourages them to explore new things on their own. The children are looking forward to an interesting walk with Mom through the woods across the street. She will point out new flowers and unusual plants along the path or they will listen to the birds sing and see who first can locate the singer. If they cannot identify them they will consult the encyclopedia at home. Hildegard has a way of making ordinary things exciting for the children.

They like to help Mother and she encourages and teaches them to accept small chores in kitchen and house. When evening comes or when they are sick, she reads suspenseful mystery or non-fiction stories to them and helps them to understand new concepts. The children love and appreciate their mother. Krista, as a young teenager, draws a birthday card for Mom, a mother bird feeding three chicks on the front cover and inside she writes.

'From one of your little fledglings.'

Dear Mom,

I love you. You're the best Mom a kid could ever have as well as being a beautiful woman of God. I want to try to be more like you, especially in the latter area. The fact that we sometimes get in each other's hair made me think what it would be like to be a mother, wanting my daughter to trust me, learn from me and be a special friend....

You rule above all. May the coming year bring much peace and joy and blessing.

Your loving daughter, Krista.

Hildegard is a person who does nothing half-heartedly. If she is asked or chooses to participate in an activity, she becomes fully involved in it, focuses on the essentials and puts all her energy into her work, which sometimes goes beyond her resources.

Hildegard has a gift of relating to younger people. The girls take her as their role model and appreciate her counsel. Young mothers admire her as a super-mom who can teach and guide her children with love.

Hildegard thinks that is quite normal and there is nothing special about it,

We want our children to grow up bilingual to benefit from the advantage which people have who speak more than one language. Our children have the advantage that both of us are fluent in German and English and we often speak German with them at home. When Michael gets to Kindergarten he knows only a few words of English and the teacher thinks he is quiet and slow. After a few months he has caught up and surpasses most of his playmates in language skills.

All three children do quite well in school and have selected a balanced curriculum, taking academic, practical and fine arts courses. Hildegard, knowing the school system from her own experience, can support the children in their endeavors, occasionally adding some information or organizational skills to complement what is taught or not taught in the classroom. In general, they are quite self-sufficient. Both Michael and Krista play supporting roles in school musicals, play in the band and sing in the choir. Krista takes two grades in one year in an open class environment in Elementary School.

Hanno is a little trickster and is drawn into the wrong crowd in Junior High School. The boys play some innocent pranks on the girls and the Vice Principal, who does not have a sense of humor or an understanding of the mentality of young boys, deems them serious misbehavior. She calls them to her office and interrogates them. His accomplices claim innocence but Hanno is honest, admits his participation, and takes the blame. When she phones us about it a few times, we take him out of the public school and enroll him in a private Christian school for a year.

Once Hildegard has to pick Hanno up for an appointment after school. They had agreed to meet in front of the school but Hanno is not there. She goes inside, sees him at the other end of the corridor and calls him. Now everybody knows she is his mom and he is embarrassed that she has come in her work-clothing, wearing purple pants.

Hildegard met Jean during the second year of her teaching at Kensington Junior Secondary. They both taught English and jointly sponsored a Christian student group in school.

Jean grew up in England as the daughter of a missionary doctor. She went to a boarding school and university there while her parents worked in Nigeria. She becomes a good friend of Hildegard and later of our family. She has a sense of humor and feels good and fulfilled when somebody needs her and she can help.

Jean leaves Kensington, after Hildegard had left teaching, and joins the pastoral team as co-pastor in her Pentecostal church. After a year she changes her work and becomes a correctional Matron in Oakalla prison, supervising correspondence courses of young offenders.

George, a young prisoner, falls in love with his teacher and proposes to her. He is much younger than Jean and is perhaps looking for a mother figure.

Krista, Michael. Hanno

Krista, Hanno, Michael

We are concerned about her relationship with George because of their age difference and the difference in education, interests and lifestyle and tell her so. but she is encouraged by a pastor who visits the prison and, after George professes faith in Christ and seems like a changed man, Jean accepts his proposal.

When he has served his time they get married and move to Golden, where Jean has been offered a position as music teacher. Not long after they had said their vows, George falls into his former lifestyle, drinking too much and experimenting with drugs. This gets him into trouble with the law again. In spite of George's reputation, Jean is able to continue teaching. When we visit them there, one summer vacation, they are both working at Smitty's, a fast food place.

Heide wants to visit us this summer and the family has planned to take her on a camping trip to hitherto unknown places of BC's interior.

Hanno cannot come along with us for the first stretch, as he has been diagnosed with a big tumor on his bladder. The doctor thinks it could be cancerous. Many people pray for him and we are relieved when the test results indicate it is benign. He is very courageous in hospital where the doctor cuts out one third of his bladder. For his comfort he sings to himself, 'The Lord is my light and my salvation, whom shall I fear?'

He has not fully recovered from his operation; so Hildegard stays at home with him. Heide offers to takes over the cooking and housekeeping in the camper for Michael, Krista and me. We set up camp in Ucluelet close to the Pacific Ocean. The water in the ocean is relatively warm and we enjoy swimming. Heide likes to lie in the sun and get a tan to make her friends and colleagues back in Heilbronn envious.

We drive on, across the Island, to Fanny's Bay to board the small ferry to Hornby Island. Hornby is a small, isolated place where many artists retreat and set up their studios. Some families have established small tourist resorts.

We find a spot at the Tribune Bay campground, level our camper and set up the tents. Mike and Krista explore the campground and the beach, while I register and Heide prepares us a lunch.

The ocean has carved two bays into the island on this side. We choose the small one which looks almost like a huge square swimming pool. The water is shallow for a long stretch and therefore warmer, ideal for children to swim and play water ball.

The west side of the bay is shielded by high rock cliffs along the Hallowell Park. It is low tide and we walk along the beach beside the cliffs and are amazed when we look at the bizarre shapes which the pounding waves have washed out of the soft sandstone of the cliff.

We have fun looking at these strange shapes and visualize them as allegorical beings or characters from Star Wars.

The summer art festival is on with its parade and artists' displays. It is a well-attended tourist attraction. Michael and Krista take part in the parade and Heide and I stroll along the displays of pottery, paintings, jewelry and weaving handicrafts. Heide buys a few souvenirs and gifts to take home to friends. I admire a beautiful vase that Hildegard would like but I want to see the rest of the offerings before I buy it; when I come back to get it, it is gone. Sometimes it is good to act on one's first impulse. In the evening, we sit on the warm rocks and watch the stars come out or we light a campfire and tell stories or sing folksongs, Heide has a good soprano voice. It is too bad that Hildegard and Hanno cannot be with us.

We leave Hornby Island and return to Parksville where we have arranged to meet Hildegard and Hanno. He has recuperated from his operation and spent a few quiet days with Mom at her sister's place in Black Creek. They join us in the camper and the whole family ferries back to the mainland and we continue our trip to the eastern part of BC. We pass Chilliwack and see the pointed Matterhorn-like Mount Cheam, still covered with snow. It is getting hot and Shasta Lake invites us for a swim. The mosquitoes are so bad that we do not stay very long. Further inland, we relive a bit of history when we walk through a few gold rush ghost towns. A century ago, they were booming centers of activity. Now the remaining buildings are empty and starting to deteriorate and collapse.

The road to the Rocky Mountains leads over Rogers Pass with beautiful vistas of the mountains. We drive through Revelstoke and stop in Golden in the foothills of the Rockies. We park our camper beside the small house in which Jean and George are living now. They are happy to see us and we have a lot to share. George has planned a fishing trip to Quartz Lake with us for the next morning. We drive their pick-up truck as far as the rough logging road takes us and park it there in the middle of the forest, no trail to follow; we walk for about four and a half hours through a pristine forest, over rock slides and along alpine meadows full of blue and yellow wildflowers.

The fir trees grow rather small at this altitude and we can see the lake glittering in the sun. I am amazed that we have found it; but George, being half native, has a special sense of direction to find his way in the wilderness. We took a fishing rod along and he shows me how to fly-fish. Skillfully I fling the fly out into the lake. As soon as it hits the water, the trout, coming up from below, snap at the bait. The water is so clear that I can almost see the bottom of the lake and see the fish coming after the fly. If they are too small I quickly pull the hook up before they bite. George and his companions go a little further along the banks where they have easier access to the water and they catch fish by hanging a line with a kernel of corn on the hook into the water. Together we catch about forty trout which we have to carry back home in our rucksacks.

It is getting dark when we arrive at the spot where we think we left the truck; we look for it but cannot find it. Heide and Ron, a friend of George, volunteer to search for it. I stay with Mike and Krista who are completely exhausted from the nine hour march and rest their heads on my lap. Heide and Ron take a flashlight and walk through the woods. Not far from our resting place, they hit the logging road, following it for a few hundred meters they find the truck. It is after midnight when we arrive at our starting place.

Jean, Hildegard and Hanno have been worried about what might have happened to us and are glad when we are back. Happy and content we slip into our beds in the camper. Krista and Mike are dead tired from this strenuous day.

Hildegard and Hanno stayed with Jean while we were on our excursion. She told Hildegard about her difficult relationship living with George. He makes no effort to find regular work and brings his friends, men and women, home and they experiment with drugs.

George mentions in a casual conversation the next day: "Jean is making enough money for the two of us and our visiting friends. Why should I work? We don't need more of it." He spends his free time making soap stone carvings, painting as a hobby and playing his guitar.

Listening to Jean's story compassionately, Hildegard suggests that she may have to end this dubious relationship if things do not change. With a heavy heart, knowing about Jean and George's unhappy life together, we continue our travels.

We stop briefly at George's work place. He has generously prepared the fish which we caught the day before and has put them on ice in a bucket for us to take along in our camper. We appreciate that very much.

Our next campground is beside the Kicking Horse River. The rushing water lulls us into sleep. Early the following morning, we get up, wash in the river and get ready for a long hike. For the first stretch, we walk along the small river then up to a high plateau into Yoho National Park. Our small trail takes us through dense forest with an occasional opening through which we have a view into a valley. We pick berries and observe a few deer grazing in a clearing. Heide wants to meet a bear and once we are startled by a movement in the bushes but it is only a hare hopping across our trail. Hildegard takes pictures of a few wind-torn snarled trees which are common at this altitude and which she loves as motifs for her paintings.

The forest clears and we are amazed about the gorgeous view over the region. Down below we look into a wide canyon. On the other side of it, we see the famous Wakaka Falls rush down over steep cliffs. We climb down to the foot of the falls and get the spray of the water rushing down.

We take a little side trip to Emerald Lake. Its name comes from the intense green color of its glacier water.

We leave BC. and enter the province of Alberta. In Banff, one of the First Nations tribes celebrates its annual pow-wow. In colorful costumes and large feathered headpieces they perform a number of solo dances and wild war dances. At the end, they invite the audience to participate in their ritual dance. There is very little response. I feel almost obliged to join them, go into the circle and dance a simple hop-dance round with one of the native woman.

We explore the town further, take the lift up to Norquay Mountain, and enjoy from its top an even more magnificent view of the Rocky Mountains.

Back in BC we turn off the main highway and drive into Fort Steele, a ghost town from the early pioneer times. It is surrounded by a stockade to protect settlers from marauding Indian tribes. At the beginning of the main road, is the Anglican Church of St. Savior, further on a saloon and the one room red schoolhouse, still with its old wooden benches, even the costume of the woman teacher hangs there. The blacksmith still hammers horseshoes in his shop and Michael is excited to walk through the doctor's office and the pharmacy with bottles of remedies. Beside the entrance are the barracks of the Royal Mounted Police, stationed here to protect the settlers and help to mediate disputes between the pioneers and the traders.

At the Moyle Lake campground, past all the National Parks on our route, Heide finally gets a chance to see a black bear. Early in the morning we hear a noise near our camper and spot a bear pillaging through a garbage can. We call Heide who is still sleeping in her tent. She rushes out with her camera and takes a photo of the young frightened bear now climbing up a tree. We continue and have one more stop in a campground in Manning Park and then we reach home.

A couple of years after our visit with Jean, she contacts Hildegard and tells her that life with George has become unbearable. He treats her like a servant girl and is not faithful to her. Hildegard advises her to leave him, which she does, and file for a divorce on grounds of adultery. To support her in this difficult time we offer Jean a home with us during the transition period. That stay extends for over a year. She fits in well with the family and is a very pleasant, unassuming and helpful houseguest.

18. Getting involved

Several years after Hildegard had resigned from teaching, she meets one of her former students, Judy, who is now a university graduate. She is happy to see her favorite teacher again and tells her about her future plans and her mother's involvements. Judy's mother lives at the end of our street. She is an idealist-communist, very community oriented. She cares for lonely old people and hosts foreign students from SFU. She gave us a big basket full of her surplus plants with which we started our garden when we moved into the area. She shares her resources for inexpensive natural foods with us neighbors. We get along quite well. She is Jewish and when my mother lived with us, she talked with her in Yiddish, a mixture of a South-German dialect, Hebrew and bits of other east European languages mixed in. The two had fun communicating with each other.

She also tells us about Frau Groß, a French milliner, who lives a little further down the hill. Her husband came from Karlsruhe in Germany and was a violinist in the Vancouver Symphony. He died and she now lives alone in her house. She is crippled with arthritis. We visit her and help with things she cannot manage anymore. The boys mow her lawn and do errands for her. Hildegard takes her shopping. She spends many a Christmas with us. The children always smile when she happily sings German Christmas songs with us, because she is a monotone.

During their conversation, Judy asks Hildegard. "You are Mennonites aren't you? You do not participate in wars and are against violence to solve problems?" Hildegard assures her that Mennonites believe there are better alternatives to settle conflicts than to violently subdue or kill one's opponents. "What do you think about American draft dodgers?" she waits for Hildegard's answer. "Do you know that the Unitarian Church has a reception centre for those who do not want to fight in Vietnam? They need homes where Draft Dodgers can stay for awhile until more permanent solutions can be found." We had heard that more and more young American men are avoiding the draft and are refusing to participate in the war in Vietnam. Hildegard tells her she will discuss this with me and perhaps the church council and let her know.

We discuss the American draft dodger situation with Erwin, our pastor. He agrees with us that we should respond to the challenge and asks us to be the liaison persons.

We notify the Unitarians of our decision. Shortly after our contact, we receive a phone call from them; they need accommodation for two people. The next day a young shy American couple arrives and we welcome them. They tell us that they are not sure how to respond to the draft which the young man has received. We share with them who we are and what we think about war. We can understand that this is not an easy decision for them to make.

The next days they inquire in town about immigration, employment and rental outlets. After they have been with us for a week, it gets very quiet downstairs where they stay. We go to their quarters and find a note on the table: "We are sorry for the inconvenience we caused you but we could not face the separation from our family and our country. We decided to go back to the USA. Thank you for your hospitality." A $10 bill lies beside it.

A week later we hear the same voice on the telephone, "Do you have room for two guys?" This time two young black men knock at our door and ask if they could stay with us. We had just finished supper and offer them something to eat. They sit down at the table, fold their hands and pray a loud and long prayer. I assume they had been told at the office that we are Christians and they want to win our trust. At the next meal their prayer is much shorter and quieter. A few days later one of them leaves, he wants to hitch-hike to Manitoba to meet with an acquaintance. Chucky stays on with us. He is a tall funny fellow, befriends our boys and plays with them. When he becomes familiar with us he asks Hildegard if she would consider taking his girlfriend in who is staying at another place. Somewhat hesitantly she agrees and makes a bed for her in the back room. Virginia is a tall, handsome British girl with red hair and a strong cockney accent. After the first night she tells Hildegard somewhat sheepishly, "Mrs. Lemke, Chucky and I have been sleeping together for some time; we do not need two bedrooms." So she moves in with him. She offers to help in the kitchen and the house. Hildegard, who has a gift for languages, unintentionally adopts her accent and Virginia asks with a smile, "Do I sound that bad?"

Soon we notice that Virginia is pregnant. Hildegard, raised in Christian ethics, counsels them about the difficulty a child born out of wedlock will face later in life and they consider getting married. We have a small wedding party at our house for them.

After they have been with us for a few months they find a small apartment and move out. One day Virginia visits us and we notice she has a black eye and her jaw is out of place. She is hesitant to tell us that Charles in a rage of anger has beaten her. We take her to the hospital and they line up her broken jaw.

Though Chuck repents humbly and asks for forgiveness, Virginia fears he might do it again to her especially in her present condition. "He hates white people", she tells us, "in spite of all the support and kindness he has received from them." Virginia gives birth to a healthy little boy and we become his godparents. Her mother and grandmother come over from England and stay with us and with her for two weeks. Chuck is a proud father. In order to be able to present his son to his family in Pennsylvania, he will have to arrange for reentry to America. We find out that he is actually a deserter and not a draft dodger. He decides to report back to his former unit and ask for a pardon. He is lucky he has to serve only six months in prison because he has a small child. Virginia's mother takes her and the little boy back to England, while Chuck is serving his sentence.

Their marriage does not work out and they get divorced. Chuck marries again, a black girl. And Virginia gets married in England. They both keep contact with us by phone or letter for a number of years.

Not long after they have left, the Unitarians send us new visitors. Richard, a young Afro-American man with his two children, little Richard and Denise, who are about the same age as our children. They have fun playing together. Little Richard lisps a little and if something bugs him he announces with a stern voice, "I am getting mad," this relieves the stress, with no further action. They are cute, well-behaved kids. Richard is looking for a job and lands one as a night school teacher of electronics and photography in North Vancouver. He shows us his new telephone installed in his rental car, which is something uncommon at that time. One day he comes home with expensive photo equipment for his job, everything on credit.

We get a little suspicious and, when he is established in his job, we ask him to find his own accommodation. He is hesitant to leave so we find him an affordable apartment down the hill and lend him the money for the first month rent. He moves out and after a while we lose contact with him and our money. A few months after his departure, we get a phone call from a police station in Idaho. They want to know details about Richard. They had arrested him for fraud. He had moved to Canada, pretending to be a draft dodger, to avoid losing custody of his children. We hope that his stay with us may have had a positive effect on his life and that of his children.

The Unitarians urgently need shelter for three draft dodgers for a couple of days only and beg us to take them. After we reluctantly agree, they tell us those three men are diagnosed with hepatitis and advise us to disinfect all utensils which they are using. This will create considerably more work for Hildegard then she bargained for but we feel we cannot refuse to help those in need. They are a little older than the ones we had before and from our conversation with them we think they are authentic draft dodgers. After four days they get their papers to immigrate to Sweden. They leave and thank us very much for our hospitality.

This has been quite a stressful time for Hildegard who had always been an accommodating, gracious hostess. The war in Vietnam comes to an end and so does the draft dodging.

Friends who are working with MCC tell us about their M2M (man to man) service organization. Their members help young offenders adjusting to society and becoming responsible citizens after their release. With other men from churches in our area I join the group. Peace and reconciliation are important concerns for us Mennonites and we will now have an opportunity to practice these principles. Oakalla prison authorities will ask young offenders if they would like to have a visit from one of the M2M members in their cell.

We have a training session to learn how to communicate with them. The prison warden requests a police record from us, briefs us and tells us what we can and cannot do.

On my first visit the warden questions me and then leads me to the cell of a young man who had indicated that he wanted to have a visit. René is a slender 19 year-old from Montreal. He is aloof and suspicious when I greet him and wonders why I have volunteered to visit young offenders. I try to convince him that I am not an interrogator in disguise, just an ordinary citizen who wants to help him adjust to the life outside when he is discharged. On the second visit he seems to trust me and is more open. He committed 65 break and entry offences on his way from Montreal to Vancouver. This time he got two years minus a day. We are allowed two visits a month with our partner. He tells me about his family and we exchange pictures. I ask about his education and what his goals are for life. He does not know. He wants to have a family one day and I ask him to try to visualize that event, how he could prepare for it and what responsibility he will have as a future father and as a citizen.

At Christmas time I try to create a bit of a festive atmosphere, I bring him some of Hildegard's delicious cookies to celebrate Christmas with him. I tell him what Christmas means to me, God's love towards us and I want to share that with him. It reminds him of his family, and he appreciates it. He is looking forward to the day of his discharge. I ask him if I should inquire about job opportunities for him but all he wants is a good beer. I offer to have him stay with us until he finds work and a place of his own and he accepts that.

I pick him up from the prison, take him home and introduce him to Hildegard and the children who know about him from my stories. Hildegard has made a good meal and I have bought a case of beer for him. During the conversation he tells her that he had never eaten at a table with a tablecloth and napkins or cups and saucers which is normal for us. He feels uneasy in this milieu. During the next days he spends most of his time in town and comes back for supper. We ask him if we can help him to write a resume for a job. "No," he says, "I applied for welfare". A few days later he tells me he has found a place to stay and would like to move out. He wants to have his 'freedom'. I take him to one of those cheap hotels which he has chosen and wish him well. I visit him there once and when I phone back again I find out he has moved and did not leave an address. I feel sad about the situation and wonder what we could have done differently. I hope that my visits with him, our conversation and his short stay with us as a family may change his outlook on life and give him hope and tools to chart a new course.

A Danish immigrant woman, Irma, goes to Jean's Pentecostal church. Jean befriends her and introduces her to us. She thinks Danes and Germans might have some things in common. Irma works in the Swedish-Canadian senior's home not very far from us.

One day I look out of the window and see a woman walking up and down our street, looking up at our houses. I go out and ask her if she is looking for somebody and recognize it is Irma. She had been looking for our house. I ask her to come in and she tells us her story. Her work manager has laid her off. She cannot understand why they don't want her any longer. She has worked hard for several years and the tenants like her. She is desperate and does not know what to do; she has no place to go. Hildegard tells her we can help her to find another job but she thinks the world has come to an end.

Jean tells us Irma is contemplating ending her life and asks us if we could take her in for a while. So we make room for Irma. She likes the atmosphere in our house so much that she stays for over a year with us. She is a simple woman, talkative to the point of being pushy. Living with us and through Hildegard's positive outlook on life and her encouraging words, Irma even regains her sense of humor. She likes our children and they in turn accept her as our permanent guest. Later she meets a bachelor in her church. They get married and live happily on his hobby farm in Chilliwack. We occasionally visit her and buy eggs and vegetables from them.

19. Spiritual Renewal – Jesus People

Young people who have joined the Hippie movement out of rebellion against the status quo become disenchanted with the lifestyle of the hippies. They hope Christianity, and a spiritual transformation will give them the inner peace and fulfillment they are searching for. They immerse themselves in the teachings of Jesus and instead of being high on acid, they are 'high on Jesus'. They become known as the "Jesus People." They are critical of the established churches and want to return to the simple lifestyle of the early Christians; many live in community.

We come in contact with them by accident. The Mennonites have deeper life meetings in the Fraser Valley and John and I attend one in the West Abbotsford Mennonite Church. The guest speaker has just finished his inspirational talk and the song leader gets up to announce the final song, when the side doors to the main nave open and through both side isles solemnly walk strangely dressed bearded young men, each one carrying a Bible under his arm. They look like the apostles in the children's Sunday School Lesson books. The song leader waits until they are seated and then announces the final song. While we are singing I suggest to John that we should talk to these latecomers and welcome them after the service. We ask the youth pastor of the church if we could invite them into the fireside room. A number of young people are as interested as we to find out who these strangers are and where they come from and they join us.

In a short introduction, we tell them who we are and what the meeting they missed was about. They introduce themselves as Jesus People. They had mistaken our Mennonite church for a Pentecostal assembly which was, as they were told, to have an evangelistic crusade at that time. They come from Whatcom County just on the other side of the US border across from Abbotsford. Quite a few of them live there on a farm, communally. They live a simple life-style and are supporting themselves by growing their own food. They share with us their frustration with society, the greed, the injustice, and pressure to conform. They yearn for personal freedom to make their own choices. Many of them are college graduates or they walked out of college before final examinations. They are searching for new values and hope to find these in Christianity. They indicate that they are looking for Christian mentors.

An older member of the church, who had sneaked into our meeting, saw this as an opportunity to give his advice. He tells them politely they should dress properly, get a decent job, earn their living, and join a church for instruction. He obviously did not listen with his heart to understand their concerns. Before we depart we tell these Jesus People about our own search and our 'Hauskreis'. They are excited and ask if they could keep in contact with us and perhaps visit us some time.

A few weeks later, on our Hauskreis night, an old pickup truck with a canopy drives up to our house and a dozen Jesus people climb out. Some bring their guitars and Bibles. It is a mild evening and we go outside, sit in a circle on the lawn in the back yard and each one briefly introduces himself. We tell them what we have planned for the evening and then Rüdiger gets his guitar and we sing a number of songs which some of our guests know too. We share our experiences during the week, listen to their stories and we pray together.

The neighbors wonder what goes on with the normally quiet Lemkes. It is getting dark; we watch a beautiful sunset and go inside. We discuss a bible text and they have many questions, especially those who come from non-Christian homes. They appreciate our input and that we include them in our discussion and our prayers.

The girls are impressed by Hildegard's thoughtful input and her friendly and positive personality and ask if they may come and visit us again.

Not long after this visit, Karen and Beth show up and stay with us for a few weeks. Others follow. At one point we have five of them sleeping in sleeping bags on the floor of our recreation room. They are on fire for Jesus and want to tell others about their new found faith. They do this on sunny evenings at the beaches and come back long after midnight, One night they get into an animated conversation with two fellows on the beach and bring them home to tell them more about their newly found joy in life. But the guys don't listen much to their message; they are interested in the girls. When the girls finally get them to leave early in the morning one of them walks out with one of the girl's sleeping bags.

We are not very pleased with this incident and tell them we have three small children and would like to know who is in the house at night. If they want to continue in that way they would have to find new quarters, perhaps closer to the beaches.

Hildegard is really concerned about the situation and finds it very strenuous. Jean hears about it and is looking for a solution. She had taken Hildegard occasionally to Pastor Bob Birch's Bible studies at St. Margaret's Episcopal Church. Since this church had incorporated charismatic teachings, it has expanded and they just added a building adjacent to their property to use as a youth centre. Jean and Hildegard talk to pastor Bob about our problem and he agrees to take our Jesus People into his youth centre.

One of them, Bob, asks us if he could stay with us for a while. As a young Christian he feels we two could help him to grow in his faith. Bobby is a sensitive, soft spoken, well-educated gay man. He had been a designer and manager of a men's dress shirt business and had become a Hippie. He had experimented heavily with drugs and alcohol. He met Jesus people, saw their happiness and positive outlook on life and wanted to have that too.

Now and then he struggles with accepting his gender identity, with guilt feelings, and questions his faith. Once he breaks down, weeps and argues with God about why he has given him the body of a man and the mind of a woman, as he expresses it. We try to build up his faith and self-esteem, encourage him and pray with him.

He is an easy house guest, is respectful, helps Hildegard in the kitchen, is particular in cleaning the house and in his gentle, humorous way teaches the kids etiquette. They love Bobby.

After half a year with us, he feels strong enough to go to Seattle and tell his former friends about his newly found joy in life. After two weeks, he comes back, downhearted and confesses he has failed miserably. He had given in to his old friends and had fallen back into his old habits. Being with us he gathers some strength again and at Christmas time he feels courageous enough to celebrate Christmas with his family in New York. They are not Christians. He wants to mend broken family ties and tell his parents and siblings about his new faith.

After three weeks he returns and tells us that it started out fine with his family but he could not sustain his stand and made a mockery of his Christian faith. This time it takes longer to recuperate from his failure. When he is with us he is confident and happy and takes part in our activities. We hope it will last.

After about two years with us he packs his suitcase again and makes another attempt to be with his family. We wish him fortitude and blessing for this event. Months pass by and we hear nothing from him and assume he has settled down. Later we get the sad news that he has died of an overdose of pills. We grieve for his untimely death. This news is a shock for our Hauskreis of which he had become a faithful member. We ask ourselves what else we could have done to save his life.

In the bulletin of St. Margaret's Church, where we attend evening services, we read that the Watsons are leading a group of 'pilgrims' to the Holy Land. The purpose of this tour is 'to provide personal contacts, give historical insight and spiritual enlightenment.' Hildegard points that out to me. She has a predilection for Israel. Her dad had told her, when she was young, about the land where Jesus had walked and taught and he had books and slides about the Holy Land which he had shown the family.

I cannot take a holiday to go with her but I encourage her to join the group and fulfill her dream and she tells Merv that she will come with them.

Merv and Merla Watson have a music ministry for Messianic Jews and have moved to Israel. Merla, of Mennonite stock, is an accomplished violinist and plays in the Jewish symphony in Jerusalem and Merv, a vocalist, accompanies their songs with guitar or accordion. They write their own songs in English and Hebrew, often based on the text of the Psalms. We have several of their recordings.

Marv has now inspired fourteen people to travel with him to Israel. He has good connections to Israeli tourist agents since they have lived in Jerusalem for several years. With them he has worked out a good itinerary. They want to visit many historical towns and places, which are important to Christians and Jews alike in biblical and in present times.

The children miss their mom. To pretend to be with her, we look up on the map of Israel the cities from her itinerary and do some research about their history and importance and imagine what she might see now. In a letter to her, we ask if she has seen in Akko the 'Knight's Hall' from the Crusaders or 'Khan El Adman' the trading post of the Ottomans or Herod's Palace and the old aqueduct in Caesarea. Some of these she has not seen or heard about.

When she comes home, she tells us all about her experiences, swimming in the Dead Sea where you cannot drown, visiting many of the places mentioned in the Bible, like Bethlehem, Nazareth and Jerusalem, going into the tomb where Jesus was laid. They wailed at the Wailing Wall and took pictures of the Muslim Mosque in Jerusalem, the 'Dome of the Rock'. They were not allowed to go inside. Two nights they spent in the guest house of the 'Kibbutz Genoas'; 500 people live in that commune. They grow all their food, have dairy cattle, vineyards and carp breeding ponds. The 'pioneers' and 'volunteers' that live there were very friendly and hospitable.

Merv's group drove through the Negev desert to the sea resort of Elat on the Red Sea which the Israelis still occupy.

20. Retracing our roots

As a family, we have traveled with our Westfalia camper through many parts of North America. Now we think our children are at an age where they can understand and appreciate the culture of other countries. We can show them another part of the world.

We told them about the places where we were born and spent our teenage years and they are excited to see them and to travel to Europe. Our relatives came to visit us here in Canada and we now have an invitation to visit them in Germany.

The children hope their knowledge of German will help them to communicate with them.

To take our camper with us to Germany would be too costly. To travel with a family of five and all our luggage by public transport is too inconvenient and expensive. And since some of our relatives and friends live out in the country where there is poor bus and train connection, public transportation is really out of the question. So Hildegard inquires from her uncle Herbert, who has connection to all sorts of people, if he knows someone from whom we can rent a camper. Uncle Herbert, a much younger half brother of Hildegard's father, traveled all over Germany and parts of Europe by bicycle, as it was customary for young journey-men at that time. In the army during the war he got an eye injury and is now almost blind. But he can still get around by train and plane and has not lost his sense of humor. He writes back that he might be able to provide a camper for us.

We arrange everything for a camping trip in Europe. For our children, this is the first time they will fly in an airplane, and they wonder what it will be like.

John and Monika and their family will spend their holiday in Germany as well and we fly with them in the same plane to Amsterdam. At the airport, Lothar, Monika's father, welcomes the Wiebe family. We know him well from our last visit and he welcomes us too.

Before we left Vancouver we packed two big BC salmon in a special box to take along as a gift. We present one to Lothar. For him it is a delicacy, hard to get in Germany and quite expensive. It is still frozen having been in the cargo section of the plane. He is very happy about it and gives us a hug,

Somewhat in the background, Max is observing us. He sees that we are being welcomed so heartily by someone he does not know and he wonders if that good-looking woman being hugged by an older man is his niece whom he has come to pick up from the Amsterdam airport. The Wiebes finally leave. We look around and Hildegard spots Max. She rushes over to him and introduces our family to him. Max is Uncle Herbert's brother-in-law. Uncle Herbert has been able to get an old Peugeot camper for us and, since he cannot drive, he asked Max to pick us up in it. He packs our luggage into the camper and there is enough room for all of us to fit in; Hildegard calls it 'the Ark'. Max is not used to driving such a vehicle. Shortly before the border he comes too close to the curb and rips the front tire open. We have no tools and have no other choice but wave at cars and wait until one stops to help us. One of them is the Dutch 'Wegenwacht,' similar to our BCAA; it stops and a grouchy driver helps us put the spare tire on. Aunt Edith has to wait two more hours to serve dinner for us.

We spend a few days with Uncle Max and Aunt Edith and explore Krefeld. Our children are surprised that everyone here speaks German and they are glad that they can understand most of it. We thank Max for picking us up and say good-bye to him and his family. Now I have to drive the Ark.

Not far from Krefeld lives Ortrun's mother, whose second husband is a painter. We bring her greetings from her daughter. Her husband shows us his atelier and his paintings, late romantic to semi-abstract canvasses. He tells us about the art scene in Germany and which art galleries and shows we should see. They serve us a delicious supper and take us to a hotel for the night. This is the only night on our trip that we spend in such a luxury, all the other nights we sleep at relatives' places or on campgrounds.

Our next visit is with Onkel Herbert and Tante Hedi in Katzweiler. Their children have left home and live closer to the place where they work. He has plenty of room for our family. Their place becomes our headquarters for the area. The next day he takes us to the owner of the Ark, an elderly deaconess, sister Margarete, a lively small person still wearing her habit. She has worked in Children's ministry and is now retired. In her old Peugeot camper she used to pick up children from near-by villages to take them to Sunday-School. The village children could recognize it by the Bible verses printed in big letters, 'Lasset die Kindlein zu mir kommen' (let the children come to me) on one side and on the other 'Jesus liebt Dich' (Jesus loves you). Our children name it the 'Jesus Bus'. We do not know what Uncle Herbert has told her about us. In our conversation we mention liability and insurance and what she expects for rent. We give her a little more than what she asks for, which we feel is very modest, and thank her very much for her kindness.

On our way back we visit our common cousin Elisabeth, we all call her Lieschen. She lives on the outskirts of the town. She welcomes us with open arms. We know her as a lively and lovely person and have a good time with her and her family. She plays with our children and they love her. Before we leave, she gives us some additional camping gear and food.

Hildegard cannot wait to show the children Kaiserslautern, the former Mennonite parsonage on Lilienstraße, where she was born. She tells the children stories about her childhood there, how they pestered the old tailor Hund who lived in the corner house across the street. They ran on their roller-blades on the street below his window, making a lot of noise and he would come running out, sometimes in socks, and chase them away with his yard stick.

The children explore the area, the house and garden where their mom had played. They are surprised to see such narrow streets but are impressed by the solid houses built of red sandstone blocks long ago.

Pastor Sigmar, who had visited us in Burnaby, has invited us to visit him and his congregation in Heidelberg. John and Monika are also invited. We have arranged to meet with them at Heide's apartment in Heilbronn. On the way there we tarry at several points of interest and miscalculate the time. It is midnight when we arrive at her place. She sits outside with a table lamp beside her, waiting for us. She lives in a nice suite on the ground floor of a private mansion with a large garden.

John and Monika spend part of their vacation with Monika's parents and siblings in Bielefeld at the same time as we are with our relatives. Friends of their parents lent them their VW camper to use while traveling in Germany. Tomorrow they will come and join us here at Heide's place.

It gets quite crowded for ten additional people in Heide's suite. Our six children sleep in their sleeping bags on the carpet in her living room and we parents in our campers. The next day we drive to Heidelberg.

Pastor Sigmar had been impressed with our house group when he participated in one of our meetings. He asked us then if we would consider speaking at their Full Gospel Businessmen's meeting in Heidelberg about our spiritual experiences. We had agreed to do so and are driving now from Heilbronn to Heidelberg.

Pastor Sigmar is on an errand so his wife, Elisabeth, welcomes us and introduces us to the family. The atmosphere in the parsonage seems somewhat tense. The children, in their late teens, are influenced by the hippie movement and their relationship with their parents is chilly. They ignore us 'strangers'. We try to find out from Sigmar what he expects us to share with the 'businessmen' this evening. We coordinate among ourselves what each one will say and in what order. We have a little time to relax. Hildegard and I go into the garden and meet their daughter, Adelgund, who sits on the stairs in her jeans and sandals and plays the guitar. We listen and when she stops, Hildegard in her open way starts a conversation with her. She tells her who we are, that Heidelberg is just a stop-over on our Europe trip and asks her what she would suggest we should see in the city. Soon we start a lively discussion and find that she is an alert young person. She wants to break out of a conservative Christian tradition where parents have a certain control of their children and do not understand the new generation. She wants to live her own life. Jörg-Martin, her brother, is in sympathy with communist ideology to the dismay of his father.

The evening comes. We gather in the Esso Motor Hotel and Sigmar introduces us as his Canadian friends to a group of about twenty people. The 'Geschäftsleute des vollen Evangeliums' is a typical transplant of the American 'Full Gospel Businessmen's Association'. The chairman and a number of the people present are Americans who work in Heidelberg. The songs we sing are choruses which we know from home. They are printed on sheets, literally translated into awkward German.

When it is our turn to speak Hildegard shares her own spiritual journey and how the Holy Spirit has worked in her life. John talks about his experience and the influence of the charismatic movement on our churches and I talk about our house fellowship. Some of the American listeners ask us for an English summary. At a social gathering afterwards we respond to their questions. The whole atmosphere is somewhat strange for us.

We spend the night in the parsonage and the next morning Sigmar shows us his church. He deplores the apathy of his church members and we talk about the problems traditional churches face in this time where individualism is the gospel. He thanks us for our contribution and we take our leave.

We stroll through Heidelberg's 'Altstadt' and visit its university, one of the oldest European educational institutions. Many Nobel Prize winners taught in its lecture halls. We walk across the old Neckar-bridge up the Kaiserstuhl hill and visit the famous castle, the 'Heidelberger Schloss'. It has weathered several wars, has been destroyed and rebuilt in many building styles from the gothic to the baroque. In the wine cellar of the castle is the largest wine barrel, I think, in the world; it has a capacity of 221,000 lt.

We drive upstream beside the Rhein, the river mentioned in many German legends and folksongs. One of the most famous, the 'Lorelei', tells of the beautiful siren, sitting on the top of the cliff, luring sailors through her bewitching singing into shipwreck on the reefs below. We take a picture of that famous rock and the children imagine the Lorelei sitting up there combing her golden hair and singing. Krista laughs and teases me, "Dad, watch where *you* are going."

Further on we come into the Black Forest. The road leads through dense dark green forest. Once in awhile in a clearing we look down on the red roofs of houses which are nestled in the valley below. Not far from the road we spot a little church on a higher plateau. We need a break to breathe the fresh air and enjoy the view. Down below is the Rhein valley and on the other side the 'Vogesen', a mountain range in Alsace, parallel to the Black Forest where we are. These two mountain ranges make the Rhine valley look like a wide canyon. We enter the church. The light shines through beautiful stained glass windows and over the altar is a modern mosaic mural; quite a surprise for such a small country church.

In Obertal at the Murg River, we camp for the first time in a German campground. It is a beautiful area but has very narrow camper spaces. We will find that in many other European campgrounds.

The 'Gasthof zur Sonne' (sunny inn) invites us for supper. The children have their first meal in a German restaurant. For breakfast the next morning, we send Hanno to the bakery on the next block, to fetch us some freshly baked German buns which we all enjoy.

Hildegard is searching for Uncle Herbert Janzen, her mother's brother, who is supposed to live in this area. She knocks at the door of Amselweg 4, the address someone gave us and an elderly lady opens hesitantly. Hildegard introduces herself and asks if a Herbert Janzen is living here. He hears it and comes running to the door, takes his niece in his arms and greets the rest of us heartily. Herbert is an outgoing person with an interesting life story. He is using his middle name, Herbert, because Isak, his first name, sounded too Jewish. He was sympathetic to the Nazis and thinks highly of the German troops who rescued many German Mennonites from the Ukraine from the 'Communist hordes'. Several of his brothers and uncles had been shot or were deported to Siberia in the Stalin era and died there. He was born in Russia, immigrated to Canada, was interned during the war as a German immigrant and deported back to Germany after the war. While in internment camp he learned several languages. This is an asset for his work as a salesman for

Rosenthal dishes. His main customers are the families of US soldiers who are stationed in Bavaria.

He invites us for supper and we have a lot to talk about.

Our tourist book mentions 'Meersburg' at Lake Constance as a 'must see'. This is our destination for the next day. We find a parking spot not too far from the castle and walk through the small medieval town. The streets are narrow and the many hanging flower baskets on the windowsills of residences, shops and restaurants give it a friendly, inviting atmosphere. It is not hard to find the castle, a Landsknecht (mercenary) in his colorful medieval battle garb and halberd stands at the front of the drawbridge and shows us the way to the gate. Meersburg is the oldest still maintained castle in Germany and dates back to the 7th century, the time of the Merowingian king Dagobert. The central tower with the torture chamber is named after him. Hanno wants a picture, having his head in the wooden headlock and Michael would like to slip into one of the knight's armor, displayed in the armory. The rooms are small and the windows narrow, the furniture is bulky and the kitchen utensils around the open fire pit rudimentary, not very comfortable. The castle is a massive structure with stone walls in the lower floors up to three feet thick. Later when it became the residence of the Bishop of Constance the upper floors were enlarged and more delicately furnished and decorated.

Not far from Meersburg is the historical museum of Unteruhldingen with the 'Pfahlbauten' (lake dwellings). The settlers, 3000 years ago in the Bronze Age, rammed wooden posts into the sea bed of Lake Constance, let them stick out about four feet above sea level, built a platform on top of them and constructed their huts on it. We enter the settlement through a fortified gate and walk on a long, narrow boardwalk bridge to the first platform. About four to six huts are built on one platform; a small boardwalk leads to the next platform with another cluster of huts. We have to bend down to go inside and look at the rather primitive furnishings. These huts are true replicas of settlements that were found on the bottom of the lake.

There are a number of castles on the banks of the Rhein. We single out Burg Rheinstein, a 'picture book' castle on a steep rock overlooking the river. We can see its slim, tall tower from afar. When we arrive at the gate, it is locked. We are disappointed. It is only five o'clock and we shout for the gatekeeper. He comes and we can persuade him to open the gate for us. Seeing the children, he even becomes friendly, and gives us a private tour. The children are fascinated. Being the only visitors gives them time to look at everything in more detail. Rheinstein is built more in the Gothic style, quite different from Meersburg. Michael had built a cardboard model of Burg Rheinstein at home and to see the real one, is exciting for him. We pass a number of other castles. Several of them are now refitted to serve as youth hostels.

In Viernheim we visit Thomas and our friend Agnes, the daughter of Pastor Erhard. They live in a communal settlement with several other families. Communal living has always interested us. They tell us they are basically quite happy with the arrangement.

It is not far from Viernheim to Cologne and soon we can see the high steeples of the Kölner Dom on the other side of the Rhein. The children had heard about the Cologne Cathedral and they are anxious to see it from the inside. We try to find a parking place as close to the Dom as possible and see a sign to a park house on the church plaza. We drive up a ramp to the parking floor and find out that our camper is too high to pass under the height barrier. We wonder why they did not put the barrier at the bottom of the ramp. We have no other choice but to back down again. It is not easy to persuade the drivers of the cars behind us to do the same. Hildegard is embarrassed seeing that all the people in the street cafés around the plaza look at our Jesus Bus with the Bible verses on its sides and find the situation hilarious.

Back in Katzweiler we pick up Uncle Herbert, our tour guide for our trip to Poland. We drive to Hillerse not far from the East German border. Mother's brother, Richard, and his family of fifteen persons, settled here after they had escaped with horses and wagons from West Prussia just before the Russian troops reached their estate in the winter of 1945. Cousin Walter is the only one left here of the family. All the others found work somewhere else. We stay over-night at his place. We had agreed with the Wiebes to meet here again. When we park our campers in his yard, Walter sees the printing 'Jesus liebt Dich' on the side of our camper. "The border police would not let you into East Germany with Bible verses on your vehicle. I would suggest you hide them before you get to the border," he tells us and brings a roll of adhesive tape. We ponder over whether we are courageous enough to make a statement of our faith or fainthearted enough to hide it. We do not want to take a chance and tape it up. Walter and Irmgard are very gracious hosts. They supply us with food and additional blankets for the trip and we leave some of our utensils which we are not allowed to take to East Germany with them. Early the next morning we leave their hospitable house heading for the border.

In half an hour we are at the end of a long line of cars waiting to cross the border to East Germany. The children are excited and a little afraid, wondering what will happen at a border between countries which don't like each other. After we wait for two hours, the border guards direct us to a barrack where we have to register. The simple wooden structure has no windows towards the road only two mailbox wide slots at waist height. Into the first one I slip our passports, not knowing where they go, who is behind the wall and what will happen to them. While they are processed, the border guards search our vehicle. With a mirror on a pole they look at the underside of our camper. We answer their questions politely and refrain from making any comments or jokes and as foreigners we are treated fairly well. A German businessman before us complains about the slow service, they ignore him for a while and then search his vehicle painstakingly. We pick up our passports from the second slot in the barrack and the customs officer tells us that we are not to leave the Autobahn on our way to West Berlin. We notice hidden police patrols at every Autobahn exit. There is no control when we enter West Berlin. We have lunch in the 'Jägerklause' and proceed to 'Checkpoint Charlie', the north east exit, which we assume is the crossing for foreigners to East Berlin, East Germany and Poland. But we find out it is only for military personnel and we cannot persuade them to let us through. We have to go back where we came from to the 'Drei Linden' crossing. We lose two hours going back and forth. But Drei Linden is the only crossing open for non-military people to get to East Germany from Berlin. From there we head straight to the Polish border, again a lengthy procedure at the Polish border. The guards just sit there and I have to go to them and ask what to do next. Passes are checked three times. On the Polish side we are asked how much money we are bringing in and we have to buy a certain amount of Zlotys at the official exchange rate for each day we will stay in Poland, (1DM =16 Zl, the unofficial rate is 25 Zl). We also have to buy vouchers for gasoline; it is against the law to accept cash at the service station to fill up the tank.

After an hour of traveling, we come to a little town, Lagowo. A man approaches us and we ask him if the town has a campground. He tells us in broken German there is one at the outskirts of the town. It is now quite dark already and we can make out some tents on the right side of the street. There is still light in the office of the compound. I walk over knock at the door and ask the attendant if he has room for two campers. He tells me in almost perfect German that this is a youth hostel, the campground is further on.

I had applied for a youth leader hostel pass from Vancouver before we left which I have with me. I show it to him and he lets us in. There is hardly anybody here. Uncle Herbert and the children can sleep in a big tent, so we do not have to put ours up and we parents sleep in our campers. We are quite tired and exhausted, going through four border crossings and are glad to have some rest.

Early next morning, I explore the town and walk up to the castle. It looks familiar to me. The tower and the castle look very much like the one on Mothers' picture postcard at home. She had completed her housekeeping training with the countess of Lagow; this must be the same town. What a coincidence! I walk along the street where my mother had walked sixty years ago. I take a peek into the chapel of the castle and am astonished to see so many people, about a dozen of them teenagers, at seven o'clock in the morning at Mass in Communist Poland.

At the lake I meet the manager of the youth hostel again. We greet each other and he mentions that he is a physical education teacher and had been on exchange in Germany. When we leave, he asks us cleverly if we have any coins, he is a coin collector. The kids empty their wallets which amounts to $4, about 100 Zlotys and he is happy. We leave the hostel and buy some supplies in the town; one loaf of bread is only 8 Zlotys.

We drive through Pommern (Pomerania). Many of the former German farm houses are either dilapidated or deserted. On the outskirts of Posen, a brand new very nice restaurant draws our attention. We have lunch there. The waitress offers us a menu. Of the 12 entries on it only three are available. Food is very cheap and not very tasty. We pay ten DM for meals for eleven people.

Uncle Herbert has arranged lodging for us with his former neighbor, Liedke, in Thiergart. We stay for a few days with his family.

They fled, when the Russians invaded West Prussia, but were overrun by the Russian army. They took his horse and wagon and everything on it and sent them home on foot. It took them a week to return. The Polish provisionary government gave them the choice to opt for Poland or be sent to a labor camp. After some consideration they decided to become Polish citizens and stay in Thiergart. After some difficulties at first, they were finally allowed to repossess their old farm. Besides running the farm they occasionally host German visitors, like us.

They welcome Uncle Herbert and he introduces us to mother Liedke and her son Peter, his wife and little son. The table is set for a good, homemade supper and we have a lot to share. Hildegard and I sleep in their guest room, the Wiebes sleep in their camper and the children pitch up a tent in the yard. Tomorrow is an important day, I will take my family to the house where I was born and lived for the first 17 years of my life. I am excited to see it again.

We get up early. Mrs. Liedke packs a lunch and comes with us. She will be our translator. All of us board our Ark and we drive along the narrow dirt road to the main street, cross the bridge over the little river Thiene and enter Alt-Rosengart, my home village. I clearly remember what it was like when I had to leave it thirty two years ago. I am eager to explain it to my family in detail,

Down from the bridge on the right side was our village inn with guest rooms, a large meeting room with a dance floor and a grocery store. I remember one year at Christmas our teacher and village party representative had organized a Christmas party for the whole community. My father was playing the violin and my sister accompanied the Christmas songs on the piano.

We drive along the Thiergarter-Chaussee. Tall chestnut trees used to stand on both sides of the road. From spring to fall their top branches formed a canopy of leaves. We gathered the chestnuts and played with them like marbles or cut little baskets out of the hard brown peel, hollowing out the white part of it. Now the road is empty, most of the trees have been cut down for firewood. At the crossing we turn right into the Thiensdorfer-Chaussee, the road that leads to the village of Thiensdorf. On the corner lived farmer Harms who ran the post office. When the weather was very bad he delivered the mail on horseback. On the right side in the run-down house lived old Mr. Riediger. It is said he was the only one in the village who voted 'nein' (no) for Hitler and got away with it.

Our village has no real centre. The farms are scattered around, some along the road, some down by the embankment of the Thiene River or off the road in the middle of their fields, like ours. A little farther down lived farmer Schoenwald. His son, Waldemar, and I were the only students who did not join the Hitler youth voluntarily the first year it was introduced. The next year attendance was compulsory.

Beside farmer Thiede's driveway was the gathering place for our milk delivery. The children have fun running up and down the ramp onto which their father had to lift heavy 20 liter milk cans. Most of the farms in our village were dairy farms.

The next building was the one room school in which I received the first five years of my public education. I still remember that time. I came from the street into the school yard and from there into the small entrance hall where we hung up our coats in the winter. We entered the large class room along the centre aisle which divided the junior classes on the window side from the senior classes, grade five to eight, on the other. I can still see myself sitting on the bench answering the teacher's questions. When I was in the senior class he sometimes asked me to supervise the beginners' class, helping them with seat work, forming their letters or adding numbers, while the teacher was instructing the seniors. I remember, and still feel the pain and embarrassment, when the teacher pulled me over the front bench and gave me a spanking with his cane.

He came a few hours late into the class room after he had slept off his boozing from a late political party meeting and was grumpy. I was bored and had played tricks on some students and they told the teacher when he finally came in. It was the only time I ever got a spanking.

Now the school is locked and several of the windows are boarded up with old wooden slabs. Tall weeds are growing around the school yard where we planted our school garden. Our children want to see the artesian well that was drilled when I was in grade four. It is still running at the entrance to the school yard.

Across the school yard we can see in the distance a cluster of tall willow trees; behind them must be our farm. We pass the little farm and tailor shop of Meister Cornelsen. My mother told me a sad story about Mrs. Cornelsen. Her husband had died years before the war and she had a hard time to keep the farm going. When the Russians came into our village in the last months of the war, they took what they found valuable from our houses, especially everything edible. It was January 1945, a cold winter and people were starving. The neighbor woman, Mrs.Preuss, had hidden some flour and the two women secretly baked bread at her place. Mrs.Cornelsen was walking home with three small loaves of bread under her apron when she suddenly saw a Russian soldier coming towards her. He asked her what she was hiding under her apron and tore it away. She begged him to leave her at least one loaf. He grabbed two of them and told her to go home with the last one. She had just run a few meters when he raised his gun and shot her in the back. They buried her in her garden.

Cornelsen's house, like many of the old East-German farmhouses with living quarters, stable and barn under one thatched roof, is in a much neglected condition. The barn may have collapsed so the present owner built a simple new stable and barn beside it.

We park the Ark behind their new barn, at the entrance to our driveway. We all climb out and walk to the gate. It hangs crookedly on its hinges and groans when I pry it open but it still holds together. I suggest we walk to our house. The last time I was here, I had to navigate it in a homemade boat across the flooded meadows. The fields in this area are below sea level and have to be drained. Only the roads are raised above sea level. Wind powered 'water mills' along the dikes of the Thiene pump the water through a network of drainage trenches and canals into the river which later empties into the Baltic Sea. The regional Polish authorities must have put the pumps in action again but I am not sure if the ground is solid enough to drive a heavy vehicle over it and I do not want to get stuck in the mud.

Flowers are blooming along the path just as they used to. I discover again the fine pink stars of the wild carnations which I like so much, recognize the yellowish blooming chamomile along the tracks and the tall stalks of the off-white clusters of yarrow waving in the wind. Mother used to make bitter-tasting tea from these. It is supposed to help against fever, indigestion and other ailments. The big yellow marsh marigolds grow partly in the water on the side of the long drainage trench which formed the border between our and neighbor Peters' fields. Peters, a Mennonite, had the largest farm in the village. He was our mayor and he wanted to prepare my father to succeed him when he retired. Scattered all over the place are the cheerful color spots of the red and white daisies.

Some of the old gnarled wind-torn willows are lining the last end of the path. We take the shortcut across a narrow bridge over the main drainage trench and the house where I was born, fifty one years ago, comes into full view. Our children run ahead to have a closer look at the old "mansion". Mrs.Liedke warns them to behave and not to go inside because we do not know the new owners. The house has aged considerably, just as I have. It has weathered two world wars, floods and new owners who do not give it the care my parents had given it for thirty-five years. It looks quite run down. The thick thatched roof has thinned out and moss is growing on top. It has been repaired in different places with tin sheets.

Mrs. Liedke hesitantly introduces us to the new Polish owners and tells them what the reason for our unannounced visit is. They are not thrilled about our coming but let us in the house. We feel Mrs.Liedke translates only half the questions we ask. We are allowed to go through the rooms but it is a little awkward and we soon leave the house. I take the children into the garden. I had told them about the tall pear tree which I had often climbed as a boy. It is gone now as are most of the other fruit trees in our orchard. They very likely made good firewood. The yard and the paths in the garden which we had to sweep and rake every weekend are now over-grown with weeds; no flowers or vegetables anywhere.

We are disappointed with our walk into the past and tell Mrs.Liedke's son Peter about it. The next morning after he has done his chores on the farm, he hitches his horse before the carriage and invites our family to get in and we drive in style back to our former home again. Peter is less inhibited than his mother. He chats with the owner and he allows us to inspect the whole house. I am of course eager to see my former room upstairs. Everything seems much smaller to me now than it was when I lived here as a boy. I hope to find some personal mementos to take along but nothing is left. I look behind the boards under the sloping roof of the attic where we had hidden our good dishes and silver but everything is gone. The owner tells us the Russians and the former residents had taken everything. When he came here five years ago, it was a mess. We go outside and I take the children behind the machine shed. It looks like a farm museum. All the equipment we had used to run the farm is still there, rusty and partially overgrown with weeds. I see an old rusty horseshoe and take it along as a memento.

For the children this is fascinating. They get a picture of how we farmed when I was their age. All my childhood memories come back and I become somewhat melancholy. Hildegard notices it, puts her arm around me and we walk quietly back to the carriage. I look back once more and feel this will be my last good-bye to the place that was once my beloved home. I never see it again.

I think this is the first time the children have driven in a horse and buggy. They love it. I let Krista hold the reins for a while and she is quite proud of this.

Uncle Herbert wants to see his former Polish farmhand with whom he had kept contact. We drive to the house where carpenter Driedger used to live. Janush lives in it now. He is happy to see his former boss again and invites us all into his house. With typical Polish hospitality, he serves each one a glass of vodka and invites us for lunch. We thank him for the invitation but tell him we just want to see how he is and drive on but he insists we stay. While we are talking, Janush's wife kills a rooster and prepares a full meal. As soon as we have taken a sip of vodka he comes and fills the glass again. I do not like it and I have to drive. I try to tell him this in a polite way. But to leave a glass half empty goes against the honor of a Polish host. We eat the prepared meal together and thank him appropriately for his hospitality. We drive the Preussisch-Rosengarter Chaussee towards our Mennonite Church.

There are still a few cherry trees standing on the side of the road. We used to climb them and pick and eat the big sweet, bing cherries until the man who had leased them chased us away. We stop at the artesian well at grandfather's driveway. It does not flow freely anymore as it has dried up to a trickle, but the water is still cool and refreshing. Hildegard and the children listen to my stories about Opa Wiehler as we drive down to his house.

They have seen photographs of him, a stately man with his long white sideburns. The big old house built with squared-off smooth logs and a thatched roof is not there anymore. Russian soldiers set it on fire, as neighbor Radke told us. He had seen them walking over shortly before it burst into flames. Both Grandparents, Onkel Bestvater, Oma's brother, and their daughter Helene died in the flames. Tante Lenchen, as we called her, had left her order as a deaconess to care for her parents especially for her blind mother. The Russians suspected she had harbored retreating German soldiers and wanted to smoke them out.

The new Polish owners have built a new house much smaller than the old one. They are friendly and let us see the rest of the farm which is still in its original state. On the dirt road behind the barn, Grandfather traveled with his wagon to visit sick and poor neighbors. He would leave some food with them, encourage the women and counsel the men to stay away from alcohol and care for their family. He took us along to train us in Christian charity.

We drive on to the Mennonite church, which we used to attend, and where I was baptized. We can get the key to unlock it and go inside. It is now used as a Catholic church. The pulpit has been moved to the side to make room for the altar. The plain off-white walls are now decorated with colorful pictures of Mary and saints. I show the children where we sang in the choir on the main balcony. The pipe organ has been replaced by an old piano. We have a few quiet moments in the church and then go to the adjoining cemetery. It is so overgrown with bushes and weeds that I cannot identify the grave of my father anymore. Most of the tombstones are removed or broken.

Not many of the Lemke relatives want to go back to their homeland so we are doing some research for them. Not far from the Liedkes is the village of Lichtfelde where my father grew up, where I watched Opa Lemke forge horseshoes in his smithy and where he let me taste the sweet honey from his beehives. His shop had collapsed and where his beehives used to stand, a plain stable has been erected.

Uncle Herbert is a good tour-guide. Hildegard remembers the name of the village where her father was born. Uncle Herbert locates the house in Kronsnest. The Polish residents who live there now are very friendly and show us every room. There are even some of the old kitchen utensils left which Hildegard inspects carefully.

On the way back we pass the Mennonite church in Thiensdorf. It is now a grain elevator and we see a tractor coming out of its main entrance door. We look inside, all benches, altar and pulpit even the floor have been removed, a sad appearance.

We spend the last night with the Liedkes, thank them for their hospitality and leave some valued Deutsch-Mark with them.

The next morning we are ready for the next adventure, the sea-resort of Kahlberg.

We spent many sunny holidays there when I was a boy. Usually, once a year at the beginning of summer vacations, our teacher took the whole school on an outing to Kahlberg. We traveled by train to the city of Elbing, from there we sailed with a small steamer across the Haff (Vistula Lagoon) followed by a large flock of sea gulls to the Nehrung, a narrow land strip separating the waters of the long inland lake from the Baltic Sea. Kahlberg is on the Nehrung. The boat docked on the south side of the village, we walked for five minutes over bumpy sand dunes through a strip of gnarled dark green pines to the white, sandy beach of the Baltic Sea.

This time we take the land route, which, until 1938, led through the Polish Corridor. Where the Nehrung starts to reach out into the sea is the village of Stutthof, a former concentration camp of the Nazis. It is now a museum. The children and we had never seen a 'KZ' before. The Nazis kept secret what was going on inside. The camp is surrounded by a high barbed wire fence. We enter through a gate with a high watch tower; nailed to its wall is a memorial plaque to remember the victims of the camp. One barrack is preserved as a museum. It shows the three-tiered wooden beds where the prisoners slept close together and in front a long wooden table with tin containers where the prisoners ate their soup. Thoughtfully we go back to our camper and drive along the narrow land strip to a more friendly place, the little sea resort of Kahlberg. We have lunch in a very nicely decorated beach restaurant. The food is simple and tasty.

It is a beautiful sunny day. The children cannot wait to get into the water. We are amazed at the white sand stretching out for kilometers. We use one of the big canopied beach chairs as a 'change room'. Lots of people of different ages and nationalities are lying on the beach or swimming in the sea. We have lots of fun in the water and on the beach and enjoy the relaxation.

The water in the Baltic Sea is not as salty as the ocean. The two bodies of water are only connected by a narrow opening north of Denmark and several large rivers flow into the Baltic Sea diluting the salt water.

Our next days will be more strenuous. I am looking forward to seeing Marienburg again, the former capital of our region. I spent my high-school years in a boarding school there. As we approach the river Nogat we can see the majestic castle built in the 13th century as the headquarters for the Order of the Teutonic Knights. Their Grand Masters resided there for two centuries. Unlike the castles on the Rhein this is built with bricks. Instead of a cliff, the Knights chose a sharp bend of the Nogat River for better protection

In 1945 German troops tried desperately to stop the advance of the Russian army. In this battle, the town centre and the castle were completely destroyed. I had seen it half a year after that battle when I traveled through the city in search of my mother. It is amazing what the Poles have done to restore most of the buildings of this famous castle. Now it is open for tourists again. For Hildegard and the children this is new territory. As we walk across the bridge, over the moat, and through the iron-toothed drop gate, they are amazed by the enormous dimension of the whole layout and structure of the castle. It is the largest secular brick building in the world. They get lost in the many inner courts and in the spartanly furnished rooms, meeting halls and the stables for the horses of the monastic knights.

From the castle we walk up to the Altstadt. The old city has changed completely. The once famous 'Hohe and Niedere Lauben', an arcade under the recessed ground floors of specialty shops and patrician homes around a cobblestone market place, had been the centre of the city. The whole area was a heap of rubble when I saw it the last time. The individually designed shops and homes are now replaced by a row of identical residential square boxes. It is not the city anymore which I remember and loved.

From Marienburg we head west and come to the old hanseatic town of Danzig, a busy port city on the Baltic Sea. The city seems not to have suffered as much destruction during the war as Marienburg or else it has been rebuilt more quickly and extensively.

The inner city with its attractive merchant and patrician houses looks as it did before the war. The Poles have rebuilt them from original plans and pictures with all the beautiful stucco ornaments and carvings, at least on the outside facades facing the street.

It is Dominican market day in the city and all the streets from Lange Gasse along the Motlau River leading to the market area have been blocked off from traffic. Crowds of people walk through the pedestrian zone eager to buy food, utensils or souvenirs. Amber jewelry is very inexpensive here and lots of it is on display. A young man has beautiful amber necklaces displayed and we approach him. He takes us aside and asks, "Do you speak English?" many of the people speak German. We make a deal in English so that the people next to him may not understand. 20DM for a dark polished amber necklace and 15DM for a long golden natural amber one, about one third of what we pay in Vancouver. He looks around and quickly puts the German currency into his pocket.

It is illegal to accept Deutschmark but everybody does it if they have a chance. We would have paid more than twice as much if we had paid in Zlotys at the official exchange rate.

From many places in the old city we can see the huge square tower of the Marienkirche (Mary's Church). It was founded in the 14th century, has been renovated and extended during the centuries and unfortunately has lost the beauty of its early Gothic style.

From the church we follow the *Frauengasse* (women's lane) to the Motlau River. It is a unique street. Most of the prominent residences have a raised terrace (Beischlag) in front of their house with ornamental stairs and railings extending to the curb. The raised terraces were to protect the entrance from occasional floods.

On our walk along the Motlau River we come to the famous Krantor (crane gate) a landmark of Danzig (Gdansk). Its picture appears in every tourist brochure of Gdansk. Built in 1442 it was the first mechanical hoist which could lift heavy loads up to 27m high.

From Danzig we drive west, back to East Germany

Before we go back to Germany, we have to spend our Polish money which we had to exchange against DM when we entered Poland. It is illegal to take any Zlotys out of the country or exchange it back into DM,

The last night we stay in Walcz (Deutsch Krone) in a campground on a small lake. Krista and I take a short swim while the others get the camper cleaned up and prepare breakfast. The Wiebes have left us already. They went south to Krakow and Vienna. We have to take Uncle Herbert back and head for Germany. When I pay my camping fee I see a sign 'breakfast from eight to ten o'clock'. I rush back and tell Hildegard, "Stop preparing breakfast we will eat out". We sit comfortably at a table in the lounge and have porridge, bread, eggs and cheese, coffee or tea and all this for 32cent per person.

We drive into town and find an art and craft store. Mike has his eyes on a beautiful hand carved chess set and Hildegard on some nicely carved and painted wooden plates and bowls and jewelry. The sales lady takes Hildegard in a back room and asks if she would mind paying in Deutsch-mark but Hildegard tells her we still have so many Zlotys which we are not allowed to take across the border. I think she gave her some German money. The border guards are not so fussy this time. They look in the back of the camper and after filling out some forms, stating how much money we spent in Poland, let us through.

We are back in Hillerse again. We repack our camper with the things which we did not want to take to Poland and had left here.

Uncle Herbert is in a rush to get home, so Walter takes him to the train station. We give him a big thank you hug and wave him off as he leaves.

We still want to make some visits in the area. Only half an hour from Hillerse is Handorf, the village where my mother and I had lived before we came to Canada. The children want to see the house which I had described to them.

We leave the camper in the parking lot beside the church and walk over the little bridge through the park-like garden to the parsonage. The old 'Fachwerkhaus' (timber frame house) still looks the same as when I left it 22 years ago. The tall chestnut tree beside our window is shedding its fruit and I show the children how to open the green prickly shells and free the brown chestnuts. They collect a few and put them into their pockets as mementos.

Pastor Brandes has now been transferred to a parish in the Solling area. The new pastor welcomes us when he hears who we are and lets us see the two rooms in which we had lived for nine years. We go through the village and I show them the farm where my mother and I had worked occasionally and the path across the meadows which lead to the railway station. It was part of my way to school before I got my bicycle.

I have fond memories of the pastor's family. We had a very good relationship with them. Pastor Brandes invited me to sing in the church choir and play the trombone in the small brass orchestra. He also asked me to lead the youth group when he was away. They named their fifth son Helmut and asked me if I would be willing to be his godfather.

Now they live in Dassel, about a two hour drive south of Handorf. We drive through the beautiful 'Weserbergland' (mountain range by the river Weser) along the 'Deutsche Märchenstrasse' (Fairy tale Road) and the 'Fachwerkstrasse'; in villages along this street are a number of picturesque old timber-framed houses, which gave this street its name.

Most of the Brandes' eight children have come to meet us. Henning, a pastor, Hans, a physician, Juergen a teacher, Dieter a church organist, Christa, a Kindergarten supervisor, Helmut training to be a pharmacist and Eckard a theology student. We refresh old memories and compare teaching methods and student behavior in Canada and Germany. They ask if we would consider teaching in Germany as they are very short of teachers. Students sometimes have to be sent home because they have no teacher for that subject. We think about it but then tell them we are not sufficiently prepared to teach in the German school system, we had better continue our work in Canada.

It is a sunny afternoon and Pastor Brandes has a special treat for our children. He shows them a German fair which is held in the marketplace this week and shows them all the different displays. He encourages them to select what they like best and he will pay for it. Our children are very modest in what they choose and ask me quietly before they take it if it is too expensive.

Our holiday is soon coming to an end and we have one more visit planned. We say good-bye to our good friends and head North for Segeberg. It is supper time when we arrive there and cousin Irmgard serves us a delicious dinner. A long time has passed since we saw them last and we have a lot to talk about concerning our families and life in Canada. The children are tired after the long trip and Joachim, Irmgard's husband, a giant of a man, finds a place for each one to sleep. The next morning we have a tour of the house and office building. He owns a well-managed tax consulting firm.

Their son, Juergen, and Michael ride their bikes to the box office of the open-air theatre to get tickets for a Karl May festival show this night. Irmgard takes the rest of the family to the workshop of the local wood sculptor, Otto Flaht. He has work in progress on mystical figures, prophets, beggars, saints and lovers, impressive sculptures of all sizes. His style is simple often showing the chisel marks. He also has a few large altar pieces and relief carvings on display. His work inspires me to pick up my wood carving tools again and create new sculptures myself

Tonight is the big event, the live performance of one of Karl May's stories about the life of Native Indians and their conflicts with the white man. The scene is played on the Kalkberg open-air-stage, the best one in Europe. Karl May wrote quite a number of fiction books about North American Indians in the late 19th century, with Chief Winnitou and Old Shatterhand, the main characters.

The Indians and cowboys ride real stallions over and around the hills, perform risky stunts and dressages and fire their guns in all directions, like a three-dimensional Western thriller. The children are spellbound and sometimes even scared because it is so real.

The Karl May Festival lasts several months during the summer. Different scenes are played every weekend. It is known by Karl May lovers all over Europe and is attended by several thousand every year.

The next day Joachim takes the day off and after breakfast he drives us to the North Sea coast. We cross the 'Nord-Ost-See Kanal' which connects the Baltic with the North Sea. It is the most traveled waterway in the world and it is amazing to watch the big ships move through the huge locks. We walk along the new dikes and the sandy beach to a small island which is accessible only during low tide. It is windy and the waves break noisily on the beach. Joachim is a native of the area and knows a lot about its geography and history, the conflicts between Denmark and Germany. He does the accounts of the estate owners and businessmen of the area and knows them well. In a running commentary he tells us interesting stories about them while we are driving past their properties on the way home.

We have covered a lot of territory today, walking along beaches, through lovely harbor villages and towns and are quite tired when we return in the evening.

Before we leave Bad Segeberg we pay a visit to Aunt Martha, my favorite aunt, Father's youngest sister. As a 14 year old, I spent a three week vacation in her holiday resort in Schreiberhau on the slopes of the 'Riesengebirge' (Giant Mountains). I had a wonderful time with her. She spoiled me, showing her love for me and her house guests took me on hikes through the mountains.

In 1945 Czech authorities, who had taken over that area from Germany, evicted her. She lived in refugee camps, worked as a nurse in an old-folks home until Joachim provided a suite for her in the neighborhood to spend her retirement there. She knows Hildegard's parents quite well and is very happy to see our family. We enjoy visiting her. Her guitar leans on the wall in one corner and we ask if she still plays it. She brings it out and sings and plays a few songs which she and Hildegard's mother used to perform when they were in my father's choir back in West Prussia.

When we say good-bye to her, we know that this will very likely be the last time we will see her. She thanks us for the visit, gives each of the children a gift and a hug and waves us off.

We are on our way back to Max and Edith. We spend our last night in Germany with them and the next morning Lilo, their daughter, takes us to Amsterdam. She wants to use the "Ark" for a short holiday before she returns it to Sister Margarethe. We pack our luggage on a cart, thank Lilo for taking us to the airport and board the plane back to Vancouver.

For our children this has been an exciting trip. The first time flying in an airplane, walking through a real castle and a huge cathedral, buildings over eight hundred years old and still looking beautiful, was very impressive for them. They appreciate having so many nice relatives in Germany and are proud to be able to speak to them in their own language and understand most of what they say.

Experiencing the culture in which their parents grew up, where they went to school and played their games was a great event for them. Realizing where their roots are, I think made them proud of their heritage, being of 'German background'.

21. Leaving Sherbrooke

Hildegard and I are aware of the changes in Germany since our last visit. Politically there is uneasiness about the growing tension between communism and capitalism, the arms race and the fear of a nuclear war. People are apprehensive of the future and are searching for a new spiritual awakening that will bring hope, trust and a closer relationship to each other and to God.

Renewal movements are born in many denominations and churches on the continent. One of the early Anabaptist visionaries, who experienced a renewal, was a Mennonite pastor, Gerald Derstine, from Minnesota. His vision of being under God's judgment and heeding his call for repentance brought amazing results for his congregation. This influenced other church leaders. Nelson Litwiller, a retired Mennonite missionary from Goshen, Indiana, had a similar experience. He was influential in forming the Mennonite Renewal and Ecumenical Charismatic Movement. It touched several Mennonite churches in the United States.

Our Sherbrooke Mennonite Church becomes aware of it through its young people. Some of them had gone to a youth retreat and a zealous counselor who was involved in that movement told them, "You will become a renewed, joyful Christian if you allow the Holy Spirit to be poured out into your heart. Every Christian can experience that renewal if he is open for it. It manifests itself often in speaking in tongues." He went perhaps too far in suggesting their parents had withheld from them that part of scripture that talks about the gifts of the Holy Spirit and its manifestations.

When the young people come home from that retreat, they approach their parents and ask why they have not been taught about the manifestations of the Holy Spirit and why speaking in tongues has never been mentioned as a gift of the Holy Spirit?

Two deacons, fathers of these young people, are very upset about these allegations. They are offended and fear their children are being led astray. They are so concerned that they call for a congregational meeting to discuss this topic. They want to bring in a resolution to ban all teachings about these gifts of the Holy Spirit especially glossolalia.

The pastor tries to calm down the heated arguments. The young people may have misunderstood their counselor and have drawn the wrong conclusions. That does not satisfy the two deacons. The rest of the congregation is not as upset and many are split in their opinion. The pastor asks the congregation how they see Helmut and Hildegard as their fellow members. Both have been involved in youth work and Hildegard is now leading a women's bible study group and the women appreciate her very much as a teacher and friend. I am congregational secretary and quite active in other church affairs.

They think we are honest, committed and loving people. But when he tells them that we received what the children are talking about a year ago, the attitude of some of them changes. Some deacons are questioning if Hildegard is teaching the true word of God and rumors go around that she is proselytizing, teaching the women how to speak in tongues which the women say is unfounded.

The church council is finally persuaded by these two deacons to issue an edict, warning the congregation of the 'false teachings' of the Charismatic Movement. We are personally asked for the benefit and unity of the congregation, to recant or leave the church. We have never coerced anyone into believing what we believe and have no intention of splitting the church over it, but we cannot renounce a gift that we have received through the grace of God. So we have no other choice but to take the consequences and leave the church which we helped to establish.

At a special congregational meeting we, the Wiebes and five other committed couples which stand with us, leave Sherbrooke Mennonite church. We are sad that we cannot work together, respect and accept each other as brothers and sisters in Christ.

We leave without ill feelings. My mother remains a member of Sherbrooke Mennonite Church. On special occasions I accompany her to church and am greeted with a friendly handshake by many members of my former congregation.

It is not easy for us to look for another church family. Hildegard and I grew up in a Mennonite Church and her father is a Mennonite minister. We were active in church and young people's work and I had put my skills as an architect at the Church's disposal. We are Mennonite Christians.

We are looking for a new Church community and that is hard for us.

Down the hill, about a ten minute walk from our house is a United Church. On a nice sunny Sunday the children and I walk down to find out what this church is like and if God perhaps wants us to join this neighborhood church. With the four of us there are seven participants in the service that morning, plus one pastor and an organist. The sermon is good but we are not used to the liturgical form of the service. The pastor thanks us for coming and mentions that many of the parishioners are on holidays, usually there are more people in church. On the way back we talk about our experience and question if we should attend next Sunday again. The decision is made for us. On the following Saturday we see black smoke coming out of the church; it burned down.

Our friend Jean invites us to come to her church, a small Pentecostal congregation of which she is co-pastor. We both accept the invitation and are welcomed by some of the members of the fellowship. The service is quite different from what we are used to. For me it would mean a big adjustment to become a member in this somewhat noisy emotional church. Hildegard does not feel at home in this fellowship either.

Another painful experience for us at this time is the dissolution of our Hauskreis. We have become an open, trusting fellowship of people from all walks of life and from different Christian backgrounds. We try to be inclusive, non-judgmental and honest with each other. This appeals to many who had difficulty accepting the more hierarchical order in their churches.

At present our group meets at our place which seems to be the most suitable facility. Hildegard's open personality draws many of our group, especially women, into her confidence. We had been meeting for several years and were confident and felt safe in our fellowship.

Unexpectedly at one of our meetings one of the members speaks up, in a very emotional almost prophetic vein. She holds against us that we are fake, pretending to have deep insight into Jesus' teachings but actually do not grasp what he really asks of us. We have a shallow faith that does not count for much.

We are stunned by her allegations. Everybody is quiet for a moment and thinks, does she talk about me? We do not know what to make of it. Hildegard is hurt because she seems to be singled out. She is questioning herself and others to find if there is any truth in what she says. I have known Hildegard long enough, and so do others; she cannot be, and is not, fake or dishonest. There must be reasons for these statements. I am puzzled by this emotional outburst. I assume it comes from built-up resentment, and perhaps jealousy. The person claims she has a lot to offer to the growth of the group but is not recognized and listened to because she cannot express her thoughts as eloquently as others, as Hildegard. In the next meeting accusations come up again. The atmosphere is tense. Members begin to stay away and the group gradually disintegrates. We are very grieved about this. We had enjoyed the open, trusting fellowship very much. We had learned from each other and grown in our faith and in our relationship.

It takes some time to realize and accept that our fellowship has so unexpectedly come to an end.

22. St. Margaret's

We decide now to attend the regular services at St. Margaret's church. We had occasionally attended the Sunday evening charismatic meetings there while we were still members at Sherbrooke Mennonite Church. Originally St. Margaret's was an Episcopal church. Pastor Bob Birch is a courageous spirit-led speaker. His sermons draw many people from different denominations to his church. Usually the main sanctuary is packed full and the overflow fills the basement assembly room where the people listen via short circuit TV. The church has become quite inclusive, welcoming seekers from all walks of life. A man in a black suit and tie can hold hands with a 'Jesus freak', barefoot, in frayed shorts, praising God together.

Pastor Bob feels that the traditional, liturgical form of the Episcopal service does not meet the needs of those who come to listen and he conducts the service as the spirit leads him. This breaking from tradition causes the bishop to ask him to withdraw from the Episcopal Synod.

Hildegard feels drawn to this kind of a fellowship and she appreciates the sincerity of Pastor Bob's sermons. I am a little hesitant at first.

More and more people flock to his service and Pastor Bob feels that he and his team cannot meet the needs of individuals, especially those of newcomers, in such a large assembly and believes it is time for another assistant Pastor. He had become acquainted with church reforms in England and invites one of their leaders, Barney, a Baptist minister from Basingstoke to come to Vancouver. Barney is an effective, Bible based speaker. He illustrates his sermons with examples from his former work as a London 'bobby'. The use of a bit of humor seems to be a good balance for the more serious sermons of Bob Birch. This arrangement seems to work out quite well at the beginning.

After having been in Canada for awhile, Barney has had time to observe the functioning of the congregation. He feels, perhaps, that the various attendees coming from different denominational or non-religious backgrounds are lacking some direction and he is looking for a solution. He thinks the church needs more structure and begins a series of sermons on obedience and discipline similar to the Old Testament hierarchical pattern. He wants to draw the men, most of whom have been absent from church functions, into church life and teach them to take responsibility for the spiritual life of their family as well as that of the church. For this purpose he arranges teaching sessions for men with potential for leadership and trains them to become home group leaders. I am one of those.

The church membership grows. People from other churches transfer their membership by a letter of recommendation; newcomers who have become believers are accepted as members by their confession of faith, and their wish to be baptized.

On one sunny Sunday morning, the church council books an outdoor public swimming pool not far from the church for a baptismal service. A number of members from different house-fellowships believe they are ready to receive baptism, among them are our Michael and Krista. Michael gives a testimony of his faith before the congregation, Krista is too shy to do the same and it is not compulsory to do so. Barney, as the pastor, together with the house-fellowship leader will step into the swimming pool and baptize the applicants by immersion. I have the privilege of baptizing our two older children and a few others from our house-fellowship. They are now official members of the church.

People who have considerable problems in their life, are depressive and are looking for guidance, seem to be lead to Pastor Bob's service.

To encourage and assist them, the leadership tries to match them up with solid Christian families who can be mentors to them and help them to grow in their faith. They think we are such a family.

Kay asks Pastor Bob for help. She had gone through a divorce, suffers deep depressions from it and needs steady supervision since she had attempted suicide. Pastor Bob asks Hildegard if she could help her.

Kay moves in with us. She responds to Hildegard's sincere concerns and opens up to her and they have honest talks together. Living with Hildegard and observing her joyful ways has a healing effect on Kay. After about half a year she wants to try to live on her own. She gets married again and we lose sight of her.

We have a short time to be alone as a family. Pastor Bob has counseled a young woman who is frightened of almost everything. She does not dare to go out of the house alone and cannot make decisions for fear of failure. Christine is a small, quiet person from a well-to-do family. She has tried everything to subdue this dreadful angst; one can literally smell her fear and her bed sheets are wet from perspiration. Her stay with us has some healing effect on her. After a few months she and her family move out of town and we lose contact with her.

We come back to caring for young offenders again, this time it is Evelyn, a young woman from Berlin, Germany. She has done time for writing bad cheques. There is little in this world she is not familiar with. She is self-confident, talks a lot and has a number of friends- a typical 'Berliner'. She claims to be a Christian and wants us to help her live her faith honestly. After she has been with us for a few weeks she gets restless and wants to go downtown to talk to her friends about Jesus. She comes home late and tells us that her friends have been responsive. The next week she comes home later and once she stays out over night. Hildegard gets suspicious and confronts her. Evelyn finally admits that she had been partying with her old friends. Hildegard tells her that she does not have to justify what she is doing but she should be honest about it. "I cannot live with somebody who is dishonest and lies to me" she tells her. Evelyn moves out after four weeks. A year later we have lunch in a restaurant on Hastings Street. Evelyn sees us and comes over to us. She tells us she is married and helps her husband in the antique store next door. She is happy and has kept out of trouble and thanks us for the time she could live with our family.

Someone introduces James, a young Métis to our church. He is coming out of prison and has no place to go. We agree to take him in. He is tall, with black hair and sprouting a small mustache. He is enterprising and quite intelligent. He soon finds a job at the City Gospel Mission, serving homeless people. Later he joins an advertising agency to become one of their ad writers. When he comes home after work he surprises our children with a 'new word' for the day, an unusual one from the dictionary and asks them what it means. If we don't know, we are to conjecture its meaning. We have fun guessing who comes closest to it and is most credible. Michael tries to trick us by embellishing his imagined meaning with details and examples. Soon everybody becomes creative. It is a good way to enlarge and improve our vocabulary and language skills.

James comes to church with us and falls in love with Dorothy, a beautiful graduate student from our house fellowship. They get married in the new sports pavilion at Burnaby Lake. Our family and the people from our house group help her parents who live in Edmonton, to make it a memorable celebration. They then establish their own home.

Barney, our pastor, introduces the practice of 'Shepherding', to the church, a British American model of mentoring young Christians. Those who want to grow in their faith, should find a mature Christian whom they trust and to whom they can go for counsel, who could disciple them.

It is emphasized that the shepherd-mentor should *never* speak into the life of the other person, if he has not been invited to do so. This theory sounds reasonable to me; it seems similar to the catholic or protestant confession. The practice, however, turns out to be disastrous in many cases. It becomes often an abuse of power.

I want to give this model a try and ask God to show me the person to whom I should relate. The next morning in my devotion I read from Revelation one, 'I am John, your brother and as a follower of Jesus, I am your partner,'... I take it as an answer and ask my friend, John, whom I could trust, if we could enter into this kind of relationship.

After a few 'confessions' he tells me, tongue-in-cheek, "You are an impossible 'sheep'. We had better stay friends and 'shepherd' each other."

Under the newly established structure in the church, roles are changing. The women are to step back for the time being and let the men grow into their position of responsibility. The man is to be the head of the family as was the custom in the Old Testament and, according to some of Paul's teachings, in the early church. Women are not to have leadership positions over men. They should serve under the leadership of their husbands. Several members find this is outdated and question whether these doctrines are applicable to our society in our time. Barney responds that those who have difficulty accepting this teaching are free to find a church of their liking. A number of people do that and leave the church. Hildegard has great difficulty with this teaching and struggles with it for years to come.

With the change of church doctrine and reorganization also comes a name change St. Margaret's becomes now: 'West Coast Christian Fellowship', a very inclusive name for a not so inclusive church. The newly introduced doctrines differ from those adhered to by the former St. Margaret's church and this causes some tension in the church council. After a while, to our surprise, Bob Birch withdraws from leadership and later leaves the church to join a sister fellowship. Many people of the congregation leave with him and join other fellowships.

Hildegard and I, together with our friends Bud and Lea, are leading a house fellowship at this time. When Pastor Bob leaves the church they decide to leave too. I think Hildegard is ready to do the same.

If we leave, I reason, it would be the second time that we change churches in a decade, first Sherbrooke Mennonite and now St Margaret's. I am by nature a loyal person and do not want to abandon the house fellowship which we helped to form and have grown fond of. So we stay and wait.

I am one of the few in our men's leadership group who openly question the procedures introduced by Barney and the elders. I ask for clarification and how to apply them effectively and what we think will be the expected outcome. This, I think, is seen as criticism and results in a visit by Vic, the Assistant Pastor from England. At first he approaches me with questions about my leadership of our home group. He tells me I have not done enough to develop leadership potential of the young men in our group. One of them is the pastor's son. He also finds it not in line with the church's teaching that Hildegard works as co-leader. She should only work under my leadership.

I am taken by surprise. I believe people in our group enjoy our fellowship. Everyone participates in it and values Hildegard's contributions, especially the women. As a group we want to grow in our faith and learn from each other how to live the teachings of Jesus: love, care, and acceptance. These are foundations for leadership but we are not a leadership training academy. We are critical thinkers, not simple conformists. This is a problem for the leadership.

I ask Vic to come to our next group meeting and explain his concerns to the whole group. He comes and speaks to us. Many are as surprised as Hildegard and I about his reasoning. Since I feel that I no longer seem to have the trust and support of the church leaders, I resign from my position. The group is then divided up and we join Fred's house group later as un-appointed co-leaders. Fred and Deanna are not as outspoken as we are.

Barney has a vision of expanding the boundaries of our church, of new church planting. He divides West Coast Christian Fellowship into five mini churches which he hopes will grow to full-fledged partner churches. One meets in the old church building, one in Burnaby, one in South Vancouver, one on the North Shore and one in Langley. This well-meant arrangement had not been prepared well enough. The new church planters are good church members but are not sufficiently equipped to be pastors and leaders of a church. Members of these groups realize this. They become disillusioned and finally leave or join other churches. One after the other of the mini-churches folds. Only Langley, in the Fraser Valley, remains as a church. The remnants of the other three groups return to the old St. Margaret's church building.

I am elected to the church council and John is appointed an elder in the new again united church.

He has accepted Barney's teaching fully, participates actively in the service with his musical contributions; he plays his violin and composes suitable music for worship. This is very much appreciated by the leadership and the congregation.

I know men are built up by Barney. Those who live up to his teaching of the reorganized church structure are appointed to leadership positions.

Those who find it difficult to accept these teachings, or think they are wrong, leave the church.

Women are expected to submit to their husbands and cannot take a leading role, even if they are better qualified and gifted than men.

Sensitive women, intellectuals and feminists see no justification for such a structure in our time, society and church. Hildegard is one of these women. She finally declares to me that she cannot be part of West Coast Christian Fellowship any more. She cannot deny herself any longer and submit to something that she does not believe in. She has become more and more disillusioned. I had been sensing this for some time. She has tried to fit in which has not been easy, and now it is impossible for her. We talk about the situation. I mention that we appreciate the worship service where we can participate uninhibited, in praising God in our own and in our spirit language. I also point out to her that our children have been baptized into this church. Several of our women friends are still in the church and do participate. Perhaps we can bring about some adjustments into the church in time.

I do not share all of the doctrines presented by Barney and the leadership either but can agree on the basic principles of our faith. I can leave behind the parts I disagree. But Hildegard cannot do that. Everything has to fit together to form a complete picture, otherwise she cannot live with it. My attempts at asking her to reconsider her decision only increase her agony and determination to leave. She tells me she will be choked and dry up completely if she stays any longer. She looks at me, and with sadness in her eyes, asks me, "Do you understand what I mean?" I am grieved and do not know how to respond. I can understand her reasons as a woman for leaving but am not fully convinced at this time that I should give up and leave with her. Perhaps I also fear the uncertainty that would follow.

She writes a letter to the church leadership about her decision and lets me read it. It is well-written. A while after Barney had received it, he invites both of us for a meeting with him and John. Hildegard was waiting for a response and now that it has come, she is nervous at first. Barney mentions as an introduction that he thinks the letter is somewhat presumptuous. Later in the conversation he asks Hildegard, "Tell me, what changes would you like to see in our church?" By now she has regained her composure and can tell him quietly, "Nothing. You can go on with what you are doing but I will not be part of it anymore." That is the end of our meeting. For John, I am sure, it must have been uncomfortable. He is caught between two loyalties.

On the way home, Hildegard mulls over the whole situation and is quiet for a while. When she finds words again she vents her resentment, "I take exception to Barney's patronizing attitude - I had hoped for more support from you - I question if you really understand the depth of my agony and hurt".

I feel crushed about this. And when I look back now, maybe at that time I did not fully understand her. If I had, I would have left with her. Now she needs my support and closeness and I am unable to give it to her. I do not understand myself either. I am in turmoil. I argue with myself and with God. I had to give up my Mennonite church family at Sherbrooke and have tried to fit into St. Margaret's and West Coast Christian Fellowship because this was Hildegard's wish. What are my alternatives now?

I wrestle with God for an answer and I seem to hear him saying, 'Do not try to pressure, persuade or argue with Hildegard; she is badly hurt and needs time to heal. Just love her. I will care for her'. I take this as a confirmation, and it always guides me in responding to Hildegard. It is not always easy. Healing takes a long time for both of us.

Many of our friends from the church whom we know more intimately and some Christian relatives withdraw from us when they hear that Hildegard has left the church and her traditional faith. For Hildegard this is very painful. She asks me, "Why do my friends avoid me and do not talk to me anymore? I am still the same person, the same Hildegard. They are my friends and my relationship to them has not changed. Why do they shun me?"

Hildegard writes to her cousin:

> To leave the church without Helmut, who could not share my conviction and suffering, was extremely hard for me. But it was important for me also that he made his decision in regards to his relationship to the congregation from his very own conviction and not because of me.'

23. A PLACE OF REFUGE

In the beginning of our time at St. Margaret's, 'End Times' prophets had fore-warned us that hard times would come upon us and we had better get prepared for them. They had advised us to look for a place of refuge for our families where we might be able to survive. Hildegard is taking these prophesies seriously and thinks we should take some action. Perhaps communal living might be the answer. She had been in a Kibbutz in Israel and we visited a few communes in Germany where several families live together and support each other. Hildegard thinks of such a commune, far enough from Vancouver, where the radiation from a nuclear bomb and the aftershocks from a devastating earthquake would not reach us. In the meantime, I add, we can use such a place as a summer vacation home for our family. We discuss this with the Wiebes and other friends.

It happens that during this time of reflection we meet Karen again, our former Jesus people friend who had lived with us.

She is married now and is well established. She had a very interesting courtship, she tells us. At St. Margaret's she met a young man of Dutch Reformed background. She liked him and after they had known each other for a while, she walked up to him and confided that 'the Lord had revealed to her that he should marry her'. He was taken aback by this unanticipated, unusual revelation.

We remember, they invited us to their wedding and that was as original as their proposal. It happened on a farm in Langley, Karen and Dick said their vows kneeling under a tree in the meadow and Pastor Bob gave them his and God's blessing. The reception hall was the barn and her musician friends played trumpet, saxophone, guitar and percussion in the shade of the open machine shed. We guests sat on hay bales on the meadow, ate healthy organic food, sang and talked. We rolled the hay bales aside to make room for folk dancing. It was a lovely colorful group of people that was moving back and forth and around on the meadow and I could even persuade Hildegard to join us.

We now talk with Karen about our idea of communal living in a place of refuge. She lives in such a commune in the USA and knows of young people who live in community in the Grand Forks area in BC, across the border. They often come over for a common Bible study. If we want to find out more about them, we should contact Sherry and Bob Dupee. We arrange a visit with them, pack our camper and drive five hundred fifty km to Christina Lake, a village on the warmest, cleanest lake in central BC.

The Dupees live on Santa Rosa Road, nine km south of the village on a gravel road up towards Castle Mountain. They are as curious to meet us as we are to meet them. Age-wise we could be their parents. Bob has a college degree and he moved to BC as a draft dodger to avoid being sent to Vietnam, like many of the other men. Sherry met him at college, she comes from a well-to-do family, wanted to get away from home and goes with him. They were the first ones to settle on the 'Mountain' on a hundred sixty acre homestead in 1972.

Now there are about eight young couples or families who live here, each one in their own unique home. They all come from the hippie scene. Roy burned his whole cannabis crop in front of his cabin when he became a Christian. All eight couples form a tightly-knit Christian commune. They live off the land. In their big gardens they grow vegetables and fruit, raise chicken, sheep and goats. Bob runs a small sawmill and is in charge of marketing the lumber, Jim cuts trees selectively from their properties and pulls them with his two Percheron horses to the portable saw. Randy is the mechanic, he operates and services the saw. He also repairs automobiles for friends and neighbors in his repair shop.

If one of them is in need of shelter or needs an addition to their abode, the men bring their toolboxes and help build it, without permit, architect or contractor. They get their know-how from 'do-it-yourself' books. The lumber comes from trees on their own property, cut to size on their sawmill. Surplus lumber they sell in the city.

We spend a week on a campground at the lake. The Dupees invite us for their Wednesday communal meal and Bible study. This time the meeting is in Bob and Sherry's living room. A latecomer, a young man with shoulder-long hair and beard, dismounts his appaloosa horse, comes in and introduces himself as Simon. He is the son of a British architect. He always wanted to become an Indian and succeeded in being initiated into the Sioux tribe. He married a beautiful half-Indian girl, moved to Canada to avoid the draft and joined the group. For a couple of years they lived in a tent, Indian style, and Juno breastfed her first baby under an umbrella to protect it from the rain seeping through the top of the tent.

Sitting around the table talking with them, Hildegard soon discovers kindred spirits among the women and they become friends. They adopt us as kind of mentors.

We tell the group of our interest in communal living and a place of refuge. Bob tells us of a place for sale about 2 km down on the Santa Rosa road, on km seven. We had seen a sign when we came up, '38 acres for sale, $22,000'. He thinks the price is far too high; we should be able to get it for half of that. We inspect the site; it has water and rocky soil for a solid foundation. I phone Mitch Silver and make him an offer. He is not ready to sell it for half of his asking price, so we leave it.

When we come home we tell the Wiebes about our intensions and they are willing to join us in this adventure to buy the property. After awhile I contact Mitch Silver again; he has had his property for sale for over a year and had no offer, so he is willing to sell. We are quite excited. I design a two-storey cabin, big enough for our two families. The next year the Wiebes and we drive to Christina Lake and park our camper and tent trailer on our own land. We have brought some tools and get to work, building first an outhouse and some benches. I survey the land and we start lining up the trenches for the foundation of our future vacation home. 1978 is a hot sunny summer and the kids like this unspoiled spot of nature and enjoy swimming in the lake.

We visit with all the people on the 'mountain'; they are very open and helpful and are looking forward to us becoming part of their community.

The next year we start building our cabin. We arrive at the beginning of our vacation. I go to city hall and apply for a building permit. All the houses on the mountain have been built without one and the owners are worried that a building inspector might give them trouble. I do not want to take the risk of building without one. With an architect's signature on the plans, they are approved without any question. I hire a backhoe and ask the operator to clear the bushes around the building site and dig a pond to drain the soggy spot on the property where a small spring bubbles up. It soon fills the pond and it will be our water supply.

When John and his family arrive, the foundation is already poured and Bob has just delivered a load of lumber. We have many helpers to build the cabin, the Shaws and Peters from our church in Vancouver and the people from the mountain and their friends. Bob and Sherry let us use the A-frame cabin in the back of their property to house all the volunteers. While we men are putting up the walls and lay the roof rafters, our women help with stapling the insulation in and other work and do the cooking and housekeeping.

Hildegard and Krista explore the surroundings in their spare time and visit the Jamiesons down the hill. They tell them they intend to sell their rustic log cabin and move to Vancouver Island. The two love it; it sits between tall pine trees on one side and a large birch on the other, right beside a small creek. "The unique little log house fits naturally into the landscape", they tell me excitedly and urge me to have a look at it. They hint that it may be available soon. I am in the middle of building our cabin and have to supervise that everything is done properly; I cannot entertain such thoughts at this time. But the two have fallen in love with that log cabin and beg me to consider buying it. When our cabin is winter ready, outside walls, floors and roof are in place, I go down and look at it. It has a beautiful view over the open meadows into the Kettle River valley with mountain ranges on the US side. The log cabin looks attractive and inviting under the yellow leaves of the big birch tree. The little creek is murmuring beside it and the tall green pines form a contrasting background. It sits on the west end of a 30 ha property, twice the size of the one on which we build our new cabin. Krista and Hildegard beseech me and I give in. I wonder if John will be interested in buying me out. He is, and we agree on a price.

In January 1981 we sign the sales contract with Jamiesons for Hildegard's dream cottage.

During our Easter vacation we have a closer look at the cabin. The interior is an open design 20 x 30 feet; the top floor is supported by two massive round centre posts and a round cross beam. The mansard roof provides more room for the upstairs bedrooms. The open design makes the interior look bigger and the proportions are pleasing.

The inside needs a lot of work. I am shocked when I look at the floor. The water from the melting snow has run down the hill, seeped through the logs and covered the particle board floor with an inch of mud. The moisture has permeated the untreated particle board and made it very brittle. When we scrape the muck up we step through the soft floor. We cover the holes with small sheets of plywood.

I inspect the structure and can see it has not been built to code. The main beam carrying the load of the second floor has shrunk and has only two centimeters support left. I quickly nail an additional support in before that section will collapse. The open stairs are made of half-rounds and the spaces between the treads are of different height, which makes it awkward to climb them in the dark. The walls and roof are not insulated and the rough wood of the logs and rafters is showing which gives it a rustic, natural look.

our cabin in Christina Lake

Interior of cabin with Hildegard

Our second shock comes when a heavy rain penetrates through eleven holes in the roof to fill the buckets underneath. The interior furnishing is very rudimentary. The kitchen counter is untreated particle board on round uprights, covered with oilcloth and underneath are open shelves. We can persuade the owner to leave the good cook stove in the cabin. The heating unit is a wood burner made from an oil drum which gets red hot when the fire is on for a while. At least the upstairs is fairly safe if it does not rain. We clean everything, try to patch the holes in the roof, and dig a drainage ditch to divert the water that runs down from the hill, into the creek. When we come back next summer, we have our work lined up.

I think of John, finishing the new house, built to building code, into which I had put so much work, and we built it for less than half the price we paid for ours. But Hildegard is happy with our unique log cabin and can visualize already the renovated, finished distinctive home and that makes me happy too. We both like to live simply and enjoy nature and we are able to do both.

When we arrive, I first have to cut the grass on the six hundred-fifty meter long driveway to get to the house. I find an old scythe in the shed, tighten the blade and whet it and have to refresh my skills to use it properly to cut the weeds and grass that have grown on the driveway and around the house, in some places over a meter high.

Our next urgent job is to put a new roof on. We chose metal because that is spark proof and durable. A metal junk dealer had just gotten a load of surplus corrugated brown steel panels, the color we wanted. It is a major undertaking for the whole family to put them in place. Some of us are measuring and cutting, some lifting them up and I place them and screw them on. We look at the finished roof with satisfaction. Now we get no more moisture inside. The next task is the floor. We have to tear the whole ground floor up. It is brittle and has holes everywhere and the wooden supports underneath are rotten.

First we build a new solid under-structure and rough in water pipes and a sewer grid for future plumbing fixtures. We get a good deal from the local lumber yard for 2"x6" tongue and groove planks. The whole family helps with nailing them to the new substructure grid. After we have sanded the floor properly, Hildegard finishes its surface with three coats of varnish. It now looks beautiful and is safe and durable.

For the first few years we live like the early pioneers and homesteaders, without electricity and telephone. We use candles and kerosene lamps, for which I had made the base on the potter's wheel. For communication with our friends and neighbors on the mountain we use a C-B radio, everybody can listen in and get the news. We dam up the little creek beside the house to form a small pond. It provides enough water to extinguish a fire, should the wood stove cause one. The cold water running through the pond acts as a fridge and keeps the container with perishable food cool.

We cook on a wood stove, so I have to cut and split firewood. It reminds me of the TV series 'Little house on the Prairie' and my early childhood in West Prussia, although there we had electricity. Year by year our living conditions improve. The Kootenay Power Co. brings in electricity. I string the electrical wires behind the exposed round beams and connect them to an electric stove and fridge, which we bought cheaply from friends in Vancouver. We have electric light, the candles are now only for special effects.

With the help of Hanno and Krista, I dig a trench to lay a cable to my workshop on the other side of the creek. To be able to use power tools now makes my job of improving and furnishing our cabin much easier.

BC Telephone Co asks us a few years later, if we want telephone service. We think it will be useful in a case of emergency, since we live far out in the 'wilderness', and we can contact family, friends, doctors and businesses in the city and out of town.

Hildegard enjoys the new kitchen counter which I had installed to replace the former open shelves. Michael had donated it when he renovated his old kitchen in Vancouver. John's brother, a contractor, had torn down some old houses and salvaged the usable kitchen cabinets for us. I install them over the counter. Now we can keep the mice out of our dishes and food.

A great relief is the new bathroom with washing machine, toilet and later a hot water tank. We do not need to go to the outhouse in the woods in the dark and in the rain anymore. There was always a possibility of meeting a coyote, a bear or a cougar on the way to the outhouse at night.

All renovations and additions we could not have done and afforded if we were not such good do-it-yourselfers. Hildegard is a faithful companion in making good suggestions and helping with so many jobs, as are the children.

There is one big excitement for the children! Jenny, Bob and Sherry's pure bred golden retriever, has a litter of eight puppies, seven golden and a black one. Little two year-old Anne, Bob and Sherry's daughter, loves to play with them. Once we find her asleep in the pen among these cute puppies. Mum Jenny did not mind having her as number nine.

Our children are crazy about these little critters and are delighted when they are allowed to select one of them. Krista chooses the black one and she is ardently teaching him to follow commands, to heel, to sit and stay and some more tricks. We call him *Thorin*, like the king of the dwarfs in the Narnia chronicles. I build a pen with an insulated hut beside the house under the window of the children's bedroom. He will be our outside watch dog; we all love him.

On our property a young German couple, Uwe and Monika Reiseleiter, have built a small cabin, an all purpose room and two small bedrooms under a mansard roof. It is well built with built in beds and cupboards. One disadvantage is that they have no water; they have to haul it in from a creek that flows a few hundred meters down in the valley. We have to walk about seven minutes through the woods to get to it from our cabin. The Reiseleiters do not live there anymore since we bought the property. We want to use it as a guest cabin. With the help of Hanno and Krista we spend a day with pickax and rake carving a new trail into the slope of the hill for a more comfortable walk for our future guests. We scrub our little cabin very thoroughly and make it comfortable. Magdalena and Gustav and Hildegard's mother and sisters are our first guests.

After the second winter, we discover with disgust that pack rats have moved in. We chase them out, close the holes they have gnawed into the walls and roof and put rat poison in the rooms before we leave for the winter. But when we come back the next year the rats are back and have built nests in the open cupboards. We chase them out, close the holes again where they came in, scrub again, put traps up and put more poison out. It does not help. The next time there are even more of them and they have young ones in their nests. They leave their droppings everywhere and gnaw at the wood of the beds and eat the upholstery of the kitchen chairs. I take Thorin into the cabin and he grabs three of the rats that jump out of their nests by the neck and kills them. But we cannot leave Thorin here over the winter. So we give up reluctantly and leave that lovely guest cabin to the rats, the uninvited guests. Our Eagle's Nest now becomes our Rat's Nest.

With time our log cabin becomes more comfortable. We cut a few windows through the logs to make it brighter inside, add some stylish antique furniture, hang pictures on walls, set vases with wildflowers on window sills and candles on tables. Hildegard inherited a Russian samovar and an old glass butter churn which fit well on our mantelpiece. She is very creative and selective in her choices to keep everything coherent, in good taste and not overly-decorated.

On our way to and from the lake we sometimes pick up flat square rocks left from small rock slides after a heavy downpour. With these different colored rocks we build a four foot high feature wall to separate the kitchen from the living room, it hides the unsightly back of the cook-stove and the stacked pile of firewood beside it, and acts as a heat storage, absorbing heat during the daytime when the stove is hot and radiating it out at night time when it gets cold.

We are far enough from civilization that we can observe undisturbed nature and untamed wildlife. Deer graze on our front lawn and elk nibble on the lower branches of our apple trees in the former orchard. I gather hay from the driveway and front lawn and store it in a covered crib for them to feed on in winter time. Sometimes we have to compete with bears for our apple crop. One morning I see a bear cub in the tree shaking the apples down and mother bear stands below enjoying our tasty red apples. I chase both of them away and harvest what they have left.

Coyotes perform a wonderful concert in the woods which sounds like staccato laughter. One night our poor Thorin was in grave danger. I hear his hoarse barking from his dog house. I go to the window and see in the moonlight a long dark shadow beside his fenced in kennel. I shine my bright flashlight on it and the light reflects from the two eyes of a large black cougar, staring at me for a moment before he takes off into the woods.

Lots of little rodents live around the sheds, squirrels, chipmunks, groundhogs. Thorin has fun or he is frustrated chasing them but never catching any. Lately a flock of wild turkeys visits us. One morning I count twenty-two of them picking grass and seeds on our front lawn and driveway. In the evening some of them fly across the meadow and settle in the big pine trees for the night. I did not know that they can fly that far.

Hildegard hangs a feeder for hummingbirds under our roof overhang. It is interesting to observe the temperament of these colorful little birds. Sometimes seven of them want to feed on four feeding outlets, some wait their turn patiently, sitting on the high back of the lawn-chair, others, aggressively, chase each other away.

Often, when I go up the driveway and pass the gate, a startled woodgrouse flies out of its nest in the bush. Sometimes we observe the chubby hens waddling to the creek to drink. They are not afraid and come so close that I can almost grab them.

Occasionally ranch cattle graze in the area, once I counted 62 heads on our meadow below the cabin. The cows keep the grass short. That reduces the fire hazard. One evening, as we are coming back from a swim in the lake, a herd of cattle is crossing our driveway, the big Holstein bull stops in front of our car, lowers his head and his horns in attack position. He remains there until all the cows have crossed the driveway, then he leaves the way free and walks off behind the cows, gentleman-like, as I would have done, I am impressed.

In late fall cowboys with lassos and cowboy hats come to our property, riding across the meadows and through the woods to look for stray cows and calves to take them home. Our children are excited to see a western movie played out on our meadows.

There are always surprises. I have my early morning walk along the Santa Rosa and am startled when I hear a bearded man on the other side of the lonely road calling me, "Do you want any tomatoes and lettuce?". I look up and there stands Bud, our new neighbor, beside his greenhouse offering me delicious big, organically-grown tomatoes and a head of lettuce. Hildegard tells me she has never tasted such good tomatoes. Bud is a retired forest warden, a quiet withdrawn man; Hildegard calls him "Rübezahl", the fairy-tale mountain ghost. Bev, his friendly, talkative wife, is a hobby painter and stained glass artist. We become good friends. They love this secluded area in the foothills of the Monashee Mountains

Of course the children, Hildegard and I love swimming in the lake. Texas Point, a peninsula which sticks out into the lake on its east side, is our favorite spot. The sandy beach is broken up into little bays, just the right size to give a family some privacy. The boys have fun jumping from the rocks into the lake. On one of the rocks we discover faded Indian Petroglyphs. If the water in the lake is getting too warm, we go swimming in the Kettle River. Sometimes we take our inflatable canoe or tire tubes along and float down the river with the current.

If Hildegard and I are alone at the cabin, we have time to talk, to read and to hike. On one of those hikes across the border, not far from the old homestead, we smell the scent of peppermint. We follow it and step into a field of peppermint plants. We cut a bunch to dry for delicious peppermint tea and dig up some clumps from the boggy area to take with us and plant beside the cabin near the creek. It grows well there. On the old homestead, a little further on, we dig up some Iris bulbs and plant them in front of our house. They multiply quickly and each spring, when we come back, we enjoy a spread of yellow irises and the flowering lilac bushes behind the chicken coop. There are many wild flowers all year around to enjoy.

In the first year on our property, we were quite energetic and wanted to try out being self-sufficient, growing our own food in our garden to see if we could survive in case of a catastrophe in the city.

While we were contemplating in our spring break how best to start our garden, we see a tractor coming down our second steep driveway one morning. A young man gets off and asks us, "Would you like to have your garden cultivated? I just did it for the people up on the hill." He looks familiar to us; we once sang in a choir together. "How did you know, we just intended to use our spades to dig it up by hand but we gladly accept your offer". Peter, a good Mennonite, does an excellent job in a fraction of the time we would have spent doing it.

We buy some vegetable seeds and potatoes and plant our garden. When we come back in the summer, we can hardly find the potato plants among the high weeds. Some vegetables had started to grow but died because of lack of moisture. We now know the soil is fertile enough to grow vegetables but we have to be here all summer to care for the garden in order to reap the fruit of it. In fall, we can harvest some potatoes. The carrots look promising but when we pull them out, only the leaves remain, rodents have eaten the roots. We have to buy our vegetables from farmers or the supermarket again.

24. Challenges in growing up

For the last two school years, I manage to enroll our children in Burnaby South Senior Secondary School where I teach. At this time, it is perhaps the best school, academically, in Burnaby. Knowing the staff and hearing what students say about their teachers, I can choose the best of my colleagues to teach and challenge our children.

Michael is quite popular among the academic students. He takes part in choir and band, playing the oboe. He has a singing part in the annual musical performance. Both are extracurricular activities. Physical Education is one course where he does not excel quite as well as in his academic subjects.

Krista, different from her brother, is a quiet, unassuming student. She takes a wide spectrum of academic courses which, unfortunately, leaves no room for art, in which she did very well in Junior High School. Perhaps she also wants to avoid having her father as art instructor. She maintains her interest in music and takes guitar lessons. Krista volunteers in the 'buddy' system of the school, to tutor weaker students during lunch hour in Math and Science.

Her teachers think highly of her as a polite, intelligent and creative student. Mr. Glover, her physics teacher, gives a silver dollar to students who reach 100% in his comprehensive tests. He tells me he did not have many takers lately until Krista came into his class. Her math teacher, Mr. Izen, challenges the top ten percent of his classes with more difficult problems. Krista responds well to that challenge and gets all problems solved correctly. He is very pleased with her achievement.

I remember one lovely incident with Krista. I walk along the main hall when Krista comes out of her classroom, she smiles at me, puts her arm under mine and we walk together arm-in-arm to the end of the hall with all the students watching. I think she is as proud of her dad as I am of her.

At the end of the school year, the school has a rewards day. Krista collects most of the academic awards for outstanding scholarship in her subjects.

The German Consulate provides rewards for High School students who excel in learning German. They have to take a qualifying examination and I encourage Krista to participate, just for fun, and she does. I show her what is required in the curriculum and she prepares a little. She is surprised when she finds out that she got the highest mark of all the contenders, though she never took any German courses in school.

We sometimes 'play' German school at home and pretend we are communicating with Grandma in Germany and tell her what we are doing. The children love it. They sometimes remind me, "Dad, let us play German school again." It is a fun way to learn a language.

Krista's high school graduation with Oma Lemke and Hanno

Our first grandchild Madison

Students who want to graduate from the academic program have to write province-wide examinations in three or four core subjects. Krista receives the highest mark of all the students in the province. The minister of Education comes to our school on rewards day to personally present her with the Governor Generals medal for best academic achievement in the province. The principal is pleased that a student of his school gets such recognition. Krista's name is added to the names of former top students on a plaque in the main hall of the school. She also receives the highly esteemed Gordon Shrum scholarship, valued at $10, 000.

Krista does not like to be singled out as a 'brain' and is embarrassed about all the fuss about her academic achievement. It is not her intent to compete with other students to get a higher mark; she competes with herself to see if she has reached her potential.

Hanno does not take school that seriously, although he has matured since Junior High. Perhaps the courses here are more demanding and interesting. He too gets on the honor roll as Michael and Krista always did.

Our school has just received a number of computers and Hanno takes the first computer science course offered in our school. He finds it challenging. With two of his friends, Mike and Allen, he spends many a lunch hour and time after school in the computer room. The teacher trusts these three and gives them the key to the room.

When I have finished my course preparations for the next day and am ready to take Hanno home, I usually know where to find him.

Les, a good friend of ours, tells John and me that he has an opportunity to get a computer through his company, BC Tel. We think our boys would be very happy and would profit from having their own computers and ask him to order one for us as well. Two weeks later, we pick up a Commodore 64 computer from his house. Hanno is the first one in our family to teach us how to use it. In the second year of his studies at Burnaby South, Mr. Heise, his teacher, tells the three boys jokingly, "You know as much about computers as I do; go ahead with your assignments while I teach the rest of the class the basics and ask me if you get stuck". The three later work in the same computer company.

Hildegard is very supportive for Hanno getting a computer that he can explore a new field of knowledge. She always takes time to listen attentively to the children's wishes, their stories and problems if they want to share them with her. She encourages and inspires them. Having their mom at home when they need her and growing up in a happy two parent family home, gives the children security and a solid basis on which to develop good attitudes and to perform well in school and life.

When our children reach the age of sixteen they apply for a driver's license. The school offers driver-training courses during lunch hour. If students pass the driver's test on the first try they get most of their fee refunded. Michael and Krista take advantage of this offer. They drive with me to school. I show them how to drive and when they have their learner's license, I let them practice driving home. Being together with them gives them and me an opportunity to talk about personal and school matters.

Krista thinks I am mean when I have her stop the car before the crest of a hill and ask her to start it again. She is a perfectionist and gets angry with me if she rolls back and kills the engine but she realizes that this is part of learning how to drive safely. Both Michael and Krista get their fee refunded. Hanno does not need extra driver training. It is in his genes and he gets his license the day after his 16th birthday.

Michael already knows in Grade nine what he wants to do in life. His dream is to become a missionary doctor. He can see himself flying to jungles or tropical islands and see native people standing around his plane waiting to be treated and healed. After high school graduation, the missionary part of that vision fades, but he definitely wants to study medicine. Since we live so close to Simon Fraser University, it is convenient for our children to start their studies there. They can live at home and walk through the woods to university or take their bike or the bus for a short ride. Simon Fraser University waives the course fees for students who have an **A** average on their final school report. Michael qualifies and, after four years, finishes his studies at SFU with a BA in kinesiology.

Dating and holding hands is not a priority in high school or university for any of our children. They have no steady girl friends or boy friend, at least not that we are aware of. The boys are popular and may sometimes flirt with girls.

Krista is far too shy and still 'socially withdrawn', as she tells me later. She is very sensitive and intense. She lives by extremely high moral standards. Any serious misbehavior in her view is, expressed in Christian terms, considered a sin. She feels she can never live up to what society and God expect of her. We are puzzled and wonder where she has acquired this belief, as we have introduced God to our children as the creator of a beautiful world and a caring and forgiving father and Jesus as a 'loving shepherd'. We assume she might have picked up this attitude from the teaching of her conservative Sunday school teacher and taken it to the extreme. We take her out of Sunday school when we notice this influence. Rationalizing with her does not seem to change this attitude neither does encouragement help much to lift her spirits. It troubles us that she is often hiding her inner feelings and emotions from us. We find it difficult to understand why she is so hard on herself. She has everything going for her; she is beautiful, very intelligent, well-mannered and respected by everybody. Occasionally Krista will open up to Hildegard who tries to assure her that she will walk with her through these difficult times to help her find her identity and support her as much as she is able, if she will let her.

School graduation time comes and it is customary for girls to be accompanied by an escort for their school's graduation banquet. Krista reluctantly accepts the invitation from a well-groomed fellow student, perhaps as shy as she is, to accompany her. We teachers are also invited to the banquet. Krista comes over to the table where I sit with her English teacher and his wife. She greets us and has a short chat with us. When she has gone back to her group, Mrs. Bailey remarks to me, "Wow! Is she a gorgeous young lady"

Krista skipped a grade in school. She needs some time to focus on her future. It might be good to wait a year after high school graduation before continuing her education at university.

Hildegard's oldest sister, Eva, has married her former employer, Leon, after his wife had died and is now wife of a well-to-do Mennonite wheat farmer. She remains in Ritzville for more than a decade when the rest of the family moves to the coast. We love to visit them. Leon, one of the typical old western pioneers, who has no children, is very fond of our three and they of him. He is the generous uncle, goes with them to town and buys them toys of their choice. Once they bought model airplanes with rubber band motors and we go to the golf course to try them out. Uncle Leon decides whose plane goes farthest. He has an air gun and takes the three to the back yard for target practice. He puts a nickel upright on a stand about thirty feet away, shows them how to aim, and if they hit it, they can keep it. I think Hanno collected most of the nickels.

Leon is quite a bit older than Eva. Not long after their marriage he has a stroke and loses his voice. He communicates by writing on an erasable tablet. His condition gets worse and he is in and out of hospital. Krista visits him and stays with Eva for awhile to help her care for Uncle Leon. She has empathy for older people, especially for those who are suffering. A few weeks later he has another stroke and dies.

When she comes home she looks for work. It is not easy at this time for a young girl without work experience to find a well-paying job. Krista plans to travel to Europe and wants to save some money for the trip. She is willing to do anything. A marketing firm is hiring people for telephone advertising. Krista applies. She is very articulate but too honest and not aggressive enough for this kind of a job. After a week she finds she is not suited for it and quits.

She does better on her next job, distributing advertising flyers in the Lower Mainland. She gets a minimum wage which does not add much to her bank account. Through connections she hears that Central City Mission is hiring staff for their relief work in downtown East Vancouver. During winter and spring of 1982 she works in their kitchen serving men with alcohol related-problems. This work is more fulfilling for Krista and the pay is better too.

At the beginning of summer she gives her notice. Her travel plans are complete and are quite adventurous. We are somewhat concerned letting her travel alone through Europe, so she finds a travel companion in Dorothy, a lovely young science student from our house-fellowship. We give Krista an address list of relatives in Germany. Some of them have visited us already and she knows them and they in return are looking forward to see the girls and are willing to help should they get into difficulty. Knowing this relieves her mom a little,

We take the two to the airport and they fly to Europe and travel all over the continent. What impresses them most in each country and city in Europe is that they 'breathe' history; they see it in the different styles of sacral and secular architecture. Each country has its own culture, customs and specialties.

They walk through the temple ruins in Greece, through art galleries and palaces in Italy and France and castles in Germany. In some of the ancient cathedrals they listen to an organ concert or take part in folk festivals in different countries.

Relatives invite them to wedding and birthday parties or sightseeing tours. The whole trip is inspiring and eye opening for them.

One drawback on this trip is Dorothy's occasional suffering from gastro-intestinal complaints. Krista tells me later, facetiously, that they know the public washrooms in most European cities.

After their return from Europe, Krista starts university. Michael is in his second year at SFU when Krista enrolls there. A former aptitude test indicates she would meet the requirements of several faculties, she chooses science. Her tuition fee, like Michael's, is waived on the grounds of her high school marks and she has the benefit of the prestigious Gordon Shrum scholarship.

She does quite well in her first year but in her second year her emotional turmoil intensifies. She begins to question her academic path. She takes courses in psychology and philosophy to find answers to the existential question, 'What is the meaning of life and how do I fit in'? Her former understanding of Christian faith and religion does not answer this question. She is searching for new values and the purpose of life and tries to find her own identity.

She sneaks out of the house at night and wanders in the dark, to be alone trying to understand this world.

We find out when one night at 3.00 am we are awakened by a loud knock at the door. I get out of bed, go to the front door and ask on the intercom, "Who is at the door, please?" a male voice answers, "Police, do you have a daughter by the name of Krista?" When I acknowledge it, he tells me, "We saw her walking on the street at night and gave her a ride home. Could you come and take her in?" I go down and Krista gets out of the car. She is embarrassed and does not look at me. We go up to the house and she goes quietly to her room." Sorry, Dad," she says, before she closes her door. Hildegard is sitting in bed when I return and looks at me with frightened eyes. She asks, "What happened?" and is scared when I tell her. "But I thought she was sleeping, I did not hear her leaving the house". I did not either. Krista is still sleeping when I go to work and I do not know what she tells her mother.

Time goes on and Krista lives a normal life outwardly and takes part in family affairs. But inwardly that search for her identity goes on. I think she feels bad for causing us grief. Hildegard is greatly troubled for her daughter. She feels incapable of helping her, since Krista gives her little access to her inner feelings. She is on a difficult journey. Hildegard writes to Agnes:

> *Krista is rejecting with intensity and passion parts of her past, we have lived through very difficult, dark and fear-filled months I must confess some of her dark journeys I cannot really understand.*

This inner journey shifts her focus away from her studies, she misses lectures and she decides to withdraw from university for a while. We give her assurance that we respect her decision. Life and work goes on.

Krista had heard about the Guardian Angels, a non-profit organization that combats crime in the streets of inner cities. It originally started in New York in 1979, to fight widespread violence and crime in New York's subways. It has now become an international organization which had just opened a chapter in Vancouver. Krista volunteers. She is interested in risky activities and, walking the streets of Vancouver at night, looking for adventure and an opportunity to help people in need, especially single women returning from night shifts, is just right for her at this time. The Guardian Angel staff trains its volunteers in basic human skills, martial arts and self-defense, since they do not carry any weapons. People who see the red berets patrolling the streets and alleys at night feel a little safer.

Krista quits after having worked with them for a short time. She does not like their 'boot camp' training style.

A study friend introduces her to skydiving. She takes instruction and does a few solo dives. Hildegard is very worried when she hears about this dangerous sport. I can dispel her fear a little, telling her calmly, I could imagine myself doing the same thing when I was her age if I had had the opportunity.

After a while of experiencing the thrills of jumping, the course becomes more theoretical and technical and the commitment becomes more time consuming and expensive and Krista stops attending.

Krista is in a difficult phase of transition. She needs to break out of the world of her parents to create her own. For her it is a painful process; perhaps difficult for us to understand its severity, especially for me. Having lost my father at age thirteen, I never went through such a phase. I did not go through a 'rebellious' age. After my father's death, I felt responsible to assist my mother.

Our children are very much a part of our life, when they hurt, so do we.

Krista decides to travel again to immerse herself in a different environment. Hildegard suggests a Kibbutz in Israel. She still has good memories of seeing the organized life in several of them from her visit to Israel with Merv and Merla five years ago. Some of our acquaintances have been in Israel recently and they think it is easy to be accepted into one. Krista is open to new adventures and Kibbutz life can be one of them. Simple lifestyle, living purposefully, is something she values. For our comfort, we know she will have shelter, food and protection there and speaking three languages should help her to communicate with other members.

Krista buys a ticket to Tel Aviv and inquires on arrival about the possibility of working in a Kibbutz. Times have changed in Israel. All of them are full and they do not accept any new foreign volunteers, she is told. She quickly has to reorganize her plans.

A Moshav, a communal settlement less structured than the Kibbutz has openings for harvesting melons. It is hard physical work. She holds out for a week in that heat. Some American co-workers, who started with her, give up after a few hours.

When the melons are harvested, she has to look for another accommodation. She goes to an affordable Arabic hotel in Jerusalem for the next night and the owner asks her if she is willing to work for him cleaning rooms in exchange for lodging and breakfast. She accepts.

A Bedouin jewelry maker sees her working at his friend's place and offers her a job helping in his art shop. She had taken art courses at high school and produced some lovely art work. A wire sculpture of an avocet still hangs in our living room and a beautiful batik wall-hanging with two sea-horses adorns the wall of our bedroom in Christina Lake. In the afternoons she works in his jewelry shop, crafting simple Bedouin jewelry pieces.

When she has saved enough money, she quits her job and starts to explore Israel. She travels to the sea resort of Elat and sleeps on the beaches of the Red Sea. She swims in the Dead Sea and climbs Mount Sinai. In the golden city of Jerusalem she walks through its historical churches, sympathizes with the Jews at the wailing-wall, and visits modern sites and places from biblical times. Bethlehem, Nazareth and Capernaum she remembers from her Sunday-School lessons. She travels past Lake Kinneret to the Golan Heights and back to Haifa and Tel Aviv.

Most of the nights during her travels she spends in youth hostels or sleeps outdoors on the beaches. Her meals consist mainly of French white bread and water. Poor hygiene conditions and malnutrition affect her health, she suffers and develops pneumonia and has no way to find treatment for it.

We do not know anything about her hardships; it would have upset her mother even more. I think her only contact with home was a phone call for Mom's birthday. After nine weeks of working and traveling in Israel, she runs out of physical strength and money for food and remembers the comfort of home.

I remember quite well a phone call on Dec. 22, 84. I lift up the receiver and a telephone operator asks, "Do you accept a telephone call from a Krista Lemke?" My heart is pounding. "Yes, gladly, where are you calling from?" I ask the operator, "From Jerusalem". I wait for a moment and then Krista asks humbly, "Dad, can I come home for Christmas?" Tears come to my eyes, "Of course, we have been waiting for news from you, take the next plane, and call us from the Vancouver airport collect and I will pick you up. Do you need any money?" "No, thank you, I have been able to exchange my return ticket and am ok," she assures me. Hildegard is greatly relieved when she hears that Krista is coming home. She had worried about her during the weeks when we had not heard from her.

We are all very happy to have Krista back again. Hildegard makes a special celebration for her daughter, like the father in the parable of the prodigal son.

The family celebrates Christmas together and Krista accompanies our Christmas carols on the harpsichord again.

I think what she experienced in Israel has made her look at life differently. She had to fight for survival for the basic things in life, like other people did, and she could do it; she feels more assured of herself.

Hildegard tells Krista that she has left West Coast Christian Fellowship. Krista admires the courage of her mother to break out of the patriarchal structure of the church. She is now a kindred spirit to her.

Krista decides to seek the support of a therapist. She is able to find one whom she can respect and trust and who can help her to sort things out

She wants to live on her own, to have her freedom and not be dependent on or a burden to her parents. She finds a small apartment in an older house. The absent Greek landlord has not maintained it very well. It looks a little run down from the outside and the rent is therefore reasonable. We help her move into her new place on the top floor under the slanting roof.

She wants to take her piano along. In her Toronto Conservatory piano course she has progressed quite well and playing piano is a creative outlet for her.

The stairwell to her upper room is very narrow and it looks impossible to get the piano through. Mike and Phillip, who lent us his truck, claim it can't be done, so let's take it back. Hanno is quiet. I tell them not to give up so easily. I measure the opening and figure if we unscrew the railing on the side we might be able to get it upstairs. We have about five millimeters space on each side. We cover the piano with a blanket, put a rope around it and Hanno and I pull from the top while Mike and Philip push from the bottom. Slowly we move it into her upstairs room. Krista is grateful. She later furnishes her room suitably and it is quite livable. She keeps contact with us.

One lovely incident with Krista comes to my mind. Hildegard is away, I think she had traveled to Bali with Lea. Knowing that I am alone at home, Krista phones me, "Dad, may I invite you for supper since Mom is not home, tomorrow around 19:00h?" "I am delighted to come", I tell her. I buy a bouquet of flowers and go up to her apartment. She has set her good china on a fine tablecloth and has lit a few candles when I enter, creating a festive atmosphere. She serves a delicious meal with an aperitif, main course and dessert. I am impressed with her art of cooking and feel really honored by my daughter. The conversation at the table is quite amiable and I enjoy the evening with her.

Krista looks for a job again.

Expo is desperately looking for suitable workers. Krista applies and for the duration of Expo she works as guide and sales clerk for different stores. We visit her when we visit the Expo exhibitions and see that she is happy and quite efficient.

We are personally involved with Expo as well. Expo management needs accommodations for visitors to the exhibit; all hotels are booked. Our children have left and their rooms are now empty. To help out we list two rooms with a rental agency. We get a number of phone calls from different people who are desperate for a place to stay. The rooms are listed 'without breakfast' but, when the guests are very interesting, we invite them to share breakfast with us.

On the last day of the exhibition, Krista phones us. She has terrible pain in her stomach area and can hardly move. Hildegard picks her up from the Expo grounds and takes her to the hospital. The doctor in the emergency asks her if she is pregnant and when she responds with a strict, 'No', he diagnoses her with an upset stomach, prescribes some pain relief medication and lets her go. It should be better in a few days, he tells her. Hildegard takes her home. It is a weekend and we wait until

Monday. Krista is in great pain, has a high temperature and feels as if she has a block of cement in her stomach area. On Monday morning Hildegard takes her to Dr. McKean, our family doctor. He urges her to take Krista to the emergency immediately. When she is operated on, the surgeon discovers a burst appendix and the whole area around it is highly infected. Hildegard visits her in hospital to keep her company and reads the Narnia Chronicles to her, which is what she had done when Krista was still small.

After her discharge from hospital she spends time with us until she has recuperated, then she wants to go back to her apartment. She looks for another job, preferably in a library. She applies at UBC but they want somebody with work experience. She finally goes to a bookstore and asks if they need help, she needs work experience, and will work without pay. For them this is an unusual offer and they try her out. After two weeks they want to hire her but in the meantime Krista had applied at Safeway and is accepted. The pay here is much better than what the bookstore can offer. She goes back occasionally on her free days to help out. Soon Krista is elevated to a full-time position of cashier because of her reliable work. At the end of the shift she often helps other coworkers to balance their registers.

Krista gains confidence again. She feels ready to go back to University. A week before she wants to give notice, she receives a letter from Safeway, asking her if she will accept a buy-out. They have to restructure. Krista agrees and receives a cheque for $17,000. Had she resigned a week earlier she would have received nothing. Now she is ready to start her final years at SFU.

25. Our new house.

Most residents on our street have deep lots with more than double the depth of normal building lots. The back of our property borders directly onto Burnaby Mountain and has no street access. Our neighbor at the end of the street wants to develop the unused back of his property. It is hard for the elderly couple in winter to drive up the steep driveway to their house. They want to build a new house on the back lot with street level entrance. To be able to do that, all neighbors have to agree to develop the back of their properties and they do. The neighbors on our street know that I am an architect and ask me to be their agent to arrange the formalities of rezoning with the City Hall. I present a site plan to the engineering department, which is approved. We now have to hire a road builder to extend Pandora Drive to the end of our properties. The engineering department asks me as 'developer' to post a bond of one hundred five thousand dollars to guarantee that road construction and services are done according to code. I have to take out a mortgage on our house to post that bond. Everything works out in the end. We now have access to the back of our property and can subdivide our lots.

My brother-in-law buys the adjacent lot from me. The proceeds from it just cover the price for the purchase of our thirty ha property with log cabin in Christina Lake.

I am looking forward to building on the now accessible back of our lot and make some sketches for a new house. Hildegard is very reluctant to build again and to think of moving. She is 'bonded' to our first house, our first achievement, the home where our children grew up. I try to look to our future. We are getting older and the children will be gone soon. There are many advantages to building again. The entrance to our new house will be from street level, wheel chair accessible, much easier than from the old one. Neighbors would not be able to look down into our backyard and private patio. We again have direct access to the park from our front door.

It makes sense to her but her heart is in our first house. She cannot imagine leaving the place into which she has put so much effort and cannot be excited about a new house design and a move. She writes in a letter to our friend Agnes:

> "After struggling with this thought of building again for two years I gave in and threw myself into the planning and later on the actual supervision of the building with a passion.- ....when we moved in the new house I suddenly realized this move was still not really voluntary. I could hardly return to the old house without crying. Although the new house is beautiful and has a lot of me in it, it still comes out on the short side of the stick.

Three property owners on our block want to build new houses, Reimers, on the south side, Ulli and Waltraud on the north side and we in the middle. All three are German-Canadians. Christine Reimer's parents were friends of ours back in Germany. Perhaps having German friends around us makes it a little easier for Hildegard to accept the idea of leaving the old house.

It is challenging for me to design a house on a steep, sloping lot. My first idea is a three story house with the floors staggered to follow the contour of the land; this seems to be a logical solution for me. A bridge from the street level to the top floor of the house will give us a level entrance; we will not have to drive down a steep sloping driveway and walk up on outside stairs, both difficult to maneuver in icy conditions. On the top floor we want to have a full suite, planned for our old age, when climbing stairs becomes difficult. On the bottom floor we plan an in-law suite for Hildegard's or my mother, if they want to live with us. In case we need help, care givers can move in with us and be available when we need them.

By presenting all these 'logical' ideas, Hildegard warms up to visualizing the new house. We drive around and look at houses built on similar sites to see how other people have solved problems. Considering different possibilities, we finally come to an agreement to build again. We incorporate some of the ideas we looked at into a good design and build a scale model with trees and even a toy car on the bridge. A photo of it looks almost real.

Our new house on Pandora Drive

Living room in new house

This time, approval from the building department takes longer; the plan checker is not familiar with a bridge design and has to consult the engineering department. I think our house is the first in Burnaby which has its main entrance from the street over a bridge.

I will not have the time, strength and expertise to do most of the construction as I did in the first house. This time I am only architect and general contractor. I hire sub-trades and do supervision and a few odd jobs.

There are a few tense moments during the construction. When the big backhoe excavates 14 feet deep for the foundation of the front wall, it hits a huge boulder; we have to get an expert to blast it out of the way.

The day before we have arranged to pour the 14 foot high foundation walls, the framing contractor gets scared and tells me he cannot take the responsibility for doing it. I find a contractor on short notice who is willing to do the concrete job the next morning but he does a poor job and is reluctant to correct his mistakes.

The night before the subfloor is to be laid I hear some noise at the building site and go up to see what is going on there. When I arrive I see a van quickly leaving the site. I mark the license number, not really knowing why. The next morning the carpenters tell me they cannot lay the floor, there are half a dozen plywood sheets missing. I call the police, they come to the site, write down the marking on the remaining sheets and the license number of the van. The next morning the missing plywood is on the site together with four long 2x8 beams which we did not know were missing. The police had looked up the owner of the van, found the missing lumber in his garage, charged him with theft, and ordered him to return the stolen goods. We are satisfied with that.

Building the bridge is quite a sight. Neighbors watch when the big crane drives to the site, lifts up the heavy 25 foot long pre-stressed concrete slabs and places them slowly and accurately on the high I-profile steel beams. The contractor finishes the slabs with a topping and in a few days we have access to our top floor. In the meantime the painters have done their job; only our finish-carpenter still has a few things to do. We move in on the 23rd of December 1983. It is a hectic Christmas celebration this year. There are still many boxes which we have not as yet had time to unpack. But we are in our new house!

It takes a few more weeks to get the finishing work done and to pour the driveway.

Our old house is for sale and our friend, Jandirk, buys it as an investment. Since he lives in Germany, he asks us to manage it for him. We rearrange the bottom floor to create four rental units for SFU students. One of them is our daughter Krista. She moved back to be closer to SFU. Jean rents the top floor and is the 'house mother'. She is very happy to have such a beautiful suite.

This works fairly well for three years but Jandirk is afraid the house prices will go down further and he sells the house and invests his money somewhere else. A few years later the price for real estate goes up sharply and ten years later it has doubled.

The proceeds from selling our old house cover the building costs of our new house so that we are debt free, without a mortgage.

Our house is unique. Hildegard had suggested some neat features. The west wall, as in the old house, is a window wall which takes in the gorgeous view of the coastal mountains, the water and part of the city. A skylight brightens up the stairwell to the lower floor. Together we furnish the house and create a comfortable cozy home for our family. Hildegard gives the house an artistic touch, which she loves doing.

We need a picture for our living room. Hildegard goes shopping in the Lougheed Mall and happens to walk into an art exhibit in its inner court. Local artists have displayed their paintings and prints. She spots one which she thinks would look good in our living room. We arrange to meet in the mall after school. I am early and look at the display and have my eye on one of the textile prints. When Hildegard comes, we go through the aisles together and she asks me, "Which one do you think would fit best into our living room?" I point out the one I had picked. She laughs and gives me a hug. "That is the same one I have chosen". We buy it and hang it on our feature wall over the sofa.

To supplement the furniture we brought over from the old house, we invest in a new living room set. Living room and dining room are only separated by the settee and the treatment of the ceiling. The dining room has a nine foot high flat ceiling, the living room a high cathedral wood ceiling. The harpsichord finds a place in a niche beside the music cabinet. Every inhabitable room, including the kitchen, my study and the small library, even the garage, share the beautiful view.

The view changes each season. When we see the first leaves sprouting on our maple tree and see the cherry and apple trees in the backyard blooming, it is spring. When the ornamental pink cherry trees lining our street are dropping their petals it looks as if we had a pink snowfall.

On a warm sunny summer day we love to sit in our lawn chairs on the spacious balcony, enjoy the sun under the extending sun roof and watch often up to forty small sailboats crossing back and forth on Burrard Inlet.

Fall is the season of color. Some mornings we come into the living room and look over a fluffy white blanket covering the city below us. The top of Capitol Hill and the coastal mountains stick out of the fog which has drifted in from the ocean during the night. When the sun dissolves the fog, a view opens to a variety of fall colors, the strong red and orange of the vine maples and sumac trees, the golden yellow of the birches and the ocher brown of the beech tree. That color palette extends to the other side of the water to Cates Park, the Indian Reservation, and up to Grouse Mountain where we see color patches between the dark green of fir and pine trees.

Winter starts earlier on the mountains than down in the city and we can see the sun glittering on the snow capped mountains when we are still harvesting the last apples. I can watch the skiers rushing down the Grouse mountain slopes through my telescope, a gift from my children for my 65th birthday, before we have any snow on our hill.

We are looking forward to spending many years in our new home; enjoying the view and the space. It provides ample room for the whole family and guests.

Our children are still with us when we move into the new house. It is ideal for them while they attend Simon Fraser University.

Michael's biology Professor, whom we know well, makes Michael aware of an opportunity to get some medical experience in a German hospital. Professor Dustman from Engelskirchen, had done research at the Toronto university and was so impressed by the welcome and help he received from his Canadian colleagues, that, as a token of thanks, he offers Canadian medical students a one year practicum at his university hospital in Germany.

Michael speaks German and has dual citizenship, so he takes advantage of this offer. He applies and is accepted. He learns a lot during that year. He is quite proud if doctors take him along as an assistant on their patient visitation. Another doctor, Juergen von Rechlin, the brother of a good friend of ours, befriends Michael and occasionally lets him drive his Mercedes.

Hanno graduates from High school this year. He has done well and as a graduation gift we buy him a flight ticket to Germany. Michael is looking forward to having his younger brother visit him. The two get along very well and have some exciting adventures on their tours across Europe from Greece to Scandinavia and the Near East. For Michael it is the second time that he tours Europe. A few years before, he explored the continent with his cousin Will.

Michael is the first one to leave home. He has received his BSc from SFU and wants to continue his education at Calgary Medical School. He has chosen Calgary because he thinks it is more progressive in its teaching methods and he can finish his studies there in three years, without semester breaks. At UBC it would take four.

At the end of the last semester at SFU Michael pays special attention to a beautiful girl in one of his science classes (or was it the other way around?). She also plans to go to medical school. Michael and Tannis' relationship becomes more intimate.

At first, when her parents realize that their daughter has the intention to marry the son of German immigrants, they have reservations. But when Michael has finished medical school and they have learned to know him better, they honor the choice of their daughter and her family arranges a big, well-organized wedding celebration. However, one thing they had overlooked. Hildegard and I go from table to table welcoming and greeting the guests. Hildegard does this very graciously. When it is time to sit down for the banquet, there are no seats reserved for the parents of the groom. This is quickly corrected and we all enjoy the festivity. Later we smile about it.

26. Metamorphosis

Hildegard was in a difficult phase of her life when we moved into our new house. Leaving the secure, familiar atmosphere of Ridge Drive and moving into the new house on Pandora Drive was scary for her but she moved into a visible, tangible place which she had helped to create and she soon got used to it and appreciated its advantages.

It is much harder for her when she leaves the church and loses the support of her 'father's house', her spiritual home. Unlike leaving our house on Ridge Drive she has no place to transfer to, there is a vacuum, her support is gone and this is frightening for her. She writes,

> Moving away from all I had ever known in terms of church life and practice was truly terrifying.

After she has struggled with the situation for awhile she becomes more assertive and writes to Agnes,

> I have inwardly moved to a space where the Christian Church as an organization with which I grew up has no relevance for <u>me</u> other than being the place where many of those dear to me find fulfillment in their life with God.

And in a letter to Irmgard:

> The solid, protecting structure of the congregation became for me a cage, when I left it, I left the familiar, the safe haven and embarked on a venture, the venture of freedom which caused some trepidation.
>
> (translated)

Family is important to Hildegard and the separation gives her pain,

> *I felt completely alone. Helmut did not understand what I was about, my birth family was shocked to the bone and in some way afraid of me.*

At the beginning of searching for her new Self, Hildegard was in a raw and touchy state of mind, her response to a letter from her younger sister, who looked at Hildegard as her 'surrogate mother', indicates that. Gertraud, an evangelical believer, is deeply concerned about Hildegard's new 'so-called journey'. She feels she has to warn her and writes in a letter, lovingly, the best way she can express it, that Hildegard is on a 'slippery slope'. She quotes scripture and shares her own belief as the biblical one, and closes her letter, 'God is still in control and loves you very much.'

Hildegard's reply is sharp:

> *Your well-meaning letter hit me like a bomb blast. I was and am devastated and deeply grieved. Part of the pain is parting with the companion of my childhood and youth – you have no idea how that hurts. – I need to face that, you neither respect and trust me, for if you did you would not so bluntly condemn me to hell. I am appalled at the arrogance of your position - as you can see I am hurt and sad and angry, I make no bones about it.*

Hildegard usually says openly if something bothers her and when she has vocalized it, she does not bring it up again. She has that special gift of bearing no grudges.

Gertraud felt strongly that she had to tell her sister her concern for her; not to lecture her or get into an argument.

It takes a short while until both sisters can communicate more amiably again with each other avoiding the issues of faith and church.

In conversation with other friends, Hildegard claims that I do not understand her. I think I can see her point but emotionally I perhaps do not understand her fully. I do not come to the same conclusion as she does.

I had noticed her evolving feminism and her growing uneasiness with the church structure. She tells the women at a retreat:

> *As I studied feminist theology there arose within me an incredible rage against the patriarchy and the sinister plot of the church to represent the divine as a triple male godhead, a rage Helmut had a hard time putting up with.*

I think I can understand and accept her reasons for leaving the church but that this means leaving her faith as well is hard for me to understand. For Hildegard everything has to fit together, if one part is off or wrong, the whole construct collapses.

My path is different. The foundation of my faith was laid by my parents and grandparents, as Hildegard's was. Our first image of God was, "Der liebe Heiland" the good shepherd, loving, caring. Added to that he was the almighty, all-knowing God, the creator of the universe and all the beauty of nature around us. We looked up to him with awe and wonder. He also knew everything about us. He was not the 'righteous Judge' who punishes us for every sin, our misbehavior, (an image that was so devastating for Krista). He was the one who forgives and does 'not hold our transgressions against us'.

We both were baptized on our personal faith. Hildegard writes to her sister,

> *We were baptized together, you out of obedience, I out of conviction.*

She grew up and lived in this protective faith environment most of her single life in her family and church. I had to test the foundation of my faith in many different situations, often alone, when I had to face the horror of war in battles and in military hospital, later in dangerous missions and as a refugee. I built my faith structure as I understood it, fitting one stone onto another, rejecting and putting away those that did not fit in.

We both felt the presence of the Holy Spirit in our lives giving us strength and joy in our faith when we were active in the charismatic movement. The building of my faith weathered many storms but still stands. I am still building and replacing.

I try to understand Hildegard's decision but I cannot walk her path and, in a way, she does not want me to do it just for her sake, though it would have been easier for both of us if I had gone with her. For Hildegard her image of God changes drastically.

> *The God image I had was just a projection. Taking back that projection I went through a difficult and scary time. It was as if I wiped the slate of my belief system clean and allowed an utter void. - I was on a spiritual quest. I needed to find out what had gone wrong, why I could no longer live and believe as I had. - I had an uncanny desire to break some of the strictest taboos of my past. I had my horoscope done, visited more than one clairvoyant with mixed results, I acquired a set of runes to help me find some answers in this bewildering new freedom. I realized that whether I read the Daily Word from the Bible, worked with the Tarot or the I Ching or the Runes for that matter, it was always getting in touch with that deep inner centre that knew.- I became reluctantly and fearfully willing and ready to live without the comfort of God and prayer. Very slowly a new way of perceiving God became possible.*
>
> *One room after another offered its riches, I read voluminously: Theology, Bible Criticism, Mysticism, Psychology, Feminism, research on the Goddess cultures. A whole new library attended that process, many intense sharings, discussions, probings with new and old friends.*

Old friends that left the church before her and would understand her 'new freedom' are Ulli and Waltraud next door. They introduce and encourage her to explore new ways. Hildegard, who needs fellowship to thrive, writes to Agnes:

> *Occasionally I get together with Ulli and Waltraud comparing notes, sharing the deep moves within us and drawing strength out of their love and vulnerability.*

Ulli shares with her his experience working with some of those 'taboos'. He also has dedicated his latest book 'New Embracing' (for the courageous, who are searching for their way) to Hildegard. He invites her out one evening to celebrate the occasion until two o'clock in the morning.

Waltraud creates intricate astrological charts on special computer software, which Hildegard uses to understand and interpret her own behavior pattern and that of family members and friends. At the beginning of her journey she frequently goes over to Ulli and Waltraud to share with them. She is often gone until after midnight. Sometimes I hear her talk to Ulli on the bridge at one o'clock, go to the window and wonder when she is coming back. I cannot sleep very well and am still awake when she comes into our bedroom.

I am pretty well shut out from all of that and we do not talk much about it. Looking back, I think she perhaps would have preferred if I had cried out my frustration and jealousy, had shared my difficulty to comprehend her actions, rather than to withdraw, which is my way of responding.

I agonize, meditate and pray to find ways to relate to Hildegard, to understand her. God answers with a vision. I am in a haze and seem to hear a voice as if God is speaking to me:

> 'Do not push Hildegard or try to persuade her, do not argue, just love her and leave her to me, I will care for her.. She is deeply hurt and needs time to heal.'

I am confident, believing this revelation will give me direction and hope.'

It is a difficult and testing time for both of us. Hildegard, too, is inwardly suffering from our inner separation. Sometimes she lies in bed beside me and weeps, I put my hand on hers but she wants me to share my feelings with her audibly and I do not know how to do it.

Outwardly life goes on. We discuss the necessary family matters and are respectful and courteous with each other. About our relationship, she writes:

> …it had become so clear to me that much of what Helmut lives he lives "off me" not really coming to his own and allowing his own personality and deep heart to express itself and grow. I feel like pushing him away but only to become himself, an opposite that I can truly love. What is happening to both of us is needful and very important. I do not wish <u>separation</u> so I muddle on willing for us to walk together but each one doing his own walking.

Hildegard had perhaps noticed that I had gradually given up some of my former independence as a student, in favor of a balanced relationship when we started our life together. Hildegard and I do have very similar interests. She is usually more assertive in pursuing these, is more articulate and makes friends more easily. I appreciate that in her. I am content with her choices, can go along most of the time and if not I make that known. Do I profit from it? Perhaps. My reasoning is, she does it so well, why should I compete? I don't think I am unable to have or defend my own opinion or make contacts. I can do it if I have to. To 'express my deep heart' is another matter. At this time, it is even more difficult for me. I have to and want to learn that.

Michael is at Medical School and Krista has her own apartment so Hildegard claims Krista's former room as her meditation room and arranges it to her present requirements. Along the wall beside the fireplace I install shelves for her own library, theology, psychology, mystery and New Age literature, books about art, goddesses and matriarchal societies.

In one corner beside the window are two drums, which she sometimes plays, one we had tried out and bought on our holiday in Scottsdale, Arizona, the other is a gift from our friends in Christina Lake; they made it themselves. On one wall besides eagle feathers and dream catchers she hangs an Icon, Madonna with child. We watched a woman artist in Mexico painting it and bought it from her. A white scatter rug covers part of the dark brown wall to wall carpet; on it, as an accent, the skin of an anteater, a gift from a missionary friend of ours who had brought it from Indonesia. Some of her selection of special shells and rocks find a spot on the mantle of the fireplace and the bigger rocks and exotic drift wood are arranged on the floor.

Artistically the appearance of her room is quite pleasing, perhaps a little too distracting for a real meditation room. Only her intimate friends and the close family are welcome in her 'sanctuary' by invitation.

Hildegard also has a number of tapes which she bought after weekend meditation workshops. I remember one which she attended with Krista, led by an Australian spiritual guru. He promises, 'attending this workshop will change your attitude towards people and life in general; your life will be less inhibited and stressful'.

I question the merits of his lauded retreat and the promises he makes and he cannot convince me to participate.

I pick Hildegard and Krista up at the end of the event in the conference hall in a hotel. They are still doing a relaxing dance and hugging each other. Several men in the group are attracted to our good looking Krista but she keeps her distance.

A month later there is to be a follow-up retreat and the participants are asked to preregister. My two women look back at it with mixed feelings and think they have had enough of it.

Hildegard is persuaded by an advertisement to order a set of meditation tapes, which promise 'increased brain activity, clearer thinking, creativity' and a few more things, all 'scientifically' researched. 'Listening an hour a day to the ethereal monotone music on the tape will definitely give results within a couple of months', they claim on the introductory tape which is free but there are several sets of tapes to follow which she has to buy.

For a number of months Hildegard faithfully meditates in her meditation room, listening to those tapes. This Buddhist approach to life does not seem to agree with Hildegard's inquisitive and creative mind, as she indicates in her journal:

> *Since I have started the holosync meditations, my inner life has gone quite flat I have been singularly unmotivated.*

She does not experience the results which the tapes promise and she discontinues these meditations. Hildegard is a trusting person, sometimes perhaps too easily persuaded but she also can discern afterwards what is helpful and what is not.

In her search for identity as a woman, she finds a new approach.

> *Then I made the most amazing discovery. As I was turfing out a lot of outdated values and bondages, I had this uncanny desire to paint and draw. I fought this upsurge in creativity literally for nine months. When I finally gave in, I discovered a way to my centre, to my identity as a woman, to my hidden dreams and desires.*

Hildegard had always admired my sketches and I encouraged her to try to draw too. But the perfectionist in her thought she could never do it that well. Now she becomes more courageous and is looking for ways to apply her creative ideas. I see an opportunity to do something together with her. I have a spare sketch book and we sit side by side sketching. We do some exercises that I used to do with my students to discover important parts and contours in an object. She accepts tips from me on how to improve her drawing skills and soon is quite impressed with the outcome of her first efforts. She starts drawing from photographs which she feels is easier. Later in Christina Lake we sit in the shade of the birch tree and draw from nature, trees, her favorite motif, and other objects.

I bring a book about watercolor painting from school which she studies carefully. We try some color mixing and blending with the primary colors, her palette fills out and she begins to enjoy painting.

On one frosty winter night, she left her painting on the balcony. When she picks it up the next morning, she discovers that the wet paint has crystallized on the paper and created an interesting texture. She applies this method in later paintings for special effects

Our holidays we spend mostly in Christina Lake, if we do not travel. The communal settlement as we learned to know it is now deserted. Our good friends, Bob and Sherry left for Oxford to study. They had been active in 'Young Life', a Christian Youth movement. He finds he needs to learn more about working with young people and gain some experience, so he takes courses which will empower him in this work. Sherry is working on her masters in English literature. Simon studies theology in England and later becomes the priest of the Grand Forks Anglican Trinity Church.

Roy makes peace with his father and goes back with his family to the States, studying chemistry and joining the company of his dad. The Jesus People have returned to the established society and are finding a place where they can contribute responsibly to it. None of our friends in the mountain community is left. We have no one with whom we can communicate and have fellowship. We have to draw on our own creativity for entertainment and find it beneficial for our relationship. It becomes more intimate again. Hildegard reflects:

> *As I strove for a certain emancipation of thought and being, our relationship was strained to the utmost. Both of us really believed in the commitment we had made to each other. In time Helmut learned to accept and respect the new me and as months and years went by I, too, became aware that there were far more aspects in our marriage that bonded us to one another than the one we just had lost: our symbiotic shared faith.*

I notice this in our relationship. We talk and share our thoughts and dreams with each other more easily. We explore the countryside on long hikes and visit the old homesteads of our friends on the mountain, which are now for sale. We sketch old machinery, sheds and utensils that still remind us of the former homestead on which we now live.

27. New Challenges

Ulli invites Hildegard to participate in a youth retreat in spring 1987 on the Hasliberg in Switzerland. Several presenters are to talk to the young people about different stages and activities in life and how to deal with them. Hildegard is asked to lead in a workshop about creativity.

The new Hildegard has gained more courage and consents somewhat hesitantly, since she is not sure what it will involve. Ulli picks her up in Zürich and introduces her to the pastor couple who lead the workshop and the other presenters. Hildegard makes friends with the people at the retreat, one of them is Gisela. She also has a challenging relationship with her husband who is a pastor in Saarbrücken, Germany. She teaches 'Dance in Worship'. Hildegard finds it very meaningful. They correspond intimately for a while afterwards and we visit Gisela later in Saarbrücken.

Before Hildegard comes home again she visits several relatives and friends in Germany among them Heide. She shares her experiences at the retreat with her.

Hildegard comes back invigorated and brings greetings from the relatives and tells me that Heide invited me to visit her when I come in the fall.

I joined the Burnaby teacher's choir because I love to sing but also because I can participate in a trip to England. The choir has received an invitation from the European Federation of Young Choirs to participate in the Loughborough Singing Week. Loughborough is Burnaby's Partner City. Grant, our choir director, selected songs which are representative of our country and culture from the pioneer times to the present. We come from the city of Burnaby named after Robert Burnaby, a famous son of Loughborough. He had been secretary to the governor of British Columbia and had resided for awhile in our town.

We are an amateur choir and cannot compete in quality with the renowned choirs from music academies in Germany and the Czech Republic and noted choirs from other European countries, but our program with songs from Canadian history is unique and finds approval. It is a wonderful experience for me to hear these professional singers perform and to sing with them in the mass choir. One Sunday we are invited to sing in a Presbyterian church. After the service we go to the cemetery where Robert Burnaby is buried and pay homage to the one from whom our city got its name.

After the singing week is over, we want to see a little more of England. With a few others of the group, I take the train to Lincoln and walk through the aisles of one of the largest early Gothic cathedrals. It fills me with a sense of awe and worship. English Gothic architecture is more decorative than the earlier pure French and German Gothic.

We travel south, to Nottingham, the traditional home of lace work. We are a part of the more than one-hundred thousand visitors from all over the world, who are attracted to the Lace Centre to look at hundreds of different lace patterns that are displayed there. I buy a small doily for Hildegard as a memento. On the way to the train station, we cross a plaza and notice a sculpture, an oversize figure of 'the king of thieves', Robin Hood, pulling the string of his bow to send an arrow towards his adversary. I remember the stories about him from our English text in school.

We drive on to Coventry to visit the new Cathedral. We enter through an arch and part of a vault, a remnant preserved from the former Gothic Cathedral which was destroyed in a German air raid in WWII. The new cathedral, designed in glass and concrete, is quite a contrast to the remnants of the old one. I am overwhelmed by the strong color and variety of themes in its modern stained glass windows, its altars and little side chapels.

From Coventry I take the train to Oxford. Our friend Bob from Christina Lake is studying there. He takes me around to the different Colleges and galleries and we end up in an old English Pub, have a warm beer and talk.

Hildegard had been in Oxford, visiting Sherry, his wife, a few months earlier. They explored the countryside and ended up in Stonehenge, the archaeological mystery in Southern England. It left a deep impression on Hildegard who has always been interested in archaeology. She later uses that image in a large silk painting.

To save hotel costs, I sleep the night on the ferry from England to Ostende and take the train to Germany. I make contact with the Lemke and Wiehler relatives in North Germany which Hildegard had left out of her itinerary.

I accept Heide's invitation to make her place my southern headquarters for a few days. From there I can visit school friends and relatives in the area, while Heide is still teaching at school. In the evening we have time together.

Hildegard had told me earlier in an unguarded moment that I should fall in love again with a woman in order to become more attentive and magnanimous, more alive, it might help our relationship. Well I keep this in mind when I drive to Ellhofen to visit Heide. We have known her for 17 years already; and she has become a very good friend of Hildegard and our family. She is single and appreciates being included in our family affairs. I always liked her.

On one warm evening, Heide sets the table for the two of us on the balcony. We are leaning over the railing on her fourth floor apartment, looking over the vineyards back on the slopes. I tell her that I like her a lot and put my arm around her. She leans towards me and says without much emotion "I, too". When we are eating supper, Heide tells me she has some difficulty becoming more intimate with men. I have noticed this and accept it. We can share quite openly, which inspires me. At night I ponder, 'Can one love two women at the same time?' A scripture verse comes to my mind 'no one can serve two masters,' – I love Hildegard and am committed to her, there is no question, but I am also very fond of Heide.

The next morning I drive back to Frankfurt. I phone her from the airport and thank her for her hospitality and friendship.

When I come home we start a correspondence. In former years I would send a routine Christmas letter to her and our German relatives sharing family events during the year. Now a letter arrives once in two or three months. I read excerpts from her letters to Hildegard, who writes to her,

> *I think something good could result from good intimate talks between you and Helmut. You can say things to him for which he seems not to be receptive, coming from me- it could be enriching and beneficial for him hearing it from another woman motivated by love.*
>
> *When Helmut came back from his trip he was more open, sensitive and energized. I really enjoyed talking to him openly and he was willing to listen and to understand me. I feel that Helmut is engaged in working on our relationship and I appreciate that.* (translated)

She writes to Gisela:

> *This trip has been good for Helmut, he describes it 'as an extension of his horizon' which is valuable for me, we can talk more openly with each other. I wish very much for myself that we can continue from now on to work on our relationship.*

After I receive several letters from Heide, I sense uneasiness in Hildegard. She writes to Heide:

> *I had difficulty accepting that you asked Helmut how I would react to a relationship between the two of you. It would have been easy to add a note directed to me personally. I felt excluded.*

Hildegard is quite open and direct in expressing her feelings. I appreciate this in her. I always know where she stands. In another letter to Heide, she writes:

> *For me this is a new experience and I could imagine that a relationship between the two of us and you could result in growth for all of us and I have always been for it.*

Strangely enough, in spite of my views and convictions about it I noticed after your letter arrived that I felt sick and fell into a depression, it makes me think about myself - do I live a lie? This split in me causes helplessness.

It seems that Hildegard's depression is a mild case of jealousy. I interpret this as a sign that she really cares about me and I respond by showing her my commitment and love.

28. Exchange teaching

Shortly before we went on our separate trips to Europe I get a phone call from Friedrich, a good friend of ours. He asks me if I would be interested in a teacher exchange with Germany. I am somewhat flabbergasted and not prepared for that. I had been thinking of taking advantage of a good buy-out from my teaching position and retiring early next year. Fred, the best calligrapher in Canada, is teaching at the Emily Carr Art College in Vancouver. He has a degree from a university in Dresden. He tells me Hildegard Banneyer, a German art and design teacher from Bielefeld, had asked the Art school for a teacher exchange. The Art College has no position open for her and the principal asks Fred, who speaks German fluently, to let her know of their decision. Fred does not want to disappoint her and phones me first to ask if I am interested in an exchange with her. I need some time to think about it.

A few years ago, I had applied for a paid leave of absence to take art courses at Greek and Italian Universities in order to study art history at the places where art history happened. Studying there, I thought, would be interesting and improve my qualifications as well.

The selection committee was too narrow-minded and did not grant me a leave. This offer now might be an alternative. Germany is much closer to Greece and Italy than Burnaby.

I ask Fred for Hildegard's address in Germany. I write to her and we exchange information about our schools. We feel good about an exchange and inform the school boards and our principals about our intentions. At first my school board rejects the application because our school is in the process of amalgamating with a Junior High school. This means we will add students from grades 8, 9 and 10 to our Senior Secondary grades 11 and 12. This, they argue, would mean for the exchange teacher to teach much younger students than she is used to which she might not want to do. "The best way to find out her feelings about this would be to phone and ask her", I suggest. "I know she wants very much to come to Canada." They agree to do this.

I quickly phone and tell her, "Hildegard, be prepared for a phone call from our district Superintendent to-morrow morning. He will point out to you what to expect here and see if you would be able to handle the situation". She practices her English and prepares possible answers all night, she tells me later. The Superintendent is satisfied with her responses in the interview and compliments her on her English. This changes his mind and he approves the exchange. I am quite excited about this which (my) Hildegard notices. One day she says to me, "Why don't you go on exchange to Bielefeld and I think I will stay here." I look at her, "Are you serious? I always took for granted that both of us would go to Bielefeld, if you do not come with me I definitely will not go." I am not quite sure if she just wants to test me.

She later writes to Gisela:

> "Happy news, Helmut and I have applied for a teacher exchange to Bielefeld. Added to our joy about it and our appetite for adventure is also a bit of angst."

We arrange with our exchange partner the conditions and expectations for our exchange. She will teach art courses at Burnaby South assigned by the vice principal in consultation with my fellow art teachers. I will teach at the Bielefeld Art and Design College, courses which she has been teaching there.

We agree to exchange homes. She can use our whole middle floor, all four rooms and bath, and the utility as her kitchen. We will join her husband in her Bielefeld apartment. I offer her our second car, the Colt. She can have it serviced in the school's automotive shop and she allows me to use her Renault in Bielefeld. Although many people warn us about car exchange, it is the easiest way for both of us, is economical, and works very well. Both vehicles are economy cars.

We are both paid by our own school-boards. She thinks she can live on $1400 a month here which Hanno will transfer from my account into hers. I will take the equivalent in Deutsch-Mark from her account in Bielefeld. We are both satisfied with this arrangement. It saves us headaches and a substantial amount on currency exchange fees. Hanno, who lives upstairs, will take care of any problems here and Hubertus, Hildegard's husband, will care for us in Bielefeld. Hildegard also wants to bring her son Wenzel with her to expose him to Canadian culture and to improve his English.

Two days before our departure the two arrive in Vancouver and I pick them up from the airport. We welcome them into our home and show them their quarters. I still have time to take her to the school where she is going to teach. The whole school has been reorganized during the holidays to incorporate the Junior High students.

At the end of the school year, I had asked Gisela, a German colleague, "Take Hildegard under your wing when she arrives, show her around and help her with language difficulties." It works out perfectly and the two later become good friends.

A problem arises when we introduce Hildegard and Wenzel to Thorin, our faithful black Labrador dog. We find out, to our surprise, that both of them are afraid of dogs. Animals usually sense that, but Thorin takes quite well to them and accepts them. Wenzel dares to take him out on the leash for a walk and his fear melts away when Thorin wags his tail and licks his hand. When Hildegard B. sees this, she slowly gets used to the kind creature as well. She tells us later that Thorin, in his affectionate, friendly way, took her fear of dogs away.

We have all the documents ready and have packed what we need to take along. Hanno takes us to the airport and we give him last words of advice before we take off.

We arrive with five suitcases at the Frankfurt airport on August 11, 1988. Hildegard describes our arrival:

> "We retrieve our luggage very quickly and in good shape, breeze through customs and through the automatic doors to the front lobby right into the warm hugs of our friends Thomas and Agnes, they live not far from Frankfurt and they surprise us here. It feels like being welcomed by family. They hand us a shopping basket filled with yellow roses, wine, bread, homemade jam and liver sausage."

After the first excitement dies down, Hubertus, who had stayed back discreetly, steps up and welcomes us with a smile. We all decide on a short break at an airport restaurant to catch up with the latest news from the Hannacks. They leave and we stash our luggage into Hubertus' Renault station wagon and start for our new home. Hildegard writes home:

> "During the three hour ride up to Bielefeld I soon discover that Hubertus is a 'kindred spirit', I feel comfortable with him. That night he makes us a delicious Italian dinner which he serves in his dining room complete with candles and wine".

At ten o'clock we are dead tired and fall into our beds. They are excellent, firm, long enough and cozy.

We spend the next two or three days moving in, punctuated by orientation sessions with Hubertus both in the house and all over Bielefeld. Our three rooms on the first floor are comfortable and furnished in very good taste. The ceilings are ten feet high the walls white, hung with gorgeous prints. We have a small stereo system where we can play records and tapes. The view out of my window is into the thickest greenery one can imagine. This must be one of the best areas of the city.

When Hubertus shows us our rooms we notice a huge flower bouquet on the side table. Hildegard goes closer and finds a card, a very thoughtful welcome gift from my cousin Irmgard, from Bad Segeberg. Two days later another gorgeous bouquet is delivered this one from Heide. Hubertus is quite impressed and wonders what kind of 'celebrities' we are.

Hubertus is a public school teacher, a kind, soft-spoken young man. Age-wise, he could be our son. He has a somewhat rocky relationship with Hildegard, his wife. I assume they agreed on the exchange in order to be away from each other for a year to find out if this will improve their relationship, if they will miss each other.

We are unpacking and Hubertus takes a peek into our room, he realizes the content of these five suitcases will never fit into the small wardrobe he has supplied. He goes to Ikea and comes back with another somewhat bigger clothes closet.

We are sharing the kitchen and bath with Hubertus. Hildegard has discussed with him the arrangement of sharing the fridge. When he sees us coming from the market with two big bags of groceries he disappears again and comes back with a reconditioned small fridge, puts it in the pantry for his use and tells us we can use the fridge in the kitchen. We find this very thoughtful and generous of him. All in all we feel really lovingly cared for.

I have a few days before school starts and we want to get acquainted with the neighborhood. Hildegard writes home,

> "On Sunday Helmut and I walk about ten km getting to know Bielefeld from the top. We climb the tower of the (castle) Sparrenburg, dating back to the 12th century and located in the middle of the city on a hill. We spend at least two hours up there enjoying a magnificent view in all directions and talking politics with some young students.
>
> We walk home through a lovely beech wood, past a Museum Village and on to a large park very close to where we live. We have great fun confirming that walking is the best way to get to know the city. We have since located the Art Museum, the swimming pool, small and large supermarkets, the bakery, post office, bank and City Hall"

We have to register at the immigration office and they require another medical examination including an HIV test before we are listed as residents and can work in Bielefeld.

Bielefeld lies in a dale of the Teutoburger Forest. The south-west slope leads down to the Bürgerpark with its large pond in the middle. Kids love to feed the swans and ducks that swim across it. On the lawn strut colorful crown peacocks. Off one side we can walk right into a beautiful rose garden; along its path are large enclosures for all kinds of birds. On the opposite side the metal sculpture of a full size moose peeks out of the bushes, a gift from an East-Prussian donor. Walking through the park to its far end and up several steps we reach the patio of a small café with a mouthwatering selection of pastries. All this is only a ten minute walk away from our apartment.

Hubertus has two bicycles reserved for us. We take them to the old empty schoolyard a block away and try them out. Hildegard is a little fearsome and shaky on hers and does not feel safe riding it in the city. I do not have that much difficulty and a few rounds of the school yard give me good control of it again.

The 'Karl Severing Schule für Gestaltung und Technik', in which I am to teach, is a conglomerate of several faculties, art, design and applied design, in different buildings, studios and workshops. A few days after our arrival I have my first visit with Oberstudiendirektor Dr. Knake and his vice principal, Herr Ludwig, in his office. Knake, a tall, clean-shaven, middle-aged man is somewhat distant and formal as if he does not trust me fully. Perhaps he is surprised about my accent-free German, too perfect for a Canadian. Mr.Ludwig, a shorter fellow with a mane of blond hair is more personal. The interview is cordial and Mr.Ludwig gives me a brief instruction about the layout of the institution and what is expected of the staff. He gives me a booklet with the prescribed curriculum and wishes me a good start.

When I come home Hildegard wants to know how it went. I tell her I had expected a little more collegiality. I show her the curriculum description but it is written in such a sophisticated, stilted German that we both have difficulty understanding it and I am supposed to teach from it.

With some trepidation I go to my first staff meeting. In contrast to the principal my colleagues are very friendly and helpful. After I get my teaching assignment I ask them about the curriculum guide, they laugh and tell me it does not make much sense to them either, "Just teach the way it makes sense to you as you have taught in Canada," but that is easier said than done. I have a responsibility to prepare my senior classes for their final examination and graduation and have to know what kind of work is required for it.

My teaching assignment is very generous. Normally a teacher here is expected to teach 25 hours a week. For me, as an exchange teacher, I am allowed to teach one hour less and, being over sixty, two more hours less.

I look at my timetable; my Monday assignment is to teach one senior class in design for a five hour stretch. On Thursday and Friday I am expected to teach seven hours a day but have no classes on Tuesday and Wednesday, provided I do not have to substitute for a colleague who is absent. Their school-board does not employ substitute teachers, as we do in Burnaby.

For the first weeks I have to spend a lot of time preparing my lessons which does not leave much time for Hildegard. My students here are older, self-motivated, eager to learn and demanding. They are more critical than my students in Burnaby and ask probing questions for which I have to have an answer.

Hildegard writes:

> *"After that euphoric late summer beginning, feelings drop to an all time low. Helmut's school has started and he goes to teach with much trepidation and uncertainty. Here things are handled differently and his confidence in his adequacy slips.*
>
> *While Helmut's attention is completely focused on his work, I go through a period of acute loneliness and isolation which lasts several weeks. I realize I have been torn out of all my relationships and feel like someone waking up in a completely strange setting after a bout of amnesia. All too aware of my predicament I decide to accept the depression and pain very consciously and to wait for a better time. That is hard – but the time comes."*

Hubertus notices this and tries to cheer Hildegard up. He invites us the next weekend to his mother's country home in Coesfeld about a two hours drive. His mother and sister, also both Hildegards, are warm-hearted people. Hildegard senior is a fellow artist and soon she and my Hildegard have a lot to share.

A week later is Hubertus' birthday. He invites us to join the party and we learn to know his friends, all young couples in their early thirties, very interesting people. Hildegard soon finds soul-mates in Christine, a tall, stately redhead with freckles, who has a responsible position in the 'Laborschule,' an experimental public school, and who writes the curriculum and tries it out with selected students. Ingrid is a 'mystic', an anthroposophist. She teaches in a Waldorf-School, an interdisciplinary school based on Rudolf Steiner's esoteric philosophy.

Hildegard regains her spunk. She hears about a painting course given in the Community Hall on Siegfriedsplatz, about a five minute walk. The instructor teaches a new art form, painting with dyes on silk. Hildegard soon discovers her talent and enjoys working in this medium.

Word gets around that we are in Bielefeld. We are here for a week and Canadian friends have discovered us. Les and Shirley travel from their son Tim's wedding party in Denmark via Bielefeld back to Vancouver. We are surprised and happy. Hubertus is very generous; he offers them his bedroom and sleeps at a friend's place. A few days later, quite unexpectedly, my cousin Kurt from Hamburg knocks on the door. He tells us his son Reinhard works as a physician in the Bethel Hospital in town and before he goes to visit him he wants to welcome us to Germany. Now we know that we have relatives in the city.

In September all foreign exchange teachers are invited by the German Department of Education to an orientation meeting in Bonn. We receive some guidelines and have an opportunity to exchange experiences of our first month teaching in Germany. On the way back I get a ride with a lively Australian teacher who drives past Bielefeld. We have a friendly exchange of ideas.

When I come home Hildegard shows me a letter from the Burnaby Teacher's Federation. The executive has worked out an agreement with the School-board that all teachers in the district have to join the teacher's union as a requirement for teaching in the district. I have to comply within two weeks or my teaching license will be revoked. Those two weeks have passed already and if I take it literally, I would be out of a job. I send a letter to the superintendent and ask him if this is the way to treat us exchange teachers, the education 'ambassador' to foreign countries. Dr. Froese writes back that I need not to worry as he will take care of the situation. I share this incident with my colleagues and they ask me, "What kind of democracy do you have in Canada? We here have a choice, we can join the union, or a professional teacher's organization or neither".

29. Visiting Italy

A week before fall vacation, our department has scheduled an excursion to Florence. My colleague, Erwin, is the coordinator of the trip. He invites Hildegard and me to come along, Hildegard as a chaperon for the girls, me as an assistant. Since I teach some of the students in the group, I feel some responsibility to prepare them for the art scene in Florence and ask Erwin what he expects of me. "Nothing in particular, just relax and enjoy the time in Italy," he assures me.

We board the tour bus, direction Florence. After we have traveled awhile we notice that the boys in the back rows empty one beer can after another and then come to the front and ask the driver to stop, as they have urgent needs. We find this appalling but Erwin does not say anything, he is stressed out, has his headphones on and listens to music. In the evening we roll into Florence. Erwin has no program prepared, so Hildegard and I tell the students the next morning at breakfast that we are setting out to explore Florence, the birthplace of the Italian Renaissance and anyone is welcome to join us.

Quite a few line up to go with us and listen to our comments as we start out with the city's landmark, the big cathedral, known as the Duomo. We enter through the wide bronze doors with reliefs of the life of the Madonna. The somewhat austere gothic interior has the shape of a basilica, forming a Roman Cross. We stand in the centre and look up into the huge octagonal copula. The largest brick dome in the world. On the way out we stop at the mural of the 'Last Judgment' by Vasari,

Beside the Duomo is Giotto's tall, square bell tower, a delicate Gothic design. We climb up the narrow winding stairs and have a tremendous view of the city.

On our way to the 'palazzo Vecchio', the Romaneque fortress-like town hall, we pass the 'Neptune fountain' with the tall statue of the god of the sea, surrounded by nixes and horses. In front of the palace stands a copy of the famous statue of 'David' by Michelangelo. We cross the 'Ponte Vecchio', the old medieval bridge over the Arno River. On its side railings 'hang' shops, like swallow nests, over the water; they sell now mainly souvenirs to tourists.

I still remember from Professor Flesche's art history lectures, the 'Palazzo Pitti' as an example of early Italian Renaissance architecture. The palace was the residence of the Medici, of the Duchy of Tuscany and, for a short time, when Florence was the capital of Italy, the residence of King Emmanuel II. It is interesting for me now to see this famous Renaissance building in reality.

It has been a strenuous day. We are tired from walking and return to our hotel for a typical Italian supper, spaghetti and meatballs. The next day we want to visit some of the well-known art galleries. The Uffizi Gallery, one of the oldest art museums in the world, houses a rich collection of Renaissance and Baroque Paintings by Giotto, Leonardo da Vinci, Titian, Dürer, Raphael and many more. In the Academia Gallery we admire paintings, mainly with religious themes, from the Gothic to the late Renaissance period but our special interest is drawn to Michelangelo's sculptures especially the over-five meter high marble statue of 'David'. It is a masterpiece of Renaissance art, an expression of strength and refinement. David is not the warrior or harp player or the famous king he is a well built contemplative young man, his body and limbs carved out in masterful detail. In the Medici chapels in the Basilica de Lorenzo, are more of his sculptures, 'Mother and Child' and the reclining figures of 'Day and Night and Dawn and Twilight' on the tombs of the Medici brothers.

Quite delightful for us are the small frescoes which Fra Angelico painted on the cell walls of the San Marco monastery.

A few days later the bus takes us to the medieval town of Siena, a unique Gothic town, dating back to the Etruscan time. It is quite different in its simplicity and clear order from the grandeur of Florence. We walk a narrow road through the city and end up on the large slightly sloping shell-shaped 'Piazza del Campo' one of the most beautiful civic spaces in Europe. Its focal point is the 'Pallazzo Pubblico' the grand gothic city hall with its slender tower. Climbing up the stairs to the look-out platform awards us a marvelous view of the piazza and the city. A number of patrician residences and its famous university surround the plaza.

I gather a number of students and we sit on the stairs to the plaza and sketch this interesting vista.

Hildegard is fascinated by the story of St. Catherine of Siena, a famous Dominican nun, a mystic and church reformer of the 14th century. Hildegard feels an affinity to her and goes with great reverence through the cells of the convent were she had lived and spent her time, caring for the poor, writing letters to Popes and princes pleading for unity and peace in the country. We see the mysterious crucifix where she had visions and got the stigmata. She was a remarkable woman for her time.

We return to Florence exploring more of its sites, this time alone as the students have other interests. We both enjoy our stay in Florence and take in from the art scene more than we can digest in these few days.

The week goes by fast and the students have to go back to Bielefeld. We travel with them in their bus until Verona; there we leave them and board the train to Venice. When it leaves the platform I have a strange feeling that we are going in the wrong direction and ask a passenger about it. He smiles and tells me in broken German this is the train to Milan. We get out at the next station, cross the platform and are lucky the train to Venice comes in twenty minutes.

I had always wanted to visit this historically interesting medieval city and now it becomes reality.

When we arrive at the Santa Lucia train station, we pick up a tourist guide and leaf through the hotel and B&B section. We had not made any hotel reservations, we like to be flexible. We write down a few addresses and pull our suitcases along the road to look for a place to stay for the week. The first hotel is not very clean; the next one is too small. Hildegard gets a bit nervous but the third one is ideal, a little off the main street at the corner of two canals. From the balcony of the first floor we can watch the mail boat, the milk and grocery delivery boats, the yachts and gondolas cruising on the canals. There are no cars allowed on the island on which Venice is built, everything is transported by boat or cart.

The first evening we walk to the Piazza St Marco to have a glimpse of the night life of this romantic city. The St Marco Basilica at one end of the large city square and the Doges Palace connected to it, look quite imposing. Hundreds of lights are reflected from the gilded mosaic arches of the Basilica and in contrast the dark arched Arcades of the Doge's palace lie in the shadow.

Venice was the trading centre for the Byzantine Empire and the Muslim World five hundred years ago. We can see the influence of these cultures in the architecture of the city. The trade brought prosperity and the wealthy merchants competed in building bigger and more splendid palaces, employing the most famous artists of that time.

The Basilica with its five big arches and a number of minarets shows a strong Byzantine influence; the facade is intricately decorated with mosaics. The Doge's palace, facing the Piazzo and the Venice Lagoon, picks up that motif in its long arcade of gothic arches.

The next day we take a cruise along the Grand Canal and branch off into some side canals to get a good overview of the city. Palaces of rich merchants built in different styles and sizes face the canal and provide good motifs for our cameras. Our boat passes under a number of bridges, each one of a unique design, Later we walk over them to look at the palaces, churches and museums from another perspective. We can walk from one end of the city to the other in a few hours.

Remnants of its golden age are still visible but a number of those palaces are now neglected. Hildegard writes home,

> "How can one describe the beauty of Venice? For me it was a very sad beauty because decay, mildew and rot were in evidence everywhere. How gorgeous this city must have been in its prime" -

Venice will have a special place in my memory.

30. Bielefeld our new home.

We take the train back to Germany Heide picks us up from the station in Heilbronn. We spend a day with her in Ellhofen.

Hildegard had shared with her on her visit last year her difficult experiences after she had left the church, grappling with her status as a woman, about the influence of feminism in her development and her emancipation as a determined individual. Having become a changed person, she wants to give expression to that by not responding to the short or endearment form of her name any more, by which her sisters, parents and friends have always called her, Hilde or Hildchen. She now wants to be called by her full name, Hildegard. Heide listens and decides to adopt *her* full name as well. From now on we call her Adelheid instead of Heide. After being with her for a day in Ellhofen she offers to drive us to Bielefeld.

The fall school holidays are staggered throughout the German provinces and hers are a little longer than ours in Westfalia. She has time and we invite her to stay a few days with us. I had been looking forward to seeing her again. At my visit with her last year she was warm and friendly but now I notice certain aloofness. I ask Hildegard about it and she suggests to me, "Why don't you talk to her?" While Hildegard is making supper I invite her for a walk through the Bürgerpark. We talk casually about Hildegard's and my experiences in Italy and about schoolwork. When we come to the more secluded Rose-garden we sit down on a bench and I mention that I notice a change in her attitude since I have returned. She replies, somewhat evasively, "This is the way I am". I ask her directly how she sees our relationship now that I am here with Hildegard. She pauses for a moment and then says, "For me you are the husband of my best friend Hildegard." I am at first somewhat taken aback and let it sink in. This change could perhaps be a reaction to Hildegard's last letter to her. I assume she might fear, consciously or perhaps unconsciously, losing her as a friend if the relationship between us continues. I understand this and accept her as 'a good friend of my wife' without much resentment.

The three of us explore the outskirts of Bielefeld on my free days, visit the historical Germanic Farm Museum, and take a long walk through the Teutoburger Wald to the Hünenburg with its look-out-tower from which we have a wonderful view over the forest. It has just turned into a sea of beautiful yellow, orange and red fall colors.

I now have more confidence in teaching my subjects. I have observed some of my colleagues in their classes, picked up some tips and found that I can keep up with them, I even introduce some topics which they had never even tried yet.

Hildegard feels more at home now too. We transform one small room into a make-shift studio for her and she enjoys experimenting with her new art form, silk-painting.

Hildegard's mother and sisters come from the USA to see where we are and how we are managing and, of course, to visit some of their friends and relatives in southern Germany. Hubertus vacates his bedroom again and they stay with us for a few days. Hildegard shows them the city and on my free day I take them to Detmold. This small once- fortified medieval town with its colorful timber-frame houses, its city hall, Renaissance Castle and the well known Music Academy has its special charm.

From there we drive through the southern part of the Teutoburger Forest to the 'Hermansdenkmal' a monument for the leader of a Teutonic tribe, 'Herman the Cherusker'. He and his cohorts defeated the Roman legionnaires in this forest in 9 BC and allegedly kept the Romans out of Germania. The 27m high sculpture of Herman, his sword stretched high up into the sky is quite impressive.

South of Detmold, a few kilometers out of the Teutoburger Forest, we discover an unusual natural phenomenon, the 'Externsteine'. In the middle of flat fields we all of a sudden approach an outcropping of colossal odd shaped rocks of different sizes; the tallest of the five is about four stories high. Hildegard is very excited about them when she finds out about their history. This megalith was the centre of religious activities through the ages. In prehistoric times, it was a sacred cult place, a Germanic pagan shrine for the celebration of summer and winter solstices. In the Middle-ages, it was a place for Christian hermits who lived in caves at the base of the rocks. Old worn-out steps cut crudely into the rock, wind up to a platform from which a small bridge leads to a now open air chamber on the top of the tallest rock. It served as a place for sacrifices and later monks gathered there for prayer. In the Nazi times, it was a sacred grove. Because of certain astronomical alignments the site has attracted devotees of Neo-Paganism and it has become a New Age mystic site. We take some of our guests to this unusual, interesting rock formation.

One day I come out of school and wait at a crossing for the traffic light to change. A driver who is in a rush cannot make the turn and slams into the door of my car. A young man gets out, a cigarette in his hand, and apologizes. We exchange data and he leaves. I wait for the police; they come after awhile and tell me if the other driver admitted his fault, they do not have to record it.

I see Dr. Nebelsieck, Hubertus' family doctor, and he thinks I should stay home for a week to recuperate from the shock. Hubertus takes care of the repair but I have to haggle with the insurance company for a decent settlement. It is a new experience for me to see how Germans deal with car accidents.

A letter from Ulli arrives, he is on a book promotion tour in Germany and will do a reading together with a German songwriter and musician and he invites us for this event. We drive up to Melle, a little town over an hour north from us, listen to the music of Siegfried Fietz, a modern folk singer, and to Ulli's reading. We enjoy their performance. It is good to have a little home atmosphere again and get personal greetings from our children,

We have the opportunity to listen to a trumpet and trombone concert of the renowned French trumpet player, Maurice André. He plays Baroque music, which is his specialty, and some modern pieces. The bright, clear tones of his piccolo trumpet still ring in my ears. He performs in Bielefeld's concert hall, the 'Oetkerhalle'. It is only two blocks away from where we live. The hall is named after Bielefeld's famous son, Dr. August Oetker. He developed a baking powder in his pharmacy; this product was so good and was marketed so successfully that he developed new products and recipes. His baking ingredients are now known all over the world and his cooking and baking books are found on the shelves of many kitchens in several countries.

The German Education Ministry invites us exchange teachers to a study session in Berlin and I accept the invitation. It is Hildegard's 55th birthday. To have company while I am in Berlin, she pays a short visit to Adelheid in Heilbronn. Her birthday is a day later than Hildegard's so they can celebrate together.

The next morning I take the Inter-Zone-Train to Berlin. It goes from the border right through the Soviet Zone to West Berlin without any stops.

Our hosts in Berlin are quite generous. I am given a private hotel room and we start our morning events with a common breakfast. For an introduction they take us on a guided bus tour to important places in the city like the Brandenburg Gate, the Charlottenburg Castle, and the new Congress Hall, which the Berliners call the pregnant oyster because of its shape. We walk around the ruins of the Kaiser Wilhelm Memorial Church, which are preserved as a reminder of the destruction of the city during WWII.

When we return, we listen to a lecture about German history and the situation in the divided city. The lecturer prepares us for our tour through the restored 'Reichstag', the parliament building. As we enter, we are issued a security tag and have to display it when we proceed to the chamber where the governments of the German Emperor and later Adolf Hitler had their sessions. We are allowed to sit in the benches where former members of Parliament sat. A guide explains to us the parliamentary procedures in former and present governments. Occasionally the West

German and West Berlin Parliaments meet here jointly. East Germans object strongly to these meetings held in 'their' capital.

Our program allows sufficient free time to explore the city on our own. I walk along the Kurfürstendamm, compare the prices in stores with ours, visit several very moving Holocaust monuments and other open air sculptures, like the 'Flame' on the Theodor Heuss Plaza. I take the subway to Friedrichstraße, one of the few transfer points to East Berlin. With my Canadian passport, I do not have much difficulty passing through the checkpoint. The once busy Alexanderplatz in Berlin Mitte, named after Russian Tsar Alexander who visited Berlin in 1805, is still surrounded by many ruins and damaged buildings from WW II. Opposite the new East German parliament building stands, somewhat isolated, the Weltzeituhr (world time clock) I check my time on it and find out what time it is for our children in Vancouver.

One of the special attractions is the Pergamon Museum not far from the Alexanderplatz. I know from my art history courses that it houses artwork from archaic to the Hellenistic Period, Islamic and Middle Eastern art and I am curious to see it now. I walk around Greek and Roman sculptures and greatly admire the huge Pergamon altar with its 113 m long frieze depicting the struggle of the gods and the giants.

Many of the art pieces from the Pergamon and other German museums were stolen, destroyed or transferred to museums in Russia, America and several European countries after WWII. Some have been returned, others disappeared and there are still negotiations in progress for the return of identified items.

A dominant building on the Museum Island is the massive neo-classicistic Berliner Dom, a protestant cathedral. It was heavily damaged in the war and has been restored in a somewhat simpler form.

I notice the contrast between West and East Berlin in many ways. Rebuilding of infrastructure is slower, people look somewhat indifferent.

I want to eat lunch in the restaurant in the new East German monumental parliament building. There are only a few people in the dining room. Three waiters lean against the counter talking to each other, none pays attention to me. After a while, I wave and one comes over and asks nonchalantly, "What would you like?" I ask for the menu. He disappears and after a while brings the menu. It does not take long for me to choose; from the dozen entries, only four are available today. No waiter in sight to take my order; I have to go to the counter and tell them that I am ready to order. It takes 45 min until he brings my lunch and another 20 min. to get the bill after I finished my lunch. It takes me almost two hours to get a one-course lunch in East Berlin. There is not much incentive to work there.

The last day we are offered tickets for a Cabaret performance 'Die Wühlmäuse' (the Burrow Mice), an interesting political satire.

On Sunday, I am glad to be back in Bielefeld with Hildegard again. In the evening, we listen to an 'Advent Vesper', pre-Christmas music, in the Nicolai Church. It prepares us for the coming season.

For the Christmas holidays, we have an invitation from Swiss friends. On the way, we stop in Ellhofen. On Christmas- eve Adelheid takes us to a nativity play in the Ellhofen village church. The next morning we head towards the Alpine Mountains.

It is thick fog and we cannot see the mountain. We have a hard time finding the house of our hosts. Dietmar and Christine, the Pastor couple of the small Grenchen congregation, welcome us. Hildegard knows Dietmar from the Hasliberg retreat. She introduces me to them and we talk about our families and church. Dietmar visits his parishioners on his bicycle to be a good example for simple living and energy-saving.

He shows us their church and the adjacent communal room, which Christine has decorated and furnished quite artistically. We sleep upstairs and when we go to bed, we find a piece of Swiss chocolate nicely wrapped on our pillows, a token of love from Christine.

The fog has not lifted when we wake up and this is quite depressing. Dietmar suggests we drive to Grindelwald, a famous ski resort higher up in the mountains. We can hardly see the road but at a higher altitude we rise above the fog and the clear blue sky opens a tremendous view of the Alps. It has snowed at higher elevations and we have to drive carefully. Grindelwald is a beautiful small Swiss Alpine town surrounded by the Eiger, Mönch, Wetterhorn and Jungfrau mountain ranges, all have peaks over 4000 m. We climb up to the Ski lift and watch the skiers perform their tricks.

On our way back to Bielefeld, we stop in Kaiserslautern, Hildegard's hometown. We drop in on our common cousin, Lieschen, surprise her on her birthday and celebrate with her. She is such a joyful and friendly person, it is fun to be with her and her family and to meet other relatives which have come to celebrate with her.

The next day she takes us to the 'Dritte-Welt-Laden', a shop where she volunteers to sell goods produced in developing countries.

Adelheid has told us about an exhibition of religious art in a museum in Wiesbaden. We meet her there and look at the display of icons, sculptures, mosaics and other art objects, many on loan from Russia. We meditate on these mystical paintings of religious symbols, sacred objects of worship for many devout orthodox Christians.

We have been here in Bielefeld for almost half a year now and have participated in many events. I am now more relaxed and enjoy teaching my adult students. I have to prepare my lessons carefully to meet their expectations and inspire them. I also want to make a good impression as a representative of my country.

Hildegard, in the meantime, takes another course in silk painting and is quite enthusiastic about new methods and materials which she tries out in our makeshift studio.

On Sunday morning, we hear the bells of many churches inviting us to worship. We have not heard the sound of church bells for a long time. There is a small fairly new Catholic church a few hundred meters beyond our garden fence. Hubertus used to go there but he had a dispute with the priest and stopped going.

I try the Mennonite 'Aussiedler' church, founded by Mennonites who returned from the former German settlements in Russia. The church is filled to the last seat. The sermon is simple, reminding the congregation of the sinfulness of society and the temptations the younger generation is facing. I do not know if I will fit in there easily. I do not speak Low German either, which most of them speak after they come out of the service.

A group of Mennonite Brethren meets in a pub, which they rent and have to rearrange for the Sunday service. They have to be out at one o'clock when it opens for the public again. The people are very friendly. Pastor Neufeld's sermon on this Sunday is entitled "We are midwives of joy" a very appropriate topic for this time.

I attend a few times but it is too far to drive.

We hear the bells of the near-by Lutheran 'Matthäus Kirche' every Sunday and I consider attending the service there. I leave when the bells begin to ring, the sound of the bells accompanies me on my walk through the park and they stop ringing when I arrive at the church. The church has a very talented young music student as a substitute organist. He plays preludes before the service and introduces each hymn later with a prelude suited for its text.

After the service, I go up and ask him, "Where do you find the music for these beautiful preludes?" "Most of them I compose myself while I am playing," he tells me. I compliment him on his creativity.

He also leads a small church choir and I ask him if he needs tenors. He is delighted. So the following Wednesday I go to choir practice. I meet the pastor who sings bass. He tells me enthusiastically about his studies in Toronto, when he finds out that I come from Canada. We have a lively conversation during the breaks.

A number of sacred concerts are offered during the Lenten period. One evening we go to the Marienkirche to listen to a Choral Passion by Diestler.

31. Holiday in Greece and elsewhere

The spring break is coming closer and we make plans for our holidays.

One reason why I agreed to the teacher exchange was so that I could take advantage of the longer spring and fall holidays in Germany. These holidays give us a chance to travel in Europe, especially to Greece, Italy and Spain. Our holidays in Burnaby are in July and August. It is far too hot for me during that season to enjoy traveling in these southern European countries.

We had seen the northern part of Italy in the fall recess, now we are looking forward to exploring Greece in the spring holidays before the tourist season starts and the crowds move in.

Hubertus drives us to the airport in Amsterdam and a few hours later we arrive in Athens, the city of my dreams. At this time of the year, it is not difficult to find a decent hotel. We spend the first day getting acquainted with the downtown area. I feel the air in the inner city is quite polluted and I develop a headache and find it more difficult to breathe. The city council is aware of this problem and tries to combat pollution. Cars with odd license numbers are only allowed to enter the inner city on odd days and cars with even numbers on even days. People who can afford two cars have one with an odd and the other with an even license plate number.

For me the most important attraction in Athens is the Acropolis, the 150 m high plateau in the middle of the city, the 'sacred rock of the gods'. We walk up the steps through the partly collapsed gate, the Propylaea with its massive marble columns. To the right on a narrow platform stands the small temple of Athena Nike, with its ionic column facade. This gem, built to commemorate the Greek victory over the Persians is well preserved.

The suspense grows when we approach the huge Temple in the centre of the Acropolis, the Parthenon, a Doric temple for the Goddess Athena. It was the most perfect, aesthetically pleasing classical building in Greece. Now, in its shell, we can just imagine that beauty. Close by, is a smaller Ionic temple, the Erechtheum. We count the Caryatids; six of these wonderfully draped female sculptures carry the roof of the 'Porch of the Maidens'.

The whole plateau of the Acropolis was once settled with residences nestled between the temples. Now remnants of these, rocks, parts of columns, capitals and sculptures lie scattered around.

From the plateau, we can see the layout of the city. Further down in the shadow of the Acropolis, lies Plaka, the oldest settlement in the centre of Athens, a village in the city. We walk the narrow winding roads and steps up to another hill. Nestled between rocks and trees are neoclassical mansions and older residences with beautiful gardens and porches overgrown with grapevines. Some friendly owners offer us a few grapes when they find out we are foreigners. We stop at a unique little restaurant on an outcropping of the road for a cup of coffee. From its terrace, we have a captivating view of this picturesque part of Athens. It is a special occasion for the two of us to walk along roads that already existed millennia ago. At each curve of the winding road, we have another view of the city down below us.

We leave Athens and take the steamer, 'Knossos', to Crete. We land in Iraklion, take a taxi from the harbor to the city and find a nice small hotel with rooms around a tranquil inner court. Its walls are overgrown with blooming creepers. We spend a few days in this lovely place exploring the harbor and the city. Not far from Iraklion are the ruins of Knossos. Hildegard is looking forward to exploring this renowned archaeological site in Crete. It does not take long by bus to get there. When we come to the entrance of the site, we are amazed by the immensity of the excavation of this former Minoan settlement. We are a little bewildered not knowing where to start when we hear someone calling, "Come and join a tour through the magnificent palace of Knossos". The guide, who called, speaks perfect German and tells us, "Four months from now this place will be packed with tourists". Now he has a hard time getting a dozen people together. "Knossos", he mentions, "was perhaps the administrative and religious centre of the Minoan culture in Crete or even in Greece, dating back to the Bronze Age". He guides us through the huge palace compound, one thousand three-hundred rooms and chambers belonged to it at one time. Most of them are in ruins now and only the foundations are left and remnants of walls. He leads us up and down ramps and stairs and explains to us what kind of buildings have stood where these heaps of rocks are now. Some of them have been partly restored to give an idea of what this town must have looked like.

We go past big basins that may have been used for ritual purification and walk through storerooms with huge storage vessels. The best-restored part of the palace is the large throne room with the built-in alabaster throne. A few walls are decorated with colorful frescos depicting mystical figures, griffins that flank the alabaster throne, other animals and plants, fishing scenes and flower gatherings. One does not see glorifications of war heroes or battles, only a few athletes doing bull jumping. The Minoans were a peaceful more matriarchal civilization.

After the guided tour, we have time to go back to the more interesting details of the big palace area. Hildegard takes a picture of me standing on the high platform of the partly restored temple beside the red columns. Unlike in Greek and Roman architecture, the columns are not built with marble sections, the Minoan columns are trunks of cypress trees painted red. Down from the palace plateau we can see the rising stone seats of the big amphitheatre.

The Knossos experience is a highlight of our visit to the island of Crete.

The next day we rent a car and drive around the periphery of Crete. It is a little more than an hour's drive on the highway along the coast to the old Mycenaean town of Rethymnon now the third largest harbor city on the island. It is known for its decorative Piazzas, fountains and churches, which survived destruction during WWII and former occupations.

It is lunchtime and we are looking for a restaurant. We pass by one, which looks unusual for Crete; it is finished in natural wood, clean and nicely furnished. We are trying in English with the aid of our hands to order a lunch, when we hear the cook speaking German to his daughter in the kitchen. Now it is much easier for us to order our meal. We ask him, "Where did you learn such perfect German?" He smiles, "We operated a Greek restaurant in Bavaria for eighteen years and returned half a year ago. We opened this restaurant a few days ago; you are one of our first customers". We ask him, "How do you feel being back again in Greece?" He replies happily, "I saved enough money in Germany and am glad to be able to start this restaurant in my home country". We ask the 15-year-old daughter the same question and she answers emphatically, "I would rather have stayed in Germany. Women are treated better over there". It sounds strange to us to hear a Greek in Crete speak German with a Bavarian accent.

From Rethymnon we drive south on rough country roads which at points have been washed out from floods. We drive through deep gorges with high vertical rock walls on both sides. Like in many parts of Greece, we pass by a number of archeological excavations of old settlements, sacred places and burial grounds. Hildegard wants to see them all. She wants to walk these small paved roads between the house foundations and imagine walls rising up from them, forming buildings and villages of a different culture.

Near the south coast of Crete, we visit the ancient half-collapsed monastery of Moni Preveli. A donkey grazes between the ruins where the monks formerly may have lived, prayed and worked their gardens.

We come down from the mountainous area and reach the small fishing village of Matala. We walk along the beach and climb up a flight of worn-out crooked stone stairs to a little restaurant and order a local fish dish for an early dinner. From the patio of our restaurant, we see a tall rock wall rising up from the other side of the bay. It has a number of different size holes in it. The waiter tells us they are openings of caves washed out by the sea when the water was still higher. During the 1960's hippies inhabited them. They swam in the sea and lay on the sandy beach; it was 'Paradise' for them. But they were too messy and the authorities ordered them to move on. When we walk over there they are not inhabited any more.

From Matala a narrow road winds around the southern perimeter of the island. As we come to a higher elevation, fog moves in from the sea. It becomes so thick that we can hardly see the road. We almost run into a car, which comes out of nowhere. We ask the driver how to get to Mitros. In sign language, he let us know we should follow him; he is going in that direction. We stay close behind him so as not to lose sight of his rear lights. After a while he stops, gets out of his car, touches his car and points to the left, then looks at us and points straight ahead. Now we are on our own on this narrow gravel road in a cloud of fog. It has become so dense that we can see only five paces in front of us. I drive on the left side where I can anticipate the upward slope of the mountain. I prefer not to look to the other side. The bank falls off steeply. If the road takes a sharp curve, Hildegard has to get out and tell me which way to turn. It takes us hours before we drive into Mitros. We are exhausted and glad to find a modest room in a rooming house to settle for the night. Some cute little girls are curious and want to make contact with us.

The next morning, the sun is shining into our room and wakes us up. We pack our things together and continue our trip along the eastern side of Crete. Once in a while, we have a good view over the Mediterranean Sea with all those small islands. We spot little fishing boats, which have anchored in small bays along the shore.

At lunchtime we arrive in Agios Nikolaos, a picturesque small harbor town nestled around the end of a bay. We look in the tourist guide for a rooming house. We find one up the hill that seems to be right. When the woman of the small guesthouse finds out we are Canadians, she offers us her best corner-room on the second floor with a balcony from which we have a magnificent view.

Agios Nikolaos is our headquarters for the next week. We acquaint ourselves with the city and explore the surroundings of the area before we have to return our rental car. We read about the Lassithi Plateau, the area of the ten thousand windmills. On our way, a herd of sheep and goats with their curved horns crosses the street and we wait until they are gone.

As we are slowly climbing up to the Plateau, we see one of those windmills beside a small farmhouse not far from the road. Hildegard notices carpets hanging on the clothes line. We turn into the driveway to have a closer look. When the artisan sees us coming, he gets up from his loom and greets us. We admire his work and ask if some of his wall hangings are for sale. He nods and shows us his finished pieces. Hildegard selects two of them; they are beautiful, original and we have met the man who knotted them. To remember this later I ask if I can take a picture of him, his workshop and the windmill. He hesitantly gives me permission.

We drive on to the crest of the hill and read on a sign, 'To the Dikton Andron Caves.' That is where we want to go. It is late afternoon by the time we climb up the steep curvy trail to the entrance of the cave. Only a few people are waiting for the last tour. The guide takes Hildegard by the hand and leads her down slippery steps to the cave. At one point, we have to climb down a ladder to the interior of the cave. There are still active stalactites inside the caves causing stalagmites to form in a variety of bizarre shapes. A little higher, the guide points to a small, hidden cave where, according to legend, Rhea hid baby Zeus, to prevent his being kidnapped by his father Cronos. Hildegard has many questions and so we are the last ones to come out of the caves.

A lonely donkey is standing not far from the entrance. His master, realizing that nobody is needing a ride down anymore, is ready to lead him back to the village. When he sees Hildegard, he asks her if she wants to ride his donkey down the treacherous trail. "I am not charging you anything," he assures her. She is hesitant and does not trust him but I encourage her to take advantage of this kind offer; it will be fun. He helps her into the wooden saddle and leads the donkey cautiously down the hill. When she dismounts, he sheepishly asks if we could buy him a 'beero' since it has been a long hot day. We do not mind and he is happy.

The next morning we have breakfast on the balcony and enjoy the sun and the view. It is Easter Sunday and we go down to the Greek-Catholic church to hear the Easter Mass presented in several languages; it is quite a colorful 'audiovisual' ceremony, which also stimulates our olfactory senses. In the afternoon, we take a leisurely stroll around the bay through narrow streets with steps to higher elevations. We visit the historical museum with exhibits of early pottery and jewelry.

I had returned my car to the rental place, so now we take the bus to Elunda, north of Agios Nikolaos, to discover the ancient submerged city of Olundas. We see some marble structures in the clear water below and pull a small piece of marble with an interesting colorful design out of the water as a souvenir. Elunda has a nice sandy beach. I take a short swim so that I can tell my colleagues and friends 'I swam in the Mediterranean Sea'. Hildegard is not courageous enough to join me; the water is still too cold for her.

On our way to Agios Nikolaos, we saw a street sign to Kritsa. It is mentioned in the tourist guide as one of the most picturesque villages in Crete. It has kept old Cretan customs and traditions alive. We board the bus again to find out if this is true. Kritsa is built on a rocky hill with narrow streets and along them interesting taverns, palaces and churches. Private residences are built around lovely inner courts.

Crete has a stirring history. Starting with the highly developed Minoan, partially matriarchal civilization in the Bronze age and followed later by Roman, Arab, Venetian and Ottoman invasions. Each one has left its mark on the culture, the customs, art and architecture of the island.

We visit the Panagia Kera the most important of the churches in Kritsa. It is a 13th century Byzantine church with three isles, clearly identifiable on the outside and crowned with a typical Byzantine dome. The inside is decorated with beautiful frescoes from different periods, depicting biblical stories, the life of Mary, saints and prophets.

It is a sunny day and Hildegard and I sit in the shadow of a tree and sketch this remarkable building surrounded by old gnarly trees.

Back in Agios Nikolaos, we have one last stroll around the harbor, watching the sunset and walking slowly through the town, saying good-bye to this beautiful place. The next morning we pack our suitcases and go down to the dock to board a boat to the island of Santorini.

When we approach the harbor, we look up to a high steep cliff rising up vertically from the sea. We wonder how we will get up to the top of it. On the boat, we learn to know a British professor, a middle-aged man with long flowing hair and a somewhat inflated ego. He claims to speak Greek and we think he could help us to find a hotel. When the boat docks, we stay close behind him. At the entrance, behind a barrier, a number of men wave and call the names of their hotels. Our new friend speaks to one of them who looks trustworthy. The price he is charging for a night is acceptable. We let him grab our suitcases and we climb aboard his minibus.

He takes us on a roller coaster ride along a road that winds in a dozen sharp serpentines up to the top of the cliff. A short drive along the ridge and we are in a newly developed suburb, south of the city. The Olympia Hotel is a brand new hotel. The bellhop takes our luggage to a bright, well-furnished room on the second floor. We look out of the window and see the lights of the city, which we will explore tomorrow.

Santorini has a very unusual history. Around 1600 BC a gigantic volcanic eruption split the island apart. About half of it broke off and sank down 400m into the Aegean Sea. The larger eastern remnant of the island, in the shape of a crescent, drops down sharply about 400 m into the sea. A few smaller islands, remnants of the west-side of the original island, surround a big caldera in the middle. After the eruption, a sixty m high layer of ashes covered the island and buried the Minoan civilization that had flourished there since the Bronze Age. A few centuries later Phoenicians, Romans and Greek settled there again. Now this beautiful island is visited by many tourists and we are two of them.

We get up early, have a quick breakfast and are on our way through vineyards and an open area to Thira or Fira as some call it. Its architecture is unique. The normal houses have smooth plastered walls and small windows. The roofs are either flat or vaulted. Walls and roofs are painted white to reflect the summer heat. Doors and window frames are usually painted blue, the Greek national colors. The churches have a rectangular tower a little higher than the roof with big rounded openings for the free hanging bells. Usually there are three beside each other and sometimes one small one above.

The city is nestled on the cliff. Since the ground is not flat, the houses are built on terraces, often around a small plaza. Some of the houses are built close to the edge of the cliff only a few flowering bushes separate them from the steep drop-off. Hildegard does not dare to come close to the edge and look down 390 m to the waters of the Aegean Sea. The roads connecting these platforms of different heights are often steep and winding. Several of the side streets are narrow, not wide enough for cars to drive through. This makes a large part of the city, which has only

12,000 inhabitants, a foot passenger zone only. On one of these narrow roads, we meet an old man riding his donkey with a filly following him, a pastoral motif for our cameras. We enjoy walking along the alleys, stopping at little art shops or street displays, looking through open gates into inner courts. Before we realize it, the houses become fewer and we are at the other end of the town. We take a rest on one of the stone benches and look back at this beautiful, picturesque city. The view from here over the caldera and the small islands, which were once part of Santorini, is breathtaking. The weather is in our favor and the sun is getting warm. A narrow, overgrown gravel path, winding along the ridge of the crescent, invites us to go further. There are very few trees at this altitude, which gives us a wide panoramic view. In the distance, we spot a white object between a cluster of trees. This challenges us to investigate. Along our path here and there are big boulders and rocks between a lush groundcover and small bushes. If we bend down, we can identify a variety of small flowers in it. It reminds us almost of Alpine meadows. After half an hour's walk around craters and boulders, we catch up with a lone man riding a donkey along the trail. We try our few Greek words on him and he starts talking excitedly to us. We hear the word 'beero' repeated several times. He turns right from our path and invites us to follow. We smell an adventure and go along. After a short distance we meet the main road and beside it a small tavern which our guide seems to frequent. It is lunchtime and the owner invites Hildegard to the kitchen, opens the fridge and asks her what she would like for lunch. She sees some eggs and orders an omelet. He serves us a simple lunch for a reasonable price. We have fun trying to get a conversation going with body language and the few German words the two men know; they have a sense of humor.

We are back on our original trail again and the white object that drew our attention turns out to be a small monastery. The building is locked. We walk along the narrow arched walkway around an inner court, try every door but none can be opened. We rest in the shade of the trees for a while and look around. Back in the distance, we can make out the white houses of Thira. North on a hill we see again a white shape which looks like another monastery. When we arrive there, it too is uninhabited. It looks, however, as if someone has been here not long ago. We are now more than ten km away from Thira. The hike in the fresh air, with the smell of the flowers from the groundcover was pleasant at the beginning. Now it is hot, and we are getting tired. Down on the north tip of the island we can see the houses of Oio, the second largest town on Santorini. That, we decide, will be our final destination. Besides the donkey rider, we have so far been the only people on the trail. Now two energetic-looking hikers come up from the town below. We recognize them as the Austrian couple from our hotel with whom we started out this morning. They are already on their way back to the hotel. They tell us we have to see Oio. When we walk down to the small sea resort, we know what they mean. The more affluent people seem to live here. Taking advantage of the sloping terrain from the cliffs down to the sea, they built their residences on terraces with patios and swimming pools on different levels, separated by flower planters and connected by winding stairs. The houses are larger with overhanging roofs providing shade from the hot sun. Window walls give them a gorgeous view of the water, the boats and smaller islands.

No large hotel blocks are dominating the town, no smoking factory chimneys; everything seems to blend harmoniously together. Most of the houses are painted white with blue accents, which is another unifying aspect. It is the same in Thira and other villages we have seen. It feels good to walk through these pleasant, wholesome unspoiled settlements.

We are too tired to walk the fifteen km back to our hotel and decide to take a bus back. We assume the bus station will be at the market place and we see a bus standing there.

We ask the bus driver when the next bus to Thira leaves. He tells us this was the last run for the day. He will resume service again tomorrow morning. We are not sure if we understand him correctly, it is only 5:30 pm. When he sees our disappointment, he offers to drive us home for two thousand five hundred Drachmas. A bystander who speaks a little English helps us to communicate with him. She tells us rather to take a taxi; its stand is only two blocks away from here. The taxi driver is eating supper with his family and asks us to wait. After twenty minutes he comes out and will take us to our hotel for eight hundred Drachmas. We accept gladly.

The next morning we sit at the breakfast table with a young Hippie couple from England. They tell us a thrilling experience. They had gone in a boat to Nea Kameni, a small uninhabited Island in the middle of the caldera that resurfaced a few centuries ago from an underground volcano eruption. They missed the boat to go back and had to spend the night on the island. They were not prepared for the cold night. Surprisingly they found a cave beside a huge crater which provided shelter and warmth. They cuddled up in it for the night and were nodding off when they suddenly heard some strange rumblings. They were afraid and looked around to see if someone might have hidden there and was going to rob or assault them. This rumbling continued all night sometimes louder sounding as if something was breaking and falling, sometimes softer like the growling of a bear. They did not close an eye all night and were on guard. The next morning they went to the dock early, waiting for the first boat to take them back. The skipper told them the island is an active volcano it makes all kinds of noises and is sometimes spewing poisonous yellow gasses in the air. It can be very dangerous to stay there. They can be glad to be still alive.

Hildegard cannot leave the island before she has explored the famous archaeological site in Akrotiri. We take the bus to the south end of Santorini. A large area has been excavated, laying open a Minoan settlement that had been buried by a thick layer of ashes from the violent eruption of the volcano several millennia ago. The excavated houses have been fairly well preserved; some of them must have been three stories high and had an advanced drainage system. The layout of the town and the houses with frescoes still visible on some of the walls, the furniture, utensils and pottery that was found there, give us an idea of the culture of that civilization.

The last day we walk down from the cliffs through small villages with gardens and olive groves to the other side of the island. The path goes down gradually towards the beach of the Mediterranean Sea. It is quite a different landscape.

The next morning we take the boat back to Athens. It takes most of the day, since we stop at several Islands en route, with names we remember from Greek mythology.

We have to find a hotel in Athens again and are told of one that is very reasonable, run by students. Since we use the room only for the night, we do not think it matters if it is not so comfortable; during the day, we are out on explorations anyway. The first night is not pleasant. It is noisy until the early morning, the bed creaks when we turn and the mattress is short and hard. The next morning we move out and find a better room in a quieter area on the side of a small park.

We have one more day in Athens and plan a day trip to Delphi. I had suggested going on our own, leaving early by bus and beating the crowds. Hildegard did not want to get up so early and suggests taking the guided tour that was offered from our hotel. The bus comes at 8:30h and picks up people from five other hotels. We finally arrive in Delphi at noon. I count about twenty tour busses on the parking lot already. The path to the excavation site is packed with people. Our short tour guide has put a yellow ribbon on the top of her umbrella, which she holds up to keep our group of fifty together. The information she gives us about Delphi is brief, unspecific and she repeats it in French again. It takes us over an hour to walk the two hundred m to the Apollo Temple. Often we have to wait until the other groups have moved on. We hardly arrive there when it is time for lunch. Hildegard and I skip lunch and wait until most of the people are crowded into the restaurants and souvenir shops. We then get a chance to go closer to the temple ruins, the place of the famous oracle of Delphi. We walk down the steps to the well-preserved amphitheater and imagine ourselves sitting there watching the plays written and performed by Greek dramatists and actors.

We join the group again when they have finished their lunch and board the bus which takes us to our hotel. The next day we fly home.

32. More adventures in Europe

Back in Bielefeld, Hildegard takes our films to the photo shop. When we look at the prints and slides, we relive the trip again and agree, this has very likely been our most memorable vacation experience so far.

Normal life returns, I ride my bike to school to teach my students for their last semester and Hildegard takes care of house arrangements.

One week after our return from Greece, Michael and Tannis pay us a surprise visit. They were married three months before we left on our exchange and this trip is a late honeymoon for them. Michael had visited his former hospital and Doctors in Engelskirchen and Dr. Rechlin had lent him his Mercedes for their vacation. They pick us up and we drive together to some of our relatives and friends in the area. They stay for a few days and then take off on their own.

The Ministry of Education invites us exchange teachers to a study conference in Berlin. My vice principal will provide a substitute to teach my classes so that I can attend.

Experienced educators give us helpful tips and study material to show us how to invigorate our German instruction.

Our hosts want to know how we are managing in our guest schools, if our exchange is valuable for us and, if not, what we would like to see changed. A lively discussion follows. Some teachers are disappointed, they are asked to teach classes they were not prepared to teach and that caused problems. I report, the exchange is very challenging and interesting for me and the staff is very helpful and accommodating to make my stay here as pleasant as possible.

On our guided tour through the city, we visit the 'Hansa Viertel', a new, modern urban district rebuilt from the ruins of the war and designed by renowned architects. We drive along the 'Straße des 17. Juni', the road on which Berliners marched in 1953, demonstrating against unfair treatment by the Soviet occupation force. We stand quietly in front of the Auschwitz Holocaust monument.

I take the lift up to the observation platform of the television tower in East Germany, the tallest in Western Europe at that time. The Berliners call the tower "Die Rache des Papstes" (the Pope's revenge). The light shining on the circular stainless steel dome of the visitor's platform reflects in the form of a cross no matter from where one looks at it. The communist authorities have tried to cover the dome with a dull non-reflecting paint but it had not helped much. The cross seems permanent.

From the visitors platform I have a splendid view of the city. I can follow the run of the 'Mauer' dividing Berlin into East and West Berlin and can see the progress in rebuilding the city after its destruction during the war in both parts of Berlin. There are still many ruins left in the East.

Back in Bielefeld, Hildegard awaits my return anxiously. German schools have a week of holiday at Pentecost and we want to visit Rome during that time. She has already packed her suitcase, I change the clothes in mine and the next day we take the train to Rome.

Ali, Hubertus' brother, has a girlfriend studying in Rome and she can accommodate us. Gina has promised to pick us up from the station but we miss each other. We take the bus to her place. At the bus stop, a passenger warns us not to leave our luggage out of sight. Thieves here are quite clever. They stand beside your suitcase with the lid of a cardboard box in their hand. If you do not watch they will slip it over your suitcase and, in seconds, they will carry the carton away with your suitcase hidden inside.

A bus ride in Rome is a special experience. At the next stop, we think the bus is full and will drive on, as they do in Vancouver, but the driver stops and more people squeeze in. We have hardly room to breathe. The air is so thick that I almost faint.

Gina lives in a suburb and we have to change busses twice. The last one is almost empty and the friendly bus driver, when he sees us two helpless foreigners, takes a detour with his bus to get closer to the area where Gina lives. He shows us the street, which leads to her house. We appreciate his kindness.

Gina, a tall blond young woman, welcomes us and apologizes for leaving the station without us. We had separated to look for her in different parts of the big main station and she had been looking for a couple.

After lunch, we make plans about how best to discover Rome. She thinks we are too ambitious hoping to see all the places we have on our list. We start out with the most sacred place in the Catholic Church, the St. Peter's Basilica in the Vatican City. We cross the huge elliptical court in front of the church, walk up the stairs to the entrance and stand under the balcony from which the pope gives his message to the multitudes. He is not there today.

Five architects were involved in the design and supervision of the building. Bramante started it in the Renaissance and Bernini, one hundred twenty years later, worked on it in the Baroque period. Each architect added his own touch to it. The first impression, when we enter the church through the Porta Santa, is overwhelming. We feel small and unimportant in this vast space of the largest Christian Church in the world. Apparently, sixty thousand people can fit into it. The sun shining through the stained glass windows only dimly lights the interior and our eyes have to get used to the dim light to focus on the details. For us the most impressive of the many chapels is the chapel of the Pieta with Michelangelo's sculpture of Jesus lying in the arms of Mary. He perfected it masterfully in every detail. Many people kneel and pray in different chapels to their favorite Saints.

Through the lantern of the huge Dome, the light shines on Bernini's lofty Baldachin hanging over the Papal Altar and the chair of St. Peter.

The conversation in the church subsides when a procession of bishops and priests in their ornate robes moves slowly past the altar to the covered corridor leading from the basilica to the Castel Saint Angelo, the pope's quarters. We leave the basilica and walk past a long line of people waiting to get into the Vatican Museum, which we want to see tomorrow. The Castel is a huge cylindrical structure originally built as a mausoleum for Emperor Hadrian. Later it was refitted as a fortress and became a refuge and residence for the pope. A large sculpture of Archangel Michael unsheathing his sword crowns the building and gives it its name, Angel's Castle. We walk over the Angel Bridge to the other side of the Tiber River and back to Gina's place. She gives us a good tip to get to the Sistine chapel tomorrow. "Line up early and when you have your ticket, walk straight to the end of the Museum corridors where the chapel is. You will have some time for yourself to see the pictures unobstructed by the crowds which will follow". It is a holiday in Italy and no buses are running, so Gina drives us to the museum. The line is still short when we arrive an hour before opening but when the doors open we cannot see the end of the row of waiting people. We take her advice and rush in. We have to forgo the temptation to stop and look at several of the paintings of well-known artists and displays especially the one of modern sacred sculptures. The sign 'Capella Sistine' shows us the way to the end of the museum halls and we reach the Sistine Chapel before the crowds arrive. We are overwhelmed by these powerful paintings. Seeing this alone is worth a trip to Rome.

Only five people are in the chapel. I am the only one who lies on the floor, not to strain my neck to study intensely Michelangelo's marvelous ceiling paintings, nine large panels describing the creation of the world. We had looked at prints of the Sistine Chapel in Hildegard's art collection and our art history-professor, had talked about it extensively in his lectures. Now we both have an opportunity to see the originals. The paintings had just been restored and now shine in their original brilliance. Michelangelo's large creation of Adam and Eve in the middle panels of the ceiling, God reaching out to Adam and transferring the spark of life to him, indicate that the 'sculptor', Michelangelo, painted these powerful figures. Very impressive is the Last Judgment, which fills the back wall over the altar. In the middle is the youthful Christ with Mary at his side and a multitude of nude figures moving up and down in the picture. Michelangelo's thesis was, 'no beauty exists outside the human form'.

We have less than half an hour to meditate on these paintings before the crowds start to move in and block our view. It is impossible to swim against the crowd to go back and see the exhibits we missed, so we are moved with it to the entrance and then start over again. The room with Raphael's large tapestries, the paintings of the old masters and the excellent exhibit of modern sacred sculptures interest both of us.

We are glad when we can unwind from the crowds inside and get some fresh air.

We walk to the Tiber, cross the Ponte Sista, and can see the famous Pantheon Copula from a distance already. We are disappointed when we see scaffolding around the eight column wide square portico and find out it is locked. The outside of the building looks ugly in its present state but the inside is supposed to be beautiful in its proportion and decoration. Since 609AD the Pantheon has been used as a church. This is the reason why it is in relatively good condition as the best retained antique building in Rome.

We walk on from here to the Piazza Navona with its three famous fountains. There are many of them in Rome. Bernini's 'Fountain of the Four Rivers' draws our special attention. We admire the masterfully sculpted four male figures grouped around a tall Egyptian obelisk with hieroglyphic inscriptions. They personify the four then-known continents and are symbols for their main rivers, Danube, Ganges, Nile, and Rio Della Plata. It is interesting for us to observe how the artist directs the water from the aqueduct to and through the fountain figures. In the Four River Fountain, the water flows like a river from under the reclining figures and spills over into the big basin. In the 'Fountain of the Moor', the water flows out of the mouth of the fabled creatures and the sea god Triton spills it out of a shell from which he is drinking.

From the fountains we meander to another popular tourist attraction, the 'Spanish Steps'. Wide stairs divided by narrow flowerbeds lead from the Piazza Spagna up to the church of Santa Trinita dei Monte. Groups of young people sit on the steps, some singing folksongs accompanied by guitars and others having lively discussions a few steps up.

A car drives up and young newly-weds with their attendants come down to the stairs to have their pictures taken besides the colorful flowers on the sides and between the divided steps. There is a coming-and-going all the time.

On the way back we walk up to Capitol Hill, one of the seven Hills of Rome. Michelangelo designed an open plaza on top of it, with palaces along its sides for nobility and for Government offices. Now they house the Capitoline Museum.

It has been an exhausting day. On our way home via the bridge over Tiber Island, we discover in the back of an old Romanesque church, partly hidden by trees, an inner court with modern sculptures. We walk back the narrow path to St.Bartholomew, an early Christian Church, and are surprised to find in its entrance hall two modern bronze statues, a three m high St.Franziscus and a tall female figure, the Annunciation. They remind me of my favorite German sculptor, Barlach. We enter the dimly lit church and see a monk in front of the altar. When we approach he turns towards us and I ask him if we can see the sculpture exhibit advertised on the poster in the entrance hall. Pater Martini, a kind monk, about my age, grabs my hand, welcomes us and leads us down a dark stairway behind the sacristy to his modest workshop. He is the sculptor and the sculptures we saw in front of the church and in the courtyard are his work. His slender semi-abstract figures are in dynamic motion and rhythm, athletes, dancers, children playing, saints blessing. We are surprised to see such lively sculptures being done by an elderly monk. He seems to enjoy talking to us, fellow artists, who appreciate his work.

This visit makes a good conclusion to this day's excursions.

In the evening, Gina invites us to a party and introduces us to a special guest. Frau Dr.Ingrid Warburg-Spinelli, from a renowned Jewish banker's family from Hamburg and New York. To escape Hitler's persecution of Jews, she immigrated to America and became active in the German resistance movement in the USA. She knew Count Klaus von Stauffenberg who tried to assassinate Hitler and Adam von Trott who had tried unsuccessfully to find support in America for the overthrow of the Nazi dictatorship. She has written several books about that time. Now she lives in Rome but her heart is still in Germany. She has no hatred against Germans. We have a very interesting conversation with her.

The next morning we take the bus to downtown Rome. Our aim is to see the Colosseum; most of this huge antique building is now in ruins. It was planned as an amphitheatre, was destroyed by fire and earthquakes, and was rebuilt to serve as an arena for spectators to watch gladiator duels, Christians falling prey to voracious lions, war games and animal hunts. They tell us that about one-half million people and one million animals have been killed within these walls.

We are overwhelmed by the immensity of the building. When we step inside, we look at a forty-eight m high wall three stories high with tall arches held up by slender columns and an arcade and attic on top of these. We look down into deep tunnels where animals and slaves were kept.

At present, the Colosseum has become a multi-purpose building, a gathering place for protestors against capital punishment, a backdrop for rock concerts and a shrine to honor the Christian martyrs of ancient times, a pilgrimage place. On Good Friday, the Pope leads a procession to the Stations of the Cross, which have been erected inside. The Colosseum is one of the most popular tourist attractions of Rome.

We walk a short distance to the ruins of the Forum Romanum, the centre of ancient Rome's activities. Some columns from basilicas and palaces of different Emperors are still standing. Emperor Augustus erected a gilded bronze monument there, the Millarium Aureum, point zero, from which the distance from Rome to other places is measured. All roads begin from here. The phrase, 'All roads lead to Rome' relates to this.

From the many basilicas and churches in Rome, we single out two. Santa Maria Maggiore, built in the 4th century, is the oldest basilica in Rome, which has retained its original design. In its interior are still a number of old mosaic murals and a beautiful Mary and Child Icon.

The other one is Il Gesu. I am very interested to see this church; it exemplifies the turning point from the Renaissance to the Baroque style in architecture. The strict rules of classical architecture of the Renaissance change to more open, decorative designs to make the new Baroque churches brighter and more joyful.

Our last day has come. Gina takes us to the railway station on her way to work. We want to take the night train and still have time to explore another part of Rome. We stroll along the former Circus Maximus. It is now a park and a few excavations on one end and the monumental Arch of Titus on the other are remnants of the famous ancient chariot racetrack.

It is lunchtime and in an authentic little Italian restaurant, we have to help the waiter figure out the price for our meal. He charged us one thousand lire too much. I do not know if this was intentional.

We take the bus to the southern part of Rome along the Via Apia to visit the catacombs. The entrance to the Sebastian catacomb is through an old basilica. We join a German tour. The guide leads us down small stairs through narrow passages often only one meter wide and shows us the burial places of early Christian Martyrs, the small caves, carved into the soft volcanic brownish-gray tuff stone. He takes us four stories down. The passageways widen to form small chapels where Christians may have gathered for a burial ceremony. Some of the walls of these chapels are decorated with simple frescos of Christian symbols and inscriptions of names and messages of hope scratched into the soft stone. The guide points out the names of Peter and Paul who may have visited here. We end up in the basilica again.

We do not want to stand and wait for the bus so we walk back on the narrow cobblestone paved Via Appia. High walls run down the sides of it and some parts are broken down. The long straight road seems to be a racetrack for sports cars. We watch one race down and pass another car so closely that we feel sure they must scratch each other. When the bus comes, we squeeze into it and it takes us right to the station.

Hildegard reserves two window seats in the sleeper car to Munich while I claim our suitcases. For a while, we enjoy our train ride through the beautiful Toscana landscape. When it gets dark, we pull our seats forward to make it into a bed and rest. The next day in the afternoon, we arrive in Bielefeld. Hubertus picks us up from the station. We have lots to share with him.

Before we went to Rome, we had seen an ad in the newspaper 'Adventure Siberia' a two week trip through Russia. Hildegard is interested; she had always wanted to see the country where her mother was born. It does not take much to persuade her to take advantage of this opportunity.

The day after our return from Rome, I take her to the bus station downtown and she boards the tourist bus to Berlin with forty other adventurers. The crossing to East Germany and East Berlin is smooth. From there they have to wait for a flight to Kiev, which leaves at four o'clock in the morning. She has a window seat and, looking out, she is amazed at the vast green spaces, fields and woods below. When she steps onto the tarmac in Kiev, she is tempted to kiss the ground; "This is the land where my mother was born 83 years ago".

A bus takes the group from the airport to their hotel, a modern 33 story building. Hildegard had already chosen a potential hotel partner in Bielefeld, Monika, a 30-year-old light-blond secretary. She has a Slavic looking face and could be a genuine Russian. When the two have arranged themselves in their hotel room, there is a knock at the door. When they hesitantly open it, a young man asks them politely if they want to exchange currency, one DM for one Ruble or two. The official rate is three DM for one Ruble. They are afraid this could be a trap and they decline. Later at the dinner table one of the group asks if anyone needs Rubles and Hildegard thinks this is safer and exchanges at the rate of 1:2. Things here are relatively cheap in price and quality. She finds that out on their first guided tour. The tour operator has arranged for translators, who are knowledgeable and speak German well. They visit a baroque palace, the one thousand year old St. Sophia Basilica with old frescos and mosaics and a 9th century Cave Monastery. This is something that communists normally do not value. Hildegard resolves to re-evaluate her image of Communist Russia, which had done so much harm to her Mother's family. She wants to be open and experience this country now without prejudice. She is annoyed about the macho men in her group who criticize everything that is different or not as comfortable as it is in Germany.

The program allows them some free time. Hildegard separates from the group, goes down to the Dnjepr River, which also flows through the former German-Mennonite settlements where her mother's family lived, and gathers some yellow sand from its bank and some dark soil from the land to take home to her mother as a memento.

In the evening, a Ukrainian folklore group performs some dances in the lobby of the hotel.

An Aeroflot Airbus flies them to Chabarowsk in the east part of Russia. The interior of the plane is so dilapidated and worn out that Hildegard is afraid to fly in it. She has a window seat again and looks down on the wide fields. When the Ural Mountains appear she thinks of her relatives who had been deported to labor camps beyond the Ural Mountains and died there.

The group was again taken to the large Intourist Hotel, a four star hotel on the outside and a two star on the inside.

The program in Chabarowsk starts with a city-tour, ending in the nature museum. They learn about the wild life of the area, the Siberian tiger, the arctic wolf and black bear. A small group hires a boat for a cruise on the mighty Amur River.

One of the highlights is a meeting with the Soviet-German Friendship Club. The members are mainly language students and staff from the teacher's college who welcome the group in the lounge. They sit in small groups to talk or play games to help break the ice. The invitation to dance does not find much response. The Germans would rather talk and learn more about the life and aspirations of their hosts.

Lena, a pretty girl in her last year of German and English instruction, is happy when she finds out Hildegard speaks English. She would like to travel when she is finished.

Time comes to leave and Lena walks Hildegard to the bus. Before they part, she asks Hildegard for her address. A few years later, we get a phone call from Seattle; Lena wants to come to Vancouver and asks if she can stay a few days with us.

The event for which all in the group had been waiting, the journey on the legendary Trans-Siberian Railroad, becomes reality. For three days, the forty people are together in close quarters and Hildegard describes in her diary her observations of the group dynamics.

Nilguen and Ilse, two social workers from Bielefeld, join Hildegard and Monika as roommates in their train compartment. These four are known as 'the Feminists'. Hildegard appreciates Monika, because of her rational attitude towards life. She seems to charm almost all men she meets and even on the street men turn their heads to see who this blond woman is. There is Oppa Otto, a gentle, widely travelled, knowledgeable geologist who has an artificial lung. The 'Goofy one', is a white haired big-bellied man with 'diarrhea of the mouth'. Christa, a sharp-tongued older nurse who has been in Russia twice, is telling everybody how to act. Her comments are not meant to be funny but she has everyone in stitches. And there is Detlev, the tour leader, who can be serious, cynical and critical, but is mostly flippant. Then again he can be a' young kid' who endears himself to almost everyone. They are an interesting mix of people. Hildegard's compartment is a magnet for many because most of the serious discussions take place here. In addition to this, Ilse has German toilet paper, Monika candies and vodka, Nilguen chocolate and Hildegard good coffee. They are well prepared.

There is a lot of flirting going on. Some people lose their temper and self-control others are very sensitive and polite. This experience brings out the best and worst in people. Being with them, Hildegard is reminded of Michael's observation, 'Germans cannot just state facts, they always make an editorial comment'.

The train rattles along for miles across swampy land, changing to hilly country with the occasional small village. Those that are not ghost towns consist of small wooden huts. They have two or three windows across the front wall and are covered with corrugated tin roofs. Once in a while, they see a cemetery between trees. Many of her relatives died in this inhospitable land while in exile. They very likely would not have been buried in a grave with a small fence around it. Occasionally they see some people working in their garden or going to work, dressed in heavy clothing since it is still cold here. It looks like a very poor area.

After almost twenty hours of travel, the train stops at a station and the passengers have time to go out and look around or buy something. Old women wrapped in black kerchiefs offer their garden produce, boiled potatoes, canned mushrooms, salted pickles and Sauerkraut wrapped in dough pockets to passengers. They are shy and do not want to be photographed. On one of these stops, Hildegard meets Genia, a 15-year-old Russian boy. She gives him a lighter, which she had brought and was told kids appreciate them. He is surprised and his eyes light up. He is travelling on the same train and makes it a habit to walk through their compartment, wink and smile at her. Finally he gets the courage to come up to Hildegard and give her his snake ring, "a souvenir from Russia" he says. He has been holidaying in Chabarowsk and is going home to Moscow. He wants to become an engineer. Hildegard is moved by this 'gift of friendship'.

The train moves through more hilly country and the villages become more frequent. Expanses of purple flowers pass by the window; they are Siberian Rhododendrons often growing under the white birches, typical for this part of Russia. The stewardess, whom Hildegard had asked for the name of the flowers, brings her a branch and she puts it in a glass on the table in their compartment.

The landscape changes again. The hills become snow-capped mountains. The country is more populated, the roads are paved and a lonely car and a few motorcycles are moving on them. The small villages grow to towns as they approach the rim of Lake Baikal. Soon the train moves into Irkutsk main station. This is the end of the train ride, for Hildegard, probably, a high point of her Russian adventure tour.

The hotel, to which they are taken, has a very impressive lobby with an artistic mural on the back wall, created with birch bark inlay The guest rooms, however, are dirty and the shower in their room is leaking, causing a small flood in front of Monika's bed.

The atmosphere in Irkutsk strikes them as completely different from that of Chabarowsk. There, tourists were a rarity and people eyed them with hidden curiosity. Here they seem to be an inconvenience and people are almost hostile, from the bus driver to the waitress in the dining room.

The next morning they are ready for the city tour. Marnia, their lovely hostess, gives them the background history of the area. They pass by a church, the oldest stone building in the city. The tour guide walks with them through the old section of town with one-story houses, decorated with colorfully painted shutters and lace-like carved decorations. In the newer section are rows of six story rectangular boxes in different pastel tones and different states of disrepair, typical for the style of the last four decades of Communist architecture. Their stroll ends in the foot passenger zone. They have time to window-shop and find that the quality of displayed goods is not as good as those in Western Europe. Hildegard and Monika stop at a huge fur collecting and sorting place with a wide variety of pelts on display. There is one from the arctic wolf, the red and blue fox and a few white ones of the smaller arctic foxes. Beside the smooth furs of the otter lie the soft mink and sable pelts. Monika takes a picture of Hildegard with a wolf fur on her lap. The wolf is a kind of mystical animal for her.

The next morning a bus takes them to the Baikal Lake. A big earthquake, millions of years ago, left a wide crescent-shaped crack in the earth crust, which filled with water. It is the deepest freshwater lake on earth and has a volume of water more than the Great Lakes in USA and Canada together. The water is a strong turquoise blue and its purity is unmatched.

The group is taken to a typical Siberian Village and given some free time to explore. Hildegard is searching for the white birch woods through which her mother had walked as a child. She gathers several flowers to press when she comes home. She will ask her mother if she still remembers them. A climb up a steep hill rewards them with a panoramic view of the lake.

On their flight to Bratsk, the plane flies low and they can follow the wide expanse of the taiga.

Bratsk was built in a hurry, they are told, with no cohesion between the eight different settlements. The old ones still have two story wooden houses, the new ones high-rises and lots of empty space in between. Bratsk supplies 3% of Russia's electricity and the group is taken on a tour to see the large dam on the Angara River. They are allowed to observe the operation of the big turbines.

In contrast to this technology, they undergo a time shift and visit a museum in the Taiga with tools, clothing and artifacts of the original inhabitants that lived there before it was industrialized.

Down at the lake they walk through a reconstructed village with houses from the time of the early Russian settlers. Hildegard wants to see the large oven in the house on which people slept in extreme cold winter nights, as her mother had told her. Now she can imagine what it was like in her mother's time.

The tour operator wants to provide the group with some Russian folklore. He has arranged for folk singers to play and sing Russian folksongs. In the evening, a band plays dance music. Hildegard enjoys listening to the music and watching her friends dance but, when the vodka consumption reaches a certain level, she retreats to her room and goes to bed.

The next day they take off for Moscow. The airplane, which takes them to Moscow, is a little roomier than the one they took to Chabarowsk. A crew member sees one of their group take pictures of the airport and the airplane. This is forbidden. He had also taken pictures illegally of the dam and the turbines. The airport security comes and confiscates the film from his camera. He is mad and curses the 'Stalinist regime' until some of the other passengers silence him.

Soon they are circling Moscow. Hildegard has a window seat again and looking out, she has a bird's eye view of the spread out city.

A bus takes them from the airport to their hotel on the outskirts of the city surrounded by parks. After Hildegard and Monika have settled in their 28th floor room, lunch is awaiting them in a plush dining room on the top floor. The waiter discreetly asks them if they want to exchange money 1:3. They do him the favor.

Detlev, their tour leader, has organized the traditional city tour. When they step out of the bus at 'Red Square' Hildegard is quite surprised by the impressive surroundings of the square. Influenced by the anti-communist propaganda she had imagined it to be a dismal place.

Christa, their new tour guide, tells her that red, in Russian, can refer to the color 'red' but it can also mean 'beautiful'. Hildegard thinks the latter applies more to what she is seeing, 'lots of lovely cathedrals, palaces and museums'. Spring has come and the park is full of blooming lilac trees and luscious green lawns. People sit on benches and enjoy the sunshine. In the park is a monument for the unknown- soldier with an eternal flame. People solemnly lay flowers down in front of it. For newly-weds, it seems to be a special occasion to be photographed in their wedding finery placing flowers on the steps of the monument.

While they are sightseeing around Red Square, they watch the changing of the guard in front of Lenin's Mausoleum. Lines of schoolchildren pass by their dead leader.

Gum, Moscow's famous department store, is nearby and many of the group like to see what is offered there and to compare prices. People line up everywhere. Christa mentions the food shortage in Moscow. Since Gorbatschow has granted the Ukraine a kind of semi-independence, they can keep the food they produce in their country and ship only the surplus to Moscow which has reduced the supply considerably. There is a need for an organized distribution system or they will have to introduce ration cards again.

In the evening, Detlev invites those who are interested to a night excursion of Moscow's 'Red Square'. They take the underground train and Hildegard is amazed at the beauty of the underground stations. They look like halls in the Tsar's castle. Different cities competed with each other to decorate one of these stations with stucco ornaments, mosaics and paintings. The group has never seen a metro that grandiose before. When they surface at Red Square, a full moon is just rising over the Basilius Cathedral. It is a moment of awe and magic. They walk around for a while but are too tired to do much else and soon return to their hotel.

For the last evening Detlev has planned a farewell party in a posh hotel, with lots of champagne, caviar and a floorshow. The consumption of food goes on all night and conversation is only possible when the music stops. It is a typical American variety show with rock and roll music. They find it strange that this kind of entertainment has penetrated Russia. It is so alien to Russian culture,

Hildegard and some of the more thoughtful people from her group find it immoral that the tourists are served food in abundance and Russian families have to stand in line for basic food items and sometimes do not have enough to feed their children. Her friend had not been able to buy milk and cheese for three months, the Russian tour guide tells them. She is quite outspoken, criticizing injustice and had been called in for questioning by the KGB (secret police) for her criticism and her connections to the West. She fears she might be sent to Siberia into a concentration camp one day.

Affected by the excessive consumption of alcohol, the party turns ugly, Hildegard, and some of her friends decide to leave.

This is the farewell to the Siberian adventure. Flying back and looking down from her window seat over Russia, on the steppe, the rivers and villages, Hildegard reflects on her Russian experience.

> 'With a heavy heart I take leave of Russia, my mother's homeland, cruising over Poland, Helmut's and my father's homeland and East Germany, a country in captivity to an idea. I have come on this journey to correct prejudices, to meet people, to bring together fact and fantasy, to be an ambassador of good will.
>
> Why can we not live together in peace and share the earth's riches and food so that everyone can enjoy life?'

They arrive in Berlin and board the tour bus to Bielefeld. The formalities at the border take only twenty minutes and, a few hours later, I pick her up from the bus station. I had bought a bouquet of roses to welcome her back and am happy that she is home again. While she was gone, I worked hard preparing my graduating classes for their final examinations. I am now in the process of marking them. Fortunately, I do not have to give oral examinations in my design and drawing classes.

To get away from schoolwork for a change, Hildegard and I take a long walk through the Teutoburger Forest. The sun is shining and the leaves and early flowers give the woods some spring color and fragrance. In the evening, we are invited to a birthday party for one of my colleagues. It is a fun party. We sit on the garden patio and sing folksongs, something we have not done for a long time. Arnold accompanies us with his guitar. They are quite surprised that we can sing most of the songs with them.

School comes to an end and I have to issue report cards. I know I have to justify every mark below an A. My students are critical but fair and when they hear my explanations for how I evaluated their work, they accept my judgment. I am glad that this part of my exchange year is over.

I have a number of mature students in my classes, fine people, and I enjoyed teaching them. With some I exchange addresses and they tell me, when I say good-bye, that they might visit me in Canada. Many of my colleagues have been wonderful and helpful friends.

Some friends from Canada, John and Lucia, from our former house-fellowship, and Sherry and Bob, from Castle Mountain, visit us in Bielefeld; we are hosts, interpreters and tour guides for them. There are many interesting places in and around Bielefeld to explore. We begin with the lovely Bürgerpark café, where we enjoy a cup of coffee with a piece of tasty Black Forest cake while listening to the news from home. Then we hike up to the Sparrenburg, take in the view of the city and the forest and walk back through the Teutoburger Wald. They love the beautiful small medieval towns around Bielefeld.

My sister phones to say that my mother has unexpectedly been admitted to hospital. At the age of 93, we do not know what may happen to her, so we decide to change our departure date and leave earlier than planned to be home with my mother when she needs me.

My school friend Rolf had offered us his summerhouse in Catalonia, near the Mediterranean Sea and we had been looking forward to spending our last two weeks in Spain but we have to cancel that,

The time comes for us to say farewell to our old and new friends, and our relatives here, before we go back to Canada. On our way to visit Hildegard's uncle Herbert, we drive through the Sauerland area. Checking the map, we see, mentioned as a special attraction, 'Atta Höhle'. To our surprise, we find out it is the largest and perhaps most attractive dripstone cave in Germany. It is not as monumental as the Carlsbad caves or the Dicton Caves in Crete but it is easier to access and better prepared for tourists. In the caves and hallways, we see the pointed stalagmites having formed bizarre spiral stalactites at the floor. Hildegard is fascinated again by this process and its shapes.

En route to Adelheid, we can see from a distance the tower of the Ronneburg castle. It invites us for a break. In the rustic restaurant of this

13th century castle, we have a snack and walk around for awhile. I still remember it from our Mennonite Voluntary Service Workers retreat where I met Hildegard's oldest sister for the first time.

We try to avoid the Autobahn and drive along country roads through picturesque villages and medieval towns.

Jutta, my former schoolmate, writes that she would like to renew our friendship and asks if we could drop in before we leave. She lives in an extended suburb of Munich. It is over 40 years since we graduated from high school together. We have a lot to catch up on and she confides to me that she had had a crush on me in school, of which I regrettably had not been aware. In her open friendly way, she quickly befriends Hildegard.

Her husband, a retired history professor in Munich, gives us a condensed, illustrated historical overview of Bavarian art and architecture. He drives us to the Wieskirche, the jewel of late Baroque Churches in Europe.

It is not so easy to say farewell to our homeland with its historical treasures and the people we love. When we are packing our suitcases, I ask Hildegard, "Do you think you could live here again?" She waits a moment, "I think I could, if our children were here too." When we have packed everything, Hubertus makes room in his station wagon for our luggage. As we slowly drive out of Bielefeld to the Amsterdam airport, we hear on the radio of our neighbor across the street the well-known German farewell song

"Muss i denn, muss i denn zum Städele hinaus… und Du mein Schatz bleibst hier"

(I have to leave this lovely town and you my darling will stay here) very suitable for our situation

We say good-bye to Bielefeld and Hubertus, a true friend. We say good-bye to our guest country, our former homeland, Germany, and fly back to Canada.

33. Retirement

Our plane from Frankfurt to Vancouver is fifty Minutes ahead of schedule. We have time to claim our luggage, go through customs and are ready for the welcoming party to arrive when we see our children coming through the gate. Hanno, Krista and Philip greet us enthusiastically and are surprised that we have been waiting for them already. We are happy to see them again and have much to share. Philip and Hanno pack our five suitcases in Philip's pick-up truck and we are on our way home. Krista tells us that Oma is in hospital for a check-up with her broken hip, so we stop by at the Richmond Hospital to pay her a short visit. Mother is glad that we are back, healthy and content and that she can see us once more. We tell her briefly about our experiences during the last year and bring her greetings from our relatives. We promise to come again soon, stay a little longer and show her pictures from our exchange year in Germany.

When we drive into our carport a big 'Welcome Mom and Dad' sign greets us, Krista's creation. The children have cleaned and decorated the house nicely and it feels good to be home again in our spacious rooms with that panoramic view of water and mountains. It will take a while to get used to the old routines again. Our neighbors and friends come over and welcome us back warmly.

While still in Bielefeld, I had written to our school superintendant that I plan to retire when I come back from my exchange year. For thirty years, I have taught grades 11 and 12 at Burnaby South Senior Secondary school. As Department Head of art and modern languages, I have been my own boss in regards to course arrangement and have practically designed my own curriculum. I have been quite active in school functions and have enjoyed teaching in this environment.

Things have changed now. Our school has amalgamated with the Junior Secondary school and the school population has almost doubled. My art facilities have been divided to create additional classrooms.

Since there are just two more years remaining before I *have* to retire, I feel that teaching under these conditions would not be worth the extra stress I would experience staying on.

Hildegard and I are aware that retiring two years earlier will reduce my monthly pension but we accept this for the benefit we believe we will gain. Our eventful exchange year in Germany is a good conclusion of my teaching career and I send the letter of resignation to the school board. We now have the time and freedom to pursue our hobbies and our love for traveling together.

It seems as if my mother had waited for our return from Bielefeld to see us once more before leaving us forever. We visited her a few times in the hospital and she was ready to be dismissed back to her Pinegrove senior's home. Her niece Eva and Herbert think aunt Selma needs some change from the hospital environment and invite her and our family to their country home. Oma always enjoys the outdoors. She lies in the lawn chair picking grapes from the overhanging vines, listening to our stories and commenting on Herbert's well-done barbeque chicken.

When we notice that Mother is getting tired, we are going to take her home. Hildegard and Magdalena help her walking back to the road. Shortly before they reach the car, she collapses and the two hold their unconscious mother in their arms. We call the ambulance and they drive her to the Abbotsford hospital. She remains in a coma and the family takes turns keeping watch beside her bed all the time. I tell her stories from my childhood and our travels together, read favorite scripture verses and quietly sing some of her favorite hymns at her bedside. I do not know whether she can still hear me and perceive them. She never regains consciousness from her stroke and, after nine days, she passes peacefully into a better world where she wanted to be. She is almost 94 years old.

Sherbrooke Mennonite Church is filled to the last seat for her memorial service. Our friend, John, sings a solo, 'In Dir ist Freude in allem Leide'

(There is joy in you, even in sorrow), a song well suited to describe her life. Many remember her as a very positive, friendly and helpful person, one who lived her faith openly and honestly, never complaining.

For us as a family and especially for me, who had lived with her through the terrible years during and after the war, she will always be an example of humility, thankfulness and encouragement. We will miss her.

After our return from Germany, I attend West Coast Christian Fellowship again. The new pastor from England is preaching. At the end of the service, during the announcements our friend Margret stands up and openly welcomes me back after my year of absence. I thank her. The pastor, as usual, dismisses the parishioners at the exit door after the service and chats with them. He also shakes my hand but does not inquire who I am. Barney always welcomed guests and strangers personally when he was pastor.

The same happens a few Sundays later when Margret expresses her condolence on behalf of the congregation at the death of my mother. The pastor does not say a word to me at the door. I also notice that some of the Elders with whom I had worked in the church council do not seem to 'recognize' me anymore. They may still have difficulty with the way Hildegard left the church. I feel somewhat alienated and it becomes clear to me, I do not belong here anymore. I write a letter to the leadership and let them know that I have decided to leave West Coast Christian Fellowship.

If I had done this six years ago, Hildegard and I might have been spared the tension in our relationship. But at that time, I still had responsibilities in church affairs, was perhaps too loyal and not yet ready to leave.

I get a form letter back from the church secretary saying that they will transfer my membership.

34. Closing the Circle

At this time, John Friesen invites us to a fund raising dinner for the *'Menno Simons Centre'*. The Premier of BC will be the guest speaker. It sounds interesting and Hildegard and I go to find out what the function of this centre is.

A group of Mennonites from different congregations, most of them related in some way to the University of BC, took out mortgages on their homes to buy a Catholic Convent which was in the process of closing its doors. They had a vision to transform the twenty-five rooms, where the nuns had lived, to student residences, especially for students who are not familiar with city and university life. *Menno Simons Center* was to become a safe place for Mennonite and other students to congregate and meet fellow students, to find support and friendship while studying at UBC. House parents are living with them and manage the place. They welcome new students, help them to adjust to communal living and university life.

Since the convent is located close to UBC, it is very suitable for this purpose. The little chapel makes a beautiful quiet gathering place for students during the week and for a supporting congregation on Sunday mornings.

Menno Simons Center brings back memories. It is the fulfillment of one of my dreams from twenty-three years ago.

At that time I was a member of the Bible School committee in Sherbrooke Mennonite Church. The old Bethel Bible School building in Abbotsford did not meet building code standards anymore and had to be closed. We had a vision to relocate it to Burnaby, near the newly established Simon Fraser University, since there was a Mennonite Brethren Bible School in Abbotsford already. Burnaby is easily accessible for Mennonites from the Abbotsford and Vancouver area. A Bible College near the campus with lecture halls, residences and a chapel could serve students from the Bible College as well as those from the university. They could enroll in courses in both institutions. The chapel of the college was planned as a gathering place for students to be shared on Sundays with a supporting Mennonite fellowship.

The leadership of the Mennonite churches did not share this vision; they felt 'the humanistic influence of the university could unsettle the faith of our students'.

I now see this vision partly realized in the Menno Simons Center and am looking forward to becoming part of this congregation that is supporting this venture.

I share with Hildegard that I plan to join Point Grey Fellowship. She finds it good but is not ready yet to join me, she still is looking for alternatives to the institutionalized church.

Since our year in Germany, Hildegard and I are able to talk about faith and church with a more open mind in a relaxed attitude. We sit in the living room together and reminisce about the past. My sculptures, which Hildegard has put on the shelf under the sky-light, express my feelings during that time of tension, in different stages in our relationship. I remember carving them thoughtfully during those years.

The first sculpture was inspired by the story of the prodigal son. It shows the dual personality and temperament of a person. One, the upright, enterprising strong one, is looking forward to mastering life, the other, reflective, humble, down on one knee, emerges from under the mantle of the first.

The next one also shows two sides, 'character traits' of the same form. A female torso is clutching a rectangular shape, 'the tablet'. One side of the torso is smooth, the other is rough, unfinished. 'The tablet' is elevated, perfect, smooth on both sides.

In another one, I carved two people from one block of soapstone. The male form, upright is looking into space, searching, slightly turned towards the female form as if listening. The female form connected to the first one at the back, is seated, looking down in the opposite direction, somewhat defiant. Her hands are pulling her knees up.

The sequel expresses again a male form standing close to a female one. This time they are turned towards each other, hands lifted, reaching out to each other. The last one is a harp player. Music draws people together, unites them, we both love music.

It seems that I can express and communicate my emotions better with my hands in art than articulate them in words. Hildegard would like me to be able to do both.

I am now attending the services at Point Grey Fellowship regularly. On the first Sunday, a familiar face greets me at the door, Rick, the youngest son of cousin Erwin. I have known him as a small boy. He is now a student and a resident at the Menno Simons Center. Rick introduces me to the other members of the congregation. Some of them I had met at former Mennonite conferences. Most of them are connected in some way to UBC. They are studying or teaching there or have been graduates of the university. At first, I am a little intimidated, sitting beside professors, doctors, lawyers and accountants, but they are very open and informal and soon I feel at home in this small congregation.

Pastor Palmer explains the order of the Sunday service to me and mentions the 'Forum', a talk about applied faith, which precedes the service, in place of Sunday school. When he learns that I am an architect and art teacher, he asks me if I am willing to give a talk about faith and art. I have never attended these forums before and do not know the format of it. I agree somewhat hesitantly.

I prepare a 'lecture' on Christian art and try to show how faith has inspired artists to create Icons and catacomb paintings, I try to explain the meaning of symbols they use in early Christian paintings, and the use of light to illuminate Rembrandt's biblical figures in the Baroque period.

I try to compare illustrations of biblical themes done by painters of different art periods.

A dozen people listen graciously. The pastor afterwards asks if I am willing to give another talk. So I prepare a 'lecture' on Church architecture. I point out that Church architecture in the early Christian era and in the Middle Ages was influenced by the people's faith, image and understanding of God. The house of God was the most important building in town, visible from far away.

People needed Saints to mediate between them and God. Artists responded by creating visible images of male and female saints in two and three-dimensional form and placed them in little chapels along the interior wall and around the apse.

The appearance of the Cathedrals depended on the use of building materials and the available technology. The barrel vault required a solid almost fortress-like structure while the ribbed vault allowed large wall openings for stained glass windows. There the architect in me was carried away, became a little too technical for the listeners and lost them. I think the purpose of the Forum was more to share how my faith influences my work as a professional. The forum is discontinued after my two deliberations.

After my last talk, Hedie, one of the members at PGF, tells me about the MCC Social Housing Society of which she is a director. They are looking for another director and she thinks I would be a suitable candidate. I am interested in finding out more about it and attend one of their board meetings. The work MCC is doing, helping people in need to find affordable housing, appeals to me and since it is in my field of expertise I accept the responsibility of becoming a director. We have a very good working relationship in the society and I soon make friends with the other directors and staff.

I have seen many changes during the seventeen years as a director, secretary and co-chair of the society. When I started in 1990 we managed one housing project, now we are building the eighth one and, in addition, manage five homes for handicapped persons, serving close to one thousand people in need.

Our church also undergoes a name change. Point Grey Fellowship becomes Point Grey Inter-Mennonite Fellowship, PGIMF. The founding members of Menno Simons Center and the congregation are from Mennonite and Mennonite Brethren churches and we feel our name should indicate this and should include our Anabaptist heritage. I make a sign from small cedar planks with the new name on it to identify our fellowship to newcomers.

We are also looking for a new pastor. The candidate we have in mind turns out to be unsuitable. We are disappointed and consider using the potential in our own congregation, Bible School graduates and university teachers, to lead our services. Our chapel is close to UBC and Regent College, the theological seminary, so we can invite teachers or graduate students to take an active part in our services. Being without a paid pastor inspires us members to become more involved in taking on responsibilities for church activities.

We are affiliated with two national Mennonite conferences and often invite itinerant pastors or conference officials to speak in our services. We take turns, encourage and help students to prepare a worship service and lead the singing. We sing from our Hymnal usually in four-part harmony.

Once on a sunny Sunday morning, a lady from Christian women's group walks by our chapel, the windows are open and she hears us singing. She comes up to the chapel after the service and tells Evan, our music professor, "I listened to your singing and liked it very much. Do you think your choir could sing at our women's retreat next week?" Evan replies, "We have no choir, it is our congregation that was singing. I will ask members of the congregation if some are willing to respond to your request". A group of fifteen of us meets at the women's retreat and we sing some of our hymns suitable for the occasion. They reward us with a delicious dessert.

We are one of the few churches that have a response time after the sermon. Questions, comments or sharing of personal experiences relating to the message, round out the service. These comments from the congregation are a meaningful, thoughtful and sometimes humorous contribution to the sermon. Afterwards, we normally congregate in the dining room, have a cup of coffee and cake and continue to discuss and share. On the last Sunday of the month, we invite all the students from the Centre to join us at a potluck meal.

Our congregation is always in flux. Graduates leave to find work opportunities in other cities.

35. Early retirement activities

It has been a long time since we have been to our summer cabin in Christina Lake. We are anxious to go back and find out what it looks like after a year of absence.

We are startled, when we arrive, to see one window nailed shut with a sheet of plywood and the window frame leaning against the door. We go inside, everything seems to be the same as we left it, only the smell tells us that there might be some dead mice hidden somewhere. After we have everything cleaned up and connected water and electricity we can cook our first meal, get the bedding out of the mouse-safe drawers and have a good nights rest.

A tree had fallen over the telephone line and the phone is not working. We go to the neighbor to phone the telephone company to repair it. Another chore is waiting for us, mowing the grass around the house and along the driveway. Our firewood supply is diminishing, I have to split wood again and pile it up in the now empty dog house.

We phone Billy, our neighbor, whom we had asked to look after the cabin, and ask him about the window. He tells us he drove by last winter in his snowmobile and saw the window lying on the snow. He got a piece of plywood from the shop and nailed the opening shut. We have no idea how that could have happened; there was no sign of a break in.

A few days later, when Hildegard has gone into town, a car drives down our driveway and stops at the chicken coop. An elderly woman gets out and looks around. When she sees me coming out of the house, she moves back towards the car. I ask her if I can do something for her. "Oh no, I am just looking at the old place," she tells me. "We used to live in the homestead down there and we often visited our friends here but they are long gone. I am sorry to have bothered you". I am interested and tell her, "I don't mind, are you by chance Mrs. Miller?" She looks surprised, "Yes, I am, how do you know?" I tell her that our friends refer to the old homestead with the apple trees west of our property as the 'Miller farm'. On our hikes along our property, we often return via the Miller farm because the road is a little better and we occasionally taste some of her apples. I mention, "Hildegard, my wife, would be delighted to meet you, do you live in the area, could we pay you a visit?" She does not mind at all and gives me her address. She lives in Grand Forks where we do our shopping. I invite her to come in but she declines, as her son, who brought her, has to go back.

Hildegard is excited about this unexpected discovery and the next time we are in town, we visit Mrs. Miller. She is quite talkative, shares with us many stories of bygone times, and digs up some pictures of the old homestead. Hildegard makes notes and tells her that she is writing a history of Castle Mountain.

On our next walk across the Miller farm, we try to imagine where the house and barns had been. Only one building is left and its walls have collapsed leaving the joints of the log structure exposed. We now know the person who lived here. Mr. Miller started to farm here at the beginning of the last century. He left the farm after 20 years because of heart problems.

Another deserted homestead is just across the US border. From our driveway we can see the brick chimney sticking out from the bushes when we go up to the Santa Rosa Road. Sometimes we sneak over the border to have a closer look at it. The roof and the outside walls have caved in, the interior walls all collapsed. A lilac bush is growing in the middle of the house; it looks like a bouquet standing on the living room table. Our children love to explore these old homesteads.

Hildegard had been at Stonehenge and was very impressed by the immensity of the stone blocks and the rituals connected with that place. Inspired by that phenomenon, she builds a place for meditation and celebration of nature on our property. She chooses a secluded spot on our property up the hill, which is shielded by tall pines and wild rose bushes. She gathers large stones from the many that lie around and places them in a circle. For the bigger ones for seats in between she needs my help to dig them out of the little quarry at the US border. Occasionally we sit there and rest. Sometimes Hildegard's women friends come over to the stone circle with their drums and they celebrate equinox and other festivals there.

She likes her intimate place and rituals.

After we return home again, it rains for weeks and we are longing for the sun. We pack our red Subaru station wagon and head south to California.

Our first stop is Ashland to visit the first Elizabethan theatre on the American continent where Shakespeare Festivals are held. It is not open yet. Some actors are working on the preparation of the stage for the first play and we talk to them about their performance.

The sun is finally coming out when we drive into the Rainbow Basin, a bonanza for Hildegard. The layers of prehistoric sedimentary rocks have been folded up vertically or diagonally by fault shifts and earthquakes and have an amazing range of colors, orange, red, brown, white, pink and green. The softer rocks are washed out, forming caves and the harder parts stand up in the bizarre shapes of hoodoos.

A little farther east we walk through the partly rebuilt ghost town of Calico. It was once a thriving silver mine town with saloons, theatres, schools, churches and banks. We still can have a short ride in the old railway cars.

Our main interest in this area, however, is Death Valley. We take the small road over the mountain ridges on the east side of the valley. Dante's View gives us a panoramic view of the long valley below us. The snow-capped Telescope Mountain greets us from the other side. We drive down past the round tops of the Twenty Mule Team Range to the Furnace Creek Inn, a luxury resort that does not fit into this desolate desert.

We park our car and walk down to Badwater. The names of the places, Furnace Creek, Funeral Mountain and Devil's Hole indicate that this is the lowest, hottest spot on the continent, eighty-six meters below sea level and a temperature of up to 57°C.

It is a strange feeling to walk on the white springy flat surface of Death Valley. We move carefully on it until we come to a spot where an underground river breaks through the surface and flows as a shallow creek on the valley floor. Now we are walking on a boardwalk along the Salt Creek interpretive trail and observe the strange fauna and flora in its swampy surroundings. The crusty build up on its sides is mostly NaCl, table salt.

When the sun is disappearing behind Telescope Mountain, we drive back on the Artist's Drive to Shoshone Inn, our abode in the Indian reservation. We chose it because of its close location. The few spacious but very simply furnished cabins are surrounded by trees and it is very quiet here. While Hildegard is preparing supper, I quickly go to the swimming pool a few hundred meters behind the cabin. It is a public pool, which is fed by the Tacoma hot springs. The mineral water flows through the pool and is renewed constantly. The native people here are very generous. Nobody is checking who is using it. The gate is open. I am the only one in the pool at this time. A few laps in the health spring make me feel relaxed and refreshed after a rather strenuous hot day. I regret that Hildegard was too tired to come along.

We have breakfast in the cabin, pack up and look for a tourist office. It is closed on Mondays. A curio shop is next to it and we ask the somewhat strange-looking sales person what she would suggest we explore in this area.

She takes us into her shack and shows us her rock collection. The floor is covered with coins on which she walks carefully for good luck. A young bearded fellow is mixing some organic juices and medicinal herbs in the background. He gives us advice on how to live healthily. It is a kind of eerie atmosphere but they give us helpful hints about natural phenomena in the area.

We take their advice and set off on a narrow country road through the East Mojave Desert past the Dumont sand dunes with their elegant contour lines. It is the place where the movie Star Wars was shot. In an oasis between the dunes, we discover a field of cacti, the buds on their thorny thick green surface are just opening. We are amazed at the variety of shapes and colors in the otherwise drab desert.

On a road crossing we see a sign, 'Devil's Playground'. We are curious to see what devils play with. We follow the gravel road. The desert here is dotted with a few blooming bushes and tall cacti and then we see their 'toys', enormous rocks, round ones and odd shaped ones piled on top of each other. In our imagination, these rock forms look like elephants, bears, monkeys and humans in different positions. In the distance, on a tall rectangular shaped bolder, we see the red shirt of a rock climber trying his skills. He makes it to the top and waves to us, a perfect motif for my camera. We drive through groves of Joshua trees and yucca bushes, until we come back to the highway that leads to Phoenix.

Phoenix is the hub of Western, Indian and Hispanic culture. The Heard Museum's large collection of Native art and artifacts gives an overview of the history and life of the different native tribes in the USA and Mexico.

We spend a few hours admiring old and modern European and American painters, sculptors and the vast display of china.

On our way out, we park beside the Biltmore Hotel, designed by Frank Lloyd Wright. Hildegard walks gracefully into the foyer and through some of the facilities as if she is a registered guest in this five star place. I am surprised at her boldness. The buildings are well integrated into the park-like property. It is an open design, with pavilions and covered walkways around the main Hotel tract. Architect Wright is known for his attention to detail. Everything has his personal touch, interior and exterior, very pleasing.

Another architectural phenomenon is the experimental, eco-friendly community of Cosanti in Paradise Valley. Cosanti and its extension, Arcosanti, in the Arizona high desert are experiments by the renowned visionary, Italian architect Paolo Soleri. He wants to combine architecture with ecology (Arcology) and create sustainable ecological human habitats. His concept of an alternative urban development is to have living and working facilities close together to minimize travel time. He experiments with apartments that are dug into the earth to balance the extreme hot and cold temperatures differences to save energy. The light comes from skylights. I look down the stairs and wonder what it would feel like living 'underground'.

Soleri wants to create structures, which can fulfill multiple purposes; it will save space. A greenhouse, orchard and bakery are part of the settlement, they supply healthy food for the community and make it almost self-sufficient. We get a taste of it when we have a meal in their communal restaurant.

Arizona lends itself to solar energy and wind power, so most of the energy they use is created on their own property.

People who want to live in Arcosanti have to attend a workshop about communal living and building technologies in theory and practice, given by Soleri and his staff. He has a triple honorary degree and gives lectures to promote his ideas all over the world. People from many countries and continents come to Arcosanti to learn from his experiments of ecological architecture and community living.

He draws volunteers, students and professionals who are interested in his vision to work on the construction of his projects. It sometimes shows in the quality of the buildings. They also build his famous, unique windbells in Cosanti and Arcosanti. Thousands of them in different shapes colors and sizes are hanging around everywhere, as single bells or in artistically arranged sets of five to ten bells. Soleri has them displayed together with his original sculptures in the gallery and visitors centre and many other places in town. Workers cast the bronze bells in their foundry and the ceramic bells in their ceramic studio.

A wind is blowing while we are visiting and the bells are ringing everywhere and give more or less harmonious sounds.

Many of the construction components are built or assembled on site as well, which provides work for many people in the community. For us ecology conscious people and for me, as an architect, this visit is a very worthwhile experience.

Another amazing settlement is the ancient Montezuma castle. We stop for lunch and sit down at a picnic table under old sycamore trees with their smooth light grey-green trunks, the leaves on their knotty, gnarled and twisted branches shield us from the hot sun. Montezuma castle has an interesting history. Almost nine hundred years ago, the Sinagua tribe built this five-story cave structure into the rock, housing hundred fifty people. It sits on a steep thirty meter high platform under an overhanging cliff, difficult to access. For three hundred fifty years, this Indian tribe lived here peacefully and then disappeared and no one knows exactly why.

Thoughtfully we go back to our car and drive on to Tucson, the former capital of Arizona. On my suggestion, we take an alternative route to see the Roosevelt Dam. At the Apache Junction, we turn into a narrow gravel road washed out by the small river, which is still flowing over the trail. I have to shift our Subaru into four-wheel drive to get up the steep slope to the Fish Creek Canyon with its high rock walls on both sides. It is a beautiful vista.

The Roosevelt Dam is a monumental structure, creating the largest artificial water reservoir. It is presently being reinforced and we cannot go close to the huge floodgates.

We get back to the highway and arrive in the evening at Tucson. The next day is a Sunday and I want to try a charismatic service in the Abundant Life Chapel close to our hotel. It is similar to our services in West Coast, perhaps a little livelier.

It is hot and we cool off in the swimming pool.

On our stroll through the town, we come into a pedestrian zone with an inner court surrounded by artists' studios and artisan shops with flowerpots and sculptures in between. Artists display their products, paintings, carvings, pottery, wall hangings, weavings and jewelry on the street. We take time to talk to fellow artists about their work and they seem to enjoy sharing with us. We both find these talks invigorating and inspiring. In the Khabub art centre Hildegard spots her dream drum, hand-made by Natives and affordable. She tries it out and we buy it.

We take a break at the Saguaro National Park. At the entrance we get a little scared when a naturalist approaches us with a gopher snake slung around her neck, crawling down her arm. "They are not poisonous," she tells us.

She informs us about the fauna and flora we might encounter in the park and we walk along the aisles trying to identify the many cacti and observe the small animals crawling on the ground and hiding under leafy plants. It is a well-arranged park.

We leave the Tucson area and cross the border into New Mexico, to the 'White Sands National Monument'. The park ranger has finished her shift for the day and does not want to open her account anymore. She lets us in for free.

For the first miles of the way, the sand is partly covered by salt cedar and sumac bushes, a few yuccas and Indian rice grass. Further on we see the clean white sand dunes, an overwhelming sight. We park our car beside one of the picnic tables with a metal sunroof and eat our sandwiches for supper. We take shoes and socks off and our bare feet sink into that virgin white sand. It is a wonderful feeling. We climb up to the top of a dune and look as far as we can see over other sand hills with their sensual soft contours. It is a peaceful, serene atmosphere. Once in awhile, a small bunch of Indian rice grass or evening primrose throws a shadow on the white sand. Our eyes follow the tracks of a roadrunner and a whiptail lizard impressed into the sand. They make an interesting design on the smooth sand surface.

We select a position on the dunes, which will provide a good view of the sunset and wait. The crowns of the dunes slowly change to a golden, orange hue and the shadows turn purple, a marvelous metamorphosis. With this astounding image in our hearts and minds, we leave the White Sands and find a simple abode for the night.

The next day we are on the road again. The park ranger at White Sands told us about the Three River Petroglyph Park on the way to Carlsbad. We make a detour and stand in front of a compilation of tall rocks and stone walls into which Indian artists have carved a number of intricate symbols, different animals, hunting scenes and geometric forms. We try to figure out what their message might be.

At a gas station where we have to fill up, high school kids have a carwash and our Subaru gets a needed clean up. They do not do a professional job but we have fun with them.

We arrive in Carlsbad. Its hot springs are similar in mineral content to the Austrian ones in Karlsbad, the bath of Emperor Karl from which it got its name, but that is about the only thing they have in common.

To us Carlsbad is important for its extraordinary caverns. The parking lot is almost full when we arrive in the morning. With the ticket, we are handed a pamphlet for a self-guided tour. We like to be independent so that we may look more carefully at parts we find especially interesting.

Soft, indirect lighting, hidden in small niches or under outcroppings of rocks, creates a mysterious atmosphere in these caves. We are amazed by the size and proportion of these 'halls'. Carlsbad has the largest explored caves in the US. We walk through the 'Natural Entrance' down from one huge chamber to another of equal beauty, through tunnels or along cliffs. The names of the different caves express the mood they create. It is difficult to describe the beauty of these miraculous rooms. The 'Hall of Giants' is the largest, six hundred meter long, seventy five meter wide and one hundred and seven meter high. The 'King's Palace' is a huge, highly decorated hall with a stalagmite structure in its centre which looks like a castle. The most beautiful room is the 'Queens Chamber', delicately decorated with curtains of stalactites hanging on the walls, and columns and open spaces in between. This room reminds us of Baroque or Rococo churches in Germany with their playful intricate decorations in pastel color tones. A small pool in the 'Green Room' reflects green light and gives this cave an eerie feeling. In the 'Spirit World' white stalactites hanging from its ceiling suggest angels floating around.

It is Sunday and it feels like attending a worship service in a church with organ pipes hanging from the walls. We are experiencing in awe the beauty of nature, of God's creation.

We do not realize that we have already spent three hours in the caves and walked five and a half km. We are tired and take the elevator up to the info-centre. We come back to reality when we see the gift shop and snack bar.

For us, seeing the caverns is perhaps the most exciting experience of our trip. We will take valuable memories with us.

Friends of ours have a summer cabin in northern New Mexico and they told us about the beauty and rich history of that area. So we drive straight north from Carlsbad to Santa Fe. It is getting quite hot and we are glad to have air conditioning. We enter the old part of the town via the old Santa Fe Trail. Most houses along the street are constructed with ochre-brown mud bricks, simple rounded forms. We have never seen so many different adobe houses. We spend most of the day exploring the artists' quarters. Almost every second house around the plaza is a gallery or artist's studio. Some specialize in Native art and artifacts others have a variety of exhibits.

Hildegard experiences a light heat stroke and we have to spend the next day mostly indoors.

On our way to Taos, we drive through several Indian reservations. The villages and houses look neglected no street or traffic signs. We go into a Catholic convent and ask what the name of the place is. The sister tells us it is Chimayo and encourages us to visit the Pilgrimage church and shrine at the end of the village, the 'Lourdes of America'.

The legend goes: A friar, doing penance, saw a light on the ground where he was praying and dug up a crucifix. He took it into the church but it disappeared three times and he found it again in the place where he first had seen it. A church was built on that spot and the crucifix is kept in a shrine inside. It has healing power and so has the 'sacred sand pit' where it had been buried. Thousands of pilgrims with aches and wounds come to the church, take some of the sacred soil and claim its healing power. We go inside this plain Adobe church to see the crucifix in the shrine but it is covered. People who have been healed left crutches, canes and braces on the wall.

We take the scenic high road to Taos, which meanders along the ridges of the local mountain range. We drive through pine forests again and have a beautiful view of the Sangre de Christo Mountains with its four thousand and eleven meter high Wheeler Peak.

In one of the small villages on our way we see a sign, 'woodcarver'. We drive up the steep driveway and are met by two dogs, a donkey and a few mules. A young Hispanic woman shows us the carver's workshop. He carves mainly biblical motifs, Noah's ark, nativity themes and saints in a folk art style. Besides his carving, he offers donkey and mule rides through the mountains.

In Las Trampas, we visit an old adobe church, the oldest still active church in the USA.

Taos is a spread out settlement in the Taos Pueblo Indian Reservation. When we enter the Pueblo Taos village, we are stopped by a sentinel who asks us for a five dollar entry 'parking fee', if we want to photograph, another five dollar and if we plan to photograph people a 'donation' is to be negotiated. We are quite surprised to see Native people being so business oriented. We know them usually as generous, hospitable and shy people. They have jurisdiction for the governance of their reservation and take advantage of the lucrative business from tourists.

The settlement is about one thousand years old and the inhabitants, mainly older people, have kept their traditions alive. Young people often live or work in the town nearby.

What amazes me is that they built multi-storied houses like apartment buildings long ago already and still live in them. The three-story high, adobe style structures are covered with the typical red brown mud plaster, have a flat roof, small deep windows and doors, painted a strong blue or green.

A somewhat shy middle-aged woman stands in front of a door and we ask if we may see the inside. We donate one dollar and she shows us her 'two bedroom apartment' an entrance-living room with a fireplace, the only source of heating. In the back are two rooms where they sleep, with an open kitchen in between. The ceiling is held up with rough round timbers and is low for my height. The floor is of tamped dirt. She does not want us to take a picture and we respect that. On the other side of the Rio Pueblo de Taos, a fast flowing mountain stream, is a building of the same size and in between are one-story adobe houses. Many of the inhabitants are artisans, carvers, weavers, potters and jewelry makers.

We plan our route home and I suggest that we go via the road, which I traveled forty years ago as an exchange student at Bluffton College, to visit the Schefflers in Ritzville.

Canyon De Chelly is on that route. I had seen it only from the upper rim at that time. We arrive in the evening and park on the campground. First, we try to find accommodation for the night. Both the Canyon De Chelly motel and the Thunderbird lodge are full. To find another motel in the Navajo reservation where people still live in Hogans and tents is very unlikely. We decide to repack our station wagon and sleep in the back of it. We have a good meal to reduce the food storage, shove the picnic basket and a carton with rocks and souvenirs under the car and pile the rest high up on the front seat. We crawl into our down sleeping bags, for comfort we need about thirty cm more room to stretch out but we manage. Shortly before midnight, we hear some noises under the car. A stray dog has smelled our cheese and sausage and wants to open the basket. I chase him away and put the picnic basket on the roof of the car. A few hours later, the noise is louder. The doggy I chased away got reinforcements and four mongrels are sniffing out our food and are disappointed not to find the basket. We are tired and in spite of these interruptions, we sleep well. In the morning, we still have time to repack our car and have breakfast on our picnic table, before we line up to board one of the special high-clearance open trucks with benches in the back. Five of them are taking us tourists through the canyon. It gets quite cold during the night at this elevation and we put warm jackets and caps on. The ride is rather rough on these washed out dirt roads. Parts of the wide-open canyon are still flooded. Our driver-tour-guide has a sense of humor. We have just rolled into one of these shallow lakes when he announces, "Oops, we ran out of gas". People get scared and he laughs, "Sorry, I looked at the wrong dial". He is very knowledgeable and gives us a good overview of the history and customs of the Navajos who live in this area and their ancestors the Anasazi. He talks about the battles between the Spaniards and the Navajos and shows us the steep rock, the 'Navajo Force', on which two hundred Navajos took refuge from the Spaniards. Only thirty survived, made peace with the enemy and settled in the canyon. He shows us cave dwellings usually built on rock outcroppings or ledges where extended families of up to one hundred lived. In one arm of the canyon is the 'White House', a two-story cliff dwelling with white rock walls. It has an extension to house a gift shop and toilets for tourists. The farther we drive into the canyon arms the narrower they get and the overhanging rock walls loom up to three-hundred meters.

The canyon is wider in the centre and leaves room for fields and meadows. The valley floor is quite fertile and the Navajos, being nomads, move down and live here during the summer month. We see some horses and cows trudging through the water. They will graze in the narrower, higher parts and between the rocks when the water is completely gone. In the winter, the Navajos move back into the village.

After our very informative half-day tour, the trucks bring us back to the tourist bureau; we have lunch and afterwards look from the upper rim road down into the canyon. This completes our canyon tour, and we are heading west again.

I vaguely remember the area I had traveled years ago. Parts of the old gravel road through the Navajo reserve are now paved but the sandstorms are still the same. We pass by the mission school in Oraibi, which I helped to build together with the Mennonite Voluntary Service workers. At that time, the Gossens were missionaries in Hotevilla. One of their parishioners had invited me to her home. She was weaving baskets with bast fibers. I bought a beautiful one from her, which I still have. She lived in a fairly well furnished Hopi style stone house. The sand is blowing and we do not want to open the car door so we go on. I want to take the North route home, through Canyon land, Zion and Bryce Canyon, but Hildegard thinks the mountain passes would still have snow and she does not like to drive in snow. So we drive through the desert again. A strong wind drives tumbleweeds across the road, one sticks to our radiator grill and gets a free ride for awhile. We see more flowers here and there. Fields of red poppies appear on the hills and the cacti, which had buds when we drove east, are now in bloom.

We have enjoyed the strange beauty of desert country but are missing our cool forests. When we drive along highway 99 north, Hildegard sees a sign 'Yosemite National Park'. We make a quick decision and make a detour to the park. We had been taking turns driving on those long stretches of highway. Now it is my turn to drive those narrow hairpin curves up to the Sierra Nevada Mountain range with the view of the four thousand meter high Ritter Peak and a dozen others. What a difference from the desert scene to see the huge Sequoia trees in the 'Mariposa Grove of Big Trees.'

Some of the passes are still closed because of the deep snow, so we drive the valley road beside the rushing 'Yosemite creek' with the spraying 'Bridal Veil Fall' in the southern and the high 'Yosemite Fall' in the northern part of the park. We look at the huge square rock massif of the 'El Capitan' reaching up from the road and the 'Cathedral Rock' with its double peak, like a Gothic church.

For the night we stay in a small motel in Groveland, on the outskirts of the park; it is quiet and cozy. The next morning we leave early and take the winding side roads along the foothills of the Sierra Nevada. It takes a little longer to drive through small towns and villages but we can stop more easily at special viewpoints and take in the beauty of the landscape.

When we reach the lowlands, we turn onto the State Highway # 5, which leads us straight to the Canadian border.

In Bellingham, we take a short rest and visit Hildegard's mother and sisters. They invite us to stay for supper and we share our adventures with them. Oma Scheffler is growing more fragile. She is always happy, having all her daughters around her.

When we come to the border, the customs officer asks the usual questions and waves us through. It is good to be home after such a long trip. We are grateful that everything went so well and are glad to sleep in our own bed again.

36. The empty nest.

Our children lived with us in our new house for a while, but now one after the other moves out. Michael and Tannis have rented their own apartment; Hanno finishes his studies at SFU. The family celebrates with him achieving his Bachelor of Business Administration degree. During his studies he kept his job open and worked part time for his computer company. After a short holiday, he works again full time with them. Since he has a good paying job now, Mom suggests that he become independent of us, move into the downstairs suite and provide for himself. He agrees, he still has his parents close by to call on if necessary.

Krista has moved back home again to finish her final year at SFU.

The trip to Israel and talks with a counselor help her to come out of her 'critical period'. In her search for new meaning in life, she abandoned her former restricting religious beliefs, which we think had an influence on her mood changes. She has set her mind now to pursue her goals. She does excellent work in her final year at university and concludes her studies with a Bachelor of Arts degree. She is the best student in the psychology department this year and is selected to receive the Psychological Association's Gold Medal. She is also awarded the Dean's medal for the top student in the faculty of arts. Krista feels at odds with the way the administration bestows these honors and decides not to attend the celebration and presentation of her degree and her awards.

We celebrate her graduation quietly; we want to respect her decision. Krista now has a more positive attitude and outlook on life, having concluded her final studies and decides to go on to medical school. She applies to several universities. With her academic standing, all medical schools will accept her. Like Michael, she chooses Calgary.

For her move, we hire a small U-haul truck. With a heavy heart, she sells her piano and buys a lighter electronic keyboard instrument, which is easier to transport. She can play it mute, with headphones, so as not to disturb her neighbors. She loves to play it for relaxation and enjoyment. We are off to Calgary and she insists on driving the truck all the way by herself.

We find a duplex in the neighborhood of Calgary's medical school. Krista can easily get from there to school on her bike. I set up some book shelves, fix the lock on the door and with some additional furniture from the thrift store we can create a comfortable place for her to live for the next years. With mixed feelings, we drive home again. We are glad she has chosen her profession and is looking forward to her future.

While Krista was still at SFU, she had classes with a young science student who spoke English with a strong accent. She talked to her and learned to know that Anna recently emigrated from Poland. She had secretly left Poland for a 'holiday' in Italy, spent some time in Germany and later immigrated to Canada. Krista wants to help her and asks us if she could not move in with us into one of our empty rooms on the middle floor. We have no problem with this and Anna moves into Hanno's former room. She shares the kitchen with him downstairs. After some time they find that it will save time and energy if they cook and eat together. It works and a friendship develops between the two of them and it deepens as time goes on.

Anna decides to visit her parents in Poland. She has not seen them since she left Poland years ago. Hanno and Anna think it might be good for both of them if Hanno learns to know her family and she can introduce him to her parents before their friendship becomes more intimate. Hanno takes some time off from his work and visits the Zygos in Lublin.

Anna's mother teaches High School and works as a curriculum consultant. Her father is an instructor in a Polish military academy. Neither of them speaks English or German, which makes it difficult for Hanno to communicate with them. Anna has to translate. To Hanno's relief, Andreas, her brother, is almost fluent in German. As a physician, he had worked occasionally in Germany to earn extra money, which enabled him to build his spacious house in Lublin.

Hanno is well received by Anna's family. The two return to Burnaby together and their relationship intensifies

Hanno and his friends, Tim and Phil, attend the Abbotsford air show. When it is finished, they want to drive home and find the parking lot packed full. Everyone is trying to get out fast. Not yielding to each other, they are blocking each other's way. Shouting and cursing does not get them moving. The three become annoyed by this behavior, leave their car, go to the exit and direct the traffic. These tall, handsome guys gain the respect of the drivers through their skillful maneuvering and in no time, the parking lot is empty. They have fun doing it and come to the conclusion that they would make good traffic cops. They enroll in a training program for the Police Reserves. Tim and Phil continue their training professionally. Tim as an RCMP officer and Phil as a Vancouver police constable. After graduation, Hanno is a member of the Police Reserve and looks official in his blue uniform; but soon he finds that his commitment to the police work requires too much of his spare time and the service requirements often interfere with his work schedule in his professional work. Since he cannot do both jobs effectively, he leaves the police reserve.

1992 is an eventful year for the family. Hanno buys his first house, a narrow three-story town house on Rumble Street in Burnaby. He is the youngest, and the first one of the children to have his own home. The whole family helps him move in.

His work situation also changes. The video game company for which he works amalgamates with 'Electronic Arts', a large firm which had done the production and marketing of their video games. 'EA' builds a large, modern design and production centre in Burnaby. Hanno's racing car design 'Need for Speed' is one of the best selling games in the firm. When our young relatives find this out, they are quite proud to have such an important 'uncle'. His work is highly valued and he is promoted to the position of Vice President and General Manager of the branch office in Vancouver. He travels occasionally to Europe to try out the driving capabilities of the Lamborghini, Porsche and Ferrari racing cars, which he emulates in his game designs. We encourage him to apply for dual citizenship, German (EU) and Canadian, which would make traveling in Europe much easier. He does and now has two passports to choose from.

Michael and Tannis have both done well in their undergraduate studies at SFU. Michael continues his studies at medical school at the University of Calgary and Tannis enrolls at UBC's medical school. Tannis starts out well in her first year but she notices a gradual change in her study habits, which manifests itself as an anxiety disorder. She cannot concentrate on her studies and falls behind. When she notices that she cannot fulfill the requirements of the courses her anxiety increases. Another attempt to catch up is unsuccessful and she decides to leave medical school for health reasons.

She needs a break and takes a job in the field of practical medical service and works in a home for disabled adults. After a year, she returns to SFU to complete her degree in Biology.

Michael graduates from medical school in Calgary and returns to BC. He completes an internship in New Westminster, and looks forward to beginning his residency in orthopedics in Vancouver, a field which he likes and enjoys.

After one year of very demanding expectations in his residency, he feels Tannis needs more of his support than the residency program will allow and asks for a leave of absence. We all find it is the right decision in this situation. However, his application to leave the program temporarily is rejected and he sees no other solution than to withdraw from it. Things at home improve and he sees an opportunity to reenter the program but he is unsuccessful. We feel the reasons given for the rejection are unfair and he is disappointed.

Michael is resourceful and has a positive attitude. He accepts a position as a GP in Riverview Hospital, BC's provincial psychiatric institute. His open and friendly way of communicating with people wins him friends and he is well-liked and respected for his honesty and attention to the needs of people by both patients and staff.

Michael has good organizational skills. They are recognized by the hospital and staff and he is elected as President of the Medical Staff. Over the next few years he completes his certificate in medical administration and is appointed as a Program Medical Director.

Already as a teenager, Michael was interested in aviation. Now he sees an opportunity to fulfill that wish. At the small Surrey airport, he takes flying lessons. One day in July, he surprises me, "Dad, I completed my pilot's license, can I take you on a flight over the Fraser Valley?" Of course, I accept. We drive to the Surrey Airport, he rents a Cessna 175, does the necessary preparations and we take off. Over Abbotsford, he asks me if I want to take over the control of the instruments for a while. Flying a plane feels good again. It reminds me of my first solo flight in a glider as a Hitler Youth air cadet, fifty years ago.

Now that Michael has a steady job with a good salary, he and Tannis think of buying a house. To save for a better down payment, his brother-in-law, Michel, suggests that Michael should do what he is doing, build a house and sell it again at a profit. The market is good at the moment. Michael and Tannis take the risk and with Michel's help and the support of the two families, they have a house completed for sale in half a year. It meant hard work but it paid off. The profit from the sale gives them a good down payment for a house in Port Moody. They now have some experience in building and with the advice of their architect father, they make extensive renovations in kitchen and bathrooms before they move in. This makes the house more suitable for their requirements.

Hildegard and I are now retired and have time to pursue our hobbies. Hildegard is painting in a makeshift set up in the utility. She has to reorganize everything when she does the laundry.

The garage has been empty since we sold our second car and now park the Subaru on the bridge. "Do you think we could transform the garage into a studio?" she asks me. We look at it with this purpose in mind. "It is possible; no point leaving the garage empty. We can pull the door up and build a solarium in front of it, to give you more light," I suggest. The estimate for the construction of a solarium is quite high, so I decide to build the framing myself and have the glazier only put the windows and skylights in. This reduces the cost by two thirds.

For painting on silk, Hildegard has to stretch her material on frames. Together we design and build adjustable ones of different sizes. I add a big worktable where she can spread them out and a sink and running water for easy clean up. An acquaintance of ours installs a gas fireplace which makes the studio comfortable to paint in during the colder season. We have fun working together transforming the garage into a spacious, bright art studio. Hildegard is delighted to have her own 'professional' workspace, as I have my workshop, and she is using it now, painting with a new vigor.

Hildegard is always eager to try out new methods in painting. She attends a demonstration lesson of new silk painting materials given by the fabric art store Miva on Granville Island. Hildegard and one of the instructors, Izabella, a silk painting and fabric art designer become friends. We invite her and her husband Jacob for a visit so that we may learn to know them better. They are impressed with our house design, especially the high cathedral wood ceiling and the skylights in our living room.

Both of them come from Gdansk in Poland, not far from where I was born, when Gdansk was still Danzig. Jacob is a painter. We visit him in his studio and Hildegard finds one of his abstract figures, a bird-like female portrait, interesting. On her 60th birthday, he visits us and presents it as a gift to her. He tells her he and his friends do not have a room high enough to hang this two meter high painting. It hangs now, very originally framed, on the high gable wall in our living room.

Hildegard, inspired by the demonstration lesson and the exchange of ideas with the young artist couple, becomes quite productive in her studio. An Anglican women's group from Christ Church Cathedral invites her to display her work along with other female artists in the foyer of its sanctuary.

Vancouver and Burnaby artist's organizations have open exhibits for local artists and Hildegard submits her paintings. Ulli shows some of his German guests Hildegard's studio. They like her work and buy several paintings, so do some of her friends.

Helmut and Hildegard at MHS art exhibit

> Members of the Mennonite Historical Society arrange an art display for Mennonite artists. Painters, quilters, sculptors and calligraphers are participating. They invite us too. This is a rare opportunity where Hildegard and I can display our artwork together, Hildegard her two dimensional paintings and I my three dimensional sculptures and pottery. We are surprised at how many Mennonite artists display their work there.

I had been in retirement from teaching for several years, when I get a phone call from Will, Hildegard's nephew. He had finished his teacher training at SFU and is offered a teaching position with a varied curriculum. His assignment includes several art courses for which he is not properly prepared. One is teaching a pottery course.

Hildegard and Madison

Helmut with his art students

He has never done this before and is a little nervous. I offer to give a demonstration lesson for him and his art class. He arranges it with his principal, who gives permission as an 'in service training'. I retrieve some of my old lesson plans, collect information about clay and glazes, kiln settings, methods of constructing and throwing pots on a wheel and leave them with him.

I enjoy seeing the surprise on the faces of the students as they come into the classroom. I gather them around and tell them about the origin of pottery, explain the makeup and plasticity of the material, show them the different methods of making pottery by hand and demonstrate throwing a pot on the potter's wheel. They watch attentively and try to do as I did in my demonstration with more or less success. I feel I could easily go back to the classroom and work with students again, even though I really have never missed teaching since I retired.

I have another challenge. Barbara, our German neighbor across the street, wants to enlarge her living space and asks me for advice. I discuss it with her and suggest an additional wing to her house and make a few sketches for it. She likes them and asks me to design and supervise the building of the addition. A contractor friend does the construction and she is quite happy with the outcome.

It brings back old memories. Thirty five years have passed since I left the architectural profession, and I am still fond of doing that kind of work.

37. OH CANADA, OUR HOME AND NATIVE LAND!

When spring comes, we are itching to travel again. One day Cousin Herbert phones and has a surprise for us. "Our neighbor wants to sell his motor home; it is in very good shape you should come and have a look at it," he tells us enthusiastically. We had never considered getting one but we tell him we will come over for a visit and have a look at it. While Cousin Eva is preparing coffee, Herbert takes us to old Bill Reitsman. He is eighty-one years old and his wife does not feel safe anymore driving with him in the motor home; she wants him to sell it. He reluctantly gives in. The Ford Frontier is in excellent condition and has very low mileage for a twelve year-old vehicle. Hildegard and I get warmed up to the idea of driving one. We figure, what we will save on motel costs when travelling this way, will pay for the price he asks. Traveling in it will be less stressful, our bed and kitchen will travel with us and be available whenever needed. We will be more flexible in choosing where to stay overnight. It sounds very reasonable and we decide to buy it.

Driving it home, we stop at the garage where Mister Reitsman usually has his vehicle serviced. The attendant assures us that the owner has not driven it very often in the last years, has it checked regularly and that the motor home is in perfect condition.

Now our dream to travel across Canada from the Pacific to the Atlantic coast will become reality. Hildegard packs kitchen utensils and food, bedding and clothing in the respective drawers and closets in the motor home. We check our maps, tour books and CB radio and are ready to explore our continent.

We will travel the first part of our trip east through the United States. Our motor home, we find out, is a 'gas-guzzler' and gasoline is much cheaper across the border.

Hildegard and Helmut with Frontier motor home

Helmut and Hildegard cruising on 'Indian Arm'

We want to show our new acquisition to Hildegard's sisters in Bellingham and they are impressed. In Seattle, we stay with Hildegard's study friend, Hanna. She is very happy to see us again. When we want to leave her place, we notice an air leak in one of the rear tires. We stop at a tire shop. The attendant points to the walls of our tires, "They are quite brittle because the vehicle has not been driven much during the last years. For safety reasons I suggests that you replace all tires". We do not want to take chances on such a long trip. An hour later, he has mounted new tires and we drive off with a safer vehicle.

We cannot pass Ritzville without visiting some of Hildegard's old friends from the time when she immigrated to that 'remote' town. We park our 'Moto' for the night in the yard of the Mennonite church. Before we leave the next morning, we go into the church and walk once more down the aisle, which we walked thirty-seven years ago as a newly married couple. Old memories come back when we drive the road to Cour d'Alene Lake. We spent a wonderful honeymoon there and I take a dip into the water again. The place has changed now and is not as romantic anymore.

From the flat, desert-like area of western Washington we come to Montana and the landscape changes. We are not far from the National Bison Range and take a detour into the park in the hope of seeing some of these animals, whose origin dates back to prehistoric times. We follow the 'Red Sleep Mountain scenic drive', a trail with narrow switchbacks and steep slopes to the 'High Point'. From the top a majestic 360-degree panoramic view of the area and the Rocky Mountains opens up to us.

On the way back through the meadows, we watch the huge animals grazing in a clearing. We also follow a herd of pronghorn antelopes and spot a few elk at the edge of the woods.

We drive on and Hildegard is overwhelmed by another sight. She comments:

> 'We drive through Maku Shika State Park where a whole new world opens up to us. Erosion has taken the cover off the hills and we can look into millions of years of earth history. Quite close to the top of the many multicolored layers is a yellow line. This, we are told, signifies the arrival of mammals. It is sobering to ponder the span of one life time in the presence of such immense spaces of time.'

Driving through an Indian reservation, we see a solitary church with a few log cabins behind it; they are part of the St.Ignatius Mission. The church is open. We are astonished to see two large paintings in the foyer. One is a Native Indian Madonna in her typical Indian garb with fringes and a headband, carrying her baby in a carrier on her back. On the other side is a painting of Jesus, a red-skinned Native Indian man with a high feather head piece, his hand pointing to a bleeding heart on his chest, encircled by a crown of thorns. We stand in front of it for a while and think, the artist tried to integrate the gospel into Native Indian cultural understanding. We would love to speak to the priest about these paintings but there is nobody around.

We have traveled across Montana and enjoyed the changing landscape from the highest mountain passes of the Rockies, to hills and plains. The weather becomes windy and rainy as we drive through North Dakota and stays that way until we come to the Great Lakes. From a distance, we see the long curve of the 'Big Mac', the fife mile long Mackinac Bridge spanning the narrows between Lake Michigan and Lake Huron. Crossing it shortens our travel time to Bay City considerably. South of it, is a German settlement, Frankenmuth that interests us. It has a unique history.

A group of conservative Lutherans from Franconia, Germany, came to this continent to do missionary work among the Chippewa Indians. They settled in four villages, one, Frankenmuth, survived and is now known as 'Little Bavaria'. We visit the old log house near the centre which served as a school and a church. On its wooden benches native and white children sat together receiving their basic education and worshipping together with their parents. We walk through the streets and see large decorative paintings on their house walls as we have seen them in Bavaria. Waitresses in 'dirndl dresses' serve German food in their restaurants. Their festivals and plays attract millions of tourists a year.

We visit the museum, look at old tools and utensils, read reports about the hard life of the first pioneers and check the passenger lists. Hildegard is surprised; the names of them are the same as those in her father's congregation back in Germany

Cemeteries tell a lot about the history of the place. Many of the first pioneers died young, in their thirties and forties, among them many children. The inscriptions, all in German, reveal the circumstances. We are moved by the endurance, the courage and ingenuity of these people.

From Frankenmuth we drive across the Lower Michigan peninsula into Canada, to Stratford. We are lucky to get tickets for the Shakespearean festival on the last day of the pre-season two for one sale. 'Anthony and Cleopatra' is on the program and we are looking forward to seeing the play. During the intermission, Hildegard and I discuss the performance. It is not what we expected. The stage is set for a modern version. Actors wear 19th or 20th century costumes and local vernacular. The Roman legionnaires wear Russian army uniforms with rifles and pistols. Anthony looks like a commissar. The Shakespearean tragedy is approaching a comedy - more silliness than passion. We are in a way disappointed although the whole experience, going to the festival, is enjoyable.

The next morning we set out for London to the University of Western Ontario. Krista has considered it for postgraduate studies in Psychiatry. We want to get a feeling of life on the campus to tell Krista about our observations. The buildings are, like many Canadian universities, in Neo-Gothic style, like Oxford, with a few modern additions. It is semester break and the lecture halls are closed, so we cannot go inside. We walk through the campus with its open green areas and think we could study here.

We stroll around in the town and visit the oldest residence in London, the Eldon House, now a heritage museum. It is a step back into history.

We shorten our stay in London because of my arrhythmia and head for Kitchener where the Bachmanns are expecting us. Gerhard and Ruth welcome us royally. I had hitchhiked with Gerhard through the States during our exchange student year. They insist that we stay in their guest room though we tell them we feel quite comfortable in our motor home. The next morning my pulse is still irregular and Gerhard and Hildegard take me to the hospital. Medication cannot bring it into normal rhythm and the doctor suggests electro shock treatment. Hildegard phones Michael and asks if I should agree to it. He assures us it is a normal procedure and safe. After the first shock, my heart gets into normal rhythm again and I can be dismissed.

At the supper table, when we exchange pictures and experiences, Ruth tells us we have to visit the St. Jacobs village.

The next morning we follow their advice. On the road we pass a couple in a horse and buggy, who seem to be heading for the same destination.

St. Jacobs, the former 'Jacobstettel' is the place where Jacob Snyder and his fellow Old Order Mennonites arrived in their Conestoga wagons in the early 19th century. The famous 'St.Jacobs Farmers' Market' has become a modern shopping mall, a tourist attraction. There is still some of that original rural atmosphere in this place, The Amish deliver their farm products by wagon and their horses drink from the old water troughs beside the parking lot. Benjamin's Inn and Restaurant, the former coach stop, still has some of its old world charm. Snider's Mennonite flour mill now houses workshops for jewelers, potters and glass blowers. The huge millstones displayed in the foyer are reminders of its original function. We buy some of the fresh food from the stands to fill our fridge in Moto.

The 'Mennonite Meetinghouse' museum is worth seeing for us. In video and pictorial displays, we relive the story of the Mennonites from the early Swiss Anabaptists and all their different moves to their final settlements in Ontario.

It is Sunday when we leave the campground in St. Jacobs. We drive along a country road. At the Amish meeting place we see their horses and buggies neatly lined up along the fence. In the next village, we notice a row of black sedans parked beside an Old Order Mennonite Meetinghouse, a step up from the horse and buggies.

We take a detour along a lonely side road and drive over a one lane covered wooden bridge, one of the landmarks in this area. Its sides are enclosed and support a roof which extends over the bridge to protect the wooden structures from rain and snow.

In Jordan, we marvel at the huge wooden cider press and wonder who can operate that monster.

We arrive in Niagara-on-the-Lake in the early afternoon and search for the Shaw Festival Theatre. It is still pre-season and we get good tickets for the 'Joan of Arc' drama. The setting has modern elements of guerilla warfare but is very convincing. The performance is excellent. The actress playing Joan is exceptional. It is after midnight when we find a campground.

The next morning we have a late breakfast and spend time exploring the city. We watch in awe the masses of water from the Niagara River plunging down over the wide cliff of the Falls. It is overwhelming.

We have arranged to meet Michael and Tannis in Fredericton. He has come here for a medical conference. We decide to take a shortcut to New Brunswick through New York State, Vermont and Maine.

We want to get another view of the falls and stop at the smaller American falls, walk down to the foot of them and look up at the enormous amount of water shooting over the escarpment. A look back at the Horseshoe Falls on the Canadian side shows us how humongous these falls are.

We drive through the beautiful rolling hills with its tidy villages and stately pioneer houses in New York State. In Vermont, we think we are in the 'Holy Land', when we enter Bethlehem and later Gilead, Bethel and Lebanon. At certain points of interest, we stop and explore. There is the Marble Museum in Procton. It has marble pieces in different colors and designs from the quarries of several mountains, which we passed in Vermont.

Another unique site is Shelburne, the most diverse museum we have ever seen with an astounding collection of 'Americana'. It is part of a museum village. Some of the thirty-seven buildings belonging to it have been reconstructed or moved to the site from different places to recreate a historic village of the pioneer times. I walk through the farm equipment hall with all sorts of horse harnesses, wagons and machinery. It reminds me of the time when I saddled horses and operated similar machinery.

Hildegard finds household utensils, artifacts and cultural objects quite fascinating. Two of them we remember distinctly, an oversize cradle for older, bed-ridden people and the collection of fifteen hundred dolls from different periods. Some are rag dolls, small and tall, sleepy and happy, dressed in beautiful costumes, some fashion dolls of the Barbie variety and those with batteries, which move or talk if one presses their belly button.

Our last campsite in the States is Sunset Point in a quiet pastoral setting with a view of the ocean. Hildegard and I take a long walk to the ocean and watch the amazing sunset before we go to bed. The next morning we bid farewell to beautiful New England, fill our tanks with the cheaper gas and drive across the border back into Canada.

Our first stop is Fredericton. Michael and Tannis are in their hotel. While Michael is attending his conference, Tannis will be our tour guide for the next week.

We board the ferry and soon see the red cliffs of Prince Edward Island, the land of Tannis' forebears, the Warrens. Her great-great grandfather is buried in one of PEI's cemeteries. Tannis has forgotten in which one of the many we pass. Fortunately, the archivist in Charlottetown's city hall can locate it for us. While we are waiting for the result of the search, she tells us that the PEI's parliament is in session now and we might get access to the chamber. We are allowed to enter the visitor's gallery and watch the parliament in action. I do not remember what they discussed. For us it was important to be in the chamber in Government House where the 'union of the provinces, colonies and territories of British North America' was formed, the birthplace of Canada. As we come out of the chamber, Tannis points out to us on the plaque opposite to the entrance the name of her ancestor, Joseph Warren, one of the Fathers of Confederation.

Most people who visit PEI want to see 'Green Gables', the site where the little freckle- faced orphan girl with her long red braids enamored many villagers. Lucy Maud Montgomery brings her to life in her novel, 'Anne of Green Gables'. Many tourists, mainly families with children, are eager to see the place where Anne roamed around. Japanese students know the story from their prescribed English texts. We follow them over the bridge to the haunted forest, seeing it, makes the story more real but changes our perception of it, which we had created in our imagination while reading it to the children.

Cavendish, the setting for Montgomery's story is close to the beach. Tannis leads us along a hidden trail through bushes and marram grass, over dunes to Greenwich Beach at the Gulf of St. Lawrence. We take our shoes off and walk for a while through the soft yellow sand. We are the only people on this beach. The sandy part ends and we climb up to the terraced red sandstone bluffs. It is quite windy and we watch the waves of the ocean pounding against the cliffs. In the distance we see a lonely lighthouse and behind it the current of the St. Lawrence River joining the water of the bay. When the sun is setting over the ocean, we return to our motor home.

We are invited to Tannis' relatives for supper. As a hors d'oeuvre, they serve steamed mussels. Hildegard, who has an aversion to crustaceans, the scavengers of the ocean, eats them for the first time and finds them delicious. I am surprised.

We say goodbye to our hosts and Prince Edward Island and head back to Fredericton to pick up Michael. It is getting a little more crowded now with the four of us. I have been driving the motor home so far, since Hildegard does not feel safe driving it. Now Michael can relieve me. He drives to St.John and we take the ferry across the Bay of Fundy. We find out, that the bay has the highest tide difference in the world.

We are now in Nova Scotia. Tannis tells us that a short distance from Digby, where we will land, is Port Royal, a place that is important in Canadian history. We park Moto and walk over to an interesting building complex. It is encircled by wooden palisades. A young man wearing breeches, a loose shirt and clogs, welcomes us at the gate and leads us into the inner court. "This is a replica of the settlement of the first European immigrants to North America," he tells us in his French accent. "A group of French pioneers settled here in 1605 and built 'l'Habitation'. They called the area, Acadia. Later the British moved in, destroyed the settlement and expelled the Acadians. They renamed Acadia Nova Scotia and l'Habitation is now part of Port Royal". He shows us the living quarters of the Acadians, the house of the governor, the chapel, the kitchen and bakery. When he shows us the common storerooms, he mentions, "The Acadians developed good relations with the native Micmac population, learned their survival skills, how to hunt and fish and traded with them. They became their allies against the British later on".

We walk around, talk to the women in the kitchen, dressed in pretty period costumes and Hildegard inquires about old recipes. Michael inspects the platform with the canon reaching through the palisades. We thank the guide for his history lesson, stroll through the rest of the town and head south across Nova Scotia.

We find a campground between the little harbor town of Mahone Bay and Lunenburg. As usual, we first visit the tourist bureau. Fitting for a harbor city, it is on the ground floor of an abandoned lighthouse. We have a friendly chat with the attendants and they supply us with maps and tour guides. Since Lunenburg is the centre of fishery, shipbuilding and marine-related industries, they suggest starting with the Fisheries Museum, the two big red buildings close to the quay. We spend hours observing the different species of fish in the aquariums and watching the skillful preparation and packaging of fish. In the next building are models of all sorts of ships, the most famous one, the schooner Bluenose, the trophy winning racing boat from Nova Scotia. In other buildings are displays of utensils and artifacts of early settlers. It leads us back into the troublesome history of the area. The British expelled the Catholic French Acadians and brought in 'Foreign Protestants' mainly from Germany and Switzerland. The rich German heritage has been maintained and promoted and has made Lunenburg a popular destination for European tourists. We walk through the old part of Lunenburg with its beautiful historic villas of the rich merchants. The Kaulbach house with its extended frontispiece, cornices, bay windows and bracketed attic dormers is one of the most elaborate ones.

As we go back to our campsite, we pass the settlers cemetery. Most of the tombstones have German inscriptions. They tell of the hardship and suffering of the first immigrants Hildegard recognizes many names on them. They are the same again as those of her father's congregation in the Palatinate.

A poem there describes well the courage and stamina of all those early pioneers.

> A race of men that had been long
> of courage and conviction strong.
> They ask no favor but to be
> loyal, independent, free.
> With nothing but the land and sea,
> their health and strength and energy,
> they cut the forest, tilled the soil
> established business with their toil.
> Schools they built for education,
> churches for their soul's salvation.
> Mighty and heroic deeds
> wrought they for their children's needs.

Nova Scotia has a number of lighthouses along its coast. One that perhaps best defines our image of a typical lighthouse, we find just outside the little fishing village of Peggy's Cove. The lone white tower with its narrow red top stands high on softly rounded granite mounds that undulate right into the Atlantic. Powerful surf pounds against them day and night. We stand there for a while and watch and listen.

Before we leave, we quickly write a card to the children and have it stamped in the post office, the only one in Canada located in a lonely lighthouse.

From Peggy's Cove, we drive the length of Nova Scotia, through changing landscapes along the rocky shore, over rolling hills and fertile farmland.

The bridge over the Straight of Canso takes us right into Cape Breton Island, one of the most beautiful parts of Nova Scotia, we are told.

Our plan is to circle the northern part of the island.

Just outside of Baddeck, we stop for lunch and visit the Alexander Graham Bell Museum. We admire the modern design of the buildings and the surrounding garden with its abstract sculptures.

Hildegard is more interested in the involved history of the Bell family, while Michael and I are impressed by 'Alec's' (as he was called by his friends,) many scientific inventions displayed in the museum. His special field was sound and speech reproduction, his main invention, the telephone.

From the rooftop garden, we look down at 'Beinn Bhreagh', the Bell estate, beautifully located on a peninsula protruding into Bras D'Or Lake. Here he lived and worked mostly during the last years of his life and here he is buried.

South of Baddeck the Cabot Trail begins; listed in some tourist guides as the No.1 Drive in Canada and we cannot dispute that. The coastline is majestic. The trail weaves along the foothills, sometimes close to the shore, then again through tree-shaded glens. From clifftops, we can look back at the wavy line of the trail we have just traveled. In Cape Breton Island, most people seem to be bilingual. Among themselves, they speak Acadian French but they answer us in flawless English.

The wind is strong and icy on the north bend of the island. We can stay outside for only a short time to take pictures. The vistas are spectacular, red striated rocks around small bays, sparsely wooded mountains interspersed with fields on which sheep graze.

History in the 18th century has been unfair to the population of the Maritimes. The governance of the country is often decided in Europe and with that decision the fate of the people. We find this evident when we drive into Louisbourg. We are very surprised to see the town being restored to look as it did in the 18th century.

It is lunchtime and we go into a local tavern. The servants and the cook are dressed in period costumes. The waitress ushers us to a long, solid wooden table and we slide onto heavy wooden benches. She brings us napkins, half the size of a tablecloth and puts a pewter dish with one spoon in front of us. The menu for the day is pea soup and bread for an entree and sole, vegetables and rice for the main course; potatoes were considered poisonous at that time. I love the atmosphere and the food. The people are very friendly and knowledgeable. They act like Acadians from two hundred fifty years ago. One waiter tells us about the history of Louisburg. "The area was settled by the French and because of its strategic location as a harbor and trading post they fortified the town. In the middle of the century, New England and British troops laid siege to the town and demolished the fortress. In 1961 the Canadian government gave a grant to rebuild part of the city and the fortress the way it was in the 18th century". They did it masterfully. We are allowed to go into some of the restored houses furnished with period pieces.

Michael has to go back to work so we drive on to Halifax. Tannis has friends in the city, Adrian and Elaine, they show us Halifax, the old town, the fortress and the harbor. It happens that the famous fishing and racing sailboat, 'Bluenose' is in the harbor, the schooner that won seventeen races for Canada. We watch it sailing quietly out of the harbor.

For the night, Adrian lets us park Moto in their parking space. The next morning Michael buys a box of lobsters to take home. He rearranges his and Tannis' luggage, we say good-bye to our hosts and drive to the airport. Looking back, we had a wonderful holiday together.

Hildegard and I are once more traveling alone, back to New Brunswick and up to Quebec. We are impressed by the beauty of the coastline, the long wooded stretches and the small villages. One of them is Pugwash, a fishing and salt mining village, a little different from the others. We notice the street signs are in English and Gaelic referring back to their Scottish heritage. The display in the windows of the Seagull Pewter manufacture looks inviting and we drop in. There are a number of tempting artifacts and knick-knacks. Hildegard buys some napkin rings, vases and a beautifully shaped pewter goblet.

A German flag in front of a building in the next village arouses our curiosity. We turn around and read, 'Café Petit Allemande', a German bakery. We have been craving good German rye bread. We buy several loaves and some crusty German buns.

There is another surprise on the way, the unique 'Village Historique Acadian' in Caraquet Park. We park Moto on the outskirts and walk into the village. We are transported back two hundred years into an Acadian settlement. All the houses are refurbished to look like the original ones. We see the children coming out of the old school house, the girls in their long dresses and white head pieces come up to chat with us. The blacksmith is hammering his hoof nails and on the corner is the trading post and the small white church. Women, wearing period dresses, sit at the spinning wheel or the loom or dyeing wool with their own colorants and give us demonstrations. Ducks are swimming on the pond, a goat is tethered to a pole and the farmer is hitching his horse to the wagon. Everything looks very authentic and we take it all in. It is getting late; we are hungry, go into the inn, and enjoy a typical Acadian supper.

The next morning we leave New Brunswick, drive over the Centennial Bridge in Campbellton and arrive in Quebec. We are looking forward to starting the scenic drive around the Gaspé Peninsula. On our first stretch to Carleton, the road becomes quite steep, a 17% incline, and Moto hardly makes it up. The engine temperature rises fast and when we finally stop on top of St.Joseph's mountain the coolant in the radiator boils. It will take time to cool off so we walk to the lookout. A magnificent panoramic view opens up over the road we just came and the Baie des Chaleurs with Dalhousie on the opposite side of the wide mouth of the St.Lawrence River. We are, however, troubled when we look east. Black clouds rise up and fog drifts in along the scenic road, on which we intend to drive. We listen to the weather forecast. For the next week, it is rain, fog, and cold winds over the eastern part of Gaspé. There is no point in going further under these conditions. We decide to change course and take the shorter way across the Gaspé to Quebec City. We fill the radiator with new water, turn around and drive through the Miguasha Park. In its sandstone cliffs, we are told, important fossils are imbedded. We go into the museum to inquire. A number of fossils are displayed, mainly those of fishes from the Devonian period, three hundred seventy Million years ago. One specimen, the best-preserved fossil of a lobe-finned fish in the world, has a special case. From it, the attendant tells us, evolved the first four-legged, air breathing terrestrial vertebrate. On several charts, the evolution goes further to the Homo erectus, our supposed ancestor. . But both of us have problems believing we were derived from a foot long fish.

In Point a la Croix, the Cross-Point, we step back into history again. Here the French and British fought the heroic naval battle of the Restigouche, which sealed the fate of New France forever.

From Point a la Croix we drive north through the Matapedia valley to Sainte-Flavie at the shore of the St, Lawrence River. From a distance, it looks as if people are swimming in the river. When we come closer, we see they are human like concrete sculptures partly submerged, floating or standing on rafts in the water, some on the lawn in front of a small gallery owned by the artist, Marcel Gagnong. His concrete sculptures, due to the material, are roughly textured, he only detailed the head, the body is a slightly bent column with a row of square buttons in front. They stand in pairs or in family groups. Inside he has his oil paintings and a number of 'tourist traps' displayed. I talk to him in English but he does not understand. I am surprised. As a businessman and well-known artist, I would have expected him to be bilingual to converse with his customers. Hildegard has to translate.

We continue on to Quebec, the medieval walled-in city. The 'Old City' with narrow steep streets, some ending in stairs, imposing buildings everywhere, is truly enchanting. We join the thousands of people, who mill about or are seated at tables along the sidewalks enjoying a leisurely Friday night. Musicians, some in medieval costumes, abound, playing music ranging from medieval to African beat. Artists sitting around beg to draw our portrait.

In the Musée de Fort we watch a sound and light show, enacting 'the battle of Abraham' where French, Indians and the British tried to settle the dominance of New France. It is raining and we continue our sightseeing from the thirty-first floor of a high-rise with a stunning view of the city and the harbor.

From the romantic provincial capital of Quebec, we drive through a lovely rural countryside to the big city of Montreal. This week the largest jazz festival in the world is on. The traffic downtown is horrendous. Hildegard writes:

> 'I would be totally claustrophobic but Helmut handles all this closeness with poise'.

We find our way to Peter and Jeanette and receive the warmest welcome from our good friends. We park Moto in their driveway and Leslie and Stephanie, their daughters, ask if they may come in to see how we live in it. With a lavish breakfast of croissants and café-au-lait, we celebrate our thirtieth year of friendship. Peter walks with us through his prestigious neighborhood, pointing out residences where present and past Prime Ministers Mulroney and Trudeau live and the home of the Bronfman family, owners of the Seagram Distillery.

Jeanette shows us the way up the hill to St. Joseph's Oratory, a church, Hildegard describes as:

> *'ugly on the outside and splendid on the inside. Helmut and I are completely taken in by the interpretation of Gothic principles into concrete forms'.*

We walk in on a sermon and some exquisite singing, which soars upwards like its columns.

Peter has prepared a delicious dinner on our return.

He has to continue his research at the McGill University, so Jeanette shows us more of the city. At the Jazz festival, we mix with the most diverse crowd imaginable, but the very loud music drives us away after a while.

On our day of departure, we take the metro to the Notre Dame Cathedral in old Montreal. We listen to a rehearsal of the Montreal Symphony playing Tchaikovsky. We look around the cathedral, a most sumptuous Neo Gothic church with a richness of décor, which is unrivalled.

After lunch, we leave for Ottawa. We find a well-kept municipal campsite out of town. A special bus, run by the campground, takes us from the site directly to town. Our first adventure is the Museum of Civilization, a vivid, joyful creation by Douglas Cardinal, a Métis architect. He has molded the outside walls of yellow sandstone like undulating drapery around an inner core. There is movement in these massive forms. Stairs, balconies and patios pick up the circular forms and give the whole a unifying touch. The inside reflects the shapes of the outside. In spacious halls are all sorts of displays, the most monumental is the exhibit of the 'Amerindians', the earliest inhabitants, from their early history to the present. A longhouse with different totem poles identifying the original Native tribes is erected inside with utensils, clothing, artifacts, carvings and prints. Hildegard is drawn to a women's fashion display and the Children's Museum.

We cross the Ottawa River and stand before the famous National Gallery of Canada, monumental steel, glass and stone structure. The outside does not indicate what is going on on the inside. It reminds me of a modern factory or library. It lacks the warmth of the museum we have just visited. The inside has well-arranged exhibits of Canadian and European art from early Icons to Shadbolt's work, with an emphasis on modern art. We spend some time going from one room to the next, recognizing some of the artists, painters and sculptors and enjoying the works of, for us, unknown ones. The time goes by and we fear we will miss our last shuttle bus to the campground but the driver of the bus in which we ride, offers to phone the shuttle bus driver asking him to wait for us, which he does.

Being in our capital city, we do not want to miss the opportunity of finding out how our Parliament works. The building inside is quite impressive but the tour, unlike the one in Quebec, is quite short and crowded.

We drive along Sussex Drive with a view of the Rideau Canal, the Governor General's mansion and the official residence of the prime minister. When we come back to our parking lot the attendant charges us only seven and a half dollar instead of fifteen for oversize vehicles. He muses, "Nice people are more important than money".

We leave Ottawa via Highway seventeen, a scenic drive along the Ottawa River, through hilly country, past marshes and occasional lakes. Each little town on the way has its special attraction, In Pembroke, we admire huge murals on houses and public buildings, they reach from the foundation to the roof. In Sault Ste.Marie is the oldest stone house in Northern Ontario, a mansion built with red fieldstones for a Swiss fur trader. It is now a heritage house.

The landscape changes. The vegetation is sparse and large rock plateaus come to the surface. We enter the Canadian Shield. The highway now runs through Lake Superior National Park. We stop at the southern end to explore the site of the Indian Petroglyphs. We hike down a steep romantic trail to the high cliffs towering over Lake Superior. The Agawe

Rock, sheer granite, slopes steeply down to the water. We can clearly make out the reddish brown Petroglyphs on it, horse and rider, animal figures, clan symbols or spirits that may have been important to Ojibwa culture. Hildegard is too fearful to go down to the lower level where the Petroglyphs reach into the water. On the way up, we drop in at a Canadian carver's shop and admire hand-carved figures done with different kinds of wood.

We continue driving west on Highway seventeen. In Wawa, I take a few pictures of its special tourist attraction, a five m high steel and concrete sculpture of a Canada goose stretching its wings to take off.

In White River, it is Hildegard's turn to take photos of its tourist attraction, Winnie the Pooh, sitting on a tree. The story, which her godson Caelin likes so much, begins here. A Canadian officer on transfer to London sees the little orphan bear cub in the arms of a trapper who had shot his mother. He finds it so cute that he buys it as a mascot for his regiment and calls it Winnipeg, after his hometown. When his regiment moves to the continent to fight in WWI, they give the cub to the London Zoo. Little Christopher Robin Milne falls in love with it during a visit to the zoo. He shortens his name to Winnie, and his father, the author A.A. Milne, writes the story of Winnie the Pooh.

This route along the north rim of Lake Superior offers us many spectacular views. It is mountainous, full of small lakes and woods. It is getting late and we see a nice campsite in Ney's Park, not far from the highway, near the water. We prefer campsites close to nature, in parks or wilderness areas. The waves from Lake Superior are rolling onto the beach and lull us to sleep.

The next morning we hike to the Ouimet Canyon. Boardwalks lead to a viewing platform from where we look into the canyon that later leads back to Lake Superior.

Further on we discover a rare quarry, an amethyst mine. The quarry attendant allows us to dig around in the waste pile of the mined mineral and after half an hour digging we emerge with our prize, three pounds of amethyst. We have to pay the attendant one dollar per pound.

Before we come to Thunder Bay, we stop at the Terry Fox monument; it marks the area where the determined young cancer victim ended his Marathon of Hope. We pay tribute to this courageous young man.

West of Thunder Bay, we drive a short gravel road to the old Fort Williams. A high palisade fence encircles a large compound. Tents and tepees are pitched on the riverside in front of the palisades. We go through the gate, get our ticket and enter a large court. We are greeted by a man in a black suit with a stiff white collar and a top hat, the junior clerk of the North West Company. We experience the vivid life of the fur trade time. A lot of people are milling around, stockholders, voyageurs, company clerks with their Métis wives, Ojibwa fur traders, a tinsmith and an apothecary. With us are tourists from different countries. We fake an injury and visit the doctor in his office and he gives us good medical advice. One tradesman demonstrates for us how to build a canoe. We stroke the furs of different animals displayed in the pelt warehouse, and find out to which animal each one belongs.

We hear some drumming outside and walk through the large opening in the wall on the riverside. The traders are welcoming the big canoe, which just arrived at the dock. It brings guests and supplies.

We have a closer look at the tents, which we saw when we arrived. They are part of the heritage site. Voyageurs and Indian trappers in their tepees lived there while they were dealing with the North West Company. The atmosphere here is more businesslike, different from the other heritage sites, which we saw in Louisbourg and the Acadian village.

We have learned quite a bit about French Canadian history on this trip.

We get back to the highway and continuing to travel west, we come upon an unexpected surprise, the spectacular Kakabeka falls. The water thunders down over two horseshoe-shaped cliffs, divided by a prominent rock, into a Precambrian Shield gorge. The falls are nicknamed 'the Niagara of the North'. One difference is noticeable, the water of the Kakabeka is amber brown from iron deposits, unlike the turquoise water of the Niagara Falls. Many Indian legends are woven around these falls.

The landscape continues to be dotted with lakes and scrawny woods. After Kenora, a picturesque resort on the beautiful Lake of the Woods, we cross over into Manitoba.

We have heard so much about Steinbach, the Mennonite centre in Manitoba. Since it is on our way to Winnipeg, it is our first stop. We start with the Mennonite Museum. At the entrance doors, we face a large granite monument honoring the early pioneer women. On several inlaid copper reliefs, they are depicted working hard in the house and in the fields. Different displays lead us through the history of our forebears. The historical village interests me. It tells more about the beginning of the first settlers and their progress in Manitoba.

We have to bend down when we go through the low opening into the sod house. It is dark inside and musty. It is hard to believe that these were the first dwellings of the settlers. The squared log houses remind me of my home in West Prussia, as do the tools and the machinery displays. Thanks to the ingenuity and hard work of the early pioneers, Steinbach is now the fastest-growing town in Manitoba, employing their residents in homegrown industry. We admire the clean and orderly homes and estates of the Mennonites in the area.

Our next stop is Winnipeg, Hildegard has relatives there and we spend most of our time with them, sharing family news, exchanging photos, and going on excursions with them.

With the warm wishes of our dear relatives, we travel on. In Portage la Prairie our road is blocked to make room for a strawberry festival parade. We walk along with them for a short stretch and then go back to our car and switch over to the Yellowhead Highway, the northern route. It is dotted on the map, meaning it is a scenic drive. The land in western Manitoba and in Saskatchewan is mainly flat. Hildegard likes the vastness of the horizon. Large fields of canola spread a yellow carpet on both sides of the highway. Occasionally a patch of vivid blue flax blossoms is woven in.

When we approached a village in Quebec, the first thing we saw was the church steeple, in Saskatchewan it is the grain elevator. Large grain fields alternate with large stretches of rangeland.

We bypass Saskatoon and drive to the Wanuskewin Indian Heritage site, an ancient wintering camp used by different First Nation tribes. Their interpretive center and museum are designed in wood and glass, beautiful and simple.

The displays, put together and operated by them, are organized by themes, like 'the Buffalo and his Brothers' or 'Mother Earth'. They also express their spirituality, their oneness with nature and gratitude to their creator.

In an amphitheatre, we see First Nation's history and life in action, elders telling stories. The visuals are supplemented by sounds of storm, rain, birdsongs and howling wolves.

In the outdoor activity centre, we watch artists demonstrate their craft and they invite us to participate. Unfortunately, we cannot take the time to get involved. We walk along a nature trail, which leads to the valley past an archeological dig. At the end of it, we stand in front of a steep cliff, the 'Buffalo kill', and we imagine these majestic animals tumbling down to their death or being crippled and then killed.

We end this memorable experience with a meal in the heritage restaurant, ordering a tasty buffalo stew with bannock and a Saskatoon trifle for dessert.

The branches of the trees along the street to Saskatoon are so low that the roof of Moto strips some of them off. We drive, decorated with greenery over the bridge to the campus of the university and end up at the 'Musee Ukraina'. A very friendly, knowledgeable young woman, a recent immigrant from the Ukraine, a doctor of ethnology and history, explains to us the displays of costumes, utensils and musical instruments. Hildegard tells her that her mother came from the Ukraine. She becomes more personal and tells us about history, customs and her own family in the Ukraine. Hildegard feels we are departing from a friend when we finally leave.

Saskatchewan and Alberta have a large number of immigrants from the Ukraine. Alberta's Ukrainian immigrants form the second largest language group in the province.

In Alberta, while looking for a campsite in Vegreville, we discover by accident a famous Ukrainian symbol, the Pysanka, a huge, three thousand pound Easter egg. It has intricate geometric designs and is mounted on a pivotal support. From our campsite we can see the ten meter high egg turning with the wind.

On the way to Edmonton, we drop in at the Ukrainian Heritage Village, a most meaningful sequel to the Musee Ukraina. The layout is similar to the Mennonite village in Steinbach. What strikes Hildegard most about it is 'the sparseness and severity that almost hurts'.

Edmonton is our next destination. Dorothy, our friend from our first Hauskreis and Krista's travel companion, has moved from Vancouver to the place of her birth. She wants to be close to her mother who had just lost her husband. We have to catch up on the latest news and share photos. After a good meal, we climb into her new Volkswagen Euro-Van for a tour of the town. She had won this brand new vehicle in a contest from an advertisement. Her little son, Joshua, wants to show us all the practical gadgets in the van. The next morning Dorothy has to go to work and we take off for the famous West Edmonton Mall, at that time the largest in the world. We cannot fathom how all the shops and stores in this vast complex can make a living. We look at the features, mainly entertainment, that is unique to this mall. One of these allurements is the Water Park with beach, artificial waves and a submarine. Others are a petting zoo, theatre, Ice Palace and golf course. Of interest to me is a replica of a European city street.

It is raining heavily while we are in the Mall, and dark rain clouds still hang over the western sky when we emerge. Initially we had planned to continue driving on the Yellowhead Highway and go via Jasper to Calgary. Now we decide to save that spectacular part of Alberta for another trip in better weather and head straight south where the sky is a little brighter.

In Red Deer, we have to fill our gas tanks and ask the attendant what is interesting to see in the town. He suggests St.Mary's church close by. When we approach the monumental, windowless round building, we do not recognize it at first as a church; the design is so unconventional. Hildegard is fascinated by the massive round form. I am struck by the simplicity of the design. The beauty of the lines, stone flowing like heavy velvet, forming pleasant curves, awes both of us. The walls are made of a warm red brick, one million of them to complete the structure. We find that the arcs of the walls, the curves of the bell tower and the rounded tower of the confessional flow organically together. They are repeated again on the inside, in the baptism stand and the pulpit. The architect designed round light shafts, hanging down from the roof, illuminating altar and pulpit and emphasizing their importance in the church service. Inside and outside are equally inspiring and we spend a considerable amount of time taking it all in. This is a masterpiece of Douglas Cardinal, the Canadian architect, who also designed the wonderful Museum of Civilization in Hull.

We are eager to get to Calgary to see our daughter. It lifts our spirits when we see the skyline of the city in brilliant sunshine and the white caps of the Rockies glittering in the far distance. A very excited Krista is waiting for us and bids us a warm welcome. We set up camp on an empty lot beside her house and have dinner with her and her friend Tom.

The next morning Krista has to write examinations, the last ones before her semester break at medical school. This gives us time to clean and reorganize Moto, get it serviced and buy some supplies. We want to take Krista with us. She brings her luggage to Moto, including her bike, which is hung tightly in the shower stall, locks the door of her apartment and we are off on the last stretch of our long journey.

We pass through familiar territory. The grandeur and majesty of the Rockies amazes us again, as does Rogers Pass and Revelstoke. We camp at Shuswap Lake, where we spent holidays with our children when they were small. Although Krista has only been with us for a day it feels to her like a holiday and she delights herself and us with her spontaneous joy and enthusiasm.

As we pass into the Fraser Valley we realize how unique and beautiful British Columbia is and how privileged we are to live here. We are happy to come home again.

On the front door of our house, we see a colorful 'Welcome Home' sign and Hanno greets us with a big hug.

Tonight we can sleep in our bedroom again after having been away for seventy days. Our speedometer shows that we have traveled 17,575km. For both of us this trip was a wonderful experience. A large part of our country from ocean to ocean we have been able to explore and relive its history. We are thankful that we could travel without haste, at a leisurely pace and without facing any big problems and that we enjoyed each other's company and support. We take possession of our home again, which our house sitter has kept in good order.

The next days we spend unpacking the motor home, going through the stack of mail on our desk and organizing and identifying our pictures.

Hildegard has a knack for collecting all the memorabilia, photos and folders and putting them together in well-organized albums. She arranges three of them from our trip.

As we do every fall, we drive to Christina Lake to winterize our cabin. It is still warm enough to swim in the lake. We meet Sherry there and she has a surprise for us. She bought a large piece of property in the village and wants to build a retreat centre on it. She takes us to the place and asks my advice about how to realize this idea. We are excited about the project. I draw a number of design sketches for it and make a small model. We discuss them and leave it at that.

When we arrive in late spring next year, we are surprised to see that the building of the project has been started already from their own more conventional design.

I am a little disappointed not to be notified about the change but follow its progress with interest.

38. Family Events and Surprises

Our family is expanding. Anna is joining us when she and Hanno announce their engagement. I think Anna's parents in Lublin are pleased with her decision and Mother Zygo wants to come to Canada for a visit.

Krista is preparing for her final examination at medical school. We are very happy that she has found her niche, is focused and enjoys and masters her studies very well. The whole family travels to Calgary and gathers in the Medical School's auditorium to see Krista walk up to the podium to receive her certificate as Doctor of Medicine and recite the Hippocratic Oath. Hildegard and I are invited to the banquet to celebrate this important event. Krista introduces us to her friends, we talk about their studies, and future plans.

For Krista a new phase now begins. She dissolves her apartment where she has lived for three years. It is her last activity in Calgary. We help to pack her personal effects in our station wagon and take her home with us. It gives us just a few days to get ready for Hanno and Anna's wedding.

Hanno makes most of the arrangements for the festivities; he just needs the occasional advice from his parents. They decide on their own marriage ritual, influenced by Polish, German and the usual Canadian customs.

Anna's mother had come a week earlier to be part of her daughter's special ceremony. We are sorry that we cannot communicate with her directly as none of our family speaks Polish and she speaks neither English nor German. We have to have an interpreter to converse with her.

On the day of the wedding everybody in the family is excited and busy. Krista and her friends help with the preparations and getting ready for picture taking. The weather is ideal for taking them outside. One of the favorite places to do this is 'Little Mountain' with its tiny waterfall and its sunken garden with a variety of flowers and shrubs in its stone terraces as a backdrop. It is a popular place for young couples to pose for their pictures. It is so popular that we have to wait until three other wedding parties are finished and leave. Hanno has asked Ulli to be their photographer.

For the marriage ceremony, we have chosen the little, historical St. Marks church where our friend Erhard had been pastor. Anna has no father to give her away so, on the spur of the moment, I accompany her to the altar where she joins Hanno. After the sermon, we take pictures of the two, exchanging rings, signing the wedding register and Michael and Krista witnessing it. After the service, we greet the guests, chat with them for a while until Anna and Hanno step into the limousine, and drive off.

Hanno has rented the Brock-House for the wedding banquet, a two and a half acre heritage estate with beach access, outdoor facilities and a restaurant. The weather allows the guests to walk down to the beach or sit in groups in the garden. The restaurant prepares a delicious dinner and Evita, Hanno's second cousin, has baked a special wedding cake artistically decorated, which the two cut and distribute to the guests. The 'Quintessence,' a woodwind quintet of Anna's friends, entertains with music, and speeches from siblings, friends and colleagues, some quite humorous, make this ceremony an enjoyable event.

Anna's Polish friends keep her mother company and we have asked Jacob, our Polish artist friend, to translate for her if necessary. She is a little disappointed that the wedding celebration last only one day; in Poland, it goes over several days.

For Krista a new epoch begins. She wants to specialize in psychiatry and is applying at several universities for acceptance into their residency program.

Her favorite choice is Toronto. She finds out that it has the best program for child and adolescent psychiatry in which she wants to specialize, and she is accepted.

She is moving again, this time to Toronto and Hildegard is going to help her to arrange her new apartment. For the next five years she will be a resident in different hospitals and departments in Toronto.

Life goes on. Cousin Herbert, inspired by his adventurous daughter, Evita, asks me if I want to join him and his son, Johnny, to explore northern BC. They want to paddle the Bowron Lakes. I ask Michael if he wants to join us and he gladly accepts.

I had heard about the Bowron Lakes circuit from Ulli and John. They and a few other friends had made the trip several years ago and found it an exciting adventure. The Bowron Lake is the last one of a row of six major lakes in northern BC, which are connected by streams and portages to form a one hundred sixteen km long rectangular waterway.

We check our canoe and gear to see if they are 'seaworthy' pack our sleeping bags and clothes in watertight bags and drive to Abbotsford. Johnny helps us to transfer our canoe from our car up to the roof of Herbert's camper, beside his and strap everything down.

Evita has prepared air-dried food for a week and labeled it for each day. She has appointed Johnny and trained him to be the cook. I bring four loaves of bread and the necessary sausages. We check our gear again, camp stove, dishes and tents and start on our way.

We had made reservations for this trip because it is quite popular for nature lovers. Only twenty-five canoes can be launched each day, as there are only limited camping spots on the beaches accessible from the lakes.

While I settle the administrative work, the others untie the canoes and carry them to the first lake. There are eight more to come. The forest warden gives me instructions and a map, which indicates where there are accessible campsites.

We slip on our life vests, push our boats from the bank and start paddling into the wildlife sanctuary. At dusk, we locate the first campsite, it is full and we have to paddle on. There is room in the second one. Between the steep slopes of the mountains there is sometimes only a small level space accessible from the water where we can pitch our tents. We pull our canoes on land and set our tents up while Johnny prepares supper. After we finished our first meal outside, we have to protect the rest of our food from the bears. Each registered campsite has a bear cache. Michael climbs the ladder to the beam erected over the top of two poles and I hand him the bags with our food. He hangs them up, high enough that the bears cannot reach them. We do this at every campsite.

Each lake has its special character. The long narrow Isaac Lake is bedded between the three thousand meter high Caribou Mountains; its steep slopes reach down into the lake. At night, we hear the haunting, wailing call of the loons echoed back by the mountains. In the morning, as we paddle on again, we see these graceful waterfowl with their beautiful dark turquoise speckled plumage crossing our path. When we get close, they dive and disappear for a while. In the distance, we can again see the long yellow beak and the white striated necklace of the males emerging. They are accompanying us for a while. When we come too close to them, they send out their yodeling alarm calls, dive and disappear.

The Isaac and Lanezi lakes are connected by the fast flowing Caribou River. It looks scary to paddle from one into the other. We stop at the bank, have our lunch and check out the situation. A few people pulled their canoes on shore and are unpacking to portage them beyond the waterfall. They say it is too dangerous to navigate. We are prepared to do the same when another canoe pulls up beside us. We ask the man and his little daughter what they are going to do. "We went through there a few years ago and made it, we are trying it again", they tell us. Michael challenges us, "If they can do it, so can we". We check our luggage, tie it to the crossbars of the canoe and slide into the water again. Our shallow boat shakes quite a bit when we go down the waterfall into the swiftly flowing river. We have to change our paddle quickly from side to side to keep the balance. We get some spray into the canoe when we go down into the whitewater. One of us bails out the water while the other keeps the canoe steady. Herbert's canoe is heavier and he has less difficulty. The whitewater is exciting and the fast flowing river takes us along quickly. However, it requires all our attention. After this excitement, we enjoy paddling on the quiet lake again. We have time to observe nature around us. Eagles circle over us and settle down on dry branches of the fir trees, a heron stands on one leg in the water and looks at us.

This tranquility ends when we see black clouds piling up behind us and the wind starts blowing. We pull the canoes on shore at a group campground and start setting up our tent. John is ready to prepare supper, when all of a sudden, a strong squall comes up from the lake, lifts up our tent and it is caught by a tree. We quickly grab the lines, hammer our pegs in a little deeper and tie it down more securely.

Another strong gust gets under one of the canoes, lifts it up in the air and throws it 12 m further tumbling into the lake. I had never seen anything like this before. I quickly swim out into the lake to catch up with the drifting canoe, pull it back on land and tie it up properly. It belongs to a German couple, who are camping with us. The strong wind is the precursor of a full-fledged thunderstorm with lightning, thunder and downpour. I am drenched when I come into the tent and change clothing. During the night, we hear again the haunting loon calls.

Thick fog has moved in when we untie our canoes the next morning. We have difficulty staying on course paddling along the lake. The fog lifts later and we notice the landscape is changing to lowland and marsh. We paddle through shallow lakes, small rivers and sloughs. Moose are grazing in them and a moose cow with calf follows us for a short distance and then disappears into the woods again.

The small river becomes so shallow that the bottom of our canoe scrapes the sand and we have to get out wade in the water and pull the canoe on the line behind us.

It is our fifth day and we come to the last of the lakes, the Bowron Lake. When we are in the middle of the lake, we hear thunder again and it starts to rain lightly. Michael steers us closer to the shore in case the wind turns to a strong storm and we have to pull our canoe ashore. The rain hits us in the face and we paddle as hard as we can to get out of the thunderstorm. The rain gradually decreases to a trickle when we land at our starting point again. We are exhausted, carry our boats to the camper, rest a little and get ready to leave.

On the way, back, we decide to visit the old gold rush ghost town of Barkerville. We drive the Wagon Road from Wells to the once largest town north of San Francisco. At the entrance to the now reconstructed heritage town, we stop at the white Anglican Church. Some young couples choose to get married here. A little further on, we visit the school, a theater, a barbershop, a few saloons and Chinatown. Interspersed are a number of houses and huts. We listen to tour guides, in costumes of that time, including the famous Hanging Judge Begbie, telling the old story. Michael and Johnny try gold panning. They get tiny sprinkles of gold in the bottom of the pan, not worth taking home.

We arrive safely in Abbotsford, and transfer our canoe to my car again. Evita wants to know all about our trip and if the food she had prepared was sufficient and edible. We praise her for her good preparations.

Hildegard is glad when she hears us stacking the canoe back on its rack. She is a little envious when we share our adventures in the wilderness, the beautiful sights and sounds and our excitement exploring undisturbed nature as a father and son team. "I am glad you had such a good time. I do not think I could have done it", she admits.

Hildegard used the quiet time to paint while I was gone. She likes to paint on a larger scale and is happy about her own spacious studio.

We know the curator of the Grand Forks Art Gallery, Richard Reed. He lives in Christina Lake. He has connections to a number of artists and selects their best works to display in the gallery. We are always inspired when we visit the Grand Forks gallery. He asks Hildegard about her painting and we arrange an exhibition of her work with him.

Relatives and friends from Germany visit us this summer and spend some time with us in our summerhouse. Some borrow our camper or rent a car to explore BC and the Rockies. They usually inform themselves about what they want to see, using the internet, before they come.

39. Meeting relatives and in-laws

The next summer we plan to travel to visit friends and relatives abroad again. We fly to Düsseldorf, rent a car and drive first to Bielefeld to Jup and Tine, our headquarters in Germany and visit old friends from our exchange year. From there we travel on to the Palatinate. Hildegard wants to reunite with her childhood friends and relatives in her hometown, Kaiserslautern, again. Not far from there is the Mennonite High School, Kirchheim-Bolanden where a family get-together is planed

The Wiehler clan, my mother's family, has an ambitious project, the 'Wiehlertag', a clan reunion. The last one was in 1928 in West Prussia, where most of them lived. Now, after the war, the Wiehlers are scattered all over the world.

Frank, with the help of Tante Mariechen, our family chronicler, had retrieved the names of many family members and invited them for the reunion. As a member of the European Parliament's staff in Luxemburg, Frank is used to organizing parties and he does it well. He and his family are the welcoming party at the Wiehlertag. They do the registration and his children take guests to their quarters. I am quite impressed with their family involvement and tell him so and we learn to know each other more closely.

He has asked some members of the larger clan to give talks about family history and family projects and we share life stories and experiences. Some of the musical Wiehlers play piano and violins and entertain us with musical interludes. We have enough time to meet close relatives and learn to know new ones. We sit together in small groups some with a glass of wine and talk about the good old times and future plans.

A photographer tries to get the two hundred fifty-one of us together to take the 'family picture'. We all enjoy this reunion so much, that we decide to meet once every five years and the next time, they think, we should meet in Canada.

Our closing Sunday service is in the church where Hildegard's father had been pastor. She just has to mention that she is the daughter of Hugo Scheffler and she gets hugs and questions from his former parishioners.

Very important on this trip, for me and I think also for Hildegard, is to find out what effect the reunification of Germany had had on former East Germany. We had left Germany after our exchange year in Bielefeld just a few months before the unexpected happened, the Berlin Wall fell and also the fence between East and West Germany.

We cross the former border at Eisenach, a medieval town in the Thuringian Forest. From a distance already we can see the tower of the 'Wartburg'. As most of the German castles, it is built on a high cliff. We park our car in the parking lot in the forest and walk across the bridge up to the castle. Passing through several gates, we come into the inner court. We have seen several castles but this one is important for us. Duke Fredrik III had taken Martin Luther to his castle to protect him from persecution. We are shown the room where he lived. Still on his writing desk is the first edition of his translation of the New Testament from Latin into German and copies of his doctrinal and polemical writings.

The Wartburg is only a few minutes from the city of Eisenach. Strolling through the town, we pass by the Luther House and visit the Bach museum in the house where the great German composer was born.

Going east, we drive to Erfurt, another medieval town, now the capital of Thuringia. There is the old University where Luther received his doctorate. The plain building close by is the oldest synagogue in Europe. We climb 175 steps up the steeple of the Aegidien Church to have a panoramic view of the wide Thuringian Forest. Typical in these rural areas are the picturesque small villages, with their red tile roofs and church steeple in the middle. Looking down at the city, we notice here and there a few ruins from World War II. Some houses look quite dilapidated. Either their owners were not able to obtain any building material to repair them during the communist rule or they abandoned them and fled to the West. We did not see any ruins in West Germany anymore.

We have lunch in Erfurt at a restaurant in the marketplace and hear some wonderful singing. It sounds like a choir, we look around and finally locate the singers, a men's quintet standing under the vault of the Kraemer Bridge. A sign on their collection box reads, 'We bring greetings from St.Petersburg'. They start a new madrigal; their melting voices and the amazing acoustic of the vault makes their quintet sound like a concert choir. Spellbound we listen for a while and give them a generous tip. When we walk through the park, we hear these Russian opera singers practicing for their next performance.

I always wanted to visit Weimar, the capital of music, art, poetry and philosophy. In 1919 the first constitution was written here for the Weimar Republic.

From our literature lessons in High School, we knew that our most famous poets, Goethe and Schiller, worked there. We are reminded of it when we stand in front of the monument depicting the two literary titans. Of course we had to visit Goethe's Garden house to see his contemplative poem 'Wanderers Nachtlied' (night song) which he had written on the inside wall. Every German High School student knew it by heart.

I am very interested in the 'Bauhaus' which is now a museum. My training as an architect was much influenced by the teaching of this school of art and architecture. Going through the displays brings back memories of my student years.

In Jena, not far from Weimar, we visit Hans-Peter, the son of my favorite cousin Käthe. I knew him as a baby, and as a young man he was tramping through Canada in the 'hippie years' and visited us. Now he introduces us to his lovely family. They have five beautiful children. For Judith, the oldest one, I arrange an 'au pair' place with a Mennonite family in Vancouver for the next year. Hans-Peter and Christiane take us on a tour through the historic city. He shows us his Christian High School, of which he is principal, the old university and the Zeiss factory, well known for its precision optics.

Most of the nights we spend in Bed and Breakfast places; there are many of them. We just look at the sign in the window of a house, 'Zimmer zu vermieten'. (Room for rent) We want to mingle with ordinary people of the area. When we knock at the door and ask if their room is still available, they see our car license plate and take us for 'Wessies' (West Germans) and are rather reserved. Their attitude changes when we tell them we come from Canada. They are more open to answering our questions about the reunification. One of our hosts is a tradesman and tells us, "Life was not too bad under the Communists. We did not have to make decisions, they were made for us. There was no rush, no unemployment, and no competition. Now we have to work harder to compete, but we are glad that we can travel, visit friends and relatives in the West and can buy what we need.

What annoys us is that West German firms take advantage of us; they use the stimulus money from the government to refurbish their own businesses in the West and send us their outdated equipment which makes it hard for us to compete".

Going on to Dresden, we see a sign 'garden house for rent', instead of the common 'room for rent', we inquire and this romantic cabin is available, just right for our 39th wedding anniversary. It has a bathroom, a small kitchenette and a balcony. In the morning, we are wakened by the cackling of a flock of geese, and sheep are greeting us when we go out to buy groceries. We love it.

In Dresden, the beauty of the city, the former 'Queen of Baroque', overwhelms us,

We park our car not far from the Elb-Terrace where we have a delicious lunch and a gorgeous view across the Elbe River, the countryside and the Elbsandstone Mountains. Looking towards the town, we can see the heap of rubble all that is left of the famous 'Frauenkirche' after the terrible bombing in February of 1945 shortly before the end of WW II which destroyed most of the city and killed countless residents and refugees who fled from the Russian army.

We are amazed to see the city being rebuilt so well again, especially the Zwinger Palace square. We walk along one wall with Puttos and figures of dwarfs, fauns and ancient gods. It leads to the gallery wing, exhibiting 'Alte Meister', Dutch, Italian and German painters and an extensive sculpture display from several centuries.

In the wing adjacent to the gallery, we happen on the prestigious porcelain collection of Elector Augustus the Strong. It is perhaps the largest, most comprehensive in the world and Hildegard finds it fascinating.

On the other side of the square, the Semper Opera and the Court Church have been restored from rubble to their old splendor.

Later, we drive into Meissen, the famous porcelain-producing city. In the entrance hall of the prestigious factory, we are overwhelmed by the display of all the old and new china designs which are produced here. We are allowed to watch the production of china from preparing the clay to the final hand painting of the plates. When we tell the artist that we come from Canada and own a set of Rosenthal china, he explains the whole procedure to us in detail.

In two days, we have to be in Berlin.

We heard that a group of Mennonites wanted to visit their former homeland, West Prussia, now Poland. We asked if we could join them and they agreed to pick us up from the Bernau metro station in Berlin.

We stay overnight with Cousin Helmut Gaestel, a retired high school teacher from former East Berlin.

We are an hour early at the Bernau station. Hildegard likes to be on time. We sit on a bench and watch people boarding and leaving the train. I notice a middle-aged woman, very straight, pulling her suitcase behind her. I point her out to Hildegard "She looks familiar to me but I do not remember where I may have met her". We walk down the stairs from the platform and sit down on a bench outside the station. Another couple is sitting there with their suitcases and we ask them if by chance they are waiting for the same bus as we are. They are Pastor Krueger and his wife from the Mennonite congregation in Berlin. We know them only from our telephone conversation, when we arranged to meet with them.

Another couple joins us; I recognize them, Ursula and Christoph. I had spent four weeks with Ursula in the Mennonite Voluntary Service Camp in Kiel some forty years ago.

The bus comes and we step on board. The woman, whom we saw at the platform, enters the bus with us. "We have kept seats for you in the back of the bus," the driver tells us. We file in and Hildegard sees a small woman in a colorful dress in the back row. She recognizes her childhood friend from Kaiserslautern. "What a coincidence, Gerda, I have not seen you for ages, how are you?" she asks her in her exuberant way and all the people in the bus turn around or wake up. There is no end to their questions and answers. The 'familiar' woman sits down before me. I finally address her "I think I have met you before but I do not remember where, I am Helmut Lemke". "And I am Hanna Kohnert, I think we sailed on the same boat from Bremerhaven to New York and participated in the same MCC student exchange program in 1951. I went to California and you to Ohio". She is now married to an art- history professor in Berlin. We are both involved in art and have a lot to talk about.

We 'Berliners' are a humorous, noisy bunch in the back and our laughter revitalizes the others in the bus. Time flies by and we cross the border to Poland without much difficulty. Distances here seem so short for us Canadians.

Our first night we spend in a comfortable tourist hotel in Warsaw. The city has suffered severe damage during the war. On our sightseeing tour, we are often reminded of that. The guide leads us to the monuments of the Jewish Ghetto uprising and the Warsaw uprising of 1944. We stand quietly before them while she tells us the story. The Polish Underground army attempted to free the city from German occupation while the Russian army advanced to the outskirts of the city. The Poles hoped they would support them in their struggle. But the Russians intentionally waited until the Polish forces had to surrender to the German army before they moved in; they could now claim to be the liberators of the city. The Poles still feel resentment towards the Russians.

Hildegard and I rent a horse and carriage for a sightseeing tour of our own and admire the well-rebuilt historical parts of the city. We go up to the thirtieth floor of the cultural centre for a view of the Polish capital from above.

The main goal of our trip is to see places where our Mennonite ancestors had settled and lived during the last four centuries. Several of our group remember the villages and farms from which their fathers, grandparents or relatives had been expelled.

They are excited now to walk 'in the footsteps of their forefathers'. Our tour leader has a list of Mennonite churches which we want to locate.

In Ober Nessau, the Catholic priest greets us and allows us to have a short evening service with singing and prayer in the former Mennonite church. We hold a collection and present it to the priest for the maintenance of the church. The organizers of the trip brought a plaque, indicating that this church had been founded by Mennonites from Holland and Germany. They were allowed to place it on the outside wall. Many of the Mennonite church buildings are now used as Catholic churches and we always have permission to go inside and have a short service. Mennonite does not sound as bad as German. Some of the smaller meetinghouses are now used as multiple family homes or farm storage buildings.

Children and older Polish people from the village often stand behind their fences and watch us coming out of the bus. Some of us go over to them and ask if they know the Wiebes, Penners and Neufelds who used to live here. The older ones, who still speak broken German, remember them. "They were good people"

An old Oma tells Hildegard she has a granddaughter in Toronto and wonders if perhaps she has met her. Hildegard tells her that is very unlikely but promises to send her greetings from her Oma. The old woman smiles, thanks her and shakes her hand.

We drive through a number of towns and villages, some of them are founded around estates of Prussian nobility. Schloss Schoenberg, the castle of count Finkenstein, is one of those. It is now a romantic ruin, overgrown with vines. The Russians blew it up three weeks after they had occupied it after the war; it was the property of a capitalist.

In Kulm we walk to the leaning tower. It is not quite as high and as far leaning as the one in Pisa. It has some Mennonite connection but I do not remember what it is.

Our interpreter, Franz, shows us his home city Graudenz, (Grudziadz) and the Goethe Schule, which he and children from the German minority and some children of the Polish nobility attended.

The next stop brings up some memories from my school years in West Prussia. At the beginning of the summer vacation, we sometimes went on an outing over the 'Rollberge' (the rolling Hills), a trip to which we always looked forward.

Now I relive this childhood experience again when we board a boat in Osterode on the highlands and sail through five small lakes connected by the Oberland Kanal down to Elbing near the Baltic Sea. The lakes are on different altitudes, with hills in between. To make the canal navigable would have required building and operating thirty-two locks. To build those would be quite expensive, so an engineer from Elbing devised a system to pull boats on a carriage on rails over the hills.

As we approach the first hill, many are anxious to find out how we will get over it. The captain maneuvers the boat slowly onto the submerged dry-dock carriage. We notice a little quivering when the boat interlocks with the carriage as it is pulled out of the water. It is a strange feeling to travel in a boat on land. We wave to the few passengers who pass us in the boat that is going down.

The captain explains the whole procedure to us. The schedule is arranged in such a way that the descending boat, through its weight, is pulling the ascending boat up the hill. For its start, it usually needs help from a pulley, which is operated by waterpower via a paddle wheel turbine. This navigational venture built one hundred years ago is unique in the world; it is economical and environmentally friendly.

Originally, the Oberland Kanal was a waterway to transport farm produce and lumber cheaply from the inland to the coast, now it is a tourist attraction.

From our boat, gliding across these shallow lakes, we have a view of my lovely, pastoral West Prussian landscape. Herons are standing on the swampy banks waiting for their prey, and storks picking some of the croaking frogs from the big water lily leaves. Other waterfowl are flying and swimming around. After we have covered about half of our ten-hour trip, a strong wind arises followed by a downpour. The captain fears the flat-bottom boat could capsize in the storm and heads for the next landing place in Hirschfeld. From there we take the bus to our hotel in Gdansk. It becomes our headquarters for further excursions. We have one day at our disposal. We phone Henryk, the Polish husband of Gerda Wiehler our third cousin, in Elbing. He offers to drive Hildegard and me to my home village. He is a retired marine engineer and has time for us.

On our 'Polrailpass' we travel from Gdansk to Elblag and meet Henryk at the station. He welcomes us warmly and leads us to his black Mercedes. Hildegard finds that he looks like a Wiehler, short and stubby, an affable and agreeable person. He apologizes for his poor German, which is not that bad. He says his two sons are fluent in German, having studied at German universities.

We drive the same roads which we drove 18 years ago in our rented motor home. I am anxious to see what my birthplace looks like now. We park the car at the Cornelsen farm, their house has collapsed, only the barn is still standing. We go with Henryk along the driveway to our house. When we come past the big willows, we are disappointed. There is no house or farm building anymore, not a brick or a post, only tall weeds, nettles and thistles as tall as I am. Only some of the old willows are still standing. The Poles in the countryside dismantle unoccupied houses and use bricks and lumber as building material or firewood for their own purposes. I am surprised that there is no trace of a building left anymore, nothing to come back to. I look over to neighbor Reddig's place. His house is gone too. It starts to rain and we go back quickly to the car. Our schoolhouse is deserted and a part of it has collapsed. More and more houses in our village have disappeared and most fields are not tilled. This was one of the most fertile regions in Germany, the breadbasket of the country. Now it is wasteland.

In Grunau, where our railway station is, I want to see what has happened to the Bartel estate. It was the largest Mennonite farm in the village and the Bartels were members of our church. The large house is badly neglected, windows broken and boarded up. The Pole who lives there wants to sell the farm to us; he is drunk and not interested in keeping it productive, he wants money for booze.

When we drive past my Grandpa's house, we do not want to enter his driveway to be saddened even more. Henryk drives through to Marienburg. I want to locate my former school which I attended for five years. The stately brick building with its large windows had been badly damaged in the last months of the war. Part of it has been rebuilt. It is lower now and covered with light grey plaster. I recognize it only when I go into the schoolyard and see it from the back. It does not look like my school anymore. It has another function as a correction centre for young adults and Henryk advises me not to go further inside.

Henryk takes us to the railway station in Marienburg; he is such a faithful companion and friend. We say good-bye to him and thank him for his kindness. We take the train to Gdansk and have a late supper in the hotel.

The main center of the Mennonite settlements in this area was southeast of Danzig, the 'Grosse Werder' (large lowlands) in the Weichsel (Wisla) Delta. Many of our people in the bus come from there or had family members or relatives living in one of the villages. The excitement is great when they recognize the house where they or members of their family used to live.

On the other side of the Weichsel and Nogat rivers, in the 'Kleine Werder' are the villages where my relatives the Wiehlers and Lemkes had settled. In Klettendorf we stop at a distinct 'Vorlaubenhaus', a timber-frame house with a portico over the entrance. One of my Wiehler relatives lived there. The present Polish owner welcomes us and lets us have a look into the rooms inside.

Not far from this estate is my home church. It is now, like several of the other Mennonite Churches, an active Catholic church. The priest opens it for us and we have a short remembrance service inside.

Our sister church in Thiensdorf is completely gutted. We go slowly through its open door, when we are inside one of us starts to sing and all join in. The sound resonates from the open vaults so that we sound like a big choir.

After the harvest, the church will be filled with potatoes and corn.

We now drive north towards the Baltic Sea. We Mennonite farmers want to visit Kadinen. Not far from the Prussian crown prince's Royal Palace was the stud farm for the Trakehner horses, the spirited warm-blood thoroughbreds which jumped for gold in equestrian competitions. They also were exceptional in dressage performances. They still breed the horses here. We can see a number of these beautiful animals grazing on the meadow behind the stables but we are not allowed to go onto the property.

Frauenburg (Frombork) at the Baltic Sea is the most northern part of our tour. We climb up to the top of the tower of the Planetarium where the astronomer Nikolaus Copernicus did his scientific experiments. We have a panoramic view of the Vistula Lagoon and the Baltic Sea. Below us, we notice a funeral procession entering the Gothic Cathedral.

This is the last day we spend with the group. The next morning after breakfast, we say good-bye to our travel friends.

As we leave the hotel, we see a couple in the hall unwrapping a bouquet of flowers. They approach us and ask, "Are you the Lemkes?" Hildegard affirms that, looks at the petit, friendly woman and tells her, "You must be Izabella's mother, she looks just like you". "And I am her father," says her husband, a balding, jovial man behind her and with a smile he hands Hildegard the flowers with a kiss on her hand, as it is custom in Polish high society.

We had phoned the Kajzers and gave them greetings from their daughter, our good artist friend from Vancouver. They have invited us but we told them we might not be able to see them because we are on a guided tour. So they have come to see us. They take us to their apartment in Oliva. "Izabella has told us so much about you, we could not miss the opportunity to meet you when you are so close here," Mrs. Kajzer tells us, as she shows us their artistically furnished place. They are such a welcoming couple. Mr. Kajzer brings Hildegard a box, "A small gift for you". Hildegard opens it carefully. It is an amber necklace from small amber pieces washed ashore which he had collected and strung together. For me he has a small sculpture, a symbol of the hanseatic town of Danzig and for both of us he adds a piece of polished amber with an imbedded insect. They are such thoughtful gifts, mementos from my home country.

They serve us a delicious lunch and drive us to the railway station. On the way, we stop at the solidarity monument, erected for the victims of the Gdansk shipyard uprising. It consists of three forty-two meter high slender crosses facing in different directions with large abstract reliefs and script at the lower section. Mr. Keizer proudly explains to us what the monument means to him, the beginning of a new era.

They wait on the platform and wave as our train leaves the station. We are really moved by their attention and kindness.

We have interesting company on the train to Warsaw. Three young Polish engineers want to practice their English, they tell us what we should know about their country, and they warn us of the crimes of Polish and Russian Mafiosi at the railway stations. That is perhaps the reason why Andreas insists on picking us up from Warsaw instead of letting us go on to Lublin on our Polrailpass. Shortly before we arrive, our train is hit by a terrible rainstorm, which tears the transmitter off the roof of our electric train. It takes two hours to repair it before we can move again. Andreas and Janina, Anna's brother and mother, are anxiously waiting for us and are relieved when we finally arrive. They greet us warmly. We present Janina with the flowers, which the Kajzers had given us. Andreas drives us to Lublin. He is a very fast driver. We ask him, "Do you ever get speeding tickets?" He smiles, "I attach a twenty zloty bill to my driver's license when I show it to the cop and I only get a warning". At home, Ceslaw, Anna's father, is excited about our coming.

We are shown our room in Andreas' beautiful home, while Janina sets the table. I am not used to Polish hospitality yet. It is late and I am hungry and help myself generously to the good Polish bread and sausage. Thinking this is the dinner, I thank Janina for the delicious meal. She smiles, takes the dishes to the kitchen and comes out with the main course, potatoes, steak, fish and vegetables, followed by a lavish dessert. I was told it is impolite in Poland to pass up food that is offered to you, so I put at least a little on my plate and continue eating. Fortunately, they accept my excuse for not drinking Vodka.

The next morning Andreas takes us on a sightseeing tour. He shows us palaces of famous Polish nobility, the Bielinski Palace that is now State property and count Zamoyski's Baroque Palace in Kolowka, modeled in part after Versailles. It is considered to be one of the most beautiful Baroque palaces in Poland and we can confirm this after we have walked through the richly furnished rooms. It survived both World Wars unscathed.

It has been a full day, maybe a little too much for me. I do not feel well and go to bed with a fever. The next morning I sleep in while Andreas shows Hildegard more of the surroundings of Lublin. Ceslaw wakes me up for lunch. He wants to know how I am but I cannot tell him, he does not understand me and Andreas is not here to translate. I have to guess what he is saying; we often shake our shoulders. With my Polish travelers language guide and dictionary, I try to fit words together. Anna had helped me with the pronunciation of this difficult language. If Ceslaw guesses the meaning correctly, he responds with a barrage of Polish words which I do not understand. It is both humorous and embarrassing and we are glad when Andreas and Hildegard come back again.

Andreas has shared with Hildegard some of his marital problems, his divorce and his concern for his young daughter, Ola. He does not have custody of her and is prevented from seeing her.

On our last day Andreas wants to show us the Lancut Palace, one of the greatest aristocratic residences in Poland. We walk through the large English garden and park to the beautiful baroque castle. It is now a museum and an art and music centre. In one of the adjoining buildings, we have a look at the largest collection of horse drawn carriages.

A traveling art exhibition has just opened in one of the wings, realistically done busts and figures of famous Communist politicians and labor leaders, not very exciting.

When we come back, Janina serves us a delicious farewell dinner and Ceslav presents us with some gifts, a man's umbrella for me, very suitable for the present weather, and for Hildegard an elegant leather handbag.

We have had a good time together and learned a little more about Anna's hometown and family and Polish customs. We have appreciated the Polish hospitality. We hug them good-bye and they are close to tears. Andreas takes us back to Warsaw and we board the train to Berlin.

We pick up a new rental car in Berlin, spend a night with my cousin and the next day drive west through the oak and pine forests of Brandenburg and through the clean and tidy villages in Mecklenburg. When we drive past Ludwigslust, I remember the place where I crawled across the border into the Russian Zone after the war and had my first encounter with the Russian military police.

Driving along the autobahn we see a sign, 'twenty km to Schwerin'. I look at Hildegard "Shall we take a detour and visit the city?" I ask her. She nods. We have a short sight-seeing tour through the town and I show her where I spent half a year in a military hospital and from where I started my adventurous trip to West Prussia to find my mother.

We turn back to the freeway to drive to Schneverdingen, cousin Günter's home. He and Hanna live on the outskirts of the town, with the Lüneburg Heath at their doorstep. They welcome us warmly and show us our quarters in their spacious guest suite. We sit on the patio, enjoying some refreshments, and talk about our life and our children. Karsten, their oldest son, is training to become a police inspector, like his father. The next day we take a walk through the blooming heather. Hildegard loves the wide, open area and the big sky. It is so quiet here and we hear the bees in the heather, the producers of that delicious heather honey.

We meet a shepherd, with his large flock of black- nosed sheep, the 'Heidschnucken', grazing on the heather. His dogs are eager to keep the flock together. It is such a peaceful scene.

Günther and I want to go further into the heath. He fits a bike for me and we ride along sandy trails, over boardwalks through marshy and sandy areas. Ducks and other birds look out of the reeds and Günther tells me their names and their habits. Hildegard does not come along; she does not feel safe anymore riding a bike on these tricky trails.

Günther and Hanna are also tour guides. When needed they take a group of tourists through the historic villages, the stone-age burial grounds marked by large boulders and the inviting country inns with their outdoor terraces and gardens.

On his free day Günther drives us around through the picturesque heath villages with their half-timbered farmhouses with low hanging reed-covered roofs and wide barn gates. Not far from here is the artist's colony of Worpswede. We stop in a few ateliers and Hildegard talks to her fellow artists about their work. We visit the museum with exhibits of local artists from the Impressionist and Expressionist periods.

We have a few relaxing days in Schneverdingen. Hanna spoils us with her delicious meals.

On our way to Bielefeld, we see a street sign 'to Lemke, three km'. We have to go there. At the entrance of the village, Hildegard takes a picture of me beside the sign with the name of the 'Lemke' village.

Jupp and Tine have beds ready for us. We feel at home when we come back to Bielefeld. They do not feel they need to entertain us and this gives us some freedom to plan our time. We still have a number of friends here from our exchange year.

Some things have changed in Bielefeld, it now has the shortest and most expensive 'U-Bahn' in Germany; the underground train has four stations.

Hildegard wants to visit friends in the city and do some window shopping. I would love to see some of my old school friends in Peine, about 150km east of Bielefeld, so we spend this day each one on his own. First I drop in at my favorite classroom teacher, Dr. Sundermeyer. He is still the kind, compassionate person I knew from my school days, interested in finding out what his former students have achieved in life. We talk about our hobbies, our literature classes in school and how much his teaching had meant to me, After a while, he walks over to his bookshelf, pulls out three small booklets with his own poems, and gives them to me as a memento of our school time. I am moved by this. He accompanies me to the door and wishes me well.

Klaus, our 'class clown', is surprised to see me again after such a long time and calls a few classmates together. We meet in a café and talk about past and present times.

I also find out that my first girlfriend, Erika, lives in Peine. I am a little hesitant to call her. She is delighted to hear from me again and gives me a big hug when I visit her. Her nice blond hair is now almost white but she still has the old spunk and remembers many incidents about our time together. She introduces me to her husband, he has heard a lot about me, he tells me.

It takes a ten-minute drive from Peine to Handorf. When we lived there, it took me three quarters of an hour to walk to school from our place. The streets and houses still look familiar to me. Past the church is the parsonage. I open the rusty gate to the garden and walk along the path to the old Tudor-style house. The new pastor greets me at the door. I tell him who I am, we exchange a few words and he lets me see the two rooms where we lived for nine years, forty years ago – old memories come back. I go out across the back yard. The old well is still there. They used to draw water from it in a pail. Neighbor Kindl still remembers me when I tell him my name.

I join Hildegard in Bielefeld again. Together we drive south to visit Adelheid in her interesting penthouse apartment. We walk through the vineyards and drive to the castle ruin of Löwenstein. Its tower and dungeon are still standing.

Back at home, Adelheid mentions an exhibition of African masks and modern wood sculptures in the Heilbronn museum. We drive over and find the masks somewhat strange. The wood sculptures are my métier and they inspire me again to sculpt.

Adelheid creates a festive atmosphere with candles and good music for our last meal together. Afterwards we sit comfortably around the fireplace and she tells us about her childhood in East Prussia, her experiences in East Germany and her present teaching challenges.

Our time passes quickly and we have to return to the airport. Our last night we spend with cousin Gerhard. In his spacious apartment, he always has room for guests. He shows us his work place and the complicated machines on which he creates precision instruments for medical research and diagnostic tests.

The next morning we take leave from the hospitable couple and fly back to Vancouver.

Shortly after we returned home, Hildegard gets an invitation from the Burnaby Arts Council to exhibit her work in their small gallery together with other local artists. Twenty guests, friends and relatives, come to see her display on her opening day and she receives good responses.

The first snow falls, a sign that Christmas is approaching. When we built our house, I planted forty small fir trees as a natural fence around the perimeter of our property. They have grown quite tall now. In the front, we keep them low but in the back, they grow undisturbed. A few days before Christmas, I cut off the top of the highest one and it becomes our Christmas tree. To decorate it, we have to make compromises. Each one of us contributes something from our home tradition. We agree to use natural, mainly handmade decorations. With some of our artistic friends we come together for a pre-Christmas workshop and assemble a variety of beautiful golden yellow straw stars. Red apples serve as weights to balance out the level of the branches. Of course wax candles are part of the Christmas tree, both of us used to have them on our trees at home. We do not want to miss the smell of the wax and the flicker of live candles. Bringing in a fresh tree shortly before Christmas Eve greatly reduces the fire hazard. We have a few rules: there is to be a pail with water on the balcony and the candles are only lit if someone is in the room.

The whole family gathers on Christmas Eve in our house. Hildegard cooks the traditional, easy-to-make Christmas dinner, 'Königsberger Klopssuppe', potatoes with a special gravy-soup, meatballs and cranberry sauce. Afterwards we all celebrate. We invited Tannis' parents to celebrate with us. We read the Christmas story and join in singing the well-known Christmas songs. We miss Krista's sensitive and joyful accompaniment on the harpsichord. So we sing a Capella in four-part harmony. Michael and I play recorders to enhance the singing and to get some variety. The Warrens have good voices and it sounds almost professional. Krista can get time off from Boxing Day to New Year and we celebrate again with her as a family.

40. Becoming grandparents

Before Christmas, I design and start to build a cradle. I have brought home some rough solid maple boards from Bob's sawmill in Christina Lake. I plane them, cut and fit them together and add a few simple decorations. It has to be perfect, Grandfather's legacy for our first grandchild. The cradle gets finished just in time.

On Epiphany 1996, Tannis gives birth to her first child. We grandparents are as excited about the little girl as her parents. They choose the name Madison. It is not a very familiar name to us and I have to get used to the sound of it. We are all glad and thankful that everything went well with mother and child. Madison looks lovely in her new baby outfit and the new cradle.

Mike and Tannis went to Point Grey Fellowship with me when they lived in Vancouver. After they bought their house in Port Moody, they joined a Baptist church in their neighborhood. Tannis has a Baptist background and it was important to them to attend a church where they can visit and communicate more easily with members of their church.

Three weeks after Madison's birth the family gathers in the Blue Mountain Baptist Church for her dedication. Their pastor asks God's blessing for her and her parents. The grandparents, standing on each side of the small family, add their blessings and best wishes for her future, as is the custom in both the Baptist and Mennonite tradition.

Winter is coming in full force now, one foot of snow overnight. I get my skis out, drive up to Burnaby Mountain and enjoy cross-country skiing on the easy slopes in the park. I have given up downhill skiing. It is too expensive and too crowded on the coastal mountain for my skiing skills and my age. Here, up on the hill, I am sometimes the only skier and I love to glide over the virgin snow. Hildegard has given up skiing for some time already.

Hildegard is offered the opportunity to see another part of the world. Her friend, Lea, phones, "Hildegard, may I invite you to be my guest on a trip to Bali? You just have to pay for the flight ticket, I will take care of the rest. I would love to have you come along". As a travel agent, she gets good promotional deals. I tell Hildegard, "Go for it, I wish she would have invited me too."

It does not take much persuasion and the two take off and enjoy the sun, the exotic landscape and culture in Bali. On their last day, after their final shopping, they hire a rickshaw to drive them back to their hotel. The traffic is quite heavy. A motorcycle rider and his accomplice intentionally force them off the road and in the confusion grab Lea's handbag and speed away.

All her papers, passport, tickets, money and photos were packed in her handbag, ready for the next day to leave. It takes her two days running around to report the accident to the police and get a new passport from the Canadian Consulate in Bali. Hildegard lends her the money for the return ticket. They are still shaken when they come home.

Whenever friends or relatives from abroad come to visit us, we explore our beautiful province with them and learn to know places, to which we ourselves have not yet been. Adelheid comes in her summer vacation and we visit again some islands off the coast. Many of them have attracted artists to live and work there, away from the hectic life on the mainland. They need peace and open space to create. That is what the potter Wayne Ng tells us when he shows us his work and house on Hornby Island. His living quarters, his studio and gallery are well integrated with the outdoors and he uses mainly natural building materials, available in the area.

On our way back from Hornby, we drive across Denman Island. We have heard about artist, Bently de Baron, but have never visited him in his studio. He is a very prolific artist, a painter, sculptor and potter. His gallery doors are open and we walk in. On the walls hang paintings, reliefs and intaglio carvings. The shelves on the outside wall are full of pottery, utilitarian and artistic, of sculptures, realistic and abstract, and reliefs of religious and Zodiac symbols. He likes to experiment and we love to talk with him about his new, very interesting creations. Adelheid is overwhelmed by the variety of his work and buys several gifts for her friends in Germany and an abstract terracotta owl for us. We had commented on its abstract simplicity.

We have a few days rest at home and then the whole family drives to Christina Lake. The children have a surprise for us. It is our fortieth wedding anniversary. Hanno rents a houseboat and we cruise on the lake, up to the north shore, which is only accessible by boat. We have our lunch on the quiet beach there. On our way back the kids jump from the boat into the water and swim beside the boat or ride in the rubber raft, pulled by it. We have lots of fun.

For dinner we have reserved a room in the Station Restaurant, the redesigned railway station. Our friends from Christina Lake join the party. We eat, talk, sing and have fun. Several of them present us with unique homemade gifts, which they think we might need in the future, elucidated with hilarious instructions.

Dawn, our good friend and 'artist in residence' at the mountain is in her mask-making phase. She has made masks of Hildegard and me and would like to complete the family 'portraits'. She approaches Hildegard, "Do you think your children would mind posing for a plaster mould of their faces?" "You can ask them," she replies. They agree and Dawn sticks the plaster soaked cloth strips on their faces. She will make clay and concrete casts from them. We get one of each later. A copy of the masks she attaches to her mask-wall on the 'castle' beside their own and other friends' masks. The castle is their interesting home which they have constructed themselves. It is complete with a view tower, guest rooms and arches only the dungeon is missing.

We hang our concrete masks, framed in rusty barrel rings, on the wall of our patio.

Two weeks after our wedding celebration, we get the shocking news from Monika that her husband, our good friend John, has suddenly died. They were driving home from a visit when he complained of a shortness of breath and asked Monika to drive him to the hospital. Before they arrived there, he collapsed in his seat and died of heart failure.

John had been diagnosed years ago of having an enlarged heart and Monika had been warned that he could die of heart failure unexpectedly. John with the big heart, physically and metaphorically speaking, has left us. It is very hard for the family to be without a caring husband and father and for us, to lose a dear friend. We assist Monika with the formalities of the funeral. The church and foyer are filled with mourners at his memorial service.

Winter starts with wet and cold weather; Hanno asks us if we want to spend a week in the sun, in his time-share resort on the Baja Peninsula in Mexico. We are delighted.

When we arrive at the airport in Cabo San Lucas, several taxi drivers approach us and offer to drive us free of charge to any resort. We are surprised by the generosity of the Mexicans and accept a ride. We find out the taxi drivers are paid to lure us to a resort where they want to sell us a time-share. The offer in the first luxurious resort is far too expensive for us. The taxi driver picks us up again, takes us to Hanno's resort and cashes in another fee. We enjoy our resort and its surroundings. On the second day we are invited to a showing of the whole resort with all its amenities. At the end of the showing, the agent takes us to the cafeteria and orders a free breakfast for us. In a casual conversation he asks us if we want to enjoy a week in their resort in future years. The conditions sound reasonable and the price for this one we could afford. After the presentation, the agent leaves us alone for a while. We both think about it. Most of the time in our life we have lived frugally, cared for other people; our children are on their own now, we can afford to spend a week in such a sumptuous place once a year. Naïve as we are, we believe all the promises they make and we sign the contract. We can now spend one week of our choice in a beautiful resort in Cabo San Lucas, have a spacious suite with kitchenette and balcony with view of the ocean. We can lie in the sun, walk along the beach, swim in the ocean or take a cruise and we will enjoy it.

When we leave, we have second thoughts. Does living in this luxury agree with our lifestyle, could the money be spent more wisely when so many people live in poverty?

Our neighbors, Ulli and Waltraud, have also made an expensive choice. They bought a piece of property up north with ocean frontage, the right place to build their dream house. With the help of an architect and experienced builder, they create a beautiful home right at the ocean, taking advantage of the rugged layout of the land.

Their house beside ours is now for sale. We have lived side by side for more than twenty years, now they are moving away. We will miss them.

Hildegard in her outgoing way wants to welcome the new owners. She invites them and the neighbors on each side and introduces them to each other. They appreciate very much being accepted so kindly. Later they tell Hildegard we are their best friends on the block.

We are quite a multicultural neighborhood on our cul-de-sac. The new family comes from Malaysia, two others from Italy, one from Poland, one from Ireland, one Canadian and we from Germany and further on live two Chinese-Canadian families. We have a good relationship with all of them. We trust each other to exchange house keys if there should be an emergency.

In early July, we get a phone call from an Ulrike Lohr, from the Youth Hostel in Vancouver. She tells us she is from Zweibrücken in Germany and has been an exchange student here. School is out now and she asks us for advice about what to do in Canada for the four weeks she still has available. I do not know how she has found out about us. Hildegard knows Zweibrücken well. It was a town in her father's congregation when he was pastor in Germany. Ulrike sounds quite interesting and we invite her to stay with us, it is easier to discuss things here rather than on the phone.

Her dream is to buy a used car, drive with her friend across Canada, and explore it from coast to coast. She is a short, energetic girl but her chances of buying a car are slim. I take her to a few used car dealers. Her budget is limited so we do not have many choices. At one dealer, we see an old Volvo in the back of the lot, quite dusty, indicating it has been there for some time. The price is right but the odometer shows over 200,000 km. We decide to check out a few more cars before we make a decision. A few days later, we are bargaining at another lot with a dealer about the price of a small Toyota, when a car is towed in. We look at it and recognize the old Volvo from the former lot. Now it is polished and looks much better. The dealer will check it out for us. When we come back in the afternoon, he tells us nothing is wrong with it and Volvos are reliable even at that mileage. We look at it again and she decides to buy it. It is big enough to sleep in and that will save them money for accommodations. Ulrike is very happy and the two girls go on their cross-country tour. We hope these young inexperienced drivers with a limited knowledge of English will survive.

Some time passes and we receive a phone call from Toronto. Ulrike tells us excitedly, "We had a wonderful trip, encountered no problems and were able to sell the car in Toronto with a profit. Thank you very much again for your help. We are at the airport and ready to fly home". We are glad it worked out well for them.

A few months later, I fly to Germany. My old high school friends had urged me to come to a class reunion of our high school in Marienburg. It is now fifty-two years since we left our school to serve in the army. All of us were refugees after the war and live now scattered over the continent. I am anxious to see them again and, since Hildegard does not feel like coming along this time, I go alone.

Our class 'survivors' meet once a year and take turns to invite the group for a gathering and entertainment in their hometown. For me it is the first time that I participate.

This year Karl-Heinz invites the class to Einbeck, a small medieval town in central Germany. The mayor of the town honors us with an official reception in the city hall. Karl-Heinz, we called him Heiner, is an economist who worked as an agricultural consultant in Winnipeg and Turkey. All the boys from class 11b are now reputable professionals. Back in our hotel, we tell stories. Benno, now a retired physician, asks me, "Do you remember our strict matron in the boarding school who sat at our bedside when we claimed to be sick? She did not trust us and suspected we wanted an excuse for playing hooky. She waited to check the thermometer to see if we had a temperature," he laughs. Willi, the dentist from Berlin, sits down beside me, "You were number three in the four scull rowing boat, weren't you, when our school beat the other contenders by three boat lengths in the regatta on the Nogat River?" I remember it well. We have a lot to share, memories from the past and events of the present.

For the night, I stay with the Brandes family who lives close by. Pastor Brandes has invited me to stay with them for the time of the class reunion.

Back in Handorf, Mother and I had lived with them in the parsonage when we arrived as refugees in the village. Some of their children drop in for a while to have a chat with me. I still remember them as babies, now they are young men and women.

While I am there, my cousin Walter dies of a heart attack and I go to his funeral. I meet many of my Wiehler relatives there. On the way to the cemetery, I have an intimate talk with Walters's older brother, Rudi. He is a Stalingrad survivor of World War II. In our conversation, he shares with me his wartime trauma, the gruesome fight for survival against superior Russian forces when they were besieged. It still comes back to him and is intensified when he thinks of the death of his only son in a motorcycle accident. He is very sensitive, close to tears and emotionally stressed. I have great sympathy for him.

From the small town and pastoral countryside, I travel to the metropolis of Berlin. I have planned a week there and can stay with Hanna, my former college partner. Werner, her husband, is an artist and art professor at the Berlin University. He shows me Berlin. A lot has changed since I saw it last. The Potsdamer Platz, the former bustling city centre, destroyed completely during the war, a No-Man's land on the other side of the wall, is now a huge construction site. It will soon become one of the most, modern business, shopping and entertainment malls in Europe. I am looking forward to seeing its completion.

Werner takes me to the Gemäldegallerie (art gallery) and we discuss and compare the exhibit of West and East German painters.

Ursula, a fellow voluntary service worker, picks me up for the evening and offers me her ticket for a Hindemith and Beethoven concert in the Berlin Philharmonie. It is an extraordinary experience, Beethoven is my favorite composer. The concert hall is famous for its architecture and acoustics. Critics call the style in which architect Scharoun built it: sculptural, expressionistic modernism.

I have a day on my own, buy a day ticket for public transportation and explore the city. I stop at the old Gedächtniskirche (memorial church), its only remnant, the spire, is in ruins, a skeleton preserved as a monument to the terror of war. It causes me to reflect upon life, death and the passage of time.

I notice doves flying in and out of it, a symbol of God's Spirit descending upon the old church. A new church has now been built beside it, an imposing octagonal glass and steel sanctuary with a hexagonal belfry, designed by the architect Eiermann. The Berliners nicknamed it, 'Eiermann's Puderdose und Lippenstift' (powder satchel and lipstick).

I get out of the tram at the Charlottenburger Schloss, walk through its park with its fountains and sculptures and admire the baroque facade. Beside the entrance, I notice a small sign advertising river cruises. I go down to the bank of the Havel River and board one of the small cruise ships. The Havel and its tributary, the Spree, meander through Berlin and widen in places to form small lakes. Our boat passes under some forty bridges, some so low that we are warned to duck in order not to hit them. On this trip, I discover the city from another perspective and see the back of buildings, parks and monuments to which I had never had access from the street. This is especially the case when we cruise around the 'Museumsinsel'. I have been in most of the museums, including the Berliner Dom (Berlin Cathedral). For me it is interesting to see them from the boat perspective.

Before I leave Berlin, I go once more to the former checkpoint Fridrichstrasse. I went a few times through these barracks going from West to East Berlin. The Berliners named it, 'Tränenpalast' (Palace of tears) for those who were not allowed to cross the border.

I make the rounds, visiting several relatives. Cousin Irmgard has found some new documents about our forebears, which I have not seen yet. She makes copies for me.

I conclude my visit in Düsseldorf and spend the last night with cousin Gerhard before I fly back to Vancouver.

Hildegard awaits me at the airport, gives me a big hug and a red rose. I am moved.

Every year, as we have done for a decade, we spend time in the summer and fall in our cabin in Christina Lake. Friends and relatives like our quaint, rustic cabin and join us there or rent it from us. Hildegard is always a gracious hostess.

Our children like to spend some time with us and this time Mike and Tannis bring little Madison for the first time to the mountain and she loves it, the attention she gets from her parents, grandparents and our gentle Thorin who likes to lick her hands and face. I have built a high chair insert for her so that she can eat with us at the table. She likes to sit in the children's furniture, which I built for her. Michael helps me to hang a swing into the big birch tree and she can swing on it in her mother's lap.

Years ago, Michael brought his fiancée, Tannis, for the first time to be with the family on the mountain. I needed sand for masonry work.

Krista and Tannis wanted to be helpful and offered to get it from a deposit on km sixteen on the Santa Rosa Road. They put two shovels on True Blue, our old blue pickup truck, and drove up the hill. An hour or so later I saw Krista driving the truck very slowly down the driveway. I anticipated a problem. I saw in the back of the truck the sand piled up above the sideboards. The weight made the back wheels bend inwards. I was afraid the old truck would collapse under the load and shouted to stop. By that time, they were already stuck in the curve. They did not know what the fuss was about. Not to look cheap, they had filled the truck generously. They did not know that a half-ton truck would not easily carry a ton of sand. We quickly unloaded part of the sand and wheeled it into the sand box.

Madison now enjoys playing in that sand. She loves the freedom to explore her new surroundings.

Hanno comes to join us for a week. He pulls his boat from Vancouver to Christina Lake to give us an opportunity to have a boat ride with him on the lake.

Sherry allows him to tie it to her dock at the lake. The children have fun cruising over the lake, water skiing and riding in the rubber tube.

When we are alone with Hanno, he tells us about his work. His car-racing computer game, 'Need for Speed,' is one of the most profitable projects of his company and he is happy about it. But work expectations are often demanding. He and his staff have to work at times long hours until late at night and into the morning hours in order to meet deadlines. Coming home, exhausted from work, his co-workers often do not have much time and energy left to talk with their spouses and play with their children. It makes planning family events difficult and can cause tension in their marriage relationships. He confides that it affects his relationship with Anna as well.

He has a responsible position at his work, a double commitment to his company and his family. We know it is not easy for him. Hildegard compassionately assures him that we understand this and will support him and Anna as much as we can. We appreciate his confidence.

Sherry tells us about their marital situation. Bob and she have mutually agreed to dissolve their marital relationship. We are sad to hear this. We have experienced them as the positive force, the life giving energy for the community on the mountain. There is no animosity between them; they just feel they need more space for themselves. To express this publicly, they plan a separation ceremony. Their friend, Simon, the Anglican priest, is willing to perform this ritual. They take off their two wedding rings, have them symbolically melted into one and present it to their only daughter.

During her formative years, Krista had struggled to find her identity. I think now, in the residence program, she has become more centered and confident and she knows what she wants to do. We are glad about it. Hildegard has a more intimate relationship with Krista again after her 'stressful years' and they can share more easily. Visiting and talking to her and observing her relationship with other people, Hildegard has the feeling that Krista has a tendency to being lesbian but she does not ask her. She even tries to hint at such a possibility to prepare me for it if that should be the case but I do not respond to it.

Krista has known several young men more closely but had not developed an amorous relationship with them. They were to her like friends or brothers. Now a woman whom she met at sports events is interested in her and they have developed a loving relationship.

Krista phones her mom and tells her about it. Hildegard does not mention anything to me.

Krista wants to tell me about it herself but does not quite know when and how to do this. She waits until she is visiting us in Burnaby and when we are alone she tells me about her sexual orientation, what she is experiencing and waits for my response. She also challenges me, "Dad, since you know this about me now, you would, according to the Bible, have to reject and condemn me."

That is hard. I am completely unprepared for this revelation. I am stunned and tears come to my eyes. I am quiet for a while and ponder over it. It takes some time and agony, before I can respond. "Krista, I could never reject you, I know what you have gone through. But I need time to deal with this emotional anguish".

Both Hildegard and I search for answers to deal with this disclosure. We talk to friends who have similar experiences, read books and articles about homosexuality and share occasionally with each other. Hildegard can accept and understand the situation sooner than I can. Krista helps us to get another perspective by suggesting a book entitled, 'What the Bible Really Says about Homosexuality'.

A while later I write a response to Krista.

"You are my daughter, a part of me; if I would condemn you, I would condemn myself. If I reject you, I would reject a valuable gift, which I have in you. In the records of the New Testament, Jesus never makes mention of homosexuality. His main theme is 'Love, and acceptance'. I have to weigh one against the other. There are warnings in the Bible against sexual abuse but no guidelines in regards to a loving same-sex relationship. My concern and wish for you is that you are happy and content and live honestly and openly. I know you as a sensitive, loving and compassionate person and I love you."

During the coming months and years, we occasionally read books, essays and articles written by theologians, psychologists, scientists and Bible commentators on this topic. We learn that homosexuality has different meanings in the original texts in the Old Testament and has to be considered in the context of that time and place. The same has to be applied to the Apostle Paul's reference to it in his letter to the Romans. In a conversation with my cousin, who taught Biochemistry at a German University, she tells me, researchers assume that homosexuals have a different hormonal balance than heterosexuals; their physical make up is somewhat different.

Bringing our newly gained understanding of scripture and scientific research together and with my love for my daughter, I can accept her sexual orientation.

We find out about a support group of concerned parents of children who are homosexuals and are not accepted by society and by their churches.

We stand with them and together we stand up for our children in a positive, respectful way and share our experiences.

Some relatives of our generation have more difficulty; they remember practicing homosexuality as a criminal offence and combined with their literal understanding of the Bible consider same-sex partners living together as a nontraditional, unnatural relationship, but they make an exception with Krista. Her friendly, loving, nonjudgmental attitude and her gracious willingness to help and give free professional advice to those who ask, wins the hearts of all of them. They welcome her little family. Seeing us accepting Krista's choice as an alternative lifestyle without value judgment, changes or softens their attitude towards homosexuality.

41. New Discoveries

For 1999, we have some ambitious plans. The year starts, like most years, with cold showery weather, snow turns to slush and the best place to be is around the fireplace. The mail brings flyers advertising sunny beaches and cheap flights to enticing places. This inspires us to look for a holiday in the sun.

Our intent has been for some time to learn Spanish properly, preferably in a country where people speak Spanish. We look for a place where we can combine these ambitions. We choose Antigua; it seems to be the ideal spot. It is known for its excellent Spanish language schools and a mild climate, so we book a flight to Guatemala and make reservations through our time-share in the Radisson Villa Hotel in Antigua.

On the plane, we overhear passengers in a row behind us talking about visiting Antigua. We meet them in the customs line-up again and ask them if they would mind sharing a taxi with us from the airport, to Antigua. They are also from BC and gladly agree.

After a forty-five minute drive from the airport the taxi driver takes us to the outskirts of the town and we get out at the Radisson. The bellhop takes our suitcases to our two-bedroom suite upstairs and we settle in. From the balcony, we have a good view of the countryside and the Antigua landmark, the 3766 m high Agua Mountain. The purplish brown cone-shaped volcano stands out against the blue sky. It is still active and a light veil of clouds hovers over its peak.

On our way to the hotel, we passed some interesting plazas and are now anxious to explore the town. We take a shortcut to the main street via the employee entrance. Walking along an arcade, we hear a croaking "Hello, Buenos Dias." There are no people around; it must be the colorful parrot swinging in the ring that welcomes us. We go up to him and answer him and he cackles. We continue, through a park-like garden with a big swimming pool and lawn chairs at the back, to the street which leads to the city.

Antigua was the area's capital at one time and a number of baroque buildings, churches, monasteries and communal structures are witness to a rich Spanish colonial culture from centuries ago. The big earthquake of 1773 and a few smaller ones afterwards have destroyed many of them. Only a few of these gorgeous buildings have been restored, some have been partially rebuilt and many are still ruins.

The next morning we are invited to an orientation meeting. A nice young woman informs us briefly about the history of Antigua, the layout and amenities of the resort and the programs they offer their guests. We enlist for an excursion through the countryside. The infrastructure in Guatemala is rudimentary. The paved road ends where we leave the town and turns into a dirt road. Our bus sways when it drives through potholes on the narrow village roads.

The bus driver has pre-arranged places where he takes tourists. It must be washing day in the small town of San Pedro. In the market place, we see rows of women washing their laundry in large spring-fed masonry basins on one side of the plaza. The school on the other side has recess and the teen-age girls play in the open court. We admire their colorful hand-woven long skirts and blouses. When I want to take a picture of them, some turn shyly away. Vendors have their goods spread out on benches or on the ground at the market place. I buy a small panpipe and manage to play a few tunes on it.

We are expected at the Valhalla macadamia nut farm. The bus drives through a large grove of nut trees to an open court where the owner welcomes us. He shows us the whole process from harvesting the nuts to the final product. "Macadamia nuts are very nutritious and have a high content of Omega 7 which is valued for skin care", he tells us. Then he invites us for a treat to try the nuts, raw, roasted or processed as nut butter on crackers. I find them delectable.

In the next room, a masseuse is demonstrating the application of refined nut oil and she asks for volunteers. None of the women responds, so I step up but Hildegard stands closer to her and she is treated first. Her face shines after she is finished with the face massage. I am next and I enjoy being spoiled.

Back in the hotel, we have a rest and then go to town to inquire about language schools.

In the small 'Eco Tours' tourist office we ask the lonely agent which language schools he would recommend. He gives us addresses of three from a dozen of them in his catalog.

We find this middle-aged, bearded man sympathetic and wonder why he chose the name, Eco Tours, for his office. He smiles, "I take eco-friendly people on tours to far out places in the country". His English is excellent and we ask him where he learned it. "I studied archeology for a few semesters in Pittsburg and am now a lecturer at the university. I run the tourist business as a sideline because I love to explore". This sounds very interesting and we ask him, "How many people do you need for an Eco tour?" He looks at us, "At least two." We make a deal. On Monday in a week's time, he will pick us up from our hotel and take us on a mystery tour. Before we leave he tells us, "I have to plan the route, so please tell me, what do you like to see and how much stress can you handle?" We come to an agreement and know this will be an exciting experience.

It is my birthday and Hildegard says, "For a birthday present, let's go to the 'Jardin Bavaria', have a delicious dinner and celebrate."

On our trips through town we had passed the Antigua Cathedral several times and wonder what it looks like inside. We find out on Sunday, when we attend a Spanish Catholic Mass.

The place before the church is crowded. Colorful vendors sit on the steps leading up to the entrance and sell their goods, candles, incense, shawls, clothing and snacks to the worshippers. We wind our way through the crowd and take a seat in the church close to the exit. The semi-baroque interior is decorated with pictures and sculptures of saints. Veils are hanging from the ceiling. Several priests or monks, all bearded, enter the church. They are wrapped in purple togas like cloaks, with a rope around their waist and wear a white headpiece. Their bare feet are in sandals. They carry small vessels with strong smelling, burning incense to the altar. The way the priests are dressed and the way they perform their ceremonies differs from what we know about Catholic services. The sermon is quite emotional; it seems to us that two religions have merged the old Mayan tradition and the colonial Spanish Catholicism.

The odor and smoke of the incense becomes so stifling that I have difficulty breathing and we leave after awhile. The side doors are open and people are coming in and going out at any time so we are not disturbing the service.

We have selected our Spanish language school, 'San Jose el Viejo', located in the ruins of a large convent. It collapsed in the big earthquake, like many other monasteries. The remaining walls and pillars are now overgrown with vines and flowering bushes. We had chosen it because of its romantic location and proximity to our hotel. Our classrooms are little gazebos, built against the wall like swallow's nests. They are open to the large inner court.

What attracted us also was the one-on-one instruction. Hildegard has Senora Lucretia as her teacher and I, Maestro Alejander. Hildegard has an advantage over me; forty-three years ago she had two years of Spanish at University, I had none. She has fun conversing with her teacher about house decorating, child rearing and entertaining. I can hear them laughing, while I try to figure out the conjugation of verbs and the proper use of tenses.

At the end, we receive a prestigious language certificate, which we still have.

A week later, at six in the morning, Jose picks us up from our hotel in his four-wheel drive pickup. In the open back of his car, he has boxes with food, drinks and blankets. We are looking forward to this adventure. He has planned his trip well.

Our first stop is at a lodge on Lake Atitlan. Jose knows the owner; he welcomes us and shows us our quarters, a new rustic wooden pavilion with a low reed roof, spacious and cozy, with a view of the lake.

Jose has hired a boat to take us on an excursion to villages along the banks of the lake. When we step into the small boat, a plain fiberglass shell with wooden benches without backrest, we know this will not be a luxury cruise.

The captain starts the outboard motor and takes off with us three passengers on board.

We cruise along the lake, turn into a bay in a small settlement, and walk up the narrow road to the workshop of a weaver. We watch her shooting the shuttle through the warp, choosing the proper colors for the pattern she is weaving. We try using our Spanish to talk to her.

A little way down from the church, a vendor with two children has set up her table. She wants desperately to sell me a hand-woven shirt and is quite pushy, but it does not suit me. Hildegard buys two little bracelets for Madison, which the children have made.

When we board the boat again, dark clouds move in and a strong wind comes up. The Lake becomes quite turbulent. Big waves lift up the light boat and let it drop down from the crest with a bang. Jose and I are afraid the shell will crack but Hildegard holds on to the roof post and seems to enjoy it. I am quite surprised, remembering a former boat ride.

We pass several villages. In one, we see several people in the lake, some in white robes. We assume it is a baptism and the captain tells us the evangelicals, as he calls all non-Catholics, win many converts in this area.

The storm has died down; we cross the lake and tie the boat onto a post at a small dock. Jose leads us on a long steep trail to San Marco, a remote Mayan village. The people live in simple huts with their goats and chicken around them. Children, some have beautiful features, play on the crooked cobblestone road. They are shy and their mother calls them back when she sees us approach. Nobody wants to sell us anything here, this means hardly any tourists come up this high. We notice people here are shorter and have a darker skin color than the people in the city.

For supper we are back at our cabin. The next morning we drive around the lake to the capital of the region, Chichicastenango. "You have to see the market there", Jose tells us. We have never seen so many people crowded together. Vendors block the street, drill holes into the pavement, put a pole in and stretch their lines, to hold up the roof and display their goods. Everything you can imagine, swords and jewelry, handicrafts, clothing, food, live chickens and pigs are for sale. It is interesting to watch but we cannot stand the mess and smell very long.

We walk up a hill on the outskirts of the town to a Mayan sacred site, a large altar fenced in with rocks. A huge stone mask of their god is in the middle and three crosses are in front of it; they are black from the smoke of animal sacrifices. Some people at the site are waiting for the priest to come to pray for healing for a sick boy and to curse their enemies. To please their god they have brought a live chicken for a sacrifice. We wait a while but the priest tarries and we leave.

We drive along hairpin curves up to a high pass from where we can see the ring of volcanoes in the distance. Jose tells us the names of them. Looking ahead, our eyes can make out the road which we are going to travel, down into the valley and up the mountain again.

Traveling this road, we pass terraced fields, which reach down to the valley. The houses in the villages are built with adobe bricks which farmers have formed from the loam and clay soil, mixed with dry grass and straw. In several places we see piles of them stacked up to dry in the sun.

The small dirt road leading to Todos Santos is in places steep, full of holes and washed out by floods. I am glad we have a 4-wheel drive vehicle. Sometimes we have to wait until a herd of cows or goats has passed. It is quite a pastoral scene.

We notice that people from different villages can be identified by their clothing. In Todos Santos, the men wear red trousers with white pinstripes and on top of them, some wear light black shorts. We watch the women in their red violet patterned blouses and dark blue skirts wash gourds made from squash in a fountain beside the church. The people here seem to be more content. They are not disturbed and affected by tourists as not many seem to come out to these remote villages. We observe for a while the simple life of these mountain villagers and talk to them. When it is getting late, we drive down to Antigua again.

We have become friends with Jose on this for us very meaningful excursion. He has given us a good insight into Guatemalan and Mayan culture and history. We really enjoyed it and we thank him for his sensitive and respectful manner of responding to us and his safe driving. When we depart, he tells us, "You were pleasant companions, very adaptable and unassuming. I could take you to places where I would not have taken other tourists."

Another trip into Mayan history is still waiting for us. We board a plane to Tikal, the old Mayan settlement in the jungle of northern Guatemala. A shuttle bus takes us passengers from the airstrip to the tourist centre.

The weather is very humid and hot, as we walk with our guide through the jungle. From the trees above us, we are entertained by the coatimundi, the howler monkeys. With howling sounds, they swing from one branch to the next, always watching us. Toucans and parrots, colorful large birds, peek out of the thick foliage. After a short walk the jungle opens up to a wide clearing and we are overwhelmed seeing the large archeological site, the remnants of the old Mayan settlement with its huge sacral and profane buildings. On the way here we could already see the tops of some pyramids sticking out of the jungle. Now when we enter the great Plaza we stand in awe in front of these ancient monumental structures. On one side of the plaza is the Great Jaguar temple; it is not accessible, since many of the steps have crumbled. Beside it is the Temple of the Masks, a limestone step pyramid. We can climb up the many steps with its high risers and narrow treads. There are no handrails on these long stairs, this makes it difficult and dangerous to ascend and half way up, Hildegard becomes dizzy. I have to hold her hand and lead her to the top platform. From here, we have a good overview of the layout of the former court with its Temples, patrician palaces and the South Acropolis. They give witness to the rich culture of the Mayan civilization, which ended a millennium ago.

The next day we want to take more time to explore the whole site on our own. We have chosen a path which we think is a shortcut, but all of a sudden it is blocked by trees and climbing and creeping plants. We feel the ground becoming spongy and we realize we are in the middle of the jungle and it is getting scary. We finally find our way out again and use the more trodden path.

We see a sign leading to Temple IV. From our guide we know it is with sixty-five meters the highest of the temples and a challenge for us to climb. On top of it are a number of small ceremonial rooms, once graced with wall glyphs, pictographs and other decorations. Through the window openings, we have a good view of the whole jungle with the temples and pyramids sticking out of the dense vegetation.

In the evening, we go back, we want to see the temples glowing in the setting sun. We bribe the park guard to let us watch it before he locks the gate, but it is not as spectacular as we were told. The many fireflies buzzing around our cabin when we come back are almost as exciting to watch.

When we fly back to Antigua, Hildegard reflects on our trip and tells me how much it has meant to her, to get a glimpse into the Mayan civilization past and present. To climb those pyramids, walk through temples and crypts, palaces and patrician house ruins and stand before masks and sculptures, altars with ancient symbols and inscriptions, was very enlightening and informative for us.

A few days later, we say good-bye to Guatemala and Antigua, this wonderful city.

Back at home again new opportunities are opening up.

Hildegard has read in a Mennonite paper about a Dnjepr River Cruise to the former Mennonite settlements in the Ukraine. That is where her mother grew up. She had a glimpse of Russia on her 'Adventure Siberia' tour years ago but she wants to learn more directly about her maternal roots and now she may have an opportunity to find out. She makes reservations for us and a few weeks later, we fly to Kiev.

We have a stopover in Frankfurt. The flight to Kiev leaves the next morning. Sabine, whom we befriended in the airplane to Tikal half a year ago, picks us up from the airport, takes us to her home for the night, and brings us back the next morning in time for our departure. A number of people, who are going on the same cruise as we, are waiting to board the plane to Kiev with us.

The Ungers, our tour organizers, meet us at the Kiev airport and help us with the formalities. Customs officers request that we buy health insurance from them. We tell them we have our own. After a long discussion, we finally settle for a five dollar donation (bribe) per person to their health system and we can leave the airport. They also make it difficult to bring in the container with medical supplies which MCC is dedicating to the Mennonite Centre in Kiev. This is a precious gift for the benefit of their own people. Another bribe is necessary to get it released.

Busses wait at the wharf to take us from the airport to our riverboat. We are two of one hundred sixty Mennonite adventurers on this trip. Hildegard and I get settled in a small cabin on the lower deck.

We have a day in Kiev before we start our cruise and the tour leader invites us to a city tour. We climb aboard the busses again and drive through the city passing interesting buildings, monuments and parks. Our Ukrainian tour guide informs us about the cultural importance of them and gives us an historical overview of the Ukraine and its capital.

At a ravine on the outskirts of the town, he points to a high concrete block to which abstract metal figures in different positions are attached; they seem to be reaching out in grief and agony. It is a Holocaust monument and the guide recounts in detail the fate of the Jews in the Ukraine.

We are amazed how many churches and monasteries from the sixth century to late Baroque have survived eighty years of an anti-Christian Communist regime.

In the evening, the Canadian ambassador gives us an introduction to 'The Ukraine today' and wishes us a pleasant stay in this country. After he is finished, a music group completes the evening with authentic Ukrainian folk music.

The Victor Glushkov is our floating hotel for the next two weeks. It is also our 'University'. We have three lecturers on board, a historian, an architect and a genealogist. They inform us about the history of the country and the lifestyle and achievements of the Mennonite settlers, which will prepare us better for our visit to the villages and towns where they used to live.

While our ship has to wait to be maneuvered through the Dnjepr lock, a ferry takes us to Dnepropetrovsk. We have some time to explore the city. One of the most moving experiences is the visit to the Museum. Part of it is the secluded 'Reparations room'. It is dimly lit and when our eyes have adjusted to the faint light, we see a large pyramid with photographs on all sides of it and candles around, commemorating the millions who perished in the Stalin terror. Hildegard and I quietly remember her relatives who were among them. On our way back to the boat we stop at an Orthodox church and attend a short Mass.

Sailing further south, we dock close to the former centre of the Mennonite settlements in the Chortiza and Molotschna colonies, the town of Zaporozhye, and spend a few days there.

We arrive on a Sunday and attend a Mennonite church service. The sermon is translated into three languages; our cruise choir contributes a few songs. We mingle with the congregation afterwards. With some of them, we can communicate in German or in English with others, we need a translator. A few of our group recognize relatives among the parishioners and they have a joyful reunion, they ask questions, exchange gifts, everyone is happy about our visit.

The next morning busses await us at the dock and drive us into different villages.

Halbstadt, one of the largest of the villages, was the former cultural centre and seat of the district administration (Oberschulzenamt). It is our main goal for the day. The Mädchenschule, (girl's school) is the best preserved of the former Mennonite schools in the village. American and German Mennonites have been able to purchase it back from the Ukrainian authorities and it has now become the 'Mennonite Centre of the Ukraine'. The Mennonite Church in Zaporoshye has the legal title for it.

The principal of the school welcomes us and we are allowed to visit classes in session. The music teacher has prepared a program to entertain us with songs.

The cruise participants had been asked to bring a school kit, a bag with normal school supplies. We present these to the students after their performance and they are overjoyed.

Walter Unger had talked to the school administrator and asked him, "How can we help you, what do you need most?" and he responded, "If you can supply us with funds to modernize our instruction, that would be much appreciated."

Walter mentions this at one of our history lectures and we decide to have a collection to help them to buy computers for the school. The principal is very thankful when Walter hands her a check for one thousand dollar US for that purpose.

The school is also a distribution centre for material and medical aid. When we registered for the cruise, Walter asked if we could bring used or new clothing for seniors and poor people in the former Mennonite villages. We have brought a suitcase full of clothing and we stack it up in the distribution centre with all the boxes and parcels, which other cruise members have brought.

From Halbstadt we drive through the countryside and Hildegard looks nostalgically at the wide black fields of fertile Ukrainian steppe. Some of our fellow travelers are anxious to revisit the house where they were born or where their parents, grandparents, uncles or aunts had lived.

The village, in which Hildegard's mother was born, is in Memrik about two hundred km east of Zaporozhye. We hire a van, a driver and translator and share the cost with the Neufelds whose uncle lived there, too. We have a good driver but he cannot read maps and a pretty student translator, Lena, who knows only textbook English.

The Neufelds find the house of their uncle, a typical solid Mennonite house with a brick fence along the road, the gable facing the road and the entrance from the side. The large house is now divided in the middle, like so many others, and houses two families. The old man who climbs down from the ladder from which he repaired his roof, shows us his half of the house. Some of the old furniture is still there.

While the Neufelds talk to the neighbors, we see some older people across the street sitting on a bench in front of their house and we join them. We tell them our forbears lived here, they were Mennonites. They nod, "We remember some of them as honest and godly people". They offer us Vodka, we decline but not to hurt them, I accept a glass of milk from their cow. They tell us they live on a very small pension and could not survive without their cow and the fruit of their big garden. They are very happy when I give them a couple of seed packages and Hildegard has some chocolate bars and chewing gum for the children.

We drive on to Nikolajevka, (Ebental). Hildegard is looking for her mother's house. She had told her, "It is the only stone house in the village. To recognize it, look for two pear trees beside it." Lena asks a woman who works in her garden. She tells us she got rocks from a foundation but does not really understand what we want. Then we see an old woman coming up the street. She remembers the stone house and tells us it burned down two years ago. It had been used as a recovery house for alcoholics. She will guide us to it. We ask her to join us in the car and we will drive there. She loves the ride so much that she is reluctant to leave the car when we arrive. We give her a handful of vegetable seed packages and she smiles at us.

Nothing is left of the house, even half of the foundation has been dug up. Neighbors have used the stones as building material for their own house additions. The two pear trees are still standing. Hildegard walks slowly through the weeds around the site towards the orchard. She is quiet for a while connecting with the spirit of the place where her mother was born and had spent the most impressionable years of her life. As a memento for her mother, she fills a vial with Ukrainian soil from her garden.

When we drive towards the setting sun, Hildegard has a feeling of gratitude and satisfaction at having accomplished what she had set out to do, discover her roots.

There is another place she wants to connect with, the orphanage in the former village of Grossweide in which her mother had lived after her parents died. Her mother did not have very pleasant memories of that time.

In Lichtenau, we stand quietly on the tracks of the railway station remembering the Mennonites, including Hildegard's uncles, who were deported from here to labor camps in Siberia after the revolution. Most of them never returned.

Paul Toews, our history professor, had lectured on the achievements of the 'Colonists', as the Russians called the Mennonites. On our way through the villages, he points out the Thiessen flourmill, the largest in the Ukraine, the Mennonite Credit Union and the well-known farm machinery and metal construction factory of Lepp and Wallmann.

When we pass a large estate, the guide tells us about its former owner, Johann Cornies. He introduced modern farming practices, which yielded better crops, raising sheep on the Ukrainian steppe and planting mulberry trees for sericulture, to produce silk. He was the first president of the Agricultural Improvement Society, worked together with Russian authorities and was a friend to crown prince Alexander.

We have a special treat. I do not know if this was especially arranged for our tour or was seasonal entertainment. A Cossack Equestrian team in very colorful tunics gives us a performance of their riding skills. They are very good. We are very aware that we are in southern Russia.

On our last night, before we leave Zaporozhye, we gather in the main lounge for a remembrance service. A pastor from the group gives an introduction, our tour choir sings a few suitable songs and we sit quietly in the dim lit room and meditate for awhile. Walter softly suggests that we may light a candle for family members who were dear to us and lost their lives or have gone missing during and after the revolution. Many go forward to light a candle. After each one, we observe a minute of silence. Hildegard gets up, takes a candle, lights it and places it beside the others,

"For my uncle, teacher and Pastor Johannes Janzen, "

Many candles are burning when we leave, quietly and thoughtfully.

The next morning we sail towards the Black Sea.

In Kherson, we have a short stop. A motorboat takes a group of us into an arm of the Dnepr delta; we tie the boat to a rusty dock and walk a short path to an open-air fair with a large display of art, crafts and all sorts of handmade objects. Hildegard likes to visit fairs and it is interesting for both of us to see what is offered in a Ukrainian one. She buys a cute blouse for three-year-old Madison and a few hand painted wooden eggs for Easter decorations.

We sail into the Black Sea. A Marine Corps band welcomes us in Sevastopol. Our group separates. Some visit the Mennonite settlements in the Crimea, and we board the bus to Yalta. The landscape in the southern Crimea varies. Mountain ranges change to open valleys with vineyards and orchards, once in awhile we have a view of the Sea. On the way to Yalta, we pass several vacation homes, prestigious residences and hotels along the southern coast of the peninsula. The driver points out Gorbatschow's Dacha. Yalta is a resort town for the well-to-do Russians and Ukrainians. The climate is subtropical; it is still quite hot when we walk along the beach promenade. We visit the palace, which Prince Vorontov built for his wife in Tudor and Neo-Moorish styles with exotic wood paneling and lavishly decorated and furnished chambers. We also have the privilege of entering the main parlor in the Livadia Palace, the room where the (in)famous Yalta conference was held, where Churchill, Roosevelt and Stalin reorganized the map of Europe.

On the last day of our stay in the Crimea, a bus takes those who are interested to explore Chersoneses, the remnants of an ancient Greek settlement on the southern tip of the peninsula, not far from Sevastopol. We have a very good guide. He explains to us the ruins of the large residences, the coinage, the temple of which only a few columns are remaining and the different patterns of the floor mosaics. His stories are so animated that we can imagine what it must have looked like two thousand years ago.

During the night, we sail across the Black Sea. We are 'rocked' into sleep by rolling waves. Breakfast and lunch is served on the swaying boat. Some of our group do not feel like eating and the dining room is half-empty. They feel better again when we land in Odessa. On our guided tour, we hear about the interesting history of the city. Founded by a Mongol Khan, it became part of the Ottoman Empire until Russia conquered it.

Odessa is a truly cosmopolitan, multicultural city. Its inhabitants have their roots in Turkish, Slavic, Greek, Romanic and Germanic cultures. To me it has a somewhat European flair. The famous Russian poet, Pushkin, who lived there for a while, said, 'In Odessa you can smell Europe.' It had been spared the destruction of WW II but many of the beautiful baroque and classical buildings are in need of repair.

A few events are planned for our last days. The captain gives a gala dinner with speeches and toasts. A few people from the cruise are specially recognized and get honorable mention. Hildegard is quite surprised when her name is called and she receives a reward for being 'the most enthusiastic and energetic passenger' and I agree, she deserves the honor. We all get a 'Certificate of Academic Achievement from the University of Glushkov for having completed a rigorous course in Mennonite Studies'.

The last day we have free time for a stroll through the city, to pack our suitcases and pay a visit to the Theatre - Opera house. On a tour through the building, the guide tells us it was built by two Viennese architects to be a replica of the Baroque Vienna Opera house. They had to make a few shortcuts because they ran out of money. At the end of the tour, we receive tickets for tonight's performance. They play excerpts from Strauss' and other operas; the singing is good, the acting acceptable.

The next morning we say good-bye to our comfortable floating hotel and the solicitous crew. We have to wait four hours for a plane that takes us back to Kiev. The Ukraine does not want to let us go. Lufthansa waits an hour in Kiev for our late plane and brings us safely back to Frankfurt.

We spend another three weeks visiting relatives and friends in Germany. Adelheid treats us to an excellent performance of the Petersburger Ballet, 'Requiem, Mein Jerusalem' a well-orchestrated harmony between music and movement on a simple, impressive stage.

We drive across the border to Luxemburg to visit Frank and Ulrike. Cousin Frank still works in the European Parliament in Luxemburg. He up-dates us on the latest happenings in Europe.

We both share an interest in history. He takes us to the abbey in Echternach into the Basilica from the seventh century. In the abbey museum, we admire the highly decorated handwritten copies of the bible. Echternach in 'Little Switzerland' was one of the centers of Christianization in the early Middle Ages.

While walking back through the woods, we find a spot with many yellow boletus mushrooms, Ulrike's favorites. She thinks what we gathered is worth about one hundred DM on the market. She uses them in a delicious dinner.

Up north, we drop in at cousin Günter's home in the heath again. After a hearty meal and time to exchange news and pass on greetings, he drives with us to Walsrode, a large bird sanctuary. We admire the colorful plumage of the many native and exotic tropical birds...

The time passes quickly and soon we have to return our Golf to the airport car rental and board the plane to Vancouver.

42. THE NEW MILLENNIUM

The advent of the year two thousand is heralded with the prediction that our economy will collapse. Our computers are only calibrated until nineteen hundred ninety-nine and therefore will break down and create chaos. Zealots preach that the end of the world has come and the arrival of the new Millennium, the second coming of Christ is at hand. This is arousing fear and anxiety in many people. Hildegard is a little apprehensive and we talk about it, what if …?

I cannot see any logic in it. This should happen just because we enter a year which ends in four zeros? This is not enough reason to get frantic. We continue to live our life as usual, peaceful and content.

We have big plans for this year. On my last visit in Luxemburg with Frank and Ulrike, I met Cousin Marianne. They were organizers of the Wiehlertag 1995. We talked about preparations for the next one and they handed me the ceremonial key to open the Wiehlertag 2000 in Canada. Having accepted it, I now take on the responsibility of coordinating this year's reunion.

I ask a few people from the clan to assist me in planning the meeting together. I delegate certain responsibilities to each one of the team.

We contact Columbia Bible College in Abbotsford and ask if we may use their campus with dormitories, lounges, dining hall and chapel, while their students are on semester break. This is possible and quite affordable. We have again over two hundred Wiehler descendants who accept our invitation.

Our program offers a variety of activities. One is listening to an interesting talk about 'The value of a family reunion' given by our guest speaker,

Dr. Klassen. In his deliberation, he reminds us to pass on our cultural and spiritual heritage to our children and grandchildren.

Two of our relatives entertain us with musical interludes. Reinhard with his trumpet and Doreen accompanies on the grand piano. Reinhard plays professionally in the Cologne Radio Orchestra.

Andre plays games with the young people and Evita has some humorous surprises for us. To give our guests a glimpse of the beauty of our land, locals lead groups on different excursions. One group visits an Indian Trading Post, which is interesting for our German guests. I take another group to a modern monastery and nature lovers hike into the mountains. We leave plenty of time for stories and visiting.

With taking on the responsibility of organizing the reunion, I have also agreed to be editor for the new, revised Wiehler Chronicle

Some of our forefathers had researched the Wiehler family history, collected life stories and historical data of the clan and put together a German Wiehler Chronicle. Now it needs to be updated and include stories and data from the many Wiehlers who immigrated to North America and other parts of the world after the war.

Some of our children, in-laws and grandchildren speak little or no German anymore, so we prepare a bilingual edition. A new edition needs a new face, so I rearrange the layout, design a new cover and we add stories, translations and new pictures. This takes a lot of work. Hildegard has been my sounding board and faithful advisor. The final product of the 'Wiehlerchronik 2000' is well received. Even historical societies and Mennonite university libraries ask for copies.

All three of our children with their families attend and enjoy the reunion. We had told them stories about our German relatives, now they have a chance to meet some of them.

I think the Wiehlertag 2000 was a success, everyone seemed to enjoy it. Now when everything is over and all the guests are gone, I am relieved and thankful; life becomes quieter for our family again.

On a sunny afternoon, Hanno asks us, "Do you want to come for an outing with us?" We gladly accept. It is always fun to undertake something with our children. We pass a number of houses in the suburbs which are for sale. Hildegard comments on this and points to a nice Tudor style house on the right. Hanno asks her, "Do you like it?" She does, and with a cunning smile he tells us, "We bought it." He still likes to surprise us. We know he was looking for a bigger house but did not expect such a quick decision. The house is much bigger than his apartment but needs some remodeling to suit his and Anna's lifestyle. The whole family helps peeling off the old wallpaper, replacing and repainting walls and halls and hanging new light fixtures. It looks lovely when all the furniture is moved in.

Krista and Lisa have bought a home in Toronto, remodeled and furnished it tastefully. We regret that we cannot help them move. All three of our children now live in their own homes.

With a heavy heart, we decide to sell our motor home. We have used and appreciated it very much on many wonderful trips in the last years, but we have no level space large enough to park it on our property and the police do not allow us to park it on the street for longer than a few days. To rent a space in a RV parking lot is expensive. Because of its age, it is difficult to get parts for it and beside that, it is a gas-guzzler. Our friend Billy in Christina Lake buys it for his family.

More sad events are happening in the coming months. Oma Scheffler is getting more fragile. We celebrated her 94th birthday last year with all her children and their families around her; she enjoys that. On a dark winter day Ruth and Eva, who care for their mother, phone Hildegard and her sister Gertraud to come to Bellingham and say a final good-bye to Mother. They feel her heart will not last much longer. All four daughters sit around her bed when she closes her eyes forever.

She lived a long, valiant life. She experienced the terrible Russian revolution in the Ukraine, raised five children in Germany and buried her only son when he was six years old. She had to start over again in a new environment when the family immigrated to America, not speaking the language. She was a wonderful mother and mother-in- law, a committed pastor's wife, supporting Dad in his many assignments as pastor in Canada, interim pastor in some German congregations and Bible school teacher in Switzerland. Many will miss her.

The six grandchildren carry her coffin from the hearse to the grave. A large congregation mourns with her children and grandchildren.

A month later Hildegard's faithful friend, Jutti, succumbs to a recurring cancer. Hildegard met her in a silk painting course and identified her quickly as a Mennonite. We became good friends. She led an eventful life, working for different organizations as a nurse, midwife and medic on four continents. She was a gracious woman, compassionate, kind and helpful, interested in people and in art. We loved her.

Not long after that, we attend another funeral of a person, who was very dear to us.

Hildur, the wife of cousin Erwin, I know her as one of the most positive and joyful people. Her joy of life was contagious and as a pastor's wife, she helped and encouraged many parishioners to look at life from a more sunny side. She went through hard times after the war. Bringing up five boys was not easy either. Her faith and positive attitude helped her through many difficulties. Even in pain from her lung cancer, I never heard her complain. She was an example to many.

The sons render their mother the last service, preparing her for the funeral. Laying her body into the coffin is a sacred ritual for them. Erwin had made two solid oak coffins, one for Hildur and one for himself. Now there is only one left. Sherbrooke Mennonite Church is not big enough for all the mourners that attend her memorial service.

Hildegard and I have become involved in the Canadian justice system. We have been called up for jury duty. Hildegard had done this a few years ago. It is my turn now. For both of us it is a new learning experience, sitting in the courtroom for weeks, listening to evidence and forming a decision. In the trial which I observe, the evidence is rather convincing and it does not take us long to reach a verdict. For Hildegard it took months to reach a verdict. The 'Squamish Five', an activist group, had committed criminal acts to express their displeasure with the complacency of our society. It was more complicated to explain and consider their motives. Hildegard's jury, too, came to a guilty verdict after long considerations and had to be protected by police from angry sympathizers of the 'Squamish Five' after the trial.

Hildegard and her sisters plan a unique holiday. They want to celebrate the fiftieth anniversary of their immigration to the USA. They have found out that the Queen Mary, the ship on which they came over from Germany, is retired and is now a floating hotel in the harbor of Los Angeles. They make reservations for the hotel and arrive in the lobby exactly fifty years after they left the ship in New York. Ruth still has the original passenger list from the Queen Mary on which their names are listed and Gertraud has a menu from its restaurant. They mention this to the registering clerk and she calls the manager. He comes, congratulates them and gives them VIP treatment. They get a preferred suite and are charged only half the price. In the restaurant Gertraud plays a trick and orders from the old menu. The chef is excited when he sees the fifty-year-old menu and asks if he may make a copy of it. He serves them a delicious free dinner because of it.

In the tourist shop, they see black T-shirts with an eye-catching white print of the Queen Mary on the front. All four of them buy one, wear them to many of the events and get the intended attention from the guests. They have to tell their story many times and have a lot of fun.

Another joyful event happens this summer, Magdalena and Gustav's golden wedding anniversary. The celebration starts in the sanctuary with a short service and afterwards, downstairs in the convention room, the children celebrate and honor their parents. They recount some meaningful and humorous events and illustrate it with pictures in a slide show. A number of friends share what Magdalena and Gustav have meant to them and what they contributed to their life and to that of the congregation.

At Magdalena's request I share about our relationship as siblings and her ambitions as a teenager, her achievements and her kindness. Benno, their son and the MC, asks us if we, as a family, could sing a German song, since most of the presentations are in English. He remembers us doing this at birthday parties and anniversaries when the children were still young. We gladly oblige, Michael, Tannis, Hildegard and I honor Gustav and Magdalena with a German hymn in four-part harmony.

Hildegard and I have our forty-fifth wedding anniversary one day after Magdalena and Gustav's and we are remembered as well.

We have some excitement in Christina Lake. One afternoon we come home from the lake on the Santa Rosa Road and notice a motorcyclist is following us. We turn into our driveway and so does he. We wonder who he is and what his intentions are. He introduces himself as Hardy Huber. He comes from Germany and was a horse breeder and trainer there. He brought eight horses to Canada and still has two left. They are grazing on Simon and Juno's meadow right now but there is not much grass left. Juno had told him about us and he asks if we would let his horses graze on our meadows. He is a gracious young man and we can communicate easily with him. We tell him we do not mind at all but he would have to put a fence up. A few days later, he comes with a load of posts and a roll of wire, installs a battery in the chicken coop, connects the wire with it and sets up an electric fence. The next day he brings three horses, Simon's and two of his own. One is a beautiful Trakehner mare. When our grandchildren are with us, they like to caress and feed the gentle horses.

Hanno has another surprise for us. He has booked an Alaska cruise and invites us to travel with them. It is a gift for our forty-fifth wedding anniversary. We are moved. Both of us are not great fans of mega cruises but we love to travel with them and gladly accept.

We have an inside cabin on the eighth deck of the Regal Princess. After we are settled, we go on deck and see the Lions Gate Bridge from below and our beautiful city from a different angle as we slowly glide out of the harbor into the open ocean.

The purser has arranged an information talk in the lounge, to acquaint us with all the facilities and safety features. Then a naturalist explains to us the places to which we will travel. He warns us of black bears and grizzlies and how we should respond to them if we are attacked. I think it would perhaps be more appropriate to give us information about polar bears.

In the evening, the chef prepares the Captain's dinner. Hildegard and Anna dress in their evening gowns, I in my black wedding suit and tie and Hanno in a rented tuxedo.

The captain welcomes us on board, introduces the crew and wishes us a good trip. We enjoy the delicious meal. The photographer moves around from table to table and takes pictures of the well-dressed guests.

The next morning we approach Juneau and see the first glaciers glittering in the sun. Whales cut the surface of the smooth water at a respectful distance. The Stellar Seals are more inquisitive and come closer.

Juneau, a former gold-rush town, now the capital of Alaska, is beautifully located. Nestled against majestic mountains, and shielded by islands from the open ocean, it has become a favored stop for cruise ships. We take a short hike through the town and admire the craftsmanship of the native carvers.

During the night, we sail from Juneau along the Lynn Canal to Skagway. This is now a typical tourist town. We are the fourth large cruise ship in the harbor. A tour bus is waiting on the quay to take us on a tour through the gold-rush ghost town section of the village. Our tour guide is a young Bellingham student who lived for seven years in Germany where her father did scientific research.

In a humorous way, she tells us the history of the area. Native people from the Tlingit tribe were fishing and hunting here. When the gold-rush fever brought more and more prospectors, the village grew rapidly to a bustling town. She told us stories about the hardship of the prospectors who tried to cross the high mountain passes to get to the Klondike goldfields. Some visionaries saw an opportunity for good business. They built a narrow gauge railway from the harbor to the gold fields in Canada. Prospectors could travel now and transport their goods via rail instead of trekking them with mules across the mountains. The railway is an engineer's marvel; it runs along riverbeds, across mountain passes, over bridges and through tunnels. It was finished when the gold rush was almost over. Now it is one of the main tourist attractions. We ride this classic old train along whitewater creeks, deep cliffs with spectacular vistas of the rugged countryside and along the marshy beach of Bennet Lake in the Yukon. When we leave, we feel we have relived to some extent a part of our Canadian history.

Our ship now turns into the open ocean. Once in a while, we pass ice floes on our way to Yakutat Bay. We take a Tlingit Pilot on board, dressed in the garb of an Elder of his tribe. In a humorous way, he talks about the relationship between his people and the newcomers since the gold rush. At 12:00 h, he and the captain have a ritual to appease the glacier as we approach it.

The Regal Princess sails as closely as safety permits to the glaciers. We steer towards the Hubbard Glacier, the biggest of them. The captain turns the ship very slowly in a circle to give all passengers a chance to have a good view of the glacier. Through our binoculars, we observe the calving of the glaciers. Great chunks of ice break off and plunge with a big splash into the ocean. It is a marvelous sight. On the way out of the bay, we pass a few small icebergs.

We leave the narrow passage and approach Sitka from the open ocean. The harbor entrance is too shallow for large cruise ships, so we have to use our lifeboats to reach land. Sitka, on Baranof Island, is an interesting mixture of Native, Russian and American culture; we can see that from the architecture and the crafts, which they display for tourists.

The tour bus driver tells us about the earlier confrontation between Natives and Russians. Eventually they came to a trading agreement. Sitka was the capital of Russian America and Alaska until 1906. We walk on boardwalks over muskeg with blueberries and conifers and end up on

Castle Hill where Russia transferred the title of Alaska to America in 1867. We visit a Russian Orthodox Church and later watch the Archangels, a Russian dance group in traditional costumes, perform old Russian and modern dances.

Two more nights we spend on the ship, going through the inside passage and see the lights of villages on Vancouver Island. The Regal Princess docks safely in Vancouver's harbor. We are home again and Hildegard can collect all these wonderful experiences in a travel album.

The year two thousand and one ends with a happy event. We had been looking forward to it for the last nine months. Tannis gives birth to a healthy little boy. We are all excited about it. She suggests a name for him, Tobin. A short form of Tobias, 'God is good'. Madison lives with us while Tannis is in hospital. She is a lovely girl and we are glad she now has a sibling.

She is very fond of her little brother and likes to hold him tenderly on her lap.

At year's end, Hildegard bakes the traditional 'porzeln', (pancake dough ladled into boiling oil) and Madison is helping Oma. She rolls the warm, irregular shapes in Sugar and piles them up in a big bowl. All of our children love Mom's porzeln. We have fun guessing what these unpredictable dough shapes look like. Krista and Lisa, who celebrate Christmas with us this year, take a bag full to Toronto. Lisa's specialty is Mom's Pfefferkuchen, traditional German Christmas cookies. Hildegard uses the recipe from my mother. We send a package of it to Toronto for Christmas every year when Krista and Lisa cannot celebrate with us. Hildegard bakes a variety of Christmas cakes and cookies from German and Russian Mennonite recipes and is known for her excellent baking.

In the Christmas mail, we receive an invitation to a class reunion of my graduation class in Germany. For this year, the reunion will be in Oldenburg in Northern Germany.

For me to meet old friends again, who now live as established professionals in different parts of Germany, is a good reason to go back to Europe.

After we have published the Wiehlerchronik, the history of my mother's family, I become interested in researching my father's ancestry. In libraries and old Church registers, I dig up information, write to older members of the Lemke clan and ask them to send me any information, pictures and data they might have of their forefathers and their family. Several mention that their parents or grandparents did not tell them much about their life experience. I supplement the information they send me with my findings, tracing our family history back to 1780. I arrange everything intelligibly and have the 'Lemke Chronik' printed just in time for our journey.

I am glad Hildegard is coming along this time; she is such a lovely and helpful travel companion.

We land at the Frankfurt airport and Cousin Christina awaits us there. She is a vivacious person and it does not take long for us to become friends with her and her husband Heinz. He is also an architect and we share our professional experiences. I ask him if he knows of the artist Hundertwasser and his exotic designs. He is one of Hildegard's favorite modern artists. Heinz tells us Hundertwasser has just finished a very interesting apartment building, 'Waldspirale', not far from here and he offers to drive us there so that we can have a good look at his very unusual architecture. It is an interesting experience for us to see this unconventional building complex built on different levels. It must have been a builder's nightmare to construct. Nothing lines up or is straight; floors are sloping, window frames are drooping, everything is individually formed and painted outside and inside. It is the very opposite of my formal 'Bauhaus' training. We ask him if people like to live in triangular and pentagonal rooms. He knows there is a waiting list to get into this prestigious building.

On our way north we drop in at Cousin Marianne and Michael's house. They recommend to us a unique building in Osnabrück, not far from where they live, the 'Felix Nußbaum Haus'. Architect Libeskind has designed it in his typical angular style. This one is especially adapted for the display of the Jewish painter Felix Nußbaum's work. His paintings are very emotional, relating to stages of his turbulent life as a German Jew. His motifs are 'Fear, Exile, Refugee and Triumph of Death'.

We travel on to Oldenburg to our class reunion. Eighteen grey-haired couples welcome us in the lounge of the Hotel when we arrive. I introduce Hildegard to them. She soon wins the hearts of my classmates with her friendly smile. In a special ceremony, she is officially initiated into the fellowship of the 'Winrich von Kniprode' School. Hildegard is given an opportunity to learn to know my classmates and their wives on a walk through a garden show and cruising together on the Zwischenahner Meer (Lake).

Our next destination is Berlin. On our way we take a break at cousin Günter and Hanna's place again, enjoy their hospitality and the walks along the sandy trails of the Lüneburg Heath.

They tell us their congregation has just finished building a new 'Eine Welt Kirche' (One World Church). Behind the altar table, the architect has placed a shelf section which looks like an altar with two wings. On the shelves stand book shaped glass containers. When members of the congregation travel to another country, they bring earth from that place or they ask visitors to bring some soil and the deacon pours it into the glass containers on the shelf. It is a symbol for peaceful coexistence. People may have a different history, speak different languages and have created their own culture and religious beliefs but we all live on the same earth, receive our food and energy from it and have to learn to live peacefully side by side. When we come home, we send them sand from the coast of the Pacific Ocean.

A number of my Lemke relatives live in and around Berlin. My niece, Monica, takes the initiative to invite some of them for a local Lemke reunion. I remember some of them as children. Now they are established professionals, medical doctors and engineers. It does not take long for Hildegard to befriend them, especially the younger women. They appreciate her openness, her ability to listen and respond thoughtfully.

All are surprised when I show them the 'Lemke Chronicle' to which several have contributed information. Many want to stay in contact with us now that they have learned to know us better.

Since Berlin has become the capital of Germany again, many things have changed. The rebuilding of the 'Potsdamer Platz' is almost finished. The tall glass facades and the huge tent-covered atrium of the Sony Centre, with all kinds of facilities around it, is very awe-inspiring. Hildegard and I take the lift to the fourth floor restaurant and enjoy a delicious asparagus dinner while having an occasional look at the happenings in the inner court below us.

One of the highlights of this trip is our two-week stay in the spa in Marienbad (Lazne Marianske) The company from which we rented our car does not allow us to take it across the border into the Czech Republic. To get around this problem we ask Adelheid, who wants to join us in Marienbad, if we can drive together in her car. When we cross the mountain range of the Erzgebirge leading into the Czech Republic, it starts to rain, a real cloudburst. In half an hour, the water flowing down from the mountain slopes transforms the road into a river and we have difficulty making out where the road ends. Adelheid courageously drives along the stream with us as navigators. Soon it stops raining and we arrive safely in the beautiful little Baroque town.

Hildegard and I have a lovely suite in the Nove Lazne Hotel, the New Spa, although it was built more than a century ago, when Marienbad was still part of the Austrian Empire. We are called to check in with the doctor. Friendly and professionally, he inquires about our health condition and prescribes corresponding health applications. He speaks an almost flawless German. Many people in this border region still speak German and the majority of the spa visitors are Germans.

In the forenoon, we are packed into dry-gas baths or swim in the hot mineral water in a large marble basin. It is surrounded by an arcade of Corinthian columns, like a Roman Bath. Masseuses pamper us with a partial or full body massage under a heat lamp or under water. It is wonderfully relaxing. I was at first embarrassed when the masseuse asked me to undress completely for a proper body massage.

We have a surprise, Sieglinde and Chuck, friends from Vancouver, shorten their visit with relatives in southern Germany and join us in Marienbad. It is fun, doing things together with them and Adelheid.

In the morning we meet at the mineral water fountains, they drink, as ordered by the doctor, two tall glasses of Rudolf Quelle and I two from the Karolinen Brunnen, which is not quite as bitter. Usually we eat our meals together in the mirror hall restaurant, reminiscent of Versailles.

In the afternoon, we normally have no applications. We stroll through the town or the park, keep fit and enjoy the fresh air on a long hike to the old Krakonos castle with its mountain spirit and other legendary sculptures.

The spa offers classical concerts and lectures. We have interesting discussions afterwards.

After we have enjoyed the spa and have been healed from our real or assumed ailments, we drive on to Praha, the capital of the Czech Republic. Our quarters are in a unique hostel. It was formerly a cloister then, during the Communist era, a prison and now, remodeled, a hostel. We have a bright room on the upper floor. The lower floor cells have enlarged windows but still have the heavy steel doors from the prison era. The Unitas hostel is in the middle of the city. We can reach all the important sites on foot.

The Jewish quarter with the remarkably decorated old Synagogue and the cemetery where the tombstones are crowded as close as plates in a dishwasher is remarkable.

The next day we cross the famous historical Charles Bridge over the Moldau (Vltava) River, a five minute walk from our hostel. We admire the thirty baroque sculptures, which line the railing of the old stone bridge, saints, historical and legendary figures. It does not take long from there to reach the old city.

The Hradschin, the castle district, is the dominant building complex of the old city. It is an interesting walk through the conglomerate of all the different buildings in different architectural styles, the Castle, the Gothic

St.Vitus Cathedral, a monastery, several palaces, museums and gardens and balconies from which we have imposing views.

Our tour guide points to a window in a wing of the Bohemian chancellery, which reaches out into the garden and tells us about the second defenestration of the year 1618. Protestant noblemen threw catholic governors, who wanted to revoke the newly established law of freedom of religion, out of the window.

Prague is a truly European city. It was the capital of two Holy Roman Empires and the seat of a Habsburg Emperor. We can see the cultural changes in its architecture. On our way back over the Charles Bridge to our hostel, we hear music. A violinist is playing classical compositions. At the other end of the bridge, a musician plays a Smetana symphony on the rims of wine glasses. The soft blending tones sound amazingly beautiful.

Before we return to Canada, we visit Jupp and Tine in their summer abode in Holland. Jupp shows us his ancestral estate, Asdong, close to the Dutch border. We take a day tour to the city of Bruges in Flanders, referred to as the 'Venice of the North'. We step into one of the canal boats and take a tour along the 'grachten' through interesting parts of the city, which cannot be accessed from the street. Seeing town squares and buildings from different centuries, enclosed in old fortifications, makes us wonder what life may have been like in this busy medieval port city a millennium ago.

Back home again we do not have much time left to spend in our summer cabin in Christina Lake. It soon gets too cold to go swimming but we can relax from our busy summer schedule.

We sit in the lawn chairs under the golden-colored autumn leaves of the big birch tree and reflect on our summer activities and how they have affected our relationship.

We enjoy traveling together. We complement each other. I appreciate Hildegard's enthusiasm, energy and creativity. At times, she feels I dampen it with my pragmatism. She has a keen sense of observation and can get excited about details, which I may overlook. We both love beautiful things. She draws occasionally from my studies of art history and architecture when we visit art galleries or walk through medieval or modern cities. She appreciates my 'solidity' and respects my calculated risk-taking that is not easily deterred by fear. Her risk-taking now is more in provocative thinking in the realm of life philosophy and spirituality where I am more conservative. I can respect her way of thinking and am challenged by it, but I cannot always follow and accept her conclusions. At first, she was hesitant to share her new ideas with me because she feared I would not understand and would reject them. Now she is more confident that I will listen and we can openly talk about issues which are important to her and, in a sense, to both of us.

We have both been brought up to be humble, honest, and to show respect. This enables us to compromise more easily. We acknowledge and accept, maybe even like our 'otherness' at times and appreciate what we have in common. A dose of humor, which both of us have, deflates an occasional argument. Our love for each other has endured and matured and can sustain mood changes. We are comfortable with each other and love to do things together.

Hanno again has a surprise for us. Shortly before Hildegard's birthday, he asks her if she would accept a two-week holiday in Hawaii which he is booking on his time-share agreement, as a birthday gift for the two of us. They will accompany us. We gladly accept.

In travel folders from Hawaii, we have admired the scenery, the waves rolling onto golden beaches with palm trees in the background under a sunny blue sky. We are now anxious to see if this is really so. It will be the first time for us to experience the beauty of these tropical islands.

Hanno has chosen a luxurious resort and we are quite comfortable in our suite. We enjoy walking along the beach and swimming in the ocean. I borrow a snorkeling outfit, dive into the coral reefs and am amazed at the variety of shapes and colors of the fish chasing each other. For a short time, I swim beside one of the huge turtles, which sometimes come close to the beach. Hanno and I have fun diving through the high waves. I notice that Hanno keeps an eye on me. When I swim out too far into the ocean he swims out too to be available if I should need help, without saying anything. He is such a sensitive, considerate son; I just love him. Hildegard is not quite as daring as I am; she and Anna stay in more secure waters.

Hanno rents a car and takes us to the other side of the 'Big Island'. A short distance from our resort we notice the landscape changing its colors. The green of the trees and the gold of the sand turn into gray and black. We are driving over solidified lava that long ago flowed red hot from the top of the volcano and covered this area down to the ocean. The volcano is still active. We stop and climb up a little higher to see the hot orange-red lava flowing viscidly from the volcano towards the ocean forming a huge cloud of steam when it hits the water. At that point, the lava disintegrates into small particles and ground fine by pounding waves, forms 'black sand.' We walk along the Punahu'u Black Sand Beach, a strange phenomenon.

We drive along the perimeter of the island on the rain forest side. Interesting for us is the bamboo forest. We did not know that bamboo grows that big and spreads out to become a forest. We spend a few more days in the sun and come home to shovel a foot of snow from our driveway.

My health condition is causing me some concern. My heart beats irregularly at times and I feel my energy level drop considerably. As this happens more often, I see a cardiologist and she thinks a heart pace maker will correct the arrhythmia. When it is installed, I feel much better and can assume regular activities in house and garden.

I make room for a small vegetable garden in the back yard using my composted soil to grow organic peas, beans, lettuce, tomatoes and cucumbers. It brings back fond memories of my childhood on the farm and it supplements our food supply during the growing season. Hildegard plants flowers and shrubbery in the front yard, which will bloom at different times of the year. Their display of color makes the house look more friendly and inviting.

As the children grew up they asked me occasionally what I did when I was young and I told them in fragments about my childhood and my war experiences. Now Krista urges me to write my life story down in sequence. "Dad, we want to know all the details of what you did as a boy, what life was like in the Hitler era and what you experienced during and after the war." So I think about it and try to relive my childhood on the farm, in the one room elementary school, my experiences in the Hitler Youth, the workforce and the army and begin to write my autobiography *'Nicht mehr als ihr ertragen könnt'*. Most vivid in my memory are my war experiences and my trip after the war to our home village in West Prussia, at that time still occupied by Russian troops, to search for my mother. Since I lived this part of my life in Germany, I wrote it in German, hoping my children will still know enough German to be able to read it. Some of my German relatives and friends read it and give me very good reviews, for which I am grateful.

Krista and family come from Toronto to pay us a visit. She has visited friends from Medical School in Calgary and extends her trip to the coast. We want to meet half way in Christina Lake but give this idea up because of the raging wild fires in the southern part of central BC. Fortunately, the fire can be contained before it reaches Christina Lake but the smoke of it fills the whole area.

This is the first time that little Justin has traveled this far and we are very happy to see him. Our whole family is delighted when Krista and family visit us. Hanno and Anna have bought a vacation home on Pender Island between Victoria and Vancouver and invite us to join them there. To be together as an extended family, is always fun. The children like to explore the surroundings and feed the deer that come close to the house. We sit on the spacious balcony, share our latest news or walk to the beach and the marina where Hanno has his boat moored.

After a few days, the boys have to go back to the city to work but Krista can stay with us for a little longer. This gives Oma a chance to enjoy little Justin.

Winter has arrived again and we feel we need some sun to store up vitamin D. We take advantage of our timeshare and book a two-week holiday in Mexico. This time we take Adelheid along to our spacious resort in Cabo San Lucas, it is a birthday gift for her and Hildegard. As usual, the concierge invites us to an 'information meeting'. This resort just opened half a year ago and I am interested to find out what facilities are available. They show us several suites and common rooms and ask us if we want to upgrade our executive suite. We decline but enjoy the free lunch. As a thank you for attending, we are given a few extra benefits, among them a free sunset cruise.

We look forward to this and stroll around the quay of Cabo San Lucas until it is time to board the boat. We notice only young people going on board. The captain turns on the radio and plays loud folk and rock music. Adelheid gets uneasy and whispers, "Let us get off, I don't like it". I am more adventurous, I want to find out why young people want to go on a sunset cruise and persuade her to stay. At my request, they turn the music down a little. We pass "Lovers Beach' and sail through the rock gate at the southern tip of the Baja Peninsula. We observe a gorgeous sunset. On the way back it becomes quite noisy on the boat and the young people start to dance in a somewhat suggestive way. It gets worse when the sun is down. We are the only older people on board and feel out of place in this company and the young people let us know this. We tell the captain, "We have been misinformed about the purpose of the cruise and feel uncomfortable, would you mind taking us back to the harbor". He tries to be accommodating and asks us, "Where is your hotel?" We can see it from the boat and point it out to him. Reluctantly he tells some of the crew to let down the lifeboat, we climb in and they take us to the beach opposite our hotel. When the boat hits the sand, I take my shoes off and walk through the water. The boat crew carry Hildegard and Adelheid through the water to the beach. We are glad when we are back in our hotel. For me it was a somewhat interesting experience to observe the lifestyle of young people in these days.

For the rest of our stay we enjoy the sun, and the amenities of the resort, swim, read, leave footprints in the sand and explore the former fishing village, which has now changed to a resort town.

We return home to BC in time for the Christmas preparations. Adelheid spends Christmas with us this year. She enjoys a traditional Christmas celebration as we have it in our family, sitting around the Christmas tree with its candles, singing Christmas carols accompanied by harpsichord and recorders with the grandchildren participating. She does not have this in her family.

Once again Hanno has a surprise for us, only he cannot keep it secret for long. On aunt Tannis' birthday, little Tomas Alexander is born. It was not an easy pregnancy for Anna. We are all happy that mother and child are well. Hanno and Anna are now proud parents and they have given us another grandson. A few months later Anna's mother and brother are coming from Poland to welcome their new grandson and nephew. Oma Zygo is delighted about her first grandson and is spoiling the little one while Andreas and his friends are exploring the countryside from the ocean to the Rockies.

43. Returning to her 'Father's House'

Our exchange year in Germany has helped to stabilize our relationship. When we moved to Bielefeld, it was a new unfamiliar environment for both of us. Hildegard was away from old friends and influences. New friends with creative ideas and other life styles came into her circle and helped her to overcome her first period of loneliness. Exchanging ideas with them gave her another perspective of living in relationship. Having an open mind, she adjusted quickly to unfamiliar conditions and found them 'invigorating'. We enjoyed exploring new opportunities and activities together and continue to do so.

I have been attending Point Grey Fellowship for several years now, at first with a little trepidation, but it does not take long before I am fully accepted and integrated into the congregation. I soon take on responsibilities. I am asked to chair the discipleship committee when the former chair left for an MCC assignment. Later, when we are looking for a new pastor, I lead the pastoral search committee and I participate in the worship service.

Hildegard becomes interested in our church service and I share with her what we are doing, who was giving the message and what I remember as being important from it. We sit in the living room with a cup of coffee and talk freely about my new friends, about Evan and Janice who 'adopted' me when I first joined Point Grey Fellowship as an 'orphan'. They sat down beside me, they told me later, to make me feel welcome. I tell Hildegard, "You would like them, also Janet, a very fine, sensitive Bible College professor and counselor. I often talk with her about the message and its application, about her faith and her relationship to her students. She sometimes asks me about my family and what you are doing".

Hildegard sees that I have found a church home and a caring fellowship.

She confides in me, "I sometimes long for a fellowship like the one in Point Grey as you describe it to me". Knowing Hildegard, I can understand her well. "Why don't you join us? You will find many like-minded people there and become friends with them". She is thoughtful but does not say much in response.

The 'Over Fifties' in our congregation come together once a month for a social evening. We gather at a restaurant, where we can share the food, 'break bread together'. After the meal, the members who live close to the restaurant invite the group for dessert at their home. We share with each other what happens in our lives, discuss books, films we have seen, or play word games. Sometimes we invite a speaker who will talk about a controversial topic and we discuss it afterwards.

We have several artists in the group, painters, authors and fabric artists. In one of our meetings, each one agrees to share about his or her work. I have rewritten my German autobiography for English-speaking family members and friends under the title of, 'Crossing Frontiers.' My contribution is reading an interesting excerpt from it.

Hildegard comes occasionally to these get-togethers and enjoys the people in the group. They are 'real' and they in turn like her as a person, her friendliness, the ease communicating with her and her intelligent contributions.

One day Hildegard gets a phone call from the editor of the 'MCC Committee on Women's concerns' publication, "Hildegard, Janice has told me about you and your life journey, would you be willing to write an article for our periodical about your experiences? We have chosen the topic, 'Why Mennonite Women leave the Church'." Hildegard is taken by surprise and responds, hesitantly, "Give me some time to think about it?" When she hangs up, she does not know what to do. I encourage her, "I think you should share the story that is so close to your heart. Apparently you are not alone; there must be other women who have had similar experiences". After a few weeks, her article is finished. She calls it 'Leaving my Father's House'. It is very honestly written, the way Hildegard is, and she sends it in for their Sept.-Oct. 2002 issue.

She receives very encouraging responses to her article from several women.

At the annual general meeting of the 'Mennonite Women in Service', the organizer asks Hildegard if she would be willing to exhibit a few of her paintings to embellish the room where they meet. Hildegard selects some from her cycle of pictures that express female symbolism and we hang them up.

They invite Hildegard to stay for the meeting. She is impressed with the high caliber of the presentations. A few women recognize her name from the article she wrote. They welcome her and include her in their discussions. She feels accepted in this group.

Hildegard and I have displayed pictures together before. MCC organized a Mennonite Peace Exhibit, a counter event to the more militant Abbotsford Air Show, and invited Mennonite artists to show their work for this event. We are personally invited and agree to participate. Hildegard chooses the trilogy painting about caring for God's creation, for our environment, our trees. I make a large 3D picture, illustrating with symbols Jesus journey of love and peace, his mission here on earth. A variety of contributions are on display, paintings, sculptures, calligraphy and quilts. My picture draws the attention of the organizer of the show and he tells me, "I could see this work hanging in a church". I am surprised and encouraged and offer it to our congregation. It now hangs as a 'permanent loan' in our chapel behind the pulpit.

Hildegard still struggles with the doctrine of the male Trinity and the hierarchical and patriarchal Church form. For me, as a male, it seems easier to deal with this concept. I do not consciously attach a gender to God and the Holy Spirit, for me they are genderless, all-encompassing. But Hildegard reminds me, "We refer to all three members of the Trinity as 'He', in German and in English.

She finds the fixation of some churches on the sacrificial death of Jesus is over-emphasized. "It diverts from the importance of his message and his mission, the emphasis should be more on Jesus' life, his revolutionizing teaching and his fearless actions. His example of love should be a guide for our own path". She dismisses sections from letters accorded to the Apostle Paul about women, given almost two thousand years ago, as being not applicable for today's situation anymore. She grapples with Elaine Pagels' Gnosticism, with Christa Wolf's feminism and Christianity and Bultman's mythology. She draws from Meister Ekkehard and Hildegard von Bingen, what she feels is important to us. She is searching for the meaning of life, for the good in human beings. This becomes more evident in her later years.

As long as her father lived she had his trust and support in building her faith, she accepted and shared her father's faith. She had a close relationship with him and her father trusted her too. When he gave her Stauffer's critical essay about the New Testament, he felt, perhaps, she needed more than he could give.

When she left home and we attended our first Mennonite church togeter, she found the sermon too simplistic and not providing answers to all her questions.

She hoped for more in Sherbrooke Mennonite Church but when our pastor had to preach an English sermon and asked us to check if his English was correct, Hildegard was tempted not only to change some incorrectly used words but also some concepts, but she never violated his trust.

She was perhaps most fulfilled in our Hauskreis where we could search together for God's ways and direction for our life. She regretted its untimely dissolution.

In St.Margaret's, Pastor Bob's sermons gave answers to her quest but when the leadership changed, sermons became too restrictive and patriarchal in outlining the position of women in the church. She could not bear it anymore and left the church and her 'Father's House'. She had to find her own faith in her own sphere and her own time. It took a while of strenuous searching, but she never gave up.

Hildegard had noticed women she met at the 'Mennonite Women in Service' meetings struggle with similar problems and reach their own conclusions. They understand and respect her. She appreciates these Mennonite women who can think clearly and independently and feels a kinship to them.

One evening we are sitting by the fireplace, watching the fire and listening to music from our former Motet choir. Hildegard looks at me and says, "I love this choral music and would like to join in again, but I cannot sing four-part harmony alone". "I know a place where you can do that," I muse, "We have some very good musicians in our congregation. Sometimes string instruments accompany the singing."

Some time passes after this conversation and one Saturday she tells me she will come to church with me on Sunday. She writes in her journal:

> *I have had this drawing for at least two years to get back into a fellowship, a larger context of commitment. After my article, 'Leaving my Father's House', was published in the MCC Women's Concerns, I clearly felt I could go back.*
>
> *It was like a 'coming out'. My life, my spiritual journey, was clearly spelled out for all to see and I seemed to need that to return. My choice was to go to Point Grey Fellowship, the church Helmut has been going to for years.*
>
> *I seemed to need the Mennonite context, since there were many aspects to my Mennonite tradition that I cherished still. Also the people struck me as loving and welcoming whenever I had attended social functions.*

I am very thankful that she has come to this conclusion and feel good about it. It seems so right, that Hildegard and I go to church together.

When we arrive at the chapel, the women, whom she already knows, welcome her warmly and so do the other members to whom I introduce her.

In the service she can again sing the old hymns joyfully with the congregation. She finds the sermon engaging mind and soul and the responses afterwards very thoughtful.

What she likes is that women are fully engaged in the service, can lead the worship or give the message.

Point Grey chapel far left Helmut and Hildegard

Our family 2005
Tannis, Michael, Hanno, Anna, Tomas, Krista, Justin, Lisa
below, Madison, Tobin, Hildegard, Helmut

On the way home, Hildegard comments positively on the sermon and the conversations at the coffee hour afterwards. She tells me, "In my opinion, this is the way a congregation should function." Later in her journal she writes:

> *Having gone there now for a while, my impression has deepened. I feel accepted and for the first time in my life, when I go to church on a Sunday morning, I do not have to leave my intellect at home. What a relief, I can see that the people making up the church can actually become my friends, quite a few at least.*
>
> *Truly, the 'Church' has moved on, in some quarters at least, in the eighteen years I have not attended. I am filled with relief and gratitude. At least here seems to be no judging in questions of dissent, just respect for the other's experience and journey.*
>
> *I must say I really enjoy these Sunday mornings, there is nothing predictable and the people are so open and honest and sincere. I really want to go and do not find it a drudgery.*

Several months later, Erna, who is the chair of the worship team this term, asks Hildegard if she would be willing to share her spiritual journey with the congregation one Sunday. She is hesitant but then reworks her written article from the women's periodical into a sermon with the topic, 'Lessons from Away' and presents it on Sunday, May 16, 2004. The audience is appreciative of Hildegard's openness and her ability to articulate her ideas clearly and she is thankful for that response.

Some of the women have seen Hildegard's paintings and wonder if she would display them in the chapel, to make our chapel something like the 'Sistine Chapel'. She agrees if other women artists will display with her. The first one is a solo show of Hildegard's work. For the next one others have gained courage to bring their work. She is then asked

to take charge of displaying artwork in the church.

Hildegard now feels fully integrated to Point Grey Inter Mennonite fellowship. It is 'her' church now. I love seeing her in the lounge with a cup of coffee in an animated conversation with other church members. I can easily identify her. She usually wears well- balanced, color-coordinated clothing with contrasting accents, designed by our Polish artist friend, Izabella. In her later years, she chooses more violet colors, from light blue purple to a rich plum color. She looks elegant with her shoulder-length grayish hair interspersed with a few white stripes.

Hildegard helps me to find a facility for our fellowship retreat. We find camp Luther at Hatzig Lake suitable and the camp committee plans a program for the weekend. We have mind-engaging presentations and discussions, go hiking or canoeing, play board or lawn games and discover some of our members' special gifts and abilities at a talent show. We enjoy being together in a relaxed atmosphere. Camp Luther becomes the location for our future retreats.

One Sunday, on our way to church, a car drives through a red light, hits our car behind the passenger seat and turns it around 180 degrees. No one is seriously hurt. This accident brings out Hildegard's concern for other people. She writes in her journal:

> *Two things are worth mentioning about this accident. First, that morning I had dreamt that our right rear wheel (of our car) was smashed and completely pushed over towards the left one. I had said to Helmut, we can no longer drive the car. And that was precisely what happened. The next was the amazing love and compassion that ruled both in two women witnesses and then between us and the woman who had driven through the red light. In the end, we parted hugging each other, crying, speaking and receiving forgiveness.*

After 18 years of searching, she has now returned to her 'Father's House' but on a different level. Her faith has grown to become more inclusive. She sees herself not only as a child of God but also as a partner in living out the commission he has entrusted to her and all of us. She expresses her faith in a new terminology, refreshing to some and a little scary to the more conservative.

We have both grown in our faith, understanding Jesus' commission for us. I have widened my outlook and my understanding and appreciation of scripture through sermons and an interchange with friends in the fellowship. Hildegard had tried this through books, tapes and retreats, more or less on her own. Now, in a relationship with a church community, she can apply or adjust these insights.

Our relationship has taken on another level of intimacy; we love each other, accept and value one another the way we are.

44. Our last journey

On our last visit to Oldenburg, we talked with our friend, Jandirk, about Hildegard's health condition. She shares with him her problem with high blood pressure. He is concerned and tells her, "From my experience as a pharmacist, the medication which you are taking can damage the kidneys; I would suggest you see a nephrologist".

We follow his advice and are shocked when the young nephrologist, who examines her, tells Hildegard that her kidneys are only working at thirty percent capacity. She suggests that Hildegard get prepared for dialysis. We cannot believe this and want to get a second opinion. Dr. de Luca, an experienced specialist, assures Hildegard, "There is no need to be upset. I know that some patients can stabilize their kidney function and live many years without dialysis; the borderline is ten percent, below that we have to consider dialysis". We feel a little better now and can make plans for our journey to Europe.

Frank has organized another Wiehlertag and we want to participate. We drive to the youth guesthouse in Oberwesel, close to the romantic castle Schönburg, a beautiful location. From the castle we have a gorgeous vista of the Rhein Valley.

Over two hundred members of the Wiehler clan have arrived and line up to register. We greet our cousins and learn to know more relatives.

For Hildegard many of them are strangers but she has fun talking to them and they in turn are interested in their new Canadian relative.

We listen to inspirational speakers, storytellers and musical performances. We share our meals together and take hikes to the legendary Rhein River area.

I introduce myself to the Wiehler clan from Rostock. In our conversation I tell them that we will be going on a Baltic Sea cruise after the Wiehlertag and it starts from Warnemünde, the sea harbor of Rostock. Manfred offers to take us with our luggage from the city to the quay where our cruise ship docks.

We enjoy being together with our relatives and are looking forward to meeting again in five years. We exchange addresses, say good-bye and everyone heads home.

From Oberwesel we drive south along the Rhein valley and look up to the medieval castles built on the cliffs of the mountain ranges on both sides of the river.

Hildegard wants to see her favorite uncle Herbert again. He had visited us three times in Vancouver and managed that without knowing any English. He was our faithful guide on our trip to West Prussia twenty seven years ago. We are glad we can still visit him at his sickbed at his youngest daughter's place. He dies shortly afterwards of heart failure.

Jutta, a school friend of mine, wants to see me again and learn to know Hildegard. In our conversation, she confides to me that I have a wonderful wife. She takes us on a country outing to Austria into a mountain inn. From our table on the patio we enjoy a panoramic view of the romantic cul-de-sac valley. We have lunch in a picturesque inn. From our table on the patio we enjoy a panoramic view of the surrounding mountains with their bizarre peaks. On the higher alpine meadows, cows are grazing and we faintly hear their bells ringing.

A gathering of people on a field in the other side of the road draws our attention. A helicopter is lowering an injured cow in a net directly in front of a waiting veterinarian. These Austrians love their cows.

On Sunday morning, we attend church with Jutta who is a deacon in her church and she introduces us to her pastor, with whom we have a short talk. We thank her for her hospitality and move on.

For supper we stop in a restaurant in Tischenreuth. We ask the waiter if he knows of a Bed and Breakfast place nearby. He does not know of any but a guest next to us has listened in and he does know of one. He phones the owner of the B&B and asks him to reserve a room for us. When he finds out that we come from Canada he tells us, "It will not be easy to find it, I will drive ahead, just follow me." He gets into his car and shows us the way to a nice little private hotel, on the outskirts of the town. We appreciate his kindness very much.

On our trip north we take a little detour and drive through the town of Nördlingen. My professor for city planning had told us about this best-preserved example of a medieval town. I want to show it to Hildegard. In the old part of it, the houses are close together and are surrounded by a solid fortification wall. We walk on the inside of the elevated wall along a covered walkway and look through its embrasures. From the watchtowers, we have a good view over the city, its layout, its Gothic churches, half-timbered houses and the town hall. It is another world, quite different from a town in Canada.

We continue our trip to Berlin. For a few nights, we stay again in the Mennoheim, the meeting place of the Mennonite Church. We are on our own there and can plan our time as we wish.

I contact Monica, the daughter of cousin Röschen. She picks us up and we drive through the Brandenburg forest to the county home of her cousins, Oswald and Beate. A few other relatives await us there already and welcome us.

Berlin has changed from our last visit. After the unification of Germany, the Government gradually relocated its departments from Bonn to Berlin. Renowned architects competed in revitalizing the empty space around the historic 'Reichstag' (parliament), designing beautiful modern buildings. Taking advantage of the challenging location along the meandering Spree River, they connected the different government departments with bridges and walkways, surrounded by creative landscaping. The new buildings are quite a contrast to the old classical Reichstag building.

Brigitte, the wife of nephew Reinhard, takes a day off and shows us another part of Berlin. Close to the former border, the city has created an outdoor museum to show its younger people how Communist East Germany used to protect its territory. There is a part of the 'Wall' that divided Berlin. Next to it a reconstructed section of the border between the former East and West Germany. It shows the barbwire fence in front of the ploughed strip of land armed with landmines, then the path, which border guards patrolled with their dogs to catch perpetrators who attempt to cross the border to West Germany. We climb up the replica of a watchtower on the other side of the street, to have the same view as the guards who controlled the border.

A few weeks before we arrived in Berlin, the controversial Holocaust Memorial was opened. On a 4.7 acre plot prime property close to the Brandenburger Tor, Architect Eisenman built 2700 sarcophagus-size concrete boxes of different heights and lined them up in rows on different sloping levels. They are separated by narrow pathways which lead from street level to underground chambers. In one of them are listed all the names of the Jewish victims of the holocaust in Berlin. It is impressive, but the general public does not honor it for the purpose for which it was designed. People sit on the slabs and eat their lunch and children hop from one box to the other, play catch and hide and seek and have fun.

On our last morning in Berlin, we again go through the park to our small bakery and order our last delicious breakfast.

We phone Manfred and tell him that we are on the way to Rostock. He picks us up from the rental car place, loads our luggage into his station wagon and drives us to the cruise ship. There is a long line up for the registration. We still have time and he takes us to a lovely harbor inn where we have lunch together.

We had asked Monika in Vancouver if she would like to join us on our cruise. She lives alone now since her husband, John, died. She gladly accepts. To have a companion in her cabin, we invite Adelheid. Both of them grew up in the area where we will stop on our cruise. We meet the two at the registration. I was able to reserve two cabins side by side for the four of us.

The sun is shining when we leave Warnemünde and we enjoy a beautiful sunset on the Baltic Sea. During the night, however, dark clouds come up and when we reach Gdansk, it starts raining lightly. It is our third visit to Danzig, so we know parts of the city. Our guide takes us through the Golden Gate, along the Langgasse with the beautifully restored patrician gable houses on each side and down to the Mottlau River with Danzig's landmark, the Krantor, an old heavy-weight lift. We spend a short time in the largest Gothic brick church, the Marienkirche. Vendors have displays of amber and other jewelry everywhere we go, on the street and in stores.

Our bus takes us to the Cistercian Monastery of Oliva with its two high towers arching over the entrance door of the Cathedral. Its construction started in the Middle Ages and was finished in the Rococo period. It has an outstanding organ.

The next morning the weather has changed and the captain announces, 'The wind has reached gale force, it will be too dangerous to navigate the narrows at Pilau, so we have to forego the trip to Königsberg.' We are all disappointed, especially Adelheid who was born there. We had been looking forward to visit the capital of our former province.

The sun returns again when we explore the two hanseatic towns of (Reval) Tilling and Riga, capitals of Estonia and Latvia. Both have been influenced in their development and history by changing governments, the Teutonic Knights, Danish, Swedish and Russian.

We have good guides who speak perfect German and are quite knowledgeable about the intriguing history of these countries.

The Estonians like to sing. When we stop at a large outdoor stadium with a wide orchestra bowl, our guide mentions that the Russians forbade them to have song festivals here and they kept the stadium locked.

During a stroll through Riga, we happen to go into an old deserted monastery. From the stone balcony of the inner court, we listen to a duet by bards in medieval garb, singing Gregorian music, accompanied by lute and flute, a lovely interlude.

We notice similarities in the culture and architecture of these Baltic States.

A special treat for Hildegard and me is the stopover at the Island of Ösel. The harbor is too shallow for our ship to land, so we board our lifeboats to get to shore. Stepping onto this peaceful island makes us feel transported back a few centuries. A bus takes us through small villages to a simple early Gothic church. On some of the cross vaults are frescos with Christian motifs interspersed with cabalistic ornaments.

The Bischofsburg, a former castle of the Teutonic Knights, is accessible over the drawbridge. From there we enter the large inner court, surrounded by thick square walls with solid towers. In the main Knights Hall coat of arms of many knights hang on the walls. On a plaque with their names engraved on it, I recognize the name of the Grand Master, Winrich von Kniprode, after whom my high school in Marienburg was named.

From the island we sail on to St.Petersburg where we spend two days, not enough time for this beautiful city. Our tour starts with the Winter Palace, the former residence of the Tsars. We admire the long white and green facade of the three story baroque building on the banks of the Neva River. What interests us most is the Hermitage, the part of the palace complex which houses one of the oldest and largest art museums in the world. Our guide tells us, "If you look at each art object stored here for one minute, it would take you nine years before you would have seen them all". It is so crowded inside that it is difficult to get close enough to see the paintings properly.

We listen to the guide's comments about the different buildings and the tragic history of the Emperors when we drive through the city. At the place where Tsar Alexander II had been assassinated, his son built a magnificent church, the Cathedral of the Resurrection of Christ, known as the 'Church of the spilled Blood'. It is built in a romantic mixture of styles, is highly decorated and crowned with a number of onion-shaped steeples. We are awestruck when we enter the church and see all the colorful decorations. Ceilings, walls, columns, cupolas and high arches are covered with fine detailed mosaic icons and pictures. I buy a photo license and am allowed to take pictures without a flash and I have plenty of motifs. A number of altars stand in niches, decorated with sculptures and traditional and modern paintings, before which some visitors are kneeling. It is almost too much to take it all in.

Driving on, we are charmed by the beautiful blue and white baroque Smolny Convent and Cathedral. The guide tells us, it was once a retirement home for widows of nobility, then a prestigious school for daughters of nobility. During the Communist rule it was closed and left to decay, like three hundred other churches in St. Petersburg. It has been restored and the beautiful Cathedral is now a concert hall.

The next morning, busses take us to Peterhof, the summer residence of Tsar Peter the Great. In some tourist guides it is called the Russian Versailles. We walk through the large park and are surprised to see small white and gold-colored baroque pavilions and palaces appear behind the spray of a fountain or a group of trees.

The main attraction of the Peterhof is the Grand Palace, a baroque building in bright white and yellow colors with gold accents. The rooms in the interior of the palace are furnished with fine French rococo furniture; the walls are covered with pastel-colored and delicately patterned silk wallpaper and paintings of the royal family. Guards let only a small number of visitors into each room at a time, so it is not that crowded. This gives us a chance to enjoy the atmosphere and take a few pictures.

From the upper rooms we have a panoramic view over the park down to the Gulf of Finland. Below the palace, the garden is terraced down with a series of fountains on each side. Gilded human and animal figures spout water into a semicircular pond. One of them, Samson, is tearing open the mouth of a lion and a high jet of water shoots out of it, splashing down into the pond. One day is not enough to explore this beautiful, spread-out estate.

We board our ship again and sail to Helsinki. Since our cruise ship is relatively small, we can go farther into the harbor, past several twelve-deck high cruise ships, and dock at the passenger quay.

I have always wanted to visit Finland. The beautiful, simple, functional Finish design in architecture, furniture and appliances was lauded and set as an example by our professors in our study of architecture.

Hildegard and I walk from the harbor towards the city. From a distance, we can see the tall tower of the Cathedral. There is a service in the church, which we do not want to disturb and we go a little further and sit on the long set of stairs overlooking the beautiful Senate Square below. The slightly sloping open rectangle is flanked on one side by Helsinki University, on the other by the Government Palais and behind us the large neoclassicist Cathedral. The plaza has pleasant proportions.

As we stroll through the city, we discover another very interesting structure, the 'Temppeliankion Kirkko', the 'Rock Temple'. We enter the church on street level through wide glass doors. Above them a heavy concrete slab lintel is supporting the roof over the wide opening. Compared to the unassuming outside, the inside is awesome. The walls are of untreated natural rock. The sanctuary is a hole, blasted out of a solid rock embankment. The light comes only from a ring of skylights in the roof. The altar table is a specially selected rock slab and so is the baptismal font. A copper-covered balcony hangs freely from one side and an organ from the other, like swallow nests. Well-designed, simple wrought iron candelabras are fastened to the rock walls and the candles reflect the light from the moist shiny rock surfaces. The sanctuary needs no pictures on the walls; its rock surface is mottled with multi-colored veins and has a soft luster. In contrast to the solid walls, the furniture is light, steel frame chairs with wooden seats padded with colorful fabric. Everything is simple, well-proportioned and balanced. It is a delight for us to be in this church.

From the outside, the church is hardly noticeable. Only the slightly domed roof sticks out over the rock embankment.

We are very pleased with our short exploration of the Finnish capital and take a detour to the boat through a small park where we pass a few noteworthy monuments. The most striking one is the 'Sibelius organ', a number of organ pipe-like forms, arranged in an unusual sculpture and beside it the bust of the celebrated composer hanging over a rock ledge.

Back on board again we have a surprise. As usual we go to the dining room to have supper together. The waiter takes our order and we wait for the meal. All of a sudden four waiters, one with a guitar, candles in their hands come out of the kitchen. We think somebody must have a birthday. They stop at our table, serenade us and present us with a special cake and a card, 'Happy Anniversary'. Adelheid and Monika had told the headwaiter that it is our 49th wedding anniversary today. The two laid a lovely bouquet of flowers in our cabin and we celebrate.

We are approaching the end of our cruise. Today we visit Stockholm, the city on fourteen islands, very similar to Helsinki. The tour guide tells us, "Stockholm was a member of the Hanseatic League and an important trading post in the late Middle Ages; half of Stockholm's city council at that time was composed of German-speaking burghers. This is different now". With a smile, she tells us, "forty percent of the Parliament and fifty percent of the Senate are women".

We have a chance to watch the changing of the guard in front of the Royal Residence. Not far from the residence is the large Gothic cathedral. As we come out of it, the guide points to a statue of Fredrik Petri, a pupil of Luther, "He brought Protestantism to Sweden."

We have a little time for ourselves and Hildegard and I explore the old town. Walking down a narrow back street, we come upon the shop of a silversmith and glassblower. The old master talks to us about his art, when he learns that we are artists and come from Canada. We watch him blowing these intricate glass forms. Hildegard is very interested in a pair of delicate abstract birds but he thinks they might be too fragile to be taken on the plane to Canada, so we just take a picture of them.

Not far from Stockholm, on the way to Copenhagen, we approach the island of Gotland, the biggest in the Baltic Sea. We dock at Visby and walk to the old part of the town. Again, it feels like stepping back a few centuries when we pass through the guarded gate in the high stonewall of the fortification. The watchtowers and walls which surround most of the old town are still in fairly good condition. Visby is the town of ruins, roses and narrow streets. Of the seventeen Romanesque and Gothic churches in the city, we are told, ten are ruins. The freestanding high arches of the Gothic and the solid columns of the Romanesque church ruins are well-preserved monuments of another era.

In the old fishing harbor, new motor boats are now tied to the dock, replacing the old fishing trawlers, and the former fishermen's abodes are nicely renovated to serve as holiday cabins for vacationers.

The guide takes us on a walk through the woods to an ancient burial ground. The markers for the captain's grave are large boulders laid out in the form of a ship.

Our last stop is Copenhagen, the largest cruise ship harbor in Europe, and we can see the crowds from several of the tall ships that are tied up on the dock milling around when we disembark.

I do not remember much about Copenhagen. Seeing one big city after the other, tires us out. Most of what we see of Copenhagen we see through the bus window on this rainy day. The guide in our bus is somewhat tight-lipped. Half of the time we cannot understand him from our seat. He gives us very few photo stops.

I remember the large parking place, I believe in front of the city hall, with hundreds of bicycles parked there and am amazed at the number of people riding bikes in the city.

Of course, we have to see the little Mermaid in Copenhagen's harbor. The poor girl has been mutilated, decapitated and drowned several times by vandals. She has been restored and sits again on a rock in the sea, close to the cruise ship pier.

In the evening we leave Copenhagen and arrive early in the morning in Warnemünde. Klaus, our tour guide, lends me his cell phone and I notify Manfred that we are back again. We try to find our luggage and say goodbye to our faithful travel companions, Adelheid and Monika. When we have located our suitcases, we see Manfred in the crowd. He takes our luggage and drives us to the Euro Car Rental. They are just preparing a new Smart forfour for us. While we are waiting, Manfred tells us about the Gertrudenkapelle, a small memorial chapel for Ernst Barlach. "You have to see it," he tells us. Hildegard and I like the work of this expressionistic sculptor and we drive to Güstrow to see his work. Standing in front of his semi-abstract bronzes, carvings and wood reliefs and reflecting on the expressive faces of his 'Beggar on crutches', 'Sitting woman',

'Avenger', 'Floating Angel' and many others, makes us thoughtful and we will be looking at our fellow humans with more compassion.

We start our trip back to the Düsseldorf airport in our Smart forfour, which we find just right for the two of us.

Schneverdingen is on the way and we stop in at cousin Günter's house and spend a day with him and Hanna. Günther has had a prostate cancer operation. The chemotherapy has caused him considerable discomfort. He now needs a cane to walk.

The heather is again in full bloom and the four of us walk slowly on the purple carpet of the Lüneburg Heath.

We take advantage of cousin Gerhard's invitation to stay overnight with him in Düsseldorf. It is opportune for us, since he lives so close to the airport. Now retired, he has picked up his father's hobby, weaving baskets with willow twigs. For his physical fitness he goes on long bicycle tours and hikes into the native forests, looking for special mushrooms. He is an expert in identifying them and often collects a basket of rare species and sells them to gourmet restaurants.

Time comes to depart. We repack our luggage to satisfy the airport security, return our rental car and board our plane for Vancouver.

45. The final story

Our children are now established in their professions, have their own families and their own homes. They still are and ever will be very much in our thoughts and hearts. Occasionally they appreciate our input and we appreciate their professional advice. Our love for each other is mutual.

Krista and Lisa want to improve their living conditions in anticipation of Justin growing up, going to school and making friends with other children. They see a single-family house for sale in a better neighborhood close by and after some consideration decide to buy it. They move from their duplex to a detached house in the new location. Mom flies to Toronto to help and give suggestions for rearranging and furnishing the new home. She plays with her grandson, Justin, and he loves his Oma.

Both of our boys are good handymen and can do basic repairs around the house, and so is Krista in a limited way she sometimes phones and asks for advice.

I had built a sturdy workbench for Hanno's workshop and helped him to install it and had suggested basic tools he might find useful in his workshop. He bought them and gradually upgrades them.

Michael did not have the time and room to arrange for a decent workshop which I think every homeowner should have. Occasionally I reminded him it would be helpful to have decent tools and a place to store them, especially because he is very handy and well organized in his work and office. I had told him I would gladly help him to establish one as long as I am still able to do this. He is now ready to take me up on it. I had drawn the plans for an extension of his small shed to include a decent workshop and had estimated the material needed to build it. Now we put it into practice. I love to work with my sons and share with them my practical experience and see them applying it.

Hanno is on the move again. He has been looking for property in a more prestigious area and found one in West Vancouver with a magnificent view over Greater Vancouver, the Lions Gate Bridge and Stanley Park,. He plans to build Anna's and his dream house there later.

While in Christina Lake, we receive a phone call from a stranger asking if we are interested in selling our place. We ask him how he got our address. He is a pilot and has flown over Castle Mountain several times and spotted our property. He liked the location and inquired at the Land Registry who the owner is and they gave him our address and phone number.

I tell him we are not yet ready to sell. A year later he phones again and has the same question. This time I tell him I will think about it.

With my arrhythmia attacks and increasing age, it has become more difficult for me to keep our little paradise in good condition. Walking up and down the hill is getting more strenuous for me as time goes on.

Tannis and Michael tell me they could take care of it and little Madison says, "But Opa you have to keep it for future generations" I ask her what she means by that. She is quite concerned, "What I mean is for me and Tobin and for our children and their children". I think she has a point.

The next year they come up in spring, before we arrive. Michael has to open up the place after the winter shutdown. He has to reconnect the water from the spring up on the hill, mow the grass along the driveway and around the house, remove the dead mice from under the sofa and split wood for the oven. He reconsiders, "If I have two weeks of holidays and have to work for the first week that is not the holiday I look forward to," he tells me, "I love it but it is not really suitable for us"

Hildegard does not want to give up our Christina Lake property either, but realizes that it is becoming harder for both of us to take proper care of two properties, especially for me to do the outside work and the repairs. She will agree to sell it under one condition, if a buyer approaches us and will take care of the business of the transfer without any hassle. So the next time I get a phone call from Ron, the caller has identified himself now, I ask him to make an offer. I have not yet met him, and I ask on the phone if he wants to use it as a vacation home and if he wants us to leave the furniture and some tools in the house. He is very nice on the phone, but rather evasive. I may leave the furniture and tools, he tells me. I am glad that I do not have to remove them all; but he does not want the old truck and our ancient grass cutter. Billy gets the truck and the grass mower and a few tools, in exchange for taking a truckload of junk to the dump.

We come to an easy agreement with Ron about the price and he does all the paperwork necessary for the transfer of the title. We just have to sign the contract at the lawyer's office and cash the cheque.

Hanno and Anna come and take some of the decorative pieces. Tannis would like to have the big round family table and the sofa from Uncle Leon. Michael hires a U-Haul truck to take it away and we add some dishes and bedding and a few heirlooms, like the old Russian samovar from Hildegard's parents.

After the children have left, Hildegard and I clean up. She washes the floor and cleans the dishes and pots and pans which will stay there. We want to leave everything in good order. Once more we look around in the house, pack the rest of our belongings into our car and then lock it and say our final fare well.

For Hildegard it is a 'traumatic' experience to leave this lovely place, our summer home for twenty-six years, where we could relax in the sun and fresh air, go swimming in a clean lake and take long hikes on our own property. For me it is not easy either, but I know it will become too hard for me; it is time for us to downsize.

A few months after the sale of our cabin we get a phone call from Phil, our neighbor, "Uncle Helmut did you know that your former property is for sale again?" I check the real estate listings and find out that Ron has the house for sale again for a considerably higher price. He also has clear-cut a section of the woods on the Miller farm road, which we had so carefully preserved. Hildegard is very upset about this.

Hildegard and I are getting older and our children are concerned about our wellbeing.

We are privileged to have two medical experts in our family.

Hildegard is aware of her precarious kidney condition and attends a seminar given by a kidney dietitian. She tries to improve her kidney function by changing her diet, preparing and eating 'beneficial' foods. She also listens to seminars about dialysis.

She gets advice from different friends to try alternative medicine, naturopathic remedies or meditation. On their recommendation she is willing to try them out.

Michael is concerned about my reoccurring arrhythmia and arranges an appointment with his cardiologist colleague. After a thorough examination, she suggests a new pacemaker and tells me, "This time you will get the 'Cadillac' of a pacemaker, an advanced model which has just been approved." I have an information meeting with the surgeon and he explains the procedure to me. He will cut the main conductor between the two heart chambers and replace it with a mechanical one. My heart rhythm, my life function will then depend on the performance of this implanted mechanical device. It is kind of scary. He tells me, however, that these are now routine operations and that he has done many of them successfully. This gives me confidence.

On the scheduled operation day, Michael picks me up in the morning and stays with me during the operation. The surgeon performs an AV node ablation, connects the wires from the pacemaker and, four hours after the operation, Hildegard takes me home again.

It takes a week for the insertions to heal but I have no more arrhythmia attacks and do not have to suffer the side effects of medication. We are very thankful for this solution and that we are still in relatively good health.

One day when Michael gets home from work, Tannis informs him she has made the difficult decision, after months of agonizing, to be admitted to hospital. The medications she is taking need to be adjusted and this can be done more quickly and effectively in hospital. Michael asks Hildegard if she can come over and be with the children when the nanny is not available and he has to work. She gladly helps out to care for her little darlings. Madison is a little worried about what will happen when her mother is in hospital. Hildegard tries to explain Tannis' condition to her and dispel her fears. She feels safe with her Oma. She tells her little brother, "I will be your mommy when Mommy is not here." They are lovely, brave children.

Sometimes Tomas comes over when Anna cannot find a babysitter during the daytime. He loves to come to Opa's and Oma's house. Oma always has creative ideas to bring simple toys to life. He loves to play with marbles; they roll down on guides from the sofa to the chair and down to the floor in pairs or singles. Toys have to be in motion and make noise.

I am always amazed at how the grandchildren in this world of abundance still love to play with very simple toys if someone spends time with them and inspires them. Oma is very good at doing that.

We have frequent contact with our grandchildren, either we go over to be with them or they come to us and Oma plays or does art work with them. Madison sometimes has sleepovers at 'Oma's House'. If somebody asks Hildegard if she is babysitting, she corrects them, "I do not 'babysit\, I am spending quality time with my grandchildren!"

Hildegard has some secret phone calls with our children. She finally tells me they are going to arrange a big party for my eighties birthday. I may suggest whom I want to have as guests. We select thirty-eight from our relatives and mostly friends from our congregation and our former Hauskreis. We look at a few localities and Hildegard decides on the prestigious heritage Hart House Restaurant. Krista has come from Toronto to help with the celebration. We are all happy to see her again.

Tannis welcomes the guests and hands them a page of an unbound guest book. Instead of writing birthday cards, they can write comments on it about what they appreciate in me and what they do not. She collects them afterwards to fill the (un)traditional guest book. Krista later adds photos, which she took of all the guests. I can then enjoy reading it later. I am very moved by the entry from Hildegard and the one from Tannis.

> *Dearest Helmut, your steadfast love and strength have been to all you love a source of comfort and reassurance, especially to me. You have given me the space to become me and for that I appreciate you, honor and respect you forever and I dearly love you*

And my dear daughter-in-law, Tannis writes,"

> *Dearest Dad, I am so grateful for you. Your loving acceptance of me from the start has been a blessing I hardly dared to wish for.... I pray my children will display your grace, love, zest for life and most of all your immovable faith. I am proud to have you as a father-in-law. I am blessed to call you Dad.*

Hildegard had asked some special guests to share their impressions of me. My children and sister tell what they remember about me. I am overwhelmed to find out what they think about me, who I am, especially what I mean to my children.

Gillian brings her harp and enriches the festivity with her musical contributions. Everybody seems to enjoy the party.

Life goes on again. I am a year older.

Our children are planning for a special event. It concerns Hildegard and me. It is our 50th wedding anniversary, our Golden Wedding. They allow us some input and Hildegard suggests celebrating it in a unique way, symbolically, sailing together on the ocean. She would like to invite our guests to a dinner cruise. I am concerned about this. It is a gamble; we are completely dependent on the weather. Hildegard is confident it will work out and I trust her.

The Vancouver Yacht Charters has the right boat for us and we arrange the conditions with them. Hildegard and Anna select the menu and I check out parking facilities. I print invitations on my new computer and send it out to friends and relatives who have accompanied us in our marriage for many years. This time the grandchildren may celebrate with us. Sue agrees to entertain them if they become unruly. Anxiously we listen for the weather forecast. Hildegard's optimism is rewarded; it is to be sunny with cloudy periods.

Hanno directs the guests from the parking lot to the Yacht Charters dock. When all the guests have arrived we move from the lounge to the dining room and the boat takes off, sailing slowly into the ocean. Sherry, our long time friend from Christina Lake, gives the introduction on a lighter note and Janet, who teaches at Columbia Bible College, has prepared a thoughtful meditation on the meaning of relationship and the metaphors of 'River, Tree and Canyon'. Her 'minstrel-husband', Ernie, has written suitable songs and accompanies them on his guitar.

Krista has composed our life story in rhyme form and the children sing it for us to familiar melodies from hymns, folk songs and hits, from 'Sheep may safely graze' - to 'Super Trooper.' Little Madison has memorized most of the words and melodies and proudly sings along with aunt Krista, uncle Michael and uncle Hanno. Krista plays a few preludes and intermissions on the recorder. Hanno entertains us with a powerful Power Point presentation of our life story. They do a marvelous job, meaningful and humorous. We all enjoy it.

After this presentation we are ready for a delicious meal of chicken breast or salmon and our ship is slowly gliding past the lights of the city.

We have no open mike but Ulli has written two poems for the occasion, which he reads to us. There is time to change seats, meet old friends or get acquainted with new ones. After a three-and-a-half hour cruise, we return to the dock again and everyone says good-bye. The family continues for a little longer at our house reflecting on this lovely event.

We have to use our time-share again and book a suite in the Camelback Resort in Scottsdale. We have been in Scottsdale before and love the artist's enclaves in town. We tour several art stores, visit artists in their studios and talk to them about their work.

From the balcony of our suite we can look into the park-like garden with all sorts of Cacti and exotic trees and plants and through our binoculars we can see people climbing the Camelback Mountain.

Right around the corner is an affluent residential district. There are some beautiful houses and adobe villas between palm trees and cacti and we point out the ones we think we could live in, mostly we choose the same ones.

The resort offers a number of entertainment options. I try my luck playing golf on the small green and Hildegard walks the native Labyrinth and takes part in Tai Chi classes.

In the swimming pool we meet a German couple from Cologne and have long talks with them. The instructor of a water gymnastics group asks Hildegard if she wants to participate with the other women. She usually does but this time she does not feel like joining. She also does not swim as long as she normally does either. We walk long stretches in the park and to town and enjoy the sunshine or we sit on the balcony and read.

Our time runs out and we have to go back again to snow and frost.

Hanno picks us up from the airport and takes us home. Anna has prepared a hot soup for us and the two put basic groceries for breakfast in the fridge. A yellow rose in a vase in the living room is a welcome-back gift from Jean. Their love and care for us warms our hearts.

Winter comes early this year. It is unusual for us to shovel snow in November. We hear our little neighbor's daughter having fun outside building a snowman with her dad. The unusual weather has caused a blackout and it is getting cold without electricity and heating. Fortunately, we can light our fireplace to keep us warm and we hang a cauldron from Christina Lake in the fire and boil water in it for coffee and tea.

Christmas Eve we celebrate with the family in the old traditional way, candles, a story for the grandchildren and singing English and German Christmas songs. Michael and I accompany or introduce them with our alto and tenor recorders, since Krista could not come and play the harpsichord this year.

Hanno and Anna invite the extended family for a gala dinner on Christmas day to their home, to make it a little easier for Hildegard whose energy is not quite what it used to be, she gets quite tired after a busy day.

Hildegard and I have a peaceful New Year's celebration, sit at the fireplace, listen to music and look back, thankfully, on our blessings and achievements of the last year. We share our wishes for the coming one. One of mine is to take Hildegard to a spa in Europe, preferably one that would invigorate her kidneys again. She is not sure if she wants to go.

We assume our daily routines again; Hildegard picks up swimming which she had neglected during the holidays. She comes back from the swimming pool one day, quite wearied and tells me, "This time I could only swim four laps, normally I swim forty. On the last one I was so exhausted, I was afraid I would drown, I barely made it home." Michael anticipates a serious problem and takes his Mom to the emergency. The diagnosis is 'water in her lung'. The nurse drains out two liters from her lung cavity. I had noticed already in Scottsdale that something was not as usual with her. The doctor orders a CT scan.

While we are waiting for the results, the nurse comes to the house periodically and drains more liquid from Hildegard's lungs. Three weeks later, on March 2007 the result from the scan comes back. 'Cancer in the lining of the lung'. The specialist calls us into her office, "I am sorry to tell you that it is terminal cancer.- Operation is not possible in this case and I would not suggest chemo-therapy or radiation either, your kidneys may not tolerate that, it would cause pain without gain. It might extend your life by a month or two."

It is a shock for us, a very unexpected discovery.

We have been looking forward to a pleasant, stimulating retirement in our beautiful home which we had designed with that in mind, enjoying being together in a loving, caring relationship and supporting each other when we get older. This dream will now take on a different perspective.

Hildegard, who prepares and eats healthy meals, is quite fit and slender and has never smoked, what could cause cancer for her? We were prepared for a possible kidney failure, but not for cancer.

After the first shock is over, Hildegard is astoundingly tranquil. She tells me when we sit quietly together "You know I am not afraid to die, in fact I am curious to find out what life is like after death and if I will find answers to my questions about the purpose of life. The one wish I have is that I will not have to suffer a painful death." She later mentions this to members of the fellowship, to those who ask her how she feels about her illness. They are astonished at Hildegard's peaceful attitude towards dying.

She takes advantage of all possible remedies for cancer. We drive to Victoria to a homeopathic doctor, a specialist in cancer treatment and we come home with a bag of expensive pills and tinctures. In the long run they do not make much difference. We have very good specialists and visiting nurses who can control the pain level very well as the illness progresses. Slowly she loses weight and energy. She still comes to the table for meals but does not eat very much. It is hard for me to see my lovely Hildegard fade away

They miss Hildegard in church and members and friends bring cards, flowers and meals and stay for a short time with her, receiving as much comfort from her as they can give. Many are amazed about her calmness, no complaints, hidden anger or angst about her situation.

Hildegard has given graciously and abundantly of her love and energy in many ways, to many people, has listened and given counsel. She now learns to receive love and care graciously.

Her journal expresses that:

> *Meanwhile Helmut is the most loving companion….he is so helpful and kind, that I feel really well taken care of and moved by his caring concern…*
>
> *During all this time my family and my friends have been wonderful. Mike has taken on to accompany my progress…and is a wonderful support. Hanno and Anna bring the most delicious food and little Tomas is my 'medicine'.*
>
> *I find our grandchildren the best medicine; Tomas continues to completely delight me with his incredible zest for life and his curiosity and quick mind…. Krista phones nightly and is a most wonderful support. I feel so loved! I have also received incredibly sensitive cards from my friends who pray for me. Did I have to get sick to find out*

how much loved I was? Of course I always knew it but this is so tangible. I am full of gratitude.

Hildegard now sleeps longer. In the evening she wants me to sit at her bedside and hold her hand. We talk quietly about the good times of our life together and what will happen afterwards. Sometimes we just enjoy each other's quiet presence. She wants me to kiss her goodnight before she falls asleep. I will miss these intimate moments with her.

She is still aware of family events. When Madison has her Irish dance competition, she does not want to miss that. It means a lot to Madison that Oma watches her dance.

Hanno wants to show his Mom his love for her and flies her to his summerhouse on Pender Island. It is a wonderful sunny day. We sit on the balcony, Hildegard, covered in a blanket in a deck chair, and enjoy the wide view of the ocean. She has always liked these unobstructed views into the distance.

On the last evening we sit together in the living room and watch a video from an interview that Lisa and Krista had made a few months ago, in which Hildegard tells about her life. For us, this is now an audio-visual-memoir. She mentions that she would like to make a special video for her grandchildren when she comes home.

We go to bed early. Tomorrow we will fly back to Vancouver.

Hildegard is still sleeping when I get up the next morning and have a quiet time and read in the room next door. A little later I hear her calling my name. She has returned from the bathroom and is lying across the bed, when I enter. She asks me to connect her to the oxygen bottle, which she has used occasionally. I cover her up, connect her to the oxygen and hold my arm around her to give her support. For a few minutes she breathes heavily, then in longer intervals and then her breathing stops. I know this is the end. I lay her down gently and call Hanno. He is struck by grief and close to tears when he looks at his Mom. He phones 911. The ambulance comes and the medics try to resuscitate her. I tell them life has gone out of her and they should leave her in peace. The doctor comes and certifies her death.

When they have all left, Anna comes in and is heartbroken when she sees Mom. We both hug and weep.

Hanno phones the funeral home with which we had made arrangements earlier and they will take care of the transfer of her body from the medical centre on Pender Island to the funeral home in Coquitlam.

Hildegard and Madison (as Irish dancer)

Hildegard and Helmut in BurnabyMarine Park 2007

I still have an hour alone to be with Hildegard, to pray and to communicate quietly with her,

> 'I love you dearly, Hildegard, my beautiful, gracious wife.
> You gave me your unconditional love,
> I always felt that and valued it.
> I tried to be a good husband to you, as I had promised when I put this ring on your finger.
> I tried to shield you from danger and unpleasant situations as much as I could.
> We shared the responsibility for accompanying and supporting our children as they were growing up and I admired you.
> We were able to solve disagreements amiably.
> We lived through a period of trial and crisis when you were shedding your old skin and growing a new one.
> It was a painful process for both of us.
> But I learned to accept and appreciate your new skin as much as the former.
> You helped me to understand you and had patience with me.
> I learned from you to be open, to be aware of and express my feelings.
> We gave each other room to live and to love each other.
> I thank you for that,
> I love you and I will miss you very much -

With a heavy heart I take final leave from Hildegard, my beloved life partner.

.

We cancel the reservation for our flight and drive home. Krista and family arrive from Toronto. The daughters dress their Mom's body in a dress she had just bought and had never worn yet, to make her presentable for the family and those who want to see her once more. She lies peacefully and beautifully, the way she lived, in the candle-lit sanctuary of the funeral home.

After we all have left, the funeral staff comes in and take her body to the crematorium.

A few days later we go back to receive her ashes, all that is left of her body.

We as a family and close friends gather at the gravesite and in a solemn ceremony the children and I pour the ashes into the earth, beside her simple gravestone, as she had wanted it.

Her spirit will be with us and live on in our memory forever.

Addendum

Aus Hildegard's (Liebes) Briefen
Exerpts from letters written by Hildegard (and Helmut)

Braunschweig, 31.8.54

Ich war etwas überrascht als ich von Evas Entlobung hörte. Ihr armen Mädchen lernt uns meistenteils durch Briefe kennen und seid nachher enttäuscht, wenn ihr uns persönlich kennenlernt mit unseren Schwächen und Angewohnheiten. Aber in Bezug auf uns beide scheinst Du ja immer noch ziemlich optimistisch zu sein....

Ich würde Dir lieber sagen, wie ich über die Stellung des Mannes denke, als darüber zu schreiben.

Prinzipiell ist für mich die Bibel die Grundlage. Der Mann ist das Haupt der Familie und trägt die Verantwortung nach außen hin für sie. Das einzige Mittel, das er anwenden darf um eine etwaige "Herrschaft" auszuüben ist die Liebe.

Die Frau ist die Gehilfin des Mannes. Sie ist ihm menschlich gesehen durchaus gleichgeordnet, sie trägt also indirekt zu gleichen Teilen mit an der Verantwortung für ein harmonisches Leben in der Familie. Dem Mann ist die Ernährung und der Schutz der Familie anvertraut. Er wird also mehr nach außen hin wirken, denn sein Beruf bringt ihn mehr mit der Öffentlichkeit in Verbindung. Er ist gewissermaßen der Repräsentant der Familie und muss sich auch dementsprechend verhalten, dass seine Familie sich seiner nicht etwa schämen muss, sondern stolz auf ihn sein kann....

Sei lieb gegrüßt,

Dein Helmut

I was surprised to hear about Eva's (Hildegard's sister) dissolution of her engagement. You unfortunate girls, you learn to know us men mainly through letters and when you meet us personally with our weaknesses and idiosyncracies you may be disappointed. But for the two of us, you seem to be quite optimistic.....

I would rather talk to you about the position of man in the family than write about it.

In principle, the Bible is the basis for me. The man is to be the head of the family and carries the responsibility for it.in the public domain. The only way, however, allowable to him to exercise this position, is love.

The woman is the partner of the man. She is naturally fully on the same level as he is and therefore indirectly,equally responsible for creating a harmonious family life. Man is entrusted to be the provider and protector of the family. He will be more involved in public life, since his profession brings him in contact with the publc. He is, so to speak, the representative of the family on the outside and has to conduct himself accordingly, .so that his family need not be embarrassed but can be proud of him ....

Seattle, 14.9.54
Über Deinen Brief und die Bilder und bes. über Deine Prinzipien hinsichtlich der Stellung des Mannes in der Familie habe ich mich doll gefreut. Du bist so lieb, Helmut! Weißt Du, ich werde mich schwer anstrengen müssen, meine Geduld zu bewahren bis nächsten Frühling.... Möge Gott Dir Kraft schenken, Liebster, daß Du Dein Studium erfolgreich beenden kannst..
Mit viel Liebe, <u>Deine</u>
Hildegard

Your letter and the pictures gave me great joy, especially what you wrote about the position of a man in the family. You are so loving, Helmut.! You know, I will have to strain myself to maintain my patience until next spring.... May God give you strength , dearest one, that you can finish your studies successfully.

17.12.54
... Wenn Du im Zusammenhang mit dem Winterfest erwähnst, daß Du von Natur aus etwas `steif bist, muß ich beinahe lachen. Meine leider sehr kleine, aber außerordentlich angenehme Erinnerung schildert Dich mir warm, lebendig, voll Scherz und Lebensfreude. Und ich bin von Herzen froh, daß Du damals nicht' steif warst, denn dann hätte ich warscheinlich nicht den Mut gehabt, Deinen ersten Gruß zu beantworten
Möge Dein Jahresanfang froh, friedevoll und gesegnet sein, möge er auch Dir die Erfüllung Deiner Wünsche bringen oder darf ich sagen, möge er uns beiden

die Erfüllung unseres Wunsches bringen?

Deine Hildegard

If you mention in connection with the winterfest that you are somewhat stiff and straight laced by nature I have to laugh. In my short but very pleasant memory you stood out as being warm, vivacious, full of humor and joy for life. I am very glad that you were not stiff when we met, otherwise I would not have had the courage to reply to your first letter....

May the new year be happy, peaceful and blessed for you and bring you the fulfillment of your wishes, or may I say for both of us the fullfillment of our wish?

23.12.54

Weiß und kalt leuchteten die Berge des Festlandes über den blauen Pacific zu uns herüber, die Schönheit überwältigte uns ganz und in Gedanken versuchte ich dieses Gefühl von Bewunderung und Anbetung, daß einen beim Anblick solch eizigartiger Größe überkommt, mit Dir zu teilen. Du mußt nicht über mich lachen, aber ich komme mit viel kleineren Gedanken und winzigen Angelegenheiten zu Dir. Du bist garnicht mehr aus meinem Gedankenleben herauszudenken. Vielleicht sollte ich das nicht tun aber es verschönert mein Leben um hundertfaches

We are completely overwhelmed by the beauty of the coastal mountains shining white and cold across the blue Pacific. In my thoughts I try to share with you this feeling of awe and adoration of this unique view of grandeur.

You should not laugh about me if I come to you with trivial thoughts and smal concerns. I just cannot keep you out of my mind. Maybe I should not do that but it makes my life a hundredfold more beautiful.

Jan.3.55

....Ganz bestimmt haben bei dieser Predigt viele Zuhörer gute Vorsätze gefasst, genau wie ich es getan habe; Gott an den Anfang zu stellen, an den Anfang dieses Jahres, eines jeden Tages, an den Anfang unseres Denkens und Tuns. Und wie du es in Deinem lieben Neujahrsbrief gesagt hast, an den

Anfang unseres großen, gemeinsamen Wunsches. Wie herrlich, daß wir beide zu Gott, unserem gütigen Vater, beten, daß wir beide ihn zum Freund haben, der uns nur gute Wege führt und der unsere Liebe zueinander reicher und geschützter macht.

Ich bin entsetzt über meine Offenheit zu Dir. Aber ich möchte Dir alles sagen können, meine innersten Gedanken und genau wie Du mir Dein Vertrauen und Liebe geschenkt hast, möchte ich Dir mein ganzes Vertrauen und meine ganze Liebe geben bei Dir sind sie in den liebsten, schönsten Händen, die ich mir denken kann.
Für heute gute Nacht, Liebster, Hab tausend Dank für Deine lieben beiden Briefe, sie machten mich so froh.

In Liebe, Deine Hildegard

I am sure many listeners to the sermon have made good resolutions, the same as I did, to put God at the beginning of this year, of every day and at the brginning of our thoughts and actions. And as you said in your kind New Years letter, at the beginning of our important, common wish. It is wonderful that both of us can pray to God, our gracious father, that we both have him as our friend who leads us only good ways and who will make the love we have for each other richer and more protected…...

I am startled about the openness which I have towards you. But I want to be able to say all my innermost thoughts to you. In the same way as you have confided your trust and love to me, I want to give you my full trust and all my love. With you they are in the most loving, most beautiful hands I can imagine.

Good night, sweetheart. Thank you a thousand times for your two lovely letters. They made me very happy.

Jan. 10.55

Wenn Du, Liebster, sagst, daß Du dich vorzubereiten sehnst, für dir größte und heiligste Gabe, dann möchte ich dir entgegnen, daß ich mich sehne bereit zu werden für die größte und heiligste Aufgabe in dem Leben einer Frau, - in meinem Leben, nämlich alles zu sein und alles zu geben, was ich nur sein und geben kann meinem Mann und später auch, so Gott will, meinen Kindern. Helmut, mein lieber Helmut

If you, my loved one, tells me that it is your desire to prepare yourself for the most important and holiest task, I want to respond that I long to be ready for the most significant and holy task in the life of a woman, in my life, namely to be and give everything I can be and give to my husband and, as God wills, to my children, Helmut, my beloved Helmut.

13.2.55

Gestern traf ich einen unserer Prof. an der Uni, der auch aus Deutschland kam. Seine ganze Art, seine klare Sprache, seine Höflichkeit und Haltung riefen starke Erinnerungen an "daheim" in mir zurück; manchmal vergesse ich vollkommen, wie schön es sein kann, wenn einer den anderen mit Abstand, Respect und Höflichkeit behandelt.

Yesterday I met one of our professors at the university who also came from Germany. His manners, his clear speech, his politeness and deportment reminded me how it was 'at home'. Sometimes I forget how nice it can be if one treats the other person with tact, respect and courtesy.

3.2.55

Mein Herzliebster! Du bist wieder einmal zu mir gekommen. Wir sitzen zusammen und ich erzähle Dir von meinen täglichen Erfahrungen.- Mein Leben wird so vielfältig, daß ich befürchten muß, das Einzelne, das Tiefe wird vernachlässigt.
Freunde, die ich hier gewonnen habe, stellen ziemlich viele Ansprüche an mich und je mehr ich ihnen gebe, desto mehr verlangen sie von mir. Oh, mein Helmut, komm bald, ich brauche Dich so nötig! Es ist ziemlich schwer, in der Tat beinahe unmöglich, eine objektive Freundin zu sein. Immer, wenn nette junge Leute Freundschaft mit einem schließen wollen, haben sie Hintergedanken und Wünsche, die einen in die schwierigsten Situationen bringen können. Ich sollte vielleicht nicht ganz so vergnügt und offen sein, aber ohne Offenheit und Frohsinn ist das Leben zu traurig und eintönig und im Grunde genommen möchte ich immer Frohsinn und Glück ins Leben anderer bringen, wenn ich nur kann, vergesse dabei aber manchmal, daß ich nicht stark genug sein könnte, die Konsequenzen zu tragen, verstehst Du mich, Liebster? Du hast mich mit auf Deinen Sonntagsspaziergang genommen; wir haben zusammen den verheißungsvollen Liedern der Vöglein gelauscht, ich war ganz eins mit Dir, denn ich wollte so gern die Antwot auf den Ausruf sein: Herr es ist nicht gut, daß der Mensch allein sei .... Oh, daß der Vater mir Kraft schenke, Dir das

zu sein, was Du brauchst und Dir wünschst, mein Herzensfreund.
Deine Briefe geben mir ein Glück, das man überhaupt nicht beschreiben kann; warscheinlich ist es ein kleiner Vorgeschmack von dem, was Deine Gegenwart bringen wird.. Es wird spät und wir müssen uns für heute abend trennen, wenn du doch bei mir bliebst.   Gute Nacht mein Liebster,

Deine Hildegard

Sweethart! You have come to me again. We sit together and I tell you about my daily activities. My life has become so versatile that I fear it loses depth.

Friends, whom I made here, put so many demands on me and the more I give the more they expect from me. Oh my Helmut come soon, I need you so much. It is rather difficult, almost impossible to be an objective friend. Always when nice young people want to start a friendship they do so with another agenda and have requests which can get one into most difficult situations. Perhaps I should not be so cheerful and open but without openness and joyfullness life is too gloomy and dull. I would always like to bring joy and happiness into the lives of others whenever I am able to do this. However, sometimes I forget that I might not be strong enough to endure the consequences. Do you understand me, dearest?

You took me along on your Sunday walk and we listened to the auspicious songs of the birds. I was in full agreement with you, for I liked to be the answer to the call : It is not good that man is alone.... Oh that God may give me the strenght to be that to you what you need and what you wish, my beloved friend.

Your letters give me an undescribable joy, it is perhaps a small foretaste of what your presence will bring..

It is getting late and we have to separate for this evening. I wish you could stay with me.   Good Night my beloved one.

25. August 1955

Wo Du wohl bist und was Du tust? In Gedanken bin ich bei Dir, muß Dir ganz schnell einmal sagen, daß ich Dich sehr lieb habe, daß ich Dir das

Weggehen aus der Heimat etwas leichter machen möchte und daß ich mich schon sehr auf Dich freue.
Ich freue mich schon im Herbst mein Studium wieder aufnehmen zu können aber ich glaube, wenn es wirklich klappt, daß ich vorher noch einige Tage mit Dir verbringen werde, verschwindet die Lust etwas vor dem großen Verlangen, bei Dir zu bleiben.
Mutti, die das Leben von einem mir unverständlichen "praktischen Standpunkt ansieht, findet es überhaupt unsinnig, daß ich noch immer studieren möchte. Ihrer Ansicht nach sollte ich arbeiten und Geld verdienen und für eine Aussteuer sorgen. Ich kann diese Ansicht einfach nicht teilen, denn ich schätze geistiges Gut doch viel höher und vor allen Dingen unverlierbar und besonders jetzt, da ich schon beinehe an meinem Ziel angelangt bin, könnte ich mir nicht vorstellen aufzuhören.

I wonder where you are and what you are doing? In my thoughts I am with you. I have to tell you quickly that I love you very much, to make your leaving home a little easier and that I joyfully anticipate your coming..

I am looking forward to continiue my studies in fall, but if it works out that I can spend a few days with you before then, this joy is replaced by my great longing to be with you.

Mom looks at life very pragmatically. She finds it foolish that I want to continue my studies. In her opinion I should work, and earn money for a dowry. I cannot share that point of view. I value spiritual and intellectual assets much higher than physical possessions and they do not wear out. And for me, it is especially important since I have almost reached my goal. I could not imagine to stop now.

Excerpts from letters of appreciation and sympathy from friends of Hildegard during her illness and at her memorial service..

Margret

You taught me to be vulnerable. Your hospitality and inclusiveness helped so many of us to dare to live more fully.

Ingrid

Hildegard was a priceless gift to you and all of those who knew her. Her grace, beauty and acceptance of others are things I admired as a young person at Sherbrooke Church and continue to admire in Hildegard. The world and the church need more people like her.

Elsie

Many times, I have thought of the huge impact you have had on my life and I thank the Lord for you. I learned so much from you in those days – so long ago – when we all got together to study the Word. You gave of yourself so gladly and unselfishly – I will never forget those times. Your love and joy in the Lord just seemed to spread over us all like a warm blanket. Your inspiration caused us to hunger for the Lord and his word – you helped change all of our lives!

Peter

I feel incredibly privileged to know you both; if there is a special place in my heart for you Hildegard, its because I see in you special qualities that eluded me in a soul mate. You two are about the classiest couple I know, and I am incredibly grateful for the glimpses into your family as it was growing, for the warmth of your soulful hospitality, the immensely significant esthetics of your lives, the spiritual wholeness, the intellectual vivacity of your pursuits and beliefs, the artistic passions and the talented, magnificent expressions of those passions.

Benno

You are very special to both of us and have always been an inspiration with your vibrant personality. - You are in our thoughts and prayers.

Caelin

I already miss the presence of Hildegard upon this world. Hildegard was the kindest, most amazing person I have ever known and am ever likely to know. I feel that she was someone who truly understood me and loved me for who I am. I know that Hildegard would want us to be happy and rejoice in her moving to a better place but as this ink flows so do my tears. However, during these days of sad I am happy that I was blessed enough to know Hildegard for these 16 years. And I know that I will only be made a stronger and better person from the influence of my Godmother. I will never forget her.

Janet

Your generosity of heart and courage speak powerfully to me, Hildegard, may you know how very, very loved you are! Ernie and I both are carrying you in our hearts…..

We loved Hildegard very much and shall always remember her beauty, elegance, wisdom and kindness

Dawn

I was just musing how you have always been a trail blazer for us girls- How you have lovingly steered us and never judged but always supported us in our small trials and tribulations – and once again you are blazing a trail into our future- always with grace.- How we all love you.

Claudia

I have so many good memories of Hildegard, especially her kindness during my turbulent teen years. She was a lovely, warm person and she will be sorely missed.

LEAVING MY FATHER'S HOUSE, - ONE WOMAN'S JOURNEY

Hildegard's article published by MCC's Committee of Women's Concerns in their *'Women's Concerns Report'* Sept-Oct. 2002 Issue,

My name is Hildegard. I was born into a Mennonite home in Germany, my father being the pastor of four congregations in the South of that country. My mother who had grown up in Russia came from an MB Mennonite orientation and was therefore somewhat stricter than the German Mennos. Generally speaking it was my father's generosity of spirit and his great sense of humour that won the day and I grew up feeling secure in the love of God and not overly concerned that I could never satisfy the strict demands of a righteous God.

This was the time of the second World War and our lives were constantly disrupted and endangered. Our city was eigthy-five percent destroyed by bombs and during that time we experienced such miracles of protection that a young and growing faith in a caring God was anchored deeply into my experience.

I remember my devotion as a teen-ager. I would get up at five in the morning to study the Bible and pray. I taught Sunday School and at fifteen years of age I was baptized on the confession of my faith. I had accepted my parent's faith and now tried to live it.

In 1951 our family decided to emigrate to the U.S. where we built up a new existence and learned to know a variety of Mennonite and other faiths that seemed as different and strange as everything else in this new land. I remember struggling at times to sort out what was important, but the solid anchor of the faith of my fathers held.

Years went by. I completed my university education, got married and moved to Vancouver where my husband and I joined our first Canadian Mennonite church. We soon found out that here we were and always would be OUTSIDERS. It seemed that membership was based on family ties and ethnic roots, on ways of doing things and ways of speaking rather than a common faith.Communion, the great fellowship meal of the Mennonites became a sham for me. We worked very hard to fit in and be accepted but to no avail. For the first time in my life I became deeply unhappy with the church realizing that my growing spiritual hunger would not be satisfied here.

Eventually a daughter church was built and we joined full of hope and joyous expectations that here we would find what we were looking for. We participated fully and in due course took over the young people's group.

Around this time we met a couple who was in charge of the young people of a Baptist church. Learning to know this couple and sharing with them ideas and faith issues challenged a nd excited me both intellectually and spiritually for the first time in my young adult life. We exchanged ideas on youth work and eventually we opened our home for week-end retreats where we explored beyond denominational boundaries what God might have in store for us and how we could grow and expand our faith horizons.

During this time I personnally opened many new doors in the house of my father's faith. Together with the other couple we started to organize an interfaith home group which for a long time met all my spiritual needs. Our time together culminated in a shared experience of the „Baptism of the Holy Spirit" which introduced a new dimension into our faith life involving our emotions to a much greater degree. We were full of excitement and zeal trying to live what we thought New Testament Christianity to be.

Unfortunately our mother churches looked very unfavorably on our beloved home group fearing that we would be led astray. At that time the matter of the Baptism of the Holy Spirit was a hugely divisive issue, not at all acceptable to either Mennonites or Baptists. Although we did not speak of our extraordinary experiences in the congregation eventually we were asked to leave the church.

I did not feel the pain of being excommunicated as keenly as I might have because life in the Spirit and in the home group gave us much comfort and reassurance that we were where God wanted us to be.

Another door had opened and closed again.

It took some time to find a new church home but eventually we joined one body of believers which thrilled us because it was spiritually alive and totally inclusive quite in contrast to our previous experience.

However when the leadership of this church changed the direction changed. We lost our freedom to think for ourselves and were systematically steered back into an Old Testament model based on strongly hierarchical and patriarchal values. Since the input of women was highly discouraged I had a growing sense of alienation which resulted in a process of separation,.

I had to separate my experience of God and his/her ways from that of the church,

I had to separate out my experience and consider it valid in the face of a different experience of my husband,

I had to SEPARATE, period.

To survive spiritually I had to leave my father's house and find my own.

I was forty-nine years old and had reached a stage in life where I needed to get rid of a lot of religious baggage. Moving from my father's house into a new one was truly terrifying. I had before me a quote from Scott Peck:

„We begin by distrusting what we already believe, by actively seeking the threatening and unfamiliar, by deliberately challenging the validity of what we have previously been taught and hold dear. The Path to holiness lies through questioning everything."

Then there was a quote attributed to Jesus in the Gospel of St. Thomas:

„If you bring forth what is within you
what you bring forth will save you.
If you do not bring forth what is within you
What you do not bring forth will destroy you."

With these thoughts as guides I began the exploration of my new house. One room after another offered its riches and perplexities: Theology, Bible Criticism, Mysticism, Psychology, Feminism. A whole new library attended the process as well as many intense sharings, discussions, probings with new and some old friends.

Needless to say, many religious idols toppled from their pedestal as I developed a new understanding of God, the Christ, the Bible and its interpretation, my own autonomy and responsibility as a grown partner rather than a child of God.

To explain to others how my concept of God was evolving I groped for words, pictures, metaphors to name the unnamable. I was deeply moved and came to adopt Meister Ekkehard's "Ground of all Being" that Tillich had picked up on in the Fifties.

I saw myself as a drop in the ocean which was God, qualitatively the same, holographically the same and I frightened my husband by declaring that I was of the essence of God just like Jesus. Another image came to me, God the Matrix (that within which or whitin and from which EVERYTHING originates, takes form or develops).

Although matrix may be given a feminine connotation it is for me at least gender neutral. In my exploration of the Goddess Cultures and the Divine Feminine I greatly benefitted from appropriating qualities for me as woman but the notion of praying to Mother God rather than Father God was not particularly helpful. Personally I felt a need to be conscious of my connection to the Source of all Being at all times.

Guided and influenced by my reading of Ethelbert Stauffer, German Theologian, Gerda Weiler, Hanna Wolff, Elaine Pagels, Matthew Fox, John Selby Spong I gradually changed my view of the Bible from the literal, definitive and final Word of God to that of a collection of stories and experiences of a people and persons with their God, highly metaphorical as all Jewish literature is , arbitrarily cut off when some Church Fathers so decreed. Couldn't anyone today speak with the same authority of her/

his experiences with God without constantly referring back to the Bible or legitimizing everything with a verse of Scripture?

When I left the church most of my friends dropped me. In reflecting back, my search and my questions concerning an authentic life of faith had become a threat to the churches I attended as well as to those that were close and dear to me. I also realized that mine was a journey into the unknown that I had to take alone however painful that was.

During those difficult years of re-birthing myself I began to have an incredible urge to draw and paint. I discovered my creative center and healed myself as woman by painting mostly semi-abstract nature forms of the female body. I wanted to restore honor and dignity to the creative processes of a woman's life.

Sometimes I have a deep longing for a larger body of people on the journey that come together in ritual to express their faith. I don't know whether that longing is comparable to an adult's nostalgia for the paradise of childhood or whether it points to something I need in my life and must therefore find.

What is holding me back from actively seeking such a body is my fear that once more I would have to compromise my integrity and authenticity of being and believing as I join another church.

What is my spiritual practice ?

I experience living in God's presence like breathing, natural , on-going with or without constant awareness. I do not separate between spiritual and non-spiritual ways of being and acting. Everything I am and do is spiritual, be that baking bread, cleaning house, painting a picture, journaling, meditating or exercising.

I meditate regularly and my prayers have changed over time to sitting in silence before the Source of all Being or to sending energetic thoughts of love, support and healing to whoever burdens my heart.

I love and carry on ritual celebrations with family and friends around the dinner table as well as doing my own quiet rituals in the woods, by the ocean or in my stone circle.

I sometimes participate in retreats that promise further growth and open myself to new thinking on old topics.

It is important to me that my actions and relationships with all people and with Mother Earth are informed by love, compassion and thoughts of peace.

Biographical Note:

Hildegard Scheffler-Lemke born in 1933 in Germany

1951 emigration to the State of Washington in the USA

1952 Studies at Bethel College, Kansas

1954-1956 University of Washington, Seattle. Bachelor of Arts in Modern Languages

1956 Marriage and move to Vancouver, B.C.

1957-1962 Teacher of French, English and German

Followed by raising three children and years of voluntary service in church and community.

1983 A new career in Art Making, specifically painting exhibits and teaching courses on painting on silk.

About the Author

Helmut Lemke was born in 1926 in West Prussia, Germany, (now Poland) He lived as a refugee in East Germany, fled to West Germany to study in the USA and at the Technical University in Braunschweig, Germany, where he received his degree in architecture. In 1955 he immigrated to Canada and worked as an architect in Vancouver and later as German and art instructor. He married Hildegard and they have three children. They spent one year in Bielefeld, Germany, where he taught in an art college.

For many years he volunteered as a director of the ' More than a Roof Mennonite Housing Society '.

In 2007 his wife died of terminal lung cancer and he began to write about her and his family.